PALESTINE 1936

Palestine 1936

The Great Revolt and the Roots of the Middle East Conflict

Oren Kessler

ROWMAN & LITTLEFIELD
Lanham • Boulder • New York • London

Published by Rowman & Littlefield
An imprint of The Rowman & Littlefield Publishing Group, Inc.
4501 Forbes Boulevard, Suite 200, Lanham, Maryland 20706
www.rowman.com

86-90 Paul Street, London EC2A 4NE

Distributed by NATIONAL BOOK NETWORK

First paperback edition 2024.

British Library Cataloguing in Publication Information Available

Library of Congress Cataloging-in-Publication Data
Names: Kessler, Oren, author.
Title: Palestine 1936: the great revolt and the roots of the Middle East conflict / Oren Kessler.
Description: Lanham, Maryland: Rowman & Littlefield, 2023. | Includes bibliographical references and index.
Identifiers: LCCN 2022033661 (print) | LCCN 2022033662 (ebook) | ISBN 9781538148808 (cloth) | ISBN 9781538193709 (paperback) | ISBN 9781538148815 (epub)
Subjects: LCSH: Palestine—History—Arab rebellion, 1936–1939. | Jewish-Arab relations—History—1917–1948. | Palestine—History—1917–1948.
Classification: LCC DS126 .K464 2023 (print) | LCC DS126 (ebook) | DDC 956.94/04—dc23/eng/20220720
LC record available at https://lccn.loc.gov/2022033661
LC ebook record available at https://lccn.loc.gov/2022033662

∞™ The paper used in this publication meets the minimum requirements of American National Standard for Information Sciences—Permanence of Paper for Printed Library Materials, ANSI/NISO Z39.48-1992

To my parents,

Ruth and David

Contents

List of Figures

Acknowledgments

Thanks are due first to the editors at Rowman & Littlefield, who took a chance on a first-time author when others—many, many others—would not. Working with Katelyn Turner, Susan McEachern, Ashley Dodge, and Laney Ackley has been a privilege. Thanks are due also to my agent, Andrew Stuart.

Michael J. Cohen was generous with his time, feedback, and expertise on the British Mandate. In Jerusalem, Mohammed Dajani and Sari Nusseibeh provided valuable historical and political insights as well as warm hospitality. David A. Weinberg offered meaningful assistance in the project's earlier stages, and Richard Cohen, Emanuel Beška, and Yardena Schwartz in the later ones. Since publication, I am grateful for the support of Dominic Green, Debra Goldberg, and the children of the late Sami Rohr: George, Evelyn, and Lillian.

Hassan Eltaher kindly supplied me with several of the images in this book. Adam Rasgon and David Daoud each lent Arabic expertise and friendship. Steven B. Wagner gifted me a treasure trove of recently declassified Peel Commission secret testimonies. Rami Hazan shared family memories of his late grandfather Israel, the first fatality of the Great Revolt.

I am especially indebted to Debbie Usher at the Middle East Center Archive, St. Antony's College, Oxford, whose fabled twice-daily mandatory breaks for tea and biscuits I look back on fondly. The Institute for Current World Affairs generously presented me with the correspondence of the organization's former fellow, George Antonius. The Library of Congress African & Middle Eastern Reading Room was a reliably productive workspace, thanks as much to its sublime surroundings as to dedicated staff like Sharon Horowitz of the Hebraic section and Muhannad Salhi of the Near Eastern.

This book is dedicated to my parents, Ruth Traubner Kessler and David Kessler, without whose loving support—editorial, emotional, and practical—it could not have been written. My brother Yarin provided indispensable commentary—unvarnished but often on-point—and informed me whenever my prose became stale, overcooked, confusing, or otherwise missed the mark.

Alongside my family, my partner Clara was my second editorial anchor, reading every word and saving me from a hundred hidden pitfalls. Even more than that, she has been an extraordinary example of love, patience, and understanding through the frustrations, doubts, and despair of what has been by many miles the most difficult thing I have ever done. *Te amo.*

Oren Kessler

Glossary of Names

Musa Alami: Jerusalem-born, Cambridge-educated attorney, civil servant, and Arab-nationalist activist.
George Antonius: Writer and intellectual, born in Lebanon, raised in Egypt, and long based in Jerusalem. Author of the influential 1938 book *The Arab Awakening*.
David Ben-Gurion: Poland-born Zionist leader, based in Palestine since 1906. Headed the *Histadrut* labor federation from 1921, *Mapai* party from 1930, and Jewish Agency from 1935. From 1948, Israel's first prime minister.
Blanche "Baffy" Dugdale: Author, Zionist activist, and biographer of her uncle Arthur Balfour, who issued Britain's 1917 Balfour Declaration backing a Jewish national home in Palestine.
Anthony Eden: Foreign secretary, 1935–1938 and twice thereafter (later, prime minister, 1955–1957).
Abdel-Rahim al-Hajj Muhammad: Tulkarem-born merchant and militant. Most important of the rebel commanders whom the British army called The Big Three.
The Viscount Halifax (Edward Wood): Foreign secretary, 1938–1940. An early supporter of appeasement in Neville Chamberlain's Cabinet.
Yusuf Hanna: Egypt-born editor of *Filastin* newspaper, Jaffa, 1931–1948. Corresponded regularly with *New York Times* Palestine reporter Joseph Levy.
Hajj Amin al-Husseini: Grand mufti of Jerusalem and president of the Supreme Muslim Council for most of the 1920s and 1930s. Founded and led the Arab Higher Committee during the Great Revolt.

Jamal Husseini: Founder and chairman of the Palestine Arab Party, dominated by the Husseini family. Cousin, acolyte, and spokesman of Hajj Amin, and brother-in-law of Musa Alami.

Hussein Khalidi: Physician and member of a leading Jerusalem family. Mayor of Jerusalem 1934–1937, until he was exiled to Seychelles with other members of Hajj Amin's Higher Arab Committee.

Vladimir Ze'ev Jabotinsky: Odessa-born writer and activist. Barred from Palestine in 1930, he founded the right-wing Revisionist Zionist movement and was titular—though not always practical—commander of the *Irgun* militant group.

Malcolm MacDonald: Colonial secretary, 1938–1940. Son of the first Labour prime minister Ramsay MacDonald.

Sir Harold MacMichael: High commissioner for Palestine, 1938–1944. Career colonial administrator and Arabist, broadly skeptical of Zionist aims.

William Ormsby-Gore: Colonial secretary, 1936–1938. Long linked to and friendly with the Zionist movement, his clashes with the Foreign Office over Palestine helped end his career.

Moshe Shertok (Sharett): Russia-born Zionist activist. An Arabic speaker, he held the Jewish Agency's second-most powerful role as head of its political department. Later, Israel's first foreign minister and second prime minister.

Sir Arthur Wauchope: High commissioner for Palestine, 1931–1938. His tenure was a heyday for Jewish immigration, investment, and land purchases. Retired amid criticism of applying insufficient force to quell the Arab rebellion.

Chaim Weizmann: Russia-born Zionist leader and chemist, long based in Britain. Key to negotiating the Balfour Declaration, he headed the World Zionist Organization for most of the interwar period. In his final years, first president of Israel.

Timeline

1882—First Jewish *aliyah* (immigration wave) to Holy Land begins

1897—Theodor Herzl calls First Zionist Congress in Basel, Switzerland

1917—Britain issues Balfour Declaration backing "Jewish national home"

1920—At San Remo, Allies form "Palestine" from 3 Ottoman districts

1923—Britain's League of Nations Mandate for Palestine officially begins

1929—Arab riots centered in city of Hebron leave 133 Jews dead

1936–1939—Great Revolt: 500 Jews, 250 Britons, 5,000+ Arabs killed

1948—Mandate ends; State of Israel declared; first Arab-Israeli war

1967—Six-Day War: Israel gains territories including West Bank, Gaza

1973—Yom Kippur War: Surprise joint Arab attack strikes blow to IDF

1987–1993—First Intifada culminates in Oslo Accords with PLO

2000–2005—Second Intifada; Israel withdraws from Gaza Strip

2023—Massive Hamas onslaught instigates fifth major Gaza war

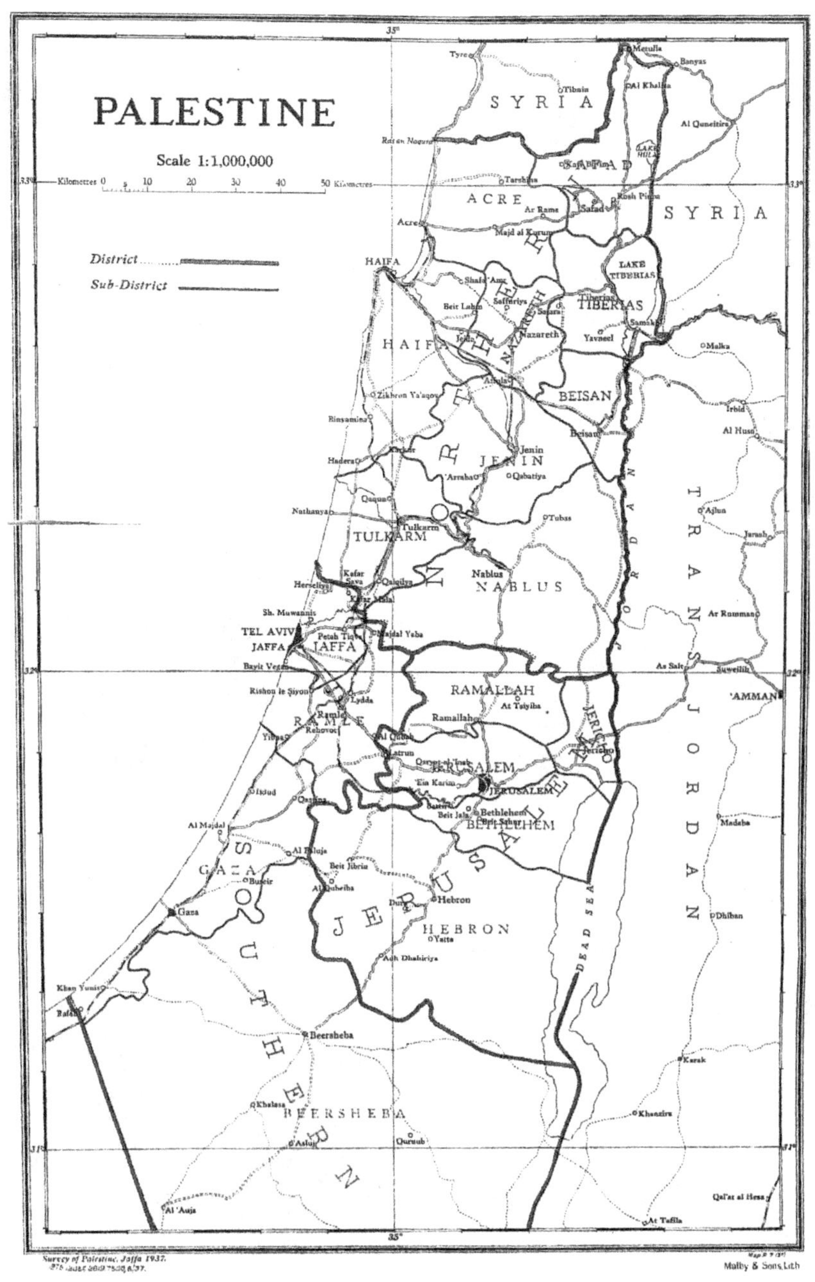

Districts of Mandate Palestine, from the 1937 Peel Commission report (Cmd. 5479)

Introduction

The Forgotten Uprising

A CERTAIN GRIM BUT FAMILIAR PATTERN TYPIFIES REPORTS FROM THE Holy Land.

Palestinians, despairing over their thwarted national hopes, wage acts of protest, boycott, sabotage, and violence. All around them Jewish settlements inexorably expand. Islamic hardliners sabotage peace talks, executing suspected collaborators and moderates. Occupation forces launch an aggressive crackdown, demolishing homes, erecting a separation wall, and drawing censure for rights abuses. The world power with the greatest clout over the warring sides pushes a partition plan, even while seeming to doubt its viability. Jewish factions are split: One is ready to give up part of the Land of Israel for peace; another demands the entire ancient patrimony, by force of arms if needed. Further bloodletting appears inevitable.[1]

These could be this morning's news alerts. Or headlines from the Second Intifada of the early 2000s, the earlier First Intifada, or any number of clashes over the three-quarters of a century since the Jewish state's creation in 1948.

Instead this is an earlier story—of Palestine's first Arab rebellion, a seminal, three-year uprising a decade before Israel's birth that cast the mold for the Jewish-Arab encounter ever since.

Five hundred Jews lost their lives—a civilian toll unmatched until the twenty-first century—and hundreds more British servicemen were killed. But the price exacted upon the Arabs themselves was heavier still, and not just in terms of body count.

The Great Revolt of 1936 to 1939 was the crucible in which Palestinian identity coalesced. It united rival families, urban and rural, rich and poor, in a single struggle against a common foe: the Jewish national enterprise—Zionism—and its midwife, the British Empire. A six-month general strike, one of the longest anywhere in modern history, roused Arabs and Muslims worldwide to the Palestine cause.[2]

Yet the revolt would ultimately turn on itself. A convulsion of infighting and score-settling shredded the Arab social fabric, sidelined pragmatists for extremists, and propelled the first wave of refugees out of the country. British forces did the rest, seizing arms, occupying cities, and waging a counterinsurgency that left thousands dead and tens of thousands wounded. Arab Palestine's fighting capacity was debilitated, its economy gutted, its political leaders banished.

The revolt to end Zionism had instead crushed the Arabs themselves, leaving them crippled in facing the Jews' own drive for statehood a decade on. It was the closest the Palestinians would ever come to victory; they have never quite recovered.[3]

To the Jews the insurgency would leave a very different inheritance. It was then that Zionist leaders began to abandon illusions over Arab acquiescence, to confront the unnerving prospect that fulfilling their dreams of sovereignty might mean forever clinging to the sword.[4] The revolt saw thousands of Jews trained and armed by Great Britain, the world's supreme military power, turning their amateur guard units into the seeds of a formidable Jewish army, complete with special forces and an officer corps.

But it was also during the revolt that some Jews—facing Fascism in Europe and carnage in Palestine—decided that mere passive defense was national suicide, and when Jewish terrorism first appeared on the landscape.

This is therefore a story of two nationalisms, and of the first major explosion between them. The rebellion was Arab, but the Zionist counter-rebellion—the Jews' military, economic, and psychological transformation—is a vital, overlooked element in the chronicle of how Palestine became Israel.

For it was then—not in 1948—that Palestine's Jews consolidated the demographic, geographic, and political basis of their state-to-be. And it was then that portentous words like "partition" and "Jewish state" first appeared on the international diplomatic agenda.

Yet ultimately the uprising also persuaded Britain that its two-decade Zionist experiment had proven too costly—in blood, treasure, and the goodwill of broad swaths of its empire. As war with Hitler loomed, the Chamberlain government determined it was high time that Palestine's doors—virtually the only ones still open to Jews—be shuttered. Few decisions in the twentieth century would carry repercussions as profound.

The reader might imagine that events of such magnitude would already have been amply investigated. This is, after all, the most written-about of the world's ongoing disputes, having earned itself the all-encompassing designation as *The* Middle East Conflict. And yet that same reader, keen to learn more, encounters scarcity: a few pages, or at most a chapter, in wider histories of this land.[5] Remarkably, no single general-interest account has yet been written of this formative but forgotten insurgency.

The few books dedicated to the topic have been confined to academia; the first in English was published only in the mid-1990s. Its author, Ted Swedenburg, wrote of being stunned by the "dearth of information about this momentous insurgency," which he realized had been "either ignored or denigrated by mainstream Israeli and Western historiography."[6]

In Hebrew there is likewise just one full-length academic study to date.[7] That gap may be understandable: Zionism's champions have always regarded it as a struggle for self-determination, not the denial of the same to others. The conventional Israeli national story progresses steadily from the early immigration waves and the Balfour Declaration through the nation-building of the 1920s and 1930s, the agony of the Holocaust, and finally the redemption of statehood. A large-scale, concerted uprising against that forward-marching tale seems an unwelcome disruption in the narrative arc.

The near-total gap in Arabic has its own reasons. Mustafa Kabha, a historian at Israel's Open University, laments that in Palestinian collective memory the rebellion has been marginalized, even silenced, "completely overshadowed by the memory of the 1947–48 Nakba ('Catastrophe')." It seems natural, he observes, "to dwell on the Nakba, due to the magnitude of the disaster and the fact that much of the blame can be attributed to external factors: the Zionists, the Arab states, the British and other actors. Dealing with 1936–39 requires much more soul-searching."[8]

It was in view of this apparent deficit that I set to work, convinced I had lit upon an undiscovered blank space on the creaking bookshelf of all things Arab-Israeli. Thus began a project spanning research on three continents, in three languages, over five years.

Still, it is a dependable rule that a writer rarely walks alone. Since I began my research, two new books on the revolt have gone to press: *Britain's Pacification of Palestine* by Matthew Hughes and *The Crime of Nationalism* by Matthew Kraig Kelly. Both are valuable, rigorous works of scholarship: Hughes's is a meticulous examination of the military and legal means Britain used to quash the rebellion; Kelly's is a study of the imperial perception of criminality and nationalism.[9]

This is a different kind of book. I am not an academic but a journalist, think-tanker, and writer, mostly on the Middle East. My aim has been to produce the first full-length, deeply researched but general-interest history of the Great Revolt: of the uprising itself, its effects on Palestine's Jewish and Arab nationalisms, the geopolitical moves it engendered, and its lasting legacies today.

As this is a narrative history, I have opted to tell it through a handful of protagonists—Arab, Jewish, and British. Most are listed in the glossary of names, but a brief summary will explain some of the less-obvious choices among them.

The primary Jewish figures will be known to readers who have some familiarity with the general terrain: Chaim Weizmann (Zionism's face and muscle abroad in the interwar years), David Ben-Gurion (unrivaled leader of Palestine's Jews from the mid-1930s on), and Moshe Shertok (later Moshe Sharett, the Jews' de facto "foreign minister"). Within a decade these would become Israel's first president, prime minister, and foreign minister, respectively. Vladimir Jabotinsky was founder of the

Revisionist movement, the forebear of Benjamin Netanyahu's Likud party and much else of right-wing Zionism.

The key British roles in this drama are the two high commissioners for Palestine (Arthur Wauchope, then Harold MacMichael) and the colonial secretaries (William Ormsby-Gore and Malcolm MacDonald) during the relevant years. Blanche "Baffy" Dugdale, a writer and niece of Arthur Balfour, occupies a distinctive place both as a woman in a mostly male arena and as a well-connected operator within both the British and Zionist elites.

On the Arab side the irreplaceable man of the period is Grand Mufti Hajj Amin al-Husseini, political leader of Palestine's Arabs and spiritual leader of its Muslims. Beside him I have chosen Musa Alami and George Antonius, two prominent Arabs who struck me as compelling, complex, yet approachable characters for an English readership.

Alami seemed particularly ripe for plucking from semi-obscurity. A Cambridge graduate, he had the rare distinction of enjoying near-universal affection and esteem from Arabs, Britons, and Jews alike. He had an unusual ability to draw close to nodes of power and influence while also preserving his own independence of mind. And though widely praised as a moderate, he cultivated bonds with hardliners—not least of them the mufti—and engaged in clandestine actions that, were they known, would have stunned his Western admirers.

Antonius was another, slightly younger, Cambridge man. A writer and intellectual, his troubled life exemplified the plight of the culturally marginal man, divided between his native Arab culture and his adopted Western one. That split identity nonetheless had its advantages: His 1938 book *The Arab Awakening* introduced the Arab national movement to the West and had an enduring impact on British and subsequent attempts to cut the Palestine knot.

Terminology is, like every other aspect of the conflict, contested ground, but I have sought wherever possible to avoid anachronistic framing or phrasing. "Palestine" is used here as it was then—the official, universally employed English name for the Holy Land. Those whom we today call Palestinians appear under the slightly unwieldy moniker of Palestinian

Arabs (or a variation thereof), for the basic reason that that is how they were almost invariably known at the time, including by their own spokesmen. It is perhaps self-explanatory that members of the *Yishuv*—Palestine's pre-state Jewish community—are not called Israelis here, though that is what they would become within about a decade.

I have similarly tried to resist the temptation to read history backwards. The main chapters that follow do not contain the word Israel (in the political sense) for the simple reason that no one—Jew, Arab, or Briton—saw him or herself as existing in the "pre-state" period. Or pre-anything else: Europe's Jews recognized they were living in fraught and anxious times; they did not know theirs was the final scene before the Holocaust. Many among Palestine's Arabs sensed their struggle had reached a decisive stage; they did not perceive their era as one they would later hark back to wistfully from their own exile and dispersion.[10]

Above all, I have attempted to place the reader in the book's time and place(s).

And yet this is no mere snapshot or time capsule—the revolt still casts its shadow over eight decades of the Arab-Israeli confrontation. Hamas's armed wing bears the name of the fighter-preacher whose martyrdom sparked the rebellion; today's boycott-Israel campaign is the direct descendant of the 1936 strike. When Israeli troops detain suspects without charge, raise checkpoints, and raze homes, they rely on tactics and laws inherited from their British forerunners. And when Washington pushes a two-state solution, it is invoking the 1937 Peel proposal, the progenitor of all later partition plans from the UN's in 1947 through the official policies of the Biden and Trump administrations.

The past is never dead—a novelist once wrote—it's not even past.[11] For Israelis and Palestinians, the revolt rages on.

Chapter 1

Flash Floods in the Desert

Jerusalem, for several centuries, was led by a handful of great families—those the Ottomans knew as the effendis, the Arabs as the *ayan*, and the English as the notables. Each family had its prerogative: the Khalidis provided civil and sharia court judges, the Dajanis minded David's Tomb on Mount Zion, the Nusseibehs kept the keys to the Church of the Sepulcher. The Nashashibis made bows and arrows for the sultan's men, while the Husseinis served as *naqib al-ashraf*—leaders of the *ashraf*, the descendants of the Prophet. The Alamis, throughout the early Ottoman centuries, supplied Jerusalem's highest religious authority, the mufti, who issued legal rulings known as *fatwas*.[1]

Like the Husseinis, the Alamis were *ashraf*, tracing their particular line to Muhammad's grandson Hassan. In the Islamic conquest's first waves, one of their ancestors left Arabia for Morocco, taking the name of Mount Alam near its northern tip. When in the twelfth century Saladin recruited men to confront the Crusaders, one Alami—a local chieftain and Sufi *sheikh*—answered the call. He apparently fought bravely in the Holy Land, emerging with vast estates including most of the Mount of Olives, where the New Testament says Jesus rose to heaven and where the Hebrew prophets say God will start resurrecting the dead.

In the 1860s the Ottomans decided Jerusalem should have a mayor. Henceforth each occupant of the office came from one of the six families, and at least four from the Alamis.[2] In 1906 the sultan named Faydallah Alami to the post, in which his father Musa had served some years before. By then the family had left Jerusalem's cramped Muslim Quarter for Musrara, a neighborhood abutting the Old City that was one of the first Arab communities outside the medieval walls. Summers they spent in a new home in Sharafat, a village on the road to Bethlehem, and winters in Jericho in the dry Jordan Valley.

Faydallah's mayoral term was tranquil: Jerusalem's headiest years would come in the following decade: the Great War, the Balfour Declaration, the demise of the empire in power for four centuries and its succession by another. And though his education was rooted in scripture—in 1904 he published a Quran concordance still in use today—Faydallah ("Faidi" to friends) was a cosmopolitan. Unlike nearly everyone in his community, he had traveled widely in Europe, and spent hours regaling guests with tales of the Continent. One oft-repeated tale was the time, in Austria, he had encountered the latest European innovation: the elevator.

The mayor's son Musa was born in spring 1897, four months before Theodor Herzl convened the first Zionist Congress in Basel. The boy lived a cloistered existence. Homeschooled until eight, he learned aristocratic pursuits like hunting but scarcely met peers. Once his father recognized the mistake, this descendant of Muhammad and servant of the Ottoman caliph sent his son to Jerusalem's Anglican missionary school. The headmaster, a Mr. Reynolds, was at first pleased to welcome the mayor's boy, but soon concluded he was unteachable and advised the effendi to apprentice him to a carpenter.

Musa started learning carpentry at the American Colony, a religious-philanthropic community led by a wealthy Presbyterian lawyer from Chicago. After six months, once it seemed possible that he was, in his words, "not entirely ineducable," he was weaned off carpentry and placed in class with the lawyer's own children. As he later told his biographer, it was only years later that he found out that Mr. Reynolds, hoping to please the mayor, had put him in a higher grade and he had not understood a word.[3]

The boy then continued to the prestigious and rigorous *Collège des Frères*. He hated every moment but excelled, particularly in history, literature, and philosophy. And having mastered English from the Anglicans and Presbyterians, Alami now learned French from the Catholics.

Musa Alami was also well acquainted with Jews. On the eve of the Great War, perhaps 7 percent of Palestine's population of eight hundred thousand was Jewish, most of them religious Jews in Jerusalem. Many hailed from Sephardic families who had lived there for centuries: They spoke the same language as the Arabs, wore the same clothes, relished the same music, and ate much the same food. One of his parents' closest friends were a Jewish couple, originally from Aleppo, who visited them nearly every night.

One local custom held that if two mothers bore sons in the same quarter at the same time, the midwife would connect between them, and each would nurse the other's boy. The children would thereafter consider each other "foster brothers" for the rest of their lives. Their families were also expected to become friends, regardless of discrepancies in religion or class. Musa's foster brother was the son of a Jewish grocer down the street. For three decades the two families visited each other, exchanged presents on feast days, and offered congratulations or condolences as life demanded.[4]

Zionism in the early twentieth century was the preserve of a small, idealistic minority of Jewry. Once, while mayor, Faidi al-Alami met with a visiting Zionist leader from Berlin. "It's not true that we oppose the Jews moving here," Alami said. "On the contrary, the Jews are wanted—they're a stimulating, fermenting, progressive force. The question is one of numbers. They are like salt in bread—a small amount is vital, but a large amount is even worse than none at all."

"You're wrong," the visitor told him. "We don't want to be salt. We want to be the bread!"[5]

A Boy Named Faithful

Adjacent to Musrara is Sheikh Jarrah, along the Old City's northern wall beside Damascus Gate. There, around the same time as Musa Alami's birth, another child was born to one of Jerusalem's great families, the Husseinis.

Where the Alamis trace their line from Hassan, the Husseinis claim descent from his younger brother Hussein. Like the Alamis, they claim to have arrived in Jerusalem in the twelfth century—not from Morocco but

Arabia—and like them, their ancestor is said to have been among Saladin's troops sent to face the Crusaders. Like the Alamis, the Husseinis had produced their share of mayors and muftis. And though the Alamis dominated the muftiship in the Middle Ages, from the late eighteenth century the post had almost always gone to a Husseini.

Taher Husseini was named mufti in 1869. Jews were already a plurality in the city; by the 1880s, augmented by large-scale religious immigration from Europe, they were a majority. In 1897 the Ottomans tapped Taher to head a panel tasked with reducing Jewish land purchases in Jerusalem.[6] The commission had some success but was fundamentally a sham: Taher Husseini, like many Arab notables, was himself involved in land sales to Jews in and around the holy city.[7]

That same year, he had a son with his second wife, the quiet and pious Zeinab. They named him Amin, meaning "trustworthy" or "faithful."

In 1908 Taher died, succeeded as mufti by his son Kamil. Next to his much older half-brother, Amin literally paled in comparison, with his fair skin, reddish hair, and blue eyes. The younger Husseini was short and frail, and self-conscious from a lisp. Little was expected of the boy: Like any good effendi's son, he attended a *kuttab*—an Islamic elementary school—and received some religious lessons at home. Like Alami, he learned French at the *Collège des Frères*, and at Jerusalem's *Alliance Israélite Universelle*, run by a Jewish (but importantly, non-Zionist) educator from Damascus.

When Amin was seventeen, Kamil sent him to Al-Azhar University, Cairo's millennium-old lodestar of Sunni learning. A year later he accompanied his mother on pilgrimage to Mecca. Throughout his life he would cling to the honorific *hajj*—his few years at Al-Azhar were insufficient for the title of *sheikh* that a genuine scholar of the faith might claim.[8]

It was in Cairo that Amin came under the tutelage of Rashid Rida. An early Salafi scholar, Rida was both modernist and fundamentalist. He recognized Muslims' technological, economic, and geopolitical lag behind the West, and encouraged them to seek knowledge in those fields from Christendom. The gap itself, however, he attributed to Muslims having strayed from the example of the Prophet and his followers. Returning to the past—to the unadulterated principles of Islam—was how Muslims could seize the future.

Rida was a proto-Arab nationalist, abandoning the Ottomans as they moved from pan-Islamism to a more secular, Turkish-centric orientation after the 1908 Young Turk revolution. Unusually among Islamic thinkers of the time, he favored the British Empire to the Ottoman, and imparted that sensibility to his student.

The British were likewise keen to cleave their Ottoman foe from its Arab subjects. Early in the Great War, Britain's high commissioner in Egypt, Henry McMahon, began a correspondence with Hussein—*sherif* of the Hashemite dynasty that ruled Mecca—promising that London would back the Arabs' independence if they rose up against the sultan.

Over nine months they exchanged ten letters. The most significant, dated October 24, 1915, pledged Crown recognition for Hussein's claims for Arab independence, but not in those "portions of Syria lying to the west of the districts of Damascus, Homs, Hama and Aleppo," which were not purely Arab-inhabited, and where Britain's ally France had historical and strategic prerogatives. London also had an "established position and interests" in Iraq that had to be taken into account. Yet the wide belt between Arabia and Syria would, after four centuries of Ottoman rule, now enjoy self-rule with British endorsement.

Years later, debate would rage over what exactly the letter had promised. Palestine is southwest of Damascus, so was it intended as part of those "portions of Syria" west of that city to which Arab claims did not apply?[9] At the time, however, Hussein deemed the British assurances sufficient: He launched an uprising against the Ottomans, and tapped his second son, the Emir Faisal, to head it. Within weeks it scored a stunning achievement, ousting the Turks from the sacred city of Mecca.

Hajj Amin was now nineteen. Drafted into the Ottoman army as an officer, but seeing little action, he heard of the revolt and dreamed of an Arab Greater Syria under Faisal's crown. He promptly deserted his post in Turkey, returning to Jerusalem to help the British recruit some two thousand Arabs for the cause.

Musa Alami was assistant military censor in Jerusalem when he learned of the uprising over the cables. Having been conscripted against his will, he thrilled at the thought of Arab independence from the sclerotic, despotic Ottoman throne. He too quit his post for Damascus, staying with a former private tutor: Khalil al-Sakakini, a Christian writer and Arab nationalist from Jerusalem. Alami had heard of young Arab nationalists haunting the cafes of Damascus and Constantinople, but had never met one before. Sakakini's home was a fulcrum for such subversive notions.[10]

Meanwhile, in spring 1916 negotiators Mark Sykes and Francois Georges-Picot reached a secret agreement to divvy the Ottomans' Levantine provinces once the Turks were routed. The British would get the swath between the Jordan River and Mesopotamia; the French would take Syria and Mount Lebanon. Palestine was to be under a later-defined Allied administration, perhaps jointly controlled by both powers.

But Sykes began to wonder if Palestine was too precious to share; for one, it was the natural bulwark guarding the Suez Canal, the vital route by which the British Empire reached India and the East. Throughout 1917, he met with Zionist leaders who pledged their reverence for Britain, that nation raised on justice, liberty, and the Old Testament. Along with Foreign Secretary Lord Arthur Balfour and Prime Minister David Lloyd George, Sykes became convinced that British and Zionist interests were one.[11]

In November 1917, as British and Commonwealth troops advanced through Sinai and southern Palestine with Jerusalem in their sights, Balfour wrote a letter to Baron Walter Rothschild. It began: "His Majesty's Government view with favor the establishment in Palestine of a national home for the Jewish people."

THE MANDATE BORN

Disparate and complex motives converged to produce what historians would call the Balfour Declaration.[12] Decades later, Lloyd George said in secret testimony that war planners had felt that the Jews, especially in America and Russia, "could either hinder us or help us very materially. . . . They are a dangerous people to quarrel with, but they are a very helpful people if you can get them on your side."[13]

Yet it would not likely have happened without Chaim Weizmann. The Russian-born British chemist's acetone-production process was crucial to the Allied explosives industry, but it was in his second occupation, as a leader of the world Zionist movement, that his charm, cajolery, and indefatigability made him a regular, persuasive presence in Whitehall.

"Individually, the Jews are intelligent and industrious; collectively they are abysmally stupid," wrote one British colonial administrator. Most of the Jewish leaders, he complained, were impatient, tactless, and self-sabotaging. Weizmann, however, was "a great chemist and a great man," who, alone among them, "had the wisdom of a Cincinnatus and knew how to wait."

As a speaker Weizmann was "almost frighteningly convincing," reminisced another official, "with all that dynamic persuasiveness which Slavs usually devote to love and Jews to business, nourished, trained, and concentrated upon the accomplishment of Zion."[14]

Five weeks after the Declaration, the British took Jerusalem. They were now military administrators, but they had a problem. Theirs was a Christian empire occupying an overwhelmingly Muslim population, whose ties to the caliph and sultan they had just severed and whose land they had pledged for a Jewish national home. Swiftly they moved to bolster local Islamic authorities. One of their first acts was elevating Mufti Kamil al-Husseini's title to one borrowed from Egypt: "Grand Mufti." He repaid the honor, assuring the public that Britain was an honorable empire and would do right by its new subjects.

It was a hard sell: Word of the Balfour Declaration was spreading in Palestine's nascent Arabic press. On its first anniversary, Musa Kazim Husseini—Jerusalem's newly appointed mayor and the mufti's uncle—wrote the military administration in the name of one hundred Arab dignitaries.

"We Arabs, Muslim and Christian, always sympathized profoundly with the persecuted Jews and their misfortunes in other countries," the mayor wrote, "but there is a wide difference between this sympathy and the acceptance of such a nation . . . ruling over us."[15]

Nine days later the war was over. Musa Alami boarded a ship to Constantinople, where his father had been representing Jerusalem in parliament but whose constituency now no longer existed. On the family's return to Palestine, the younger Alami—"daydreaming as usual," he later recalled—fell through a coal shoot and injured his ribs. He was treated by the only doctor aboard: an Arabic-speaking Jewish veterinarian from Jerusalem.

It was on the same journey that Musa first encountered a new kind of Jew: the European Zionist. They waved the Jewish national movement's star-and-bars banner over the railings and belted the movement's anthem "Hatikvah." Alami thought he detected contempt in them, not just for Arabs, but also for Oriental Jews like the vet who mended his ribs.[16]

In January 1919, Weizmann crossed the Jordan to meet Faisal, hero of the Arab Revolt, at his desert camp. There they signed an agreement, brokered by T. E. Lawrence ("of Arabia"), in which the emir effectively endorsed the Balfour Declaration's call for significant Jewish immigration to Palestine, which would stay separate from Faisal's future Arab state in the rest of the Levant.

In a joint statement, the two leaders wrote that they were "mindful of the racial kinship and ancient bonds existing between the Arabs and the Jewish people, and realizing that the surest means of working out the consummation of their natural aspirations is through the closest possible collaboration in the development of the Arab State and Palestine." Still, Faisal conditioned the agreement on the fulfillment of broader Arab dreams of independence at the upcoming Paris Peace Conference; should that fail, he warned, he would not be bound "by a single word" of the pact.[17]

America was also on board. President Woodrow Wilson, who had approved the Balfour Declaration before its publication, now reaffirmed his support: "I am persuaded that the Allied nations, with the fullest concurrence of our own Government and people, are agreed that in Palestine shall be laid the foundations of a Jewish Commonwealth."[18]

The following year, at San Remo on the Italian Riviera, the Allies formalized the division of the Levant. "Palestine" was born from the former Ottoman district of Jerusalem and parts of the provinces of Beirut and Damascus, and granted to the United Kingdom as a mandate under the newly created League of Nations.

The Jews were already busily building a proto-government in the Holy Land: There was the Palestine Zionist Executive—later renamed the

Musa Alami, 1918 (Public Domain)

Jewish Agency—handling everything from immigration, settlement, and agriculture to education and finances. It in turn answered to the Zionist Organization (later renamed the World Zionist Organization), the umbrella body founded by Herzl and now headed by Weizmann in London.[19]

Weizmann's tendencies were liberal, even capitalistic, but the Yishuv was dominated by Labor-Zionists who in turn favored immigrants of a similarly socialist bent. The Laborites ran the Histadrut, the formidable labor-union federation of which three-quarters of Palestine's working Jews were members, and which lobbied for the rights of Jewish—but only Jewish—workers. And they dominated the Jewish National Fund, which purchased land, drained swamps, and planted forests.

The Arabs had little to match these. Only after the Great War did the first Arab civil-society groups, called Muslim-Christian Associations, spring up in Palestine. At first, they looked not to Jerusalem but Damascus. Palestine's Arabs generally shared in their neighbors' dreams of a Greater Syria, potentially in a wider union with Iraq and the Hejaz. In the months after the armistice, Hajj Amin had promoted Faisal as king of such a realm, and had written articles to that effect for the short-lived Jerusalem newspaper *Suriya Al-Janubiya* ("Southern Syria").

In early 1919, a group of notables in Jerusalem had convened the first annual Palestine Arab Congress, denouncing imperialism and Zionism and demanding Palestine's inclusion in an Arab Syria. In Damascus months later, Arab leaders reaffirmed that "the southern part of Syria, known as Palestine," must be part of an independent Greater Syria.[20]

All this time Musa Alami was attending Cambridge—likely the very first Arab from Palestine to do so. More mature, even aloof, than the other students, his friends were primarily among the dons. He studied law but read widely, particularly in philosophy, as well as a history of Zionism by Nahum Sokolow, a future head of the Zionist Congress (the introduction was by Arthur Balfour).

One day Alami was invited to the home of some Jewish students, relatives of family friends in Jerusalem. His fellow guests assumed a Cambridge law student from Palestine must be a Jew; they greeted him with "Shalom" and asked how soon before their brethren "finished with the dirty Arabs."[21]

Istiqlal!

Palestine in April. "The fields and hillsides became covered with white, purple and pink cyclamen and scarlet anemones," one Colonial Office Arabist wrote. "The farmlands showed green with young wheat and barley, and the stony stream beds were pink with oleander blossom. Only those who have seen it can understand the Solomon's Glory of spring in Palestine."[22]

Spring in Palestine also meant the festival of Nebi Musa—the Prophet Moses—an annual Islamic procession from Jerusalem to a shrine by the Dead Sea believed to hold the lawgiver's tomb. In 1920, men poured in from around the country and neighboring lands, bearing flags, and even weapons. The crowd was far larger than during the war years—as many as sixty thousand. Cries rang out of "*Istiqlal!*"—"Independence!"[23]

"We won the country by the sword," they intoned—hailing the Arab conquests of more than a millennium before—"We will keep the country by the sword!" Hajj Amin, now twenty-five, held up a portrait of Emir Faisal and shouted, "This is your king!" Mayor Musa Kazim Husseini urged Arabs to "spill their blood" for Palestine.

Mobs in the Old City attacked Jews and vandalized synagogues and shops. Alami's former tutor Khalil al-Sakakini saw one man seize a Jewish shoeshine boy's box and beat him until he ran off bleeding. Some Jews started prowling the streets with knives. Sakakini walked to the municipal garden, his "soul nauseated and downcast by the madness of the human race."

The British declared temporary martial law, but took three days to reimpose order. By then five Jews had been killed and over two hundred injured. Four Arabs were also dead, including a girl who fell from a window when a stray bullet hit her in the temple.

"The acuteness of Arab feeling against the Jews is probably not realized in England," the Reuters news wire observed dryly.

Police arrested more than two hundred people, nearly a quarter of them Jews. In the Jerusalem home of Vladimir Jabotinsky—the Zionist activist who co-founded Britain's Jewish Legion in the Great War—they found a handful of rifles and pistols and 250 rounds of ammunition. They sentenced him to fifteen years in prison.[24] Mayor Musa Kazim Husseini was removed from office for incitement; his nephew Amin got ten years but fled across the Jordan. Ragheb Nashashibi, head of a rival clan to the Husseinis, was installed in the mayor's office.

In Damascus, Emir Faisal had declared himself king earlier that year. Yet when the Allies instead gave Syria to France, he refused to submit. The French easily routed his forces in a four-hour battle, inaugurating their own Syrian Mandate.

Palestine's Arabs were forced to recalibrate. As Musa Kazim Husseini told colleagues: "We must introduce a basic change in our plans here. [Palestine as] southern Syria no longer exists. We must defend Palestine."[25]

The British hoped that replacing the military regime in Jerusalem with a civilian high commissioner might help calm tempers. Their choice for the job, however, only underscored their commitment to the Jewish national home: Herbert Samuel, who as the first Jew in Britain's Cabinet had been an early and enthusiastic champion of the Zionist vision.[26]

The Jews were hardly wasting time. The 1920 riots had prompted the Labor-Zionists to create an armed unit to guard their settlements: the *Haganah* ("Defense"). The group was officially illegal, but the British looked away provided it limited itself to defense.

London was not done with Faisal: Meeting in Cairo in spring 1921, its Middle East mandarins installed the short-lived Syrian monarch as king of Iraq. Meanwhile the Crown created a new polity, Transjordan, loosely attached to Palestine but with Faisal's brother Abdullah as emir. The Zionists—particularly Jabotinsky's more militant acolytes—never forgave what they deemed an amputation. Colonial Secretary Winston Churchill hoped securing both Iraq and the lands east of the Jordan for the Arabs would soften their ire over the Jewish national home.[27]

It did not.

Mufti of Muftis

Two rallies in Jaffa were planned for May Day 1921, both by Jews. One was organized by Labor-Zionists; their rally was authorized. The other was by Marxists hoping to build a Soviet Union of Palestine; theirs was not. When the Marxist procession ran into the Laborites', fists flew. Then some Arabs joined in, having heard that all or most Jews were Bolsheviks, and that Bolsheviks opposed property, marriage, and religion. Soon it was a mob attack. Jews were assaulted in their homes and shops, and women, children, and even the elderly came after to loot.[28]

The crowd then turned on the immigrant hostel, the first stop for all Jewish arrivals. Arab policemen arrived, but they too began shooting at the hostel and helping the mob break past the gate. Other Jews were beaten to death with blunt objects outside the building. Troops arrived only hours later, and by day's end twenty-seven Jews were dead and more than one hundred wounded.[29]

The Haganah forbade acts of revenge, but not all its members heeded. One killed an Arab hunchback, with his children, in an orange grove. Another called together volunteers to break into Arab homes and destroy everything, sparing only the children. They achieved "good results," he recalled. Yet another had to point his gun at a Jewish man to keep him from beating Arabs with an iron rod. "The Jews are doing terrible things," said a high school student in Tel Aviv.[30]

The riots spread to a handful of other Jewish villages before the British finally restored order after a week. One hundred people were dead, equally split between Jews and Arabs; about 150 Jews and 75 Arabs were wounded.

The 1921 riots were the first mass-casualty event in British-controlled Palestine. But like the carnage the year before, authorities deemed them discrete events, limited in time and space. One British officer likened them to flash floods in the Negev desert.[31]

A commission of inquiry was formed. Arab fury, it concluded, came from fears of Jewish demographic, economic, and political domination. It said the Zionist leadership had failed to allay the Arabs' fears—in fact it had only magnified them—and recommended Britain clearly and publicly enunciate its plans for Palestine.

That enunciation came in the form of the 1922 White Paper, known to posterity as the Churchill White Paper but largely written by High Commissioner Samuel himself. It reaffirmed the Balfour Declaration's vision of a Jewish national home *in* Palestine, but rejected any idea of creating a wholly Jewish Palestine, one "as Jewish as England is English." Such a project would be impracticable, it said, and is not Britain's aim. Crucially, it determined that immigration should continue, but only insofar as allowed by the country's "economic capacity . . . to absorb new arrivals."[32]

Shortly after the previous year's riots, Samuel had pardoned two local leaders—one Jew and one Arab—in a bid to calm tempers. He ordered Jabotinsky freed from Acre's medieval prison, and allowed Hajj Amin al-Husseini back from Transjordanian exile.

Jabotinsky was already an established thinker, a regular contributor to newspapers like *Haaretz*. As a wunderkind in Odessa, he had taught himself the major European languages as well as Greek, Latin, and Esperanto; in prison he translated Dante. Had he wished he could have been a force in Russian literature. Instead he pledged his life to Zionism, one of a particularly muscular variety in which self-defense and self-determination took precedence over any notion of God's will or the brotherhood of the working man.[33]

Amin, by contrast, was a lackluster scholar with middling theological credentials, who but for Samuel's intervention would likely have been lost to history. Having repatriated him, the high commissioner went further still, arranging for him to succeed his recently deceased brother as grand mufti, a lifetime position that made him de facto leader of Palestine's Muslims. It was, after the Balfour Declaration, Britain's most fateful decision on Palestine, with consequences more profound than anyone at the time conceived.[34]

Shortly after, Samuel birthed a second Islamic institution—the Supreme Muslim Council—to oversee sharia courts, mosques, and religious schools. It also supervised the shrines and lands held as *waqf*, or charitable trust, established by wealthy donors and kept in their name for posterity. In short, it managed everything once handled by the Ottoman Islamic authorities. History would remember him as grand mufti, but it

GOVERNMENT OF PALESTINE

APPLICATION FOR LAISSEZ-PASSER

(Application must be in English, but Arabic or Hebrew may also be used)

حكومة فلسطين

ממשלת פלשתינה (א"י)

طلب تذكرة مرور

בקשה לרשיון נסיעה

Name (in capitals) HUSSIENI

Names (in capitals) AMIN

Place of Birth Jerusalem date 1896

Nationality Nat of Palestine

Occupation Proprietor

GOVERNMENT OF PALESTINE

APPLICATION FOR LAISSEZ-PASSER

(Application must be in English, but Arabic or Hebrew may also be used)

حكومة فلسطين

ממשלת פלשתינה (א"י)

طلب تذكرة مرور

בקשה לרשיון נסיעה

Name (in capitals) HAJ MOHAMMED AMIN EL HUSSEINI

17164

Place of Birth Jerusalem. date 1896

Occupation President of Supreme Sheri Moslem, Council, Jerusalem.

Amin al-Husseini, 1921 and 1923, before and after his selection as grand mufti (ISA P-3051/26)

was as president of the Supreme Muslim Council that Hajj Amin carried his biggest stick.[35]

Negotiation over the Mandate's precise wording had begun even before the Paris Peace Conference and stretched over three years. In summer 1922 the League of Nations finally confirmed the final text enshrining the Balfour Declaration's call for a Jewish national home in

Palestine, provided nothing be done to prejudice the civil and religious rights of the Holy Land's non-Jews.

That "dual obligation" embodied in the Mandate would engender endless headaches for the imperial power. For the Zionists, however, the Mandate's ratification was an unmistakable triumph: Five years after the Balfour Declaration, the Jewish national project was now an internationally recognized fact.

And still, when the high commissioner moved to form an Arab Agency as a counterpart to the Jewish one, the Arabs resisted. The offer was a gambit, they said, to force their assent to the Jewish national home: They had never recognized the Jewish Agency and therefore needed no counterweight. Samuel's attempts to create a deliberative body of both Jews and Arabs likewise foundered: The former wanted equal representation despite their minority status; the latter balked at such funny arithmetic.

In 1924 Musa Alami was back in Palestine, having graduated Cambridge with honors and been called to the Bar at the Inner Temple. That year also brought his marriage to Sa'adiya Jabri. Genteel and quick-witted, she was like him an Arab aristocrat, the daughter of a preeminent pan-Arabist intellectual from Aleppo.[36] Now the new groom needed a job.

Samuel believed the attorney general's office should hire an Arab. He wrote to Colonial Secretary Leo Amery—a fellow drafter of the Balfour Declaration and, like him, Jewish—endorsing Alami. The secretary protested, noting the candidate had no practical experience at the Bar. Samuel persisted: "I am satisfied that he is a young man of intelligence and excellent character," and besides, "no other Palestinian Moslem has any English legal training." Amery relented, and in summer 1925 Alami joined the administration as a junior legal advisor.

The job included preparing cases for Norman Bentwich—Palestine's Jewish-British attorney general—at times filling in as public prosecutor, and advising him on Islamic religious law and Arab affairs.[37] The work was absorbing but disheartening, as if he were being pulled in three directions at once. He found the British uninterested in their subjects, apart from a few Arab intellectuals—generally Christians—and the most gifted European-Jewish immigrants. His own Arab society seemed increasingly self-absorbed and defensive, with rival factions trampling each other for favors from the administration.

The Jews also appeared ever more closed-off: As their numbers and clout grew through the 1920s, their interactions with Arabs correspondingly dwindled, as if no longer needing them. Even Alami's Jewish foster brother began avoiding eye contact on the street.[38]

Days of Quiet

The "disturbances" of the early 1920s had not impelled Britain to reassess its fundamental guiding principle for Palestine: It would facilitate a Jewish national home while simultaneously protecting individual Arab life and liberty. The blessings of British administration combined with Jewish capital and energy would be self-evident. At some future point, the Crown would grant greater self-rule to Palestine's inhabitants, but the precise constellation thereof remained undefined.

In the absence of violence, the Jewish leadership could largely ignore the Arab issue. Despite an economic downturn in mid-decade, it was a time of growing development, infrastructure, and connectedness to the Empire's markets. Jews from abroad funneled in at least forty million pounds during the Mandate's first decade, and agricultural settlements doubled to over a hundred in number. In 1925 the Hebrew University opened on Mount Scopus with a gala and a speech by Lord Balfour. Albert Einstein and Sigmund Freud sat on its board.

Land purchases doubled in the 1920s, from 650,000 to 1.2 million *dunams*—the Turkish measurement for the earth a pair of oxen can plow daily (roughly a quarter acre). Often those selling were the same Arab leaders who most vituperatively railed against the practice. At least a quarter of the Palestine Arab Congress Executive sold land to Jews, including its president and former Jerusalem mayor, Musa Kazim Husseini, and the mayors of Jaffa and Gaza.

The second half of the 1920s was the Mandate's calmest chapter. Eighty thousand Jews arrived in those years, as many as in the two decades before. Some were moved by the same Zionist ethos that had drawn earlier immigrants; others were driven out of Europe by burgeoning post-war nationalism, as in Poland and Hungary. Many would have gone to the United States had it not drastically cut quotas in its Immigration Act of 1924. By decade's end, Jews amounted to over 160,000 of Palestine's population of one million.[39]

It was Jabotinsky, on Zionism's right flank, who knew the quiet could not last. His 1923 essay "The Iron Wall" predicted that Palestine's Arabs would not just reject any Jewish polity but actively work to destroy it, stopping only once they were convinced it could not be undone. The Jews, he believed, should stop playing coy with their ambitions: What they sought was not a "national home" or autonomy but statehood. Weizmann demurred, and Jabotinsky quit the World Zionist Organization, which the former headed. In spring 1925, he founded a new movement: Revisionist Zionism.

Justice, Jabotinsky wrote, does not mean that a people that forcibly seized territory must retain it for all time, or that a people forcibly removed from its land—even millennia ago—must remain homeless. "Self-determination means revision" of land, so that "those nations who have too much should have to give up some of it to those nations who have not enough or who have none, so that all should have some place on which to exercise their right of self-determination."

His message was unpopular, as it denied the Jewish mainstream—and the British Crown—the confidence that binational cooperation was around the corner, that blood would be the exception and not the rule. "The tragedy lies in the fact that there is a collision between two truths," Jabotinsky maintained. "But our justice is greater."

"The Arab," he contended, "is culturally backward, but his instinctive patriotism is just as pure and noble as our own; it cannot be bought, it can only be curbed by . . . *force majeure*."[40]

DAYS OF WOE

In Jerusalem, Musa Alami was ill. A doctor's note from 1925 shows him with colitis; another one says gastritis. In 1926 it was hives, in 1927 bronchitis, then fever and acute cold. The following year a doctor diagnosed him with incipient pulmonary tuberculosis and recommended he travel to Syria for treatment. He took three months' sick leave, then another six.

His tenuous health notwithstanding, Alami's bond with Bentwich was robust: He typically began his letters "My dear chief" (the attorney general was also chief prosecutor), even as Bentwich opted for the more proper "Dear Alami." Bentwich personally lobbied for him to get a raise, informing the high commissioner that he had "gained considerably in experience and confidence," and that it would be regrettable to lose "a Palestinian Moslem officer of exceptional legal qualifications."[41]

Bentwich's exhortation came as the tranquility that had prevailed through most of the 1920s looked increasingly fragile. The focus was the Western Wall.

Through the first decades of the twentieth century, Jewish rights at the wall had remained tightly circumscribed. It was property of the Islamic waqf, as was the plaza behind it that Jews called the Temple Mount and Muslims the Haram al-Sharif, or Noble Sanctuary, home to Al-Aqsa Mosque. Islamic tradition says the wall is where Muhammad tied his winged steed, Buraq, on his ascent to heaven.

The lane between the wall and the adjoining Arab homes was just eleven feet wide, often strewn with residents' refuse and donkey excrement. The status quo technically banned Jews from raising their voices or even praying at all, though the authorities typically tolerated worship so long as it remained muted. On high holidays, Jews were generally allowed to use benches, a *shofar* (ram's horn), and a screen to divide the sexes.

On Yom Kippur Eve 1928, an Ashkenazi beadle brought a larger Torah ark than usual to the site, and some mats, lamps, and a screen. Police sought to have it removed, but the beadle would not let go—when a constable threw it down the twenty-foot, cactus-filled valley running out from under the Old City, the beadle went tumbling down with it.

Bloodshed had been avoided, and London swiftly issued a White Paper reaffirming the status quo ante: The wall belongs to the Islamic waqf.

Grand Mufti Hajj Amin al-Husseini was satisfied, but only partly. Zionist newspapers were demanding the wall's "redemption"—at least one of their pamphlets showed the Star of David atop the Dome of the Rock. He began a building and public-relations blitz termed the "Buraq Campaign" to solidify Islamic ownership of the wall and the plaza above it. "Having realized by bitter experience the unlimited greedy aspirations of thc Jews," he told the government, "Muslims believe that the Jews' aim is to take possession of the Mosque of Al-Aqsa gradually on the pretense that it is the Temple, by starting with the Western Wall of this place, which is an inseparable part of the Mosque."

He created a "Committee for the Defense of the Noble Buraq" and a "Society for the Defense of Al-Aqsa Mosque." He authorized new construction—a four-foot wall atop the existing wall—ostensibly to shield Arab women on the Haram from men's gazes in homes nearby. The Jews cried foul: The construction violated the status quo, and bricks were falling on the faithful below. Zionist leaders launched their own, even bolder campaign—to purchase the wall itself—but came up short.

Ill winds were blowing. In June 1929 some Arab youths beat up the wall's long-suffering beadle. During a Friday night the next month, Muslims on the Haram banged drums, gongs, and cymbals, part of a recently revived Sufi ceremonial chant. The district commissioner demanded they stop, but the mufti then built a *zawiya*, a small mosque, atop a nearby house; there he installed a *muezzin*, a Muslim summoner to prayer. His incantations, five times daily, seemed to the Jews to grow steadily louder by the week.[42]

The Wall Is Ours

August 15, 1929, fell on the eve of the Ninth of Av, the most mournful date on the Hebrew calendar. On that day in 586 BC, the Babylonians demolished the First Temple in Jerusalem, and in the year 70, the Romans razed the Second. On the same date in the year 135, Rome quashed Bar-Kochba's revolt, exiling Judea's last remaining Jews and rebranding the province *Palestina* after the Philistines in and around Gaza. England expelled its Jews in the thirteenth century, France in the fourteenth, Spain in the fifteenth—all on that same day.

On the Ninth of Av in 1929, some Jews were warning of an impending calamity that, judging by descriptions at the time, rivaled those of history: Britain had reaffirmed the wall as Islamic property, where no screens, benches, or any other objects were to be placed. Even blowing the shofar on high holidays, it seemed, was an affront to Muslim sensibilities. Six thousand Jews massed in Tel Aviv and three thousand at the wall to decry "the gross insult of our holy possessions and national and religious feelings."

The next morning, Friday, another three hundred youth from Jabotinsky's Revisionist movement marched to the wall; they observed two minutes of silence, waved the Zionist flag, and sang "Hatikvah." "The wall is ours!" they chanted.[43]

The same day was the prophet Muhammad's birthday. That morning the mufti's Supreme Muslim Council led a march to the wall. Led by the Al-Aqsa imams, it drew two thousand people. The tumbling beadle was again roughed up and his table overturned. Some marchers burned Jewish holy books and the scraps stuck between the wall's stones.[44]

The next day a seventeen-year-old Jew was attacked after his soccer ball rolled into a tomato patch in Lifta, a village on Jerusalem's outskirts. A Jewish mob turned on an Arab teenager, stabbing him. The Arab teen survived; the Jewish one did not. His funeral four days later was punctuated by cries of vengeance—over the next seventy-two hours, Jews attacked Arabs at least twelve times and Arabs attacked Jews at least seven.[45]

The next Friday before sunrise, several thousand men from nearby villages streamed into Jerusalem. By late morning, twelve thousand worshippers had filled the Haram. At Al-Aqsa, the imam called on them to lift their hands and vow to defend their holy places to the death.

"Then go," he said, "pounce upon your enemies and kill that you in doing so may obtain Paradise." Emotion ran so high, the governor of Jerusalem remembered, that many rushed out of the mosque, sobbing and declaring they could not pray. Some bore daggers and swords; others, pistols and rifles. Exiting the Old City through Jaffa Gate, they killed two Jews, then ran up Jaffa Road attacking passersby and setting stores aflame.[46]

Thirty miles southwest lay Hebron. There Abraham bought a burial plot for his wife Sarah—the Bible's first land sale and its first interment—and was later laid to rest himself by his sons Isaac, patriarch of the Jews, and Ishmael, father of the Arabs.

In 1929, twenty-four thousand Arabs lived in the city alongside seven hundred Jews. Most of the latter were long-established Sephardim, but some were Ashkenazim, including students from America and Lithuania attending a storied yeshiva that had recently relocated from Europe.

More than a decade after the British arrived in the country, the Palestine Police remained a barebones affair: 1,500 men for the entire country, the vast majority of them Arab, led by 175 British officers. In Hebron, conditions were particularly dire: One British superintendent, Raymond Cafferata, oversaw thirty-three constables—thirty-two of them Arab, half of them elderly, and only one Jewish. In Hebron as in Jerusalem, most "native" police did not carry firearms. Amid the nationwide manpower shortage, his urgent requests for reinforcements were rebuffed.

That Friday, as riots racked Jerusalem, a man arrived by motorcycle to Hebron, recounting tales of hundreds of Arabs said to have been killed by Jews and enjoining Hebronites to take revenge. An inflamed crowd gathered at the yeshiva and lynched a student. The only other person present, the head of the yeshiva, survived by hiding in a well.

Superintendent Cafferata received local Jewish leaders and instructed them to concentrate their community in one or a few houses. It seemed a risky proposition, but they trusted Great Britain, the Arab notables, and above all the Almighty. They even declined an offer by the Haganah to send a dozen armed men. Later Cafferata received a delegation of *mukhtars*, headmen of Arab villages, from the area. They told him the mufti was demanding they join the fight and threatening to fine them if they refused. He assured them the city was now calm and told them to go home.

The next morning, the Jewish Sabbath, saw atrocities unlike Palestine had ever known.

A disabled pharmacist and his wife were murdered, their 13-year-old daughter gang-raped and also killed. Another couple survived by rolling in the blood of the others and lying still. Limbs, testicles, and eyes were cut from living people, some of them old men and children. Only one person died by bullet; the rest experienced blunter methods of execution.

In a single day, sixty-seven people were killed and more than fifty wounded.[47]

Amidst the brutality were tales of heroism.

"God, blessed be He, in His great mercy, sent us an Arab who lived in back of our house," wrote Aharon Bernzweig, an American who had retired to Tel Aviv and was summering in Hebron. The neighbor was Abu Mahmoud al-Kurdiya, who with his wife stood outside the home insisting to the rioters they had seen no Jews. The Kurdiyas had left their ten-year-old son inside the house to reassure the terrified Jews that they would not give them up. They coached the boy on words to yell from inside: "There are no Jews here—they all ran away!"

All told, two dozen Arab homes opened their doors, saving at least 250 Jews. Cafferata believed that if not for those rescuers, not a single Jew in Hebron would have remained.[48]

Yet over the following days the assaults spread to two dozen locations across the areas of Palestine's Jewish settlement: along the coast between Tel Aviv and Haifa, down the Jezreel Valley, and into the Galilee. Safed, the hilltop hub of medieval Jewish mysticism, saw the goriest scenes of Hebron repeated.

In all, six days of terror had left 133 Jews dead. Almost as many Arabs were killed by British forces, but seven of them were believed to have been killed by Jews. More than three hundred Jews and two hundred Arabs were wounded.[49]

The riots made headlines worldwide; the *New York Times* devoted most of its first four pages to them. Twenty-five thousand people gathered at Madison Square Garden, where the MC read a message from President Herbert Hoover expressing the American people's "fine sympathy" for the Zionist project. One thousand New Yorkers registered their names to defend Palestine's Jews.[50]

Cairo's *Al-Ahram* newspaper wrote that peace would elude Palestine until the government made clear to the Jews it was an Arab land. "The Arabs will fight in defense of their interests," it vowed, and "if the government practices the policy of silence, it will be the silence of the flame, which will suddenly burst forth."

In Britain, some papers questioned whether Palestine was worth it. The *Evening News* reproved the "insensate folly" of the Zionist experiment; the *Evening Star* said it was the maddest of all Britain's post-war adventures. Others counseled patience. The London *Times* said hesitation there would invite unrest elsewhere in the Empire; the *Daily News* sighed, "However much we may dislike the job, we must go on with it or submit to the derisive condemnation of the civilized world."[51]

Per habit, London called a commission of inquiry, this one headed by Sir Walter Shaw, a former supreme court justice in Ceylon and Singapore. Over two months and sixty sessions, it heard from 140 witnesses.

One was Hajj Amin al-Husseini. The mufti testified for three days straight but left a dreary impression. He likened himself to Jesus, who he said suffered a similarly grievous injustice at Jewish hands during the "Mandate of the Romans." As evidence of Zionist designs on Islamic holy places, he had brought with him the *Protocols of the Learned Elders of Zion*. Asked if he knew it was a Czarist-era forgery, he responded calmly, tersely in the negative.[52]

Another testimony came from Vladimir Jabotinsky. His name had not been on the list, but as it regularly arose in other testimonies the commission summoned him as its final witness. He was traveling in London at the time, and addressed the panel there in January 1930.

Jabotinsky cut to the point. Europe was infected with "incurable anti-semitism" and its Jews faced disaster. No one wanted them, not even America, which since the 1924 Immigration Act had all but closed its gates to immigrants from Eastern Europe. At least thirty thousand a year needed to come to Palestine. The aim was a Jewish majority, a Jewish state. Such a polity need not enjoy full sovereignty, at least not at first, but should enjoy as much self-government as, say, "the State of Nebraska." Jabotinsky said those objectives may sound extreme, but were ultimately the same ones held by Weizmann and by the Labor-Zionists. The only difference, he suggested, was his candor.

It was more than Britain was prepared to tolerate. Days later, Jabotinsky was informed he would not be allowed back to Palestine. He would never set foot there again.[53]

The Shaw Commission released its report in spring 1930. It lamented the mufti's provocations during the "Buraq campaign" and his failure to calm tempers in the weeks before the riots, but nonetheless acquitted him of overall culpability for the slaughter. The Revisionist march to the wall, it said, was the disturbances' proximal cause. Still, the report rejected

Arab assertions that the Jews had drawn first blood: "The outbreak in Jerusalem on the 23rd of August was from the beginning an attack by Arabs on Jews." Jewish acts of violence, it said, "though inexcusable, were in most cases in retaliation for wrongs already committed."

The commissioners weighed the very viability of the Mandate. "From the beginning the two races had no common interest. They differed in language, in religion and in outlook," they wrote. "Though Jewish immigration and enterprise have been of great advantage to Palestine, the direct benefit to individual Arabs . . . has been small, almost negligible." The Jews had simply brought in more immigrants than the country could handle.[54]

The commission had probed the cause of the bloodshed; now London dispatched another delegation to determine what to do about it. Released in October 1930, the so-called Hope Simpson report condemned the Jewish Agency and Histadrut labor federation, refuting their insistence that Arabs were benefiting from the new economy. There was scarcely any land left for Jews to buy, it said, and absent a revolution in Arab cultivation, further Jewish purchases could lead to a serious landlessness crisis.[55]

The same day it released those findings, the government issued a White Paper announcing Jewish immigration quotas would now be contingent on Arab unemployment levels (not just Jewish ones, as previously), and restricting major land sales. It was a coup for the Arabs and a ruinous blow for the Jews. Weizmann resigned as World Zionist Organization president. In Warsaw, fifty thousand marched in protest.

Arab triumph was short-lived. Soon Britain performed yet another turnaround, of the kind that would characterize much of the Mandate period and cast doubt over whether it had any Palestine policy at all.

A Zionist public-relations and lobbying blitz—enlisting influential figures like Churchill, Herbert Samuel, and Lloyd George—ramped up pressure on Ramsay MacDonald, Britain's politically vulnerable first Labour prime minister. Ultimately the campaign worked: The premier wrote Weizmann a letter effectively annulling the Hope Simpson report and the White Paper it had birthed.[56]

In February 1931 MacDonald read the letter in Parliament. The government did not intend to prohibit further land sales, he said, and large-scale immigration could continue. The Mandate's commitments were "solemn international obligations," and Jewish settlement was the Mandate's "primary purpose."[57]

The Arabs called it the Black Letter.

SOME KIND OF AUTOBIOGRAPHY

Lord Balfour died in March 1930. "Near the end of his days," wrote his niece Blanche Balfour Dugdale, "he said to me that on the whole he felt that what he had been able to do for the Jews had been the thing he looked back upon as the most worth his doing." Known universally as Baffy, she was, like him, a committed Christian. Like him, she was a Zionist.

Six months after her uncle's death, she was in Germany during elections in which the previously fringe National Socialist Party swelled its mandate nearly tenfold to become the Reichstag's second-biggest faction. Her husband Edgar was a translator of German.

"I gather, from references in the foreign papers I have read this week, that Hitler has written some kind of Autobiography," she wrote him in a letter. "I am certain that if that has not been translated already, a publisher would consider it just now . . . I know nothing more about the matter than that."[58]

Hitler had published *Mein Kampf* five years prior, but interest in Britain and America had been anemic and no English translations had been commissioned. Even in Germany the seven-hundred-page screed sold poorly, its genocidal reveries going largely unread.

"If, with the help of the Marxian creed, the Jew conquers the nations of this world, his crown will become the funeral wreath of humanity," Hitler wrote. "By warding off the Jews I am fighting for the Lord's work."

In the final chapter, Hitler likewise mused:

> *If, at the beginning of the War and during the War, twelve or fifteen thousand of these Hebraic corrupters of the nation had been subjected to poison gas such as had to be endured in the field by hundreds of thousands of our very best German workers of all classes and*

professions, then the sacrifice of millions at the front would not have been in vain.[59]

Elections in 1932 made the Nazis into parliament's largest party, and on January 30, 1933, Hitler became chancellor. With extraordinary speed he set to overhauling republican Germany into an autocracy. In March his government opened its first concentration camp, at Dachau, for political prisoners; two days later it passed legislation letting him enact laws without the legislature's consent.

In Jerusalem the German consulate began flying the swastika flag, despite repeated efforts by Revisionist youth to remove it. On March 31, 1933, two months after Hitler had taken office, Hajj Amin al-Husseini arranged a meeting with Germany's consul-general.

"Today the mufti told me that Muslims inside and outside of Palestine greet the new regime in Germany, and hope for the spread of Fascist and anti-democratic state authority to other lands," the consul cabled Berlin, and Amin was ready to promote any anti-Jewish boycotts the Nazis may lead.[60]

The very next day Germany held its first, one-day boycott of Jewish-owned stores. The following week Jews were barred from working in government, or as teachers or professors, and soon after, as lawyers, doctors, accountants, and even musicians. The burning of all books by Jewish authors started the month after.

Several weeks later the consul again met the mufti and other Palestinian notables, this time at the desert shrine at Nebi Musa. They proclaimed their admiration for the new Germany and sympathy for Hitler's anti-Jewish measures. They asked one thing: that the government do all it could to keep Jews from Palestine.[61] The irony was thick: Hitler's rise was one of the primary reasons Jews were reaching the country in record numbers.

Edgar Dugdale published the first English excerpts of *Mein Kampf* in *The Times* in summer 1933, then in abridged book form in Britain and America. Still, it drew meager interest. In the three years after publication it sold barely seven thousand copies.[62]

Hitler did share one goal with the Zionists: ending Europe's role as the center of the world's Jewish life. Just months after Hitler's election, Zionist officials traveled to Berlin for negotiations on an agreement that would become known as *Haavara* (Hebrew for "transfer"). The deal allowed emigrants from Germany with at least one thousand pounds to deposit their capital into a Zionist-run banking trust. The bank would use the money to buy German manufactured goods that would then be exported for sale in Palestine. In Palestine the bank would eventually return the new immigrant most of his capital.

The Haavara agreement sparked rancorous debate in the Yishuv. The Labor-Zionist leadership championed it as a pragmatic solution to German Jewry's plight, and one that would benefit the Yishuv economy. Jabotinsky, in European exile, decried the deal as "ignoble, disgraceful and contemptible." The agreement's chief architect, Haim Arlosoroff, was assassinated on a Tel Aviv beach in June 1933; suspicion fell on Jabotinsky's acolytes, but the case was never solved. Ultimately the Haavara would bring tens of thousands of Jews and $35 million in capital to Palestine.[63]

For Hitler, ridding Germany of Jews was only a first step: Zionism could never offer a permanent answer to his Jewish question. "They have no thought of building up a Jewish state in Palestine so that they might perhaps inhabit it," he wrote in *Mein Kampf*, "but they only want a central organization of their international world cheating." Any such state would serve merely as "a refuge for convicted rascals and a high school for future rogues."[64]

Musa Tells Me Otherwise

Sir Arthur Grenfell Wauchope was a member of that upper-class caste of British colonial administrators that oversaw a vast swath of the Earth in the second half of the nineteenth century and first half of the twentieth. Seriously wounded in the Boer War, he served a decade in India before commanding an infantry battalion in France and Mesopotamia during the Great War. In late 1931 he was named high commissioner for Palestine.

Unusual for his class and time, Wauchope (pronounced "Walk-up") harbored no prejudices against Jews and even seemed to like them. The Zionist movement would make massive strides during his tenure.[65] He took the Balfour Declaration as a binding commitment, and the buildup of the national home as the Mandate's fundamental task. The editor of *Filastin*, Yusuf Hanna, grumbled to *New York Times* reporter Joseph Levy—an American-born, Jerusalem-raised, Beirut-educated anti-Zionist Jew—that Wauchope was "more Zionist than the Zionists."[66]

But Wauchope also took the Mandate's "dual obligation" seriously. Soon after arriving in Jerusalem, he concluded that he needed an Arab—astute, discreet, and independent of mind and loyalties—among his advisors. He found one in Musa Alami, whom he named as a personal secretary for Arab affairs on the first day of 1933.[67] For Alami, who had begun his civil service career under Bentwich, the appointment was the second time he would report to a senior official wholly committed to the Jewish national home.

Wauchope was a rich bachelor with no need for a salary: Alami believed he probably spent far more than he was paid. An aristocrat and a humanist, his passions were music, theater, and books—not least the Bible. Alami could hardly find a single text on Palestine with which Wauchope was not acquainted.[68] He seemed to have viewed the post—the last of his career—as an intellectual, anthropological, and even spiritual project.

The high commissioner admired the kibbutzim, but was dedicated to improving the lot of the Arab peasant, the *fellah*. Sometimes he would embarrass his staff by stopping his car in villages, questioning farmers on their opinions and needs. "His eyes," Alami recollected, "would fill with tears at some tale of woe or recital of wrongs, and he would dole out *backshish*"—bribes—"under the firm impression that by giving out fifty piastres he had won a supporter." Wauchope's advisors soon found that their reports on Arab issues would be met by a rejoinder: "Musa tells me otherwise."[69]

Jewish immigration to Palestine was burgeoning, a result of the Yishuv's more established economy, and of Wauchope's arrival in Jerusalem and Hitler's in Berlin. In 1931, just four thousand Jews arrived;

in 1932 their numbers reached ten thousand. By 1933 the figure topped thirty thousand, with at least twenty-two thousand more entering illegally.[70]

In October 1933, Arab notables called for a rally and strike in Jerusalem to demonstrate "the wrath of the Palestinian Arab Nation." The work stoppage lasted a week—the first general strike in Palestine's history. Unlike the riots of 1920, 1921, or 1929, however, demonstrators directed their ire not at Jews but at the British alone.[71]

In Jaffa protesters broke through police cordons, swinging clubs and throwing stones. Some ran toward the government headquarters in the city, and police opened fire. Twenty-six people were killed and some two hundred wounded over the coming days in Nablus, Haifa, and Acre.[72] One of the wounded was the mufti's uncle, ex-mayor Musa Kazim Husseini, who was clubbed by police and died several months later, likely of his injuries. Zionist leaders insisted it was Amin himself who lay behind the riots, just as they believed he had in 1929.

"It was an awful day," remembered one British constable. "Little did we realize what the years ahead would bring."[73]

Alami wrote to authorities in London. Palestine's Arab youth, he warned, were fast concluding that working with the government was getting them nowhere: "If all that can be expected from the present policy is a slow death, it is better to be killed in an attempt to free ourselves of our enemies than to suffer a long and protracted demise."[74]

His health was suffering exactly that: First it was flu, then tonsillitis and bronchitis. "Confined to bed regret can not attend today," he telegraphed Wauchope from the family's winter home in Jericho. The next day he followed up: "Still ill will someone take appeal cases please." Doctors' notes were taking on a more psychological hue: "fever with general malaise," said one; "gastritis and nervous exhaustion," said another.[75]

Meanwhile, unbeknownst to Alami, the Jewish Agency had begun a campaign to sideline him. In London, Zionist emissaries painted him as soft on terror, and with undue influence: He was the "grand vizier" whispering in the ear of "Sultan" Wauchope.[76] Allied MPs prodded the government to dismiss him as Wauchope's secretary. In late 1933 he returned to the justice system as government advocate. Alami no longer had the high commissioner's ear, but his clout remained: He was the first non-Englishman named to such a senior post in Palestine's courts.[77]

David Ben-Gurion was head of the Federation of Hebrew Workers—better known simply as the Federation, or *Histadrut*—and of Palestine's dominant Jewish political faction, the Workers' Party of the Land of Israel—better known by its Hebrew acronym *Mapai*. He was co-director of the Jewish Agency's political department—its de facto foreign ministry—and would soon chair the agency itself.

Born David Gruen in Russian-controlled Poland, he arrived in the Holy Land in 1906 at age twenty. Like Musa Alami, it was on a ship to Palestine that he first encountered his future antagonists. "We met a few, and they clung to us for the whole journey," he wrote his father, referring to Arabs. "They sang for us, entertained us, and tried to amuse us as much as possible. . . . They are nearly all good-hearted, and are easily befriended. One might say they are like big children."

Alighting in Jaffa was less congenial: "The harbor suddenly was filled with skiffs, and Arabs clambered up the sides of our ship. The shouting and shoving were awful." Per custom, Arab porters lifted both passengers and baggage in their arms, depositing them into the smaller boats, then at shore picked them up again and placed them on dry ground. Arabs literally carried Ben-Gurion to the Land of Israel, but his diaries offer no recognition of the irony of that fact. Jaffa itself was a dusty and indolent disappointment (Tel Aviv was still three years from inception), and he spent as little time there as possible.

Hebraicizing his surname (Joseph Ben-Gurion was a Jewish rebel leader against Rome), the new immigrant dabbled in work in the farming settlements and in local Zionist politics. He spent a year in Salonica, Ottoman-controlled Greece, to learn Turkish. The Ottomans, after all, ruled the Promised Land, and he was convinced Zionists like him needed to speak the sovereign's language. Passing his language exams, he enrolled in Istanbul University law school, grew a mustache, and donned a fez.[78]

After graduation he returned to Palestine, but his bid to court the Turks came to naught: When the Great War broke out, they expelled him from the country along with thousands of other subjects of their Russian enemy. He rode out the war conducting Zionist activism and fundraising in New York, where he also picked up a bride, the Russian-born Paula. The Balfour Declaration spurred him to volunteer for Britain's Jewish Legion, but dysentery left him bedridden in a Cairo hospital as His Majesty's Armed Forces conquered Palestine.

With an aptitude for languages, Ben-Gurion was fluent in Yiddish, Hebrew, Russian, Polish, and English, with some knowledge of German and French. In later life he learned Spanish and, to read Plato, Ancient Greek. He achieved rapid fluency in Ottoman Turkish, a language written in Arabic characters and infused with Arabic vocabulary. Nonetheless, aside from some brief efforts at a Galilee commune and in Salonica, he never made a sustained effort at Arabic and never mastered its basics.

Throughout the 1920s, as he rose up the Labor-Zionist ranks, Ben-Gurion's interactions with Arabs could be counted on one hand. It was only after the 1929 riots that the otherwise farsighted activist began to contemplate whether Zionism's success might lay not exclusively with the ruling empire but also in an accommodation with the land's other inhabitants. The Zionist movement, he came to believe, needed a decade of peace to build up a Jewish majority, and for that it depended on quiet in the land.[79]

"I decided to meet a certain Arab who had a reputation as a nationalist and a man not to be bought by money or by office, but who was not a Jew-hater either," he later wrote. The man was "extraordinarily intelligent," judicious, and trustworthy. "The man was Musa Alami."[80]

In March 1934, Ben-Gurion called Alami to a meeting in the Jerusalem apartment of Moshe Shertok, his co-director in the political department. Russian-born, Shertok had arrived in Palestine as a child and lived for a time in an Arab village near Ramallah. In the Great War he served the Ottomans as an interpreter, and as the only top-level Zionist official who spoke Arabic,[81] he fancied himself something of an Arabist.

Shertok began with an extended discourse in familiarly soothing terms, comparing Palestine to a "crowded hall in which there is always room for more people," and to which Jews could enter without harming the Arabs. On the contrary, he said, Jewish capital and energy would benefit them immensely.

Ben-Gurion, of gruffer disposition, interrupted: The Jews had nowhere to go but Palestine, and the Arabs had vast, undeveloped expanses at their disposal. He wanted to know if there was a deal to be had: We want unlimited immigration, he said, and we want to become the majority. Was there a chance of the Arabs coming to terms with those aims?

Alami said he saw no reason to negotiate on that basis.[82]

What if, Ben-Gurion continued, the Zionists supported the creation of an Arab federation of which Palestine would be part? Alami thought for a moment, and said the idea was worth considering. He rejected Jewish-Arab parity in a legislative council, but did not rule out an equal share of the Mandate's executive authority, which was held solely by the British.

Now the floor was Alami's. The Arabs were nearing the breaking point, he said. The best lands were coming under Jewish ownership, and only a minority of Arabs were benefiting. The major industrial concessions like the Palestine Electric Corporation and the Dead Sea potash plant were Jewish-owned. Arabs were paying higher taxes than their brethren in neighboring countries, and the entire Arab economy had been knocked out of joint.

To Shertok's contention that Arabs stood to gain from Zionism, he answered that he would rather the country remain poor and desolate for another hundred years until the Arabs could develop it themselves.[83]

Until that meeting, Ben-Gurion recalled, the Zionists' presumption had been that they were bringing blessings to the Arabs, who therefore had no cause to oppose them. In his first talk with Musa Alami, "that assumption was shattered." For the first time, Ben-Gurion heard an articulate expression of the litany of Arab grievances, from someone he deemed "sincere, straightforward and sensible," and a genuine "Arab patriot."

Still, Ben-Gurion left the meeting satisfied. His two major proposals—a Jewish state within an Arab federation and equal executive authority—had not been summarily rejected,[84] and he felt Alami was a man of his word. Alami was similarly impressed by Ben-Gurion's candor, and they parted on friendly terms.

Even so, the meeting also marked the final stage of Alami's education on the Zionist movement's intentions. He had been, in his own words, "incredibly naive" about its goals. His biographer wrote that until that encounter he had "regarded the Zionists rather as a Kenya farmer regards elephants: dangerous creatures always liable to destroy his property and quite capable of being lethal, which he expects the Government to keep under control but against which he feels no personal enmity."

Alami had hitherto accepted Zionist assurances that their plans remained within the limits defined by the Mandate: a national home *in* Palestine. Now, having engaged two of mainstream Zionism's principal decision-makers, he had no doubt: Their ambition was a Jewish state, and in as much of Palestine as they could claim.[85]

Six months later, Ben-Gurion again reached out. Alami replied that while it would "give him the greatest pleasure" to meet, he was indisposed.

> *My dear Mr. Ben-Gurion,*
>
> *Many thanks for your note of today; I am very sorry that I was unable to get in touch with you sooner but I was not at all well. I am still in the village + if it will be convenient to you I shall be very glad if you would come to tea with me tomorrow afternoon at any time that will suit you.*
>
> *Au revoir till tomorrow.*[86]

Ben-Gurion traveled to Alami's village on the road to Bethlehem. They met under an oak in the yard that the host said was the oldest and largest in Palestine. Alami wanted to talk economics; he asked why the Zionist Labor movement employed only Jews. Ben-Gurion replied: In the diaspora, Jews were cut off from the land and accused of living off the toil of others. In the Land of Israel, they had no intention of being lords of the manor: Without doing the work themselves—skilled and unskilled, easy and hard, in factories and fields—they could not claim it as their homeland.

Alami did not rule out compromise, suggesting some form of Jewish autonomy around Tel Aviv as part of an Arab federation under British guardianship. That, he said, could constitute the Jewish national home the Mandate envisioned. He was even willing to contemplate Ben-Gurion's proposal for free Jewish immigration, as long as it came after the formation of that Arab federation.

They met twice more that month. The second time, Alami—who was in Jerusalem seeing a doctor Ben-Gurion had recommended—personally drove his guest back to his own home. Alami said he had told the mufti of their talks. Hajj Amin, he said, greeted the news like a "bombshell"—he had never imagined there were Jews who sincerely wished for an agreement with the Arabs. The mufti had no issue with the talks continuing, and asked only that the Zionist leader issue a public declaration that could mollify Arab opinion about Jewish designs. Ben-Gurion was amenable. Again they parted amicably.

Ben-Gurion hurried off a note to a colleague sketching the outlines of how an agreement as discussed with Alami might look: Jewish national ambitions did not conflict with broader Arab ones but complemented them, and the Palestine question was one to be settled by the entire Jewish and Arab peoples. The Palestinian Arabs could stay where they were, and would receive assistance in health, finance, and science. Jews could settle in Palestine without restriction. Eventually a Jewish-majority Palestine would arise, but one linked to an Arab federation so that the country's Arabs would be part of a regional majority. The Jews would help the Arab lands develop and unify.

After their meeting, Alami telephoned Ben-Gurion in Tel Aviv, suggesting he meet privately with the mufti. Alami and Amin may have been near-opposites in outlook, but they had family ties: Alami's sister was married to the mufti's cousin and political ally Jamal Husseini.

Alami also put another family member at Ben-Gurion's disposal: his father-in-law. Based in Geneva, Ihsan Jabri co-edited the preeminent newspaper of 1930s Arab nationalism, *La Nation Arabe*, with the Druze intellectual Shakib Arslan. Ben-Gurion was confident that serious negotiations with Hajj Amin were within reach, and that the road to him led through Geneva. He and Alami agreed that on his return from Switzerland, he would meet with the mufti.[87]

The Geneva rendezvous lasted three hours. Ben-Gurion told his hosts he foresaw the rise of a Jewish polity that would absorb as many as eight million immigrants. Arslan balked: The Jews could try building their national home behind British bayonets, but the Arabs could never agree to such a thing. A Jewish-majority state, even in an Arab federation, was a dream, he said. Even if the Jews gained independence, the Arabs would never recognize it. Jabri, Alami's father-in-law, was more congenial in demeanor, but the substance was the same.

Immediately after Ben-Gurion left, his hosts published the contents of the supposedly secret summit in their paper. They dismissed his "childish and illogical proposals" as "nonsense" toward which it was hard to keep a straight face. The whole encounter was portrayed as a know-your-enemy ruse.[88]

Ben-Gurion felt betrayed, the optimism stoked by his meetings with Alami dashed. On hearing of the affair, the latter said he felt "embarrassed and ashamed." Over a decade would pass before the two would meet again, and Ben-Gurion never met the mufti. A year and a half would pass before he held any more talks with prominent Arabs at all.

Later he would remember the whole enterprise as "the experiment that failed."[89]

Chapter 2

The Bloody Day in Jaffa

Izz al-Din al-Qassam was born in 1882 near Latakia, Syria, the son of a Quran teacher who headed a local Sufi order. Like Hajj Amin, he matriculated at Al-Azhar in Cairo, and like him, fell under the sway of the Salafi thinker Rashid Rida, and Rida's mentor, Muhammad Abduh. These men believed the Islamic establishment had grown stale and sterile, allowing Muslims to fall behind the Christian West in technological, economic, and political prowess. Returning to the example of the Prophet's time, while also promoting reason and modern science, would revitalize Islam in its confrontation with modernity.[1]

Thus galvanized, Qassam returned to Syria, preaching in a village mosque and exhorting the faithful against gambling and drinking and toward keeping the Ramadan fast. Once he expounded on the *hadith*—a saying attributed to the Prophet—that the difference between the praying and non-praying man is like that between a living one and a corpse. To illustrate the point, he instructed a disciple to seize an impious local, place him in a coffin, and carry him around the village.[2]

Qassam's conception of *jihad* melded the individual and political: Muslims' spiritual struggle was inseparable from their temporal battles. He tried, unsuccessfully, to travel to Libya to resist the invading Italians, served the Ottomans as a chaplain in the Great War, and, back in Syria, enlisted in a succession of militias loyal to Faisal in his rebellion against the French. Each day he would teach his men a Quranic verse, explaining its meaning in the context of jihad. For months he led fighters harassing the French from a coastal mountain redoubt, once held by the Crusaders, curiously called Jabal Sahyun—Mount Zion.[3] When the French condemned him to death, he fled south to Haifa.

Hajj Amin appointed Qassam as imam at a new mosque his Supreme Muslim Council had built in Haifa. The preacher's charisma and his credentials as an Azhar graduate and freedom fighter earned him a committed band of devotees. He started a night school for literacy and tried to lure wayward young Muslims from crime. Sometimes he preached with a sword or gun in hand. Once he exhorted a young shoeshiner to trade his brush for a pistol and shoot the next Englishman who sat on his stool.[4]

In 1929 the Haifa sharia court made him marriage registrar, requiring him to travel the towns and villages of northern Palestine. That year's riots and the 1931 Black Letter convinced him the time was ripe to act. He founded an armed group, the Black Hand, widely known as the *mashayekh*: the sheikhs. The villains of Qassam's early preaching had been the British; now they were the Jews. In April 1931 three members of Yagur, near Haifa, were ambushed at the kibbutz gate. The next year four others were killed in Galilee agricultural settlements, including a father and son whose home was firebombed in Nahalal.[5]

The early 1930s brought transformation to Haifa. In 1933 the government inaugurated Palestine's first modern port there; the next year it opened the country's first international airport and laid the terminus for the oil pipeline to Iraq. Palestine Railways was headquartered there, as was the Nesher cement works—the country's largest company, owned by a Jewish industrialist from Russia. Jews were pouring in, powering the city's building boom, creating new garden suburbs outside it, and giving the city a Jewish majority by mid-decade.[6]

Attracted by work opportunities, Arab men were also streaming into Haifa—from surrounding villages and as far as Syria's Hauran region. Yet their reception once they arrived was starkly different: Jewish workers were represented by the Histadrut, which built them modern living quarters and convinced the government to pay them as much as 50 percent more than their Arab counterparts on the pretext that their living standard was higher. Arab workers had no such representation and occupied shantytowns on the city outskirts.[7]

Qassam lived with and ministered to Haifa's new urban proletariat: stevedores, railwaymen, and construction workers. Some were former tenant farmers whose lands were now Jewish-owned; many were illiterate. "He laughed like a child, and spoke with the simplicity of a child," one student remembered.

Qassam quoted *hadiths* on martyrdom by memory. New followers pledged their loyalty with a pistol or dagger beside a Quran, which they then carried at all times. He gave them basic military and endurance training: Recruits would walk barefoot, forgo food and water, and sleep outside in the cold.[8]

Palestinian Arabs' national ambitions appeared to be in mortal danger. Britain had allowed 30,000 Jewish immigrants in 1933, 42,000 in 1934, and a record 62,000 in 1935. And that was before counting the tens of thousands of Jews who had arrived illegally. There were now nearly 400,000 Jews in the country—almost 30 percent of the population—having doubled in just four years. Tel Aviv's population had tripled over the same short period. In 1933 there had been 650 land sales to Jews totaling 37,000 *dunams* (9,000 acres); by 1935 the number of sales made and acreage acquired had both doubled. The country's Jewish-dominated banking, industrial, and construction sectors flourished even as much of the world remained sunk in depression.[9]

In Germany, Hitler declared himself *Führer* in summer 1934, and the next winter defied the Versailles Treaty to reestablish a German air force. In autumn 1935 Mussolini's troops invaded Ethiopia, annexing it to his Fascist "Italian Empire." Despite Britain's strategic interests in East Africa—Ethiopia was surrounded by British colonies, and enemy control there could threaten the Suez Canal—London acquiesced. The Arabs of Palestine started to wonder if Western democracies were declining relative to the Fascist powers that seemed everywhere on the march. And they wondered whether a world war was looming, one that might rid their country of Britain and the Jews for good.[10]

"The Middle East in its entirety is awaiting this opportunity and is doing what it can to hasten its arrival," wrote the pro-Husseini Jaffa newspaper *Al-Difa* ("The Defense"), "in the belief that war is the only means whereby the Arabs could achieve their national aspirations and put an end to the Zionist threat."[11]

In mid-October, Arab workers at Jaffa Port discovered an arms cache hidden in a cement shipment from Europe and addressed to Jews. Arab opinion was inflamed, sparking protests nationwide. Qassam moved to seize the moment.[12]

On November 6 he and two dozen companions sold their belongings (including their wives' jewelry) to buy arms. Next to a cave in the hills that the Arabs called Faquah and the Jews called Gilboa, they encountered a Jewish police sergeant and two Arab constables searching for petty criminals who had broken into a kibbutz grapefruit grove. They killed the sergeant, Moshe Rosenfeld, and let his comrades go.[13]

Qassam and his band were now hunted men. Two weeks after departing Haifa, they found themselves surrounded in a forest near Jenin. Police called on them to surrender, but Qassam fought on. In a battle lasting four hours, he and three others were killed.[14] He was buried in Balad al-Sheikh, beside the Nesher plant overlooking Haifa Bay.

Overnight, a cult hero was born. On its front page, *Al-Difa* called him the "Martyr Sheikh Izz al-Din al-Qassam Effendi, who fell for religion, faith, and principle." Jaffa's *Filastin* newspaper dubbed him "His excellency the martyr Sheikh Izz al-Din al-Qassam."

"God's mercy upon him," it wrote, "he was a true Muslim."[15]

Ben-Gurion instantly grasped the event's significance. This was not petty politics between the mufti and his detractors or the eternal bickering between Husseinis and Nashashibis. Here was a man not driven by power or lucre but by an ideology that, whatever one's judgment of it, was authentic and deep. His death gave the Arabs "moral power" they had hitherto lacked. Qassam's example was certain to inspire others, stamping Palestine in the world's imagination as a land not of growth and regeneration but of terror, thereby jeopardizing the entire Zionist project.

"This is the first time the Arabs have seen that a man could be found ready to give his life for an idea," he said. Now there would be "dozens, hundreds, if not thousands like him."[16]

Hewers of Wood

"The right honorable and gallant gentleman would not quarrel with me if I said most Jews really want the whole of Palestine, or else, alternatively, to reduce the existing population to the position of the Hittites in the Bible, namely, 'hewers of wood and drawers of water.'"

The speaker was Anthony Crossley, a Conservative backbencher.

"The Gibeonites," grumbled Eustace Percy, a high-born Minister without Portfolio.

It was late March 1936 and the House of Commons was debating High Commissioner Wauchope's proposal for a legislative council for Palestine that would grant the Arab majority a far greater voice in its own administration.

"Was it the Gibeonites?" Crossley continued, undeterred. At any rate, Britain's Palestine policy was a mistake, he said, a contradiction in terms. A small land could not become a national home for a scattered population of millions without prejudicing the rights of its existing inhabitants. The country ought to be divvied into cantons, like Switzerland, before its Arab society collapsed from excessive taxation, debt, and fast-diminishing farmland. "The fellah is neither lazy nor unintelligent," Crossley said, he just needed a sporting chance.

Douglas Clifton Brown, a fellow Tory, concurred: "We are all most sorry for the Jews and their sufferings"—six months prior, Hitler's Nuremberg Laws had stripped German Jews of citizenship—but it was nonetheless reasonable to understand how deeply "the Arabs fear the invasion of the Jews." If the high commissioner's initiative failed, he cautioned, the turmoil in Palestine and the entire region could dwarf anything seen before.

Change was roiling the Middle East. In 1932 Britain had granted Iraq independence (while keeping military privileges) under King Faisal. In early 1936, Syrians launched a fifty-day general strike that led to talks over a French withdrawal from the country. Egypt would soon begin similar negotiations with the British Crown. Only in Palestine, it seemed, were Arab aspirations not just stalled but under mortal threat.

Yet Crossley and Clifton Brown were alone in favoring Wauchope's plan. A dozen MPs from both the governing coalition and the opposition rose to denounce any move to proportional representation, which they warned would give the Arabs veto power over the Jewish national home's growth. One by one they saluted Zionism's achievements.

Henry Procter, a Conservative, called it "the greatest social experiment that has taken place in the world." Two Labourites deemed it a "modern miracle." A third, Josiah Wedgwood, said British rule had been Arab peasants' "salvation," proving that by "the use of civilization we can help natives instead of destroying them." Liberal leader Archibald Sinclair noted that "vast sums of Jewish capital have flowed into Palestine, expanded the revenues, fertilized the soil and increased the population of the country, both Jewish and Arab."

Winston Churchill, excluded from the Cabinet for seven years (he called them, biblically, his wilderness years), was in the early stages of his crusade against Hitler. He too railed against any step toward self-government for Palestine, which would trap Germany's Jews in the Third Reich. Those half-million souls were

> *subjected to most horrible, cold, scientific persecution, brutal persecution . . . their blood and race declared defiling and accursed; every form of concentrated human wickedness cast upon these people by overwhelming power, by vile tyranny . . . when that is the case, surely the House of Commons will not allow the one door which is open, the one door which allows some relief, some escape from these conditions, to be summarily closed.*

The House of Lords saw a similar display of support. Just one member endorsed the legislative council; several others agreed that facilitating the Jewish national home was the Mandate's fundamental purpose. One peer remarked that he could not recall any other debate with such unanimity of opinion.[17]

In London, across the diaspora, and in Palestine, Jewish leaders exulted.[18] They could not have known the calamities ahead.

The Man from Salonica

Israel Hazan was a recent immigrant living in Florentin, a neighborhood between Jaffa and Tel Aviv inhabited mostly by fellow Jews from Salonica. At nearly seventy, he had not planned to work in his new home, but when his son lopped off some digits in a carpentry mishap he found himself back in the labor pool. He joined the same industry he had left behind in Greece—poultry—buying chickens from Arab farmers around Nablus and bringing them to the Florentin market for slaughter and sale.

On the morning of April 15, 1936, Hazan set out in a truck piled high with empty coops. It was driven by his young neighbor Zvi Dannenberg, a Haganah member and the grandson of a founder of Tel Aviv.[19] All day they traversed the Arab villages, filling the vehicle with their clucking commodities.

As darkness fell, Hazan and Dannenberg began their return. In the hills between Nablus and Tulkarem they spotted a roadblock guarded by a handful of armed Arab men, their faces covered with keffiyehs. Bandits seeking bribes or loot were common on these rural roads, but these men ordered each passing car to pay up for a single purpose: buying arms to avenge the death of Izz al-Din al-Qassam.[20]

When their turn came, the two Jews were told to turn off the headlights and hand over their money.

Another vehicle arrived, this one with a Jewish driver and a passenger from a German-Templar village near Tel Aviv. The men instructed the German to stay seated and told the driver to surrender his cash and sit with the other two Jews in the truck.

Hazan began to murmur to himself: "What will be our end?"

More cars passed, all driven by Arabs. The armed men asked each for contributions. Returning to the Jews, they demanded more money from Dannenberg, who said he had none. The older man from Greece begged for mercy, but they shot all three on the spot.[21]

Two of them were seriously wounded. Israel Hazan became the first victim of what in time would be known as *al-Thawra al-Arabiya al-Kubra*, the Great Arab Revolt.

The Jewish newspapers seethed. "We have learned from experience in this land and are far from self-delusion concerning the cultural level of part of the population," proclaimed an editorial in *Haaretz*, newly acquired by the Schocken family, liberal Jews who owned department stores in Germany.[22]

The Zionist *Palestine Post* blared a similar theme on its front page. "On one side, the forces of destruction, the forces of the desert, have risen, and on the other stand firm the forces of civilization and building," it said, quoting a speech by Chaim Weizmann. The paper denied any political motivation for the act, deriding its perpetrators as highwaymen and brigands.

"The bandits professed 'nationalist' slogans," marveled a Hebrew daily's headline in scoff-quotes.[23]

The next night two armed Jews in khaki shorts walked into Appelbaum's banana plantation near Petah Tikva and knocked on a worker's hut at random. A fruit picker, Hassan Abu Rass, opened the door and was met with eleven pistol bullets. His shack-mate Salim al-Masri was wounded and would die shortly after. They would be the revolt's first Arab fatalities.[24]

Hundreds attended Hazan's funeral the next morning in Florentin. The casket was carried to Eliyahu Hanavi, the Greek synagogue on Levinsky Street where the dead man had prayed. By the time the procession reached Allenby, the city's main commercial street, it numbered at least 1,500 people, forcing stores, workshops, and factories to close for hours. It was the largest Jewish demonstration Palestine had ever seen.

Crowds blocked mourners from placing the coffin in a waiting car, insisting on carrying it on their shoulders. Rumors spread that Dannenberg, the driver, had also died. Some in the crowd, likely members of Jabotinsky's Revisionist movement, brayed for revenge, urging the crowd to Arab-majority Jaffa.[25]

Hazan was buried Friday morning in Tel Aviv's old cemetery on Trumpeldor Street. Afterward around a hundred Jews started walking south—toward Jaffa, police feared—and were met by British batons. Some of the marchers responded with stones.[26]

Over the course of the Sabbath, from Friday to Saturday evening, Arabs plying their trades in Tel Aviv complained to police of harassment or assault. An Arab man collecting a debt in the Yemenite Quarter was beaten, an Arab bus stoned. Ali Shauki's greengrocery was broken into and vandalized. Shoeshine boys, pretzel sellers, and ice deliverymen were roughed up, their wares strewn into the street.

Some Jewish youth broke the lamplight of a horse-cart taxi driver. They then turned to his passenger, a Jew who owned an orchard nearby: "Jewish blood is shed, and you're traveling in an Arab cart?" They were refugees from Hitler and spoke in German. In broken Arabic, they threatened the coachman's life if he did not return to Jaffa. Others inveighed against the government or raised the cry of Jabotinsky's youth movement, Betar: "In blood and fire Judea fell! In blood and fire Judea shall rise!"

The Jewish leadership dismissed the incidents as the workings of a few "street urchins" riled up by Revisionists. By Saturday evening quiet returned, and Arabs and Jews alike went home to ready for the start of the workweek in the morning.[27]

That next morning was Sunday, April 19. Rumors began to circulate among Jaffa's Arabs that the poultry driver had died and that the Jews were planning a second funeral rally, accompanied by the intimidation and violence of the first. Three other pieces of hearsay circulated simultaneously: Jews had killed two Arabs in Tel Aviv, another four in Jaffa, and three more in an orange grove outside town. A crowd developed demanding to see the purported victims' bodies. The commissioner of Jaffa district, a Mr. Crosbie, denied the gossip, as did the imam of Mahmoudiya Mosque, the city's largest, but to little effect.[28]

A soda-factory owner named Eliezer Bichutsky was attending to some business in Manshiya—Jaffa's closest quarter to Tel Aviv, centered around Hassan Bek Mosque. Decades earlier, after the Great War, he had fought off pogromists in Ukraine. Now he was in his forties and heavier. A group of men emerged from a cafe wielding barstools, wood and metal rods, and knives. A Jewish carriage driver had spotted the trouble and was trying to flee. Bichutsky tried to jump in, pleading in Yiddish—"Jews, let me on, I'll never forget it!"—but the panicked horse galloped off and within seconds he fell off. The mob smashed his skull, leaving him face-down in a sandy alley outside the mosque.

At a government office near the Ottoman clock tower, Jews waited for the rage to subside. Spotting an opening, three of them—two young men and a woman—tried to escape Jaffa. A throng perhaps one hundred strong pursued them, led by smartly dressed men in European attire. The woman and one of the men eluded them, but a handful reached the third, a legal clerk, and ambushed him with knives, hammers, and stones. "I heard his screams," a witness said, describing onlookers as clapping. Someone went into the bloodied man's pockets and calmly walked away. He was taken to a private home but lay for forty-five minutes before help arrived. The man was later named as Haim Pashigoda, age twenty.[29]

He was killed a few hundred feet from Jaffa's central police station. So was Yitzhak Frenkel, who worked at a bus garage and was felled by a log or iron rod—accounts differed—with stones and bricks finishing the job. Witnesses said the main culprit wore European dress and a red fez. They said more than a dozen Arab and British police, armed only with clubs, watched the homicide unfold.

None of the victims was shot. All met death from objects either blunt—pipes, beams, stones, bricks, chairs, fists, and feet—or sharp—pocketknives and daggers. One was nearly eighty.

An electrician with a passion for Russian poetry had spent the morning repairing the wiring at Mahmoud Hamoud's cafe on Salehi Street. More than a dozen men burst in, knocked him off his ladder, and stabbed him in the back.

Plasterers named Kornfeld and Kupermintz were employed at a grand Arab house on King Faisal Street. Both were active in the Labor movement; Kornfeld, trained as a teacher in Vienna, was learning Arabic. A group set upon them, ignoring Arab residents' calls from their balconies to desist. Within moments the two men stopped moving. They lay dying beside Perlin's lumber warehouse for an hour before police appeared.[30]

There were other onlookers who showed humanity. Arab stevedores carried Jewish coworkers to safety by boat. Arab women took in one of the plasterers who had been working with the slain men. The manager of the hardline newspaper *Al-Jamia al-Islamiya* offered to escort Jews to Tel Aviv, and a certain Imam Issa had his chauffeur drive some Jewish strangers there in their own car, returning himself on foot. A carter stood watch over the abandoned wagon of a Jewish colleague and fed his hungry mules. The guard of the garage that employed Yitzhak Frenkel warded off assailants with a knife. And Mahmoud Hamoud, eponymous owner of the cafe-turned-crime-scene, spirited out a second electrician by outfitting him in a waiter's jacket and persuading police to falsely arrest him for theft.[31]

The Jews were not entirely passive, either: In the morning some knocked over Arab-owned chicken coops and vegetable carts, and others stoned cars heading to Jaffa on the assumption that Arabs were behind the wheel. The sight of drivers with broken bones and smashed windows raised tensions in Jaffa to the breaking point.[32]

Attacks continued through the early afternoon. Laborers from Syria's Hauran region set fire to Tel Aviv's Yemenite Quarter, a narrow shantytown of wooden huts, burning it to the ground.[33] Its residents joined some twelve thousand Jewish refugees from Jaffa and adjacent neighborhoods taking shelter in synagogues, factories, and homes in Tel Aviv.[34]

By 2:00 p.m., five hours after the riots began, police and troops had restored calm. Nine Jews were dead and nearly sixty wounded. Two Arabs had been killed by police and some thirty were wounded.[35]

A mass grave was dug at the old cemetery next to that of Israel Hazan, the poultry merchant. Three victims could not be identified. Later it emerged that one was a bank manager. The other, an orphan of the pogroms, was a milk-truck driver from Be'er Tuvia, Jewish Palestine's southernmost settlement, near the Arab town of Isdud.[36]

Again the Zionist papers were infuriated. "The Bloody Day in Jaffa," howled a banner headline in Tel Aviv's *Davar*, the organ of the Histadrut labor federation. "The riot's gravest implication," the *Palestine Post* editorialized, was a "contempt for human life which it revealed among, we hope, only the scum of Jaffa's population."[37]

The Arabic press in Jaffa told another story, playing down the Jewish body count and emphasizing the two Arabs—Muhammad Abu Zeid and Abed Ali—killed by police. More than anything they raged against perfidious Albion and world Jewry for bringing Palestine to such a state.

"Jaffa changed in a single minute," ran the front page in *Al-Difa*. *Al-Jamia al-Islamiya* horrified readers with tales of armed, merciless

Jews hunting defenseless Arabs. *Filastin* blamed Britain for the accursed Balfour Declaration, and the Arab leadership for its divisiveness and venality.[38]

The government rushed through emergency regulations letting it search and occupy buildings, impose curfews, censor letters and the press, arrest without warrant, and even deport rioters from the country. Troops were dispatched to Jaffa to augment police. In Jerusalem authorities requisitioned taxis and buses amid rumors that residents of nearby villages planned to descend on the city. The small Jewish populations of Hebron—with memories still fresh of 1929—and Beersheba were transferred to Jerusalem. Police arrested dozens of Arabs in Jaffa for violence, rioting, and incitement, and at least fifty Jews in Jerusalem suspected of taking up arms.[39]

"Palestine is not a picnic," concluded New York's progressive *The Nation*. "Two powerful forces are colliding. Blood is inevitable. It has flowed in the past, it is flowing today; it will flow in the future until one side emerges victorious."[40]

And so it did. The next morning Selig Levinson and Shlomo Marsum were helping evacuate residents of Tel Aviv's Shapira quarter when they were shot dead from an orchard. A recent arrival from Warsaw was killed in Jaffa and one from Budapest at the entrance to the neighboring village of Abu Kabir.[41]

A seventy-seven-year-old rabbi from Afghanistan was stabbed in his home and died the next day. A Yemenite floorer, twenty-eight, met the same fate on the street that the British and Jews called King George and the Arabs still called Jamal Pasha. Just before midnight an electrician, twenty-one, rushed to Jaffa to offer help and was cut down on Herzl Street.[42]

Zvi Dannenberg, the poultry driver, expired after five days in hospital. The Zionist press memorialized him as a "man of iron" who could lift the side of a truck single-handed.[43]

All were laid in a communal grave in Tel Aviv, not far from the victims of 1921 and 1929.

Two days of carnage in Jaffa had left twenty-one people dead: sixteen Jews killed by Arabs and five Arabs by police. Some 150 people were wounded, roughly equally split between Jews and Arabs.[44]

A Tremendous Moral Force

George Antonius was Arab Palestine's most gifted man and perhaps its most troubled.

Born to a Greek-Orthodox family in a Lebanese mountain village, he was raised in Alexandria, a multiethnic hub a tenth of whose denizens were foreign-born: Greeks, Italians, British, Ashkenazi and Sephardic Jews, and Levantine Arabs like the Antoniuses. His father was a wealthy cotton merchant, his mother an eccentric bohemian who kept a bustling literary salon.

Antonius received a world-class education, first at Alexandria's British-run Victoria College and then, like his close friend Musa Alami, at Cambridge. He was drawn to the fledgling Arab nationalist movement, particularly *Al-Fatat* ("The Youth"), a secret anti-Ottoman society founded in 1911 in Paris. He moved there after university, returning a year later to Alexandria ready to aid the cause of Arab liberation.

Just then the Great War began, and with it, it seemed, the possibility of slipping the long Turkish noose. A lifelong Anglophile, Antonius worked for the British as a military censor. His primary pastime, however, was books. He befriended the English writer E. M. Forster, a conscientious objector working in Egypt for the Red Cross.

The young Arab patriot seemed tormented, even then. "Dear Antonius," Forster wrote him in early 1917, months before the Balfour Declaration. "Have you ever considered telling all your troubles to one single person? It seems to me that your suffering has four separate sources at least and that the confusion and weariness in your mind must be terrible."

His was a brooding sort of charisma, carefully spoken but armed with a sharp, waggish wit. Though not tall, he had soulful brown eyes, a prominent nose, and a high forehead leading to slicked-back black hair.

After the armistice Antonius settled in Jerusalem, taking Palestinian citizenship and entering the nascent Mandate's Education Department. He toured the country, recommending dramatic reforms to Arab schooling and expounding to the *fellaheen* on the role literacy and learning could play in advancing self-determination. His recommendations for decentralized, locally focused governance were rejected; his assertions of professional—and national—autonomy clashed against British expectations of a "native" colonial civil servant, even if he was a Cambridge man.

Stifled, Antonius resigned and joined the newly created, Washington-based Institute for Current World Affairs. The organization was the work of Charles Crane, the idiosyncratic heir to a Chicago plumbing fortune who had grown weary of his inherited world of pipes, valves, and fittings. A major Democratic donor, Crane had invited himself to the postwar peace talks and earned the notice of Woodrow Wilson. The president made him co-chair of a U.S. fact-finding delegation to tour the defeated Ottoman Empire and gauge its former subjects' wishes.

That two-month mission reached an unequivocal conclusion: The Arabs of the Levant preferred an American over a British mandate, one inspired by that cherished Wilsonian ideal of popular representation. A Jewish state had no place in that arrangement, the delegation determined, because Palestine's Arabs uniformly opposed it and because it would flout the Balfour Declaration's pledge to protect non-Jewish rights.

The report was never made public, surfacing only years later once the British Mandate was already in force. Crane saw in Antonius a vehicle to continue his work, signing him to a generous ten-year fellowship in which he was to send regular reports on regional affairs back to the Washington office. Thus financed, Antonius and his wife Katy moved to an imposing stone mansion built by Hajj Amin in Jerusalem's Sheikh Jarrah quarter. It was known as *Karm al-Mufti*, the Mufti's Vineyard.[45]

Throughout the 1930s Antonius was consumed with researching and writing what he hoped would become the seminal English book on Arab nationalism. At the time the very concept remained virtually unknown in the West. He wished to show that the movement had deep roots, dating well into the previous century with the first Arabic literary circles. He proposed to demonstrate that Britain had promised Arab independence—including Palestine—to the *sherif* of Mecca during the war. And he wanted to prove that Arab nationalism enjoyed the backing not just of the elites but of millions, in Palestine and across the Arabic-speaking lands.[46]

Two days before the Bloody Day in Jaffa, Antonius hosted David Ben-Gurion in secret at Karm al-Mufti.

He began by lamenting that the Jews had mobilized Britain and the world into quashing plans for the legislative council. He favored Arab-Jewish understanding but insisted it was the Jews, as the aggressor party, who had to take the first step. He understood "all the arguments of the Jews," Ben-Gurion recalled, but those aspirations, if realized in full, were irreconcilable with the Arabs'.

Neither side's ambitions could be fully realized, Antonius said. Yes, Arabs had to accept the fact of Jews in the country, but what of Zionism's demand for a majority? Ben-Gurion pointedly rebuffed his appeal to limit immigration for any reasons other than economic. Violence would not deter him: If the choice were between pogroms in Poland and Germany and pogroms in the Land of Israel, he would choose the latter.

They met twice more in the aftermath of the Bloody Day. Antonius grilled his guest on why he insisted on political Zionism rather than a "spiritual center" of the kind advocated by the writer Ahad Ha'am. Ben-Gurion expressed surprise: Did he, an expert on the Arab world, believe a Jewish spiritual center could survive in the "Arab environment"? Although we Jews were "an Oriental people," he told him, "we had been Europeanized, and wanted to return to Palestine in the geographic sense only."

According to Ben-Gurion it was Antonius who unexpectedly waxed poetic about the potential for Jewish-Arab cooperation. The two peoples coming together would constitute "a tremendous moral force that would conquer world public opinion," particularly in the rising power of America. Thus united, they could oust France from Syria, with Palestine—including a Jewish autonomous province or "establishment"—absorbed into a new Greater Syria. A federal system, like those of the United States or Switzerland, would allow the provinces self-government, with Britain having some role in administering the Jewish one. The Jews' energy, education, and funds would help develop the whole Eastern Mediterranean.

That Jewish "establishment," per this proposal, would be known as *Eretz Israel*—its language would be Hebrew and the majority of its population Jewish. It would stretch roughly from Gaza to Haifa and out to the Jezreel Valley, alongside an Arab state called Palestine centered in the hills from Hebron to Nablus. It was a landmark proposition—no less than cleaving the Holy Land in two—but Ben-Gurion dismissed it outright: Joining a Syrian federation was itself a major concession, and accepting just part of the Land of Israel was further than he could go.

Nonetheless, the talks appeared to be advancing. They decided to leave the prickly problem of immigration for later, to float the idea with their respective colleagues and reconvene.[47]

A few days later Antonius left for a visit to Turkey and never saw Ben-Gurion again. It's unclear exactly why. Perhaps because talks for Syrian self-government were already in motion: Within months France would recognize the country's independence and begin a phased military withdrawal. Perhaps he was occupied with his book, or his faltering health, or his wife's changeable moods.

Whatever the case, for Ben-Gurion, Antonius's disappearance appears to have closed off any thought of an agreement with the Arabs in the near future. He would live another four decades, but these would be among his last-ever meetings with a prominent Arab in Palestine.[48]

Strike and Counterstrike

On April 20, 1936, a day after the Bloody Day in Jaffa, notables in Nablus announced the creation of an "Arab National Committee" and called on workers to strike. Soon these local committees (they were "national" only in terms of ideology) sprang up in Arab cities and towns across the country, imploring the public to cease paying their taxes. Arab leaders had been caught off-guard by the outburst of rage the day before. Now they scrambled to catch up, to place themselves at the head of a rising groundswell of indignant but leaderless urban youth.

On April 25 the mufti announced the birth of the Arab Higher Committee, a nationwide leadership council, chaired by himself. The AHC declared the general strike would continue until London drastically altered its Palestine policy. That meant three things: an end to Jewish immigration, a prohibition on land sales, and the establishment of representative government to reflect the country's Arab majority.

In early May the committee began touring Arab cities across the country—starting with a visit to Qassam's grave—to rally support for the strike. Hajj Amin was now in explicit, public confrontation with the British authorities that had raised him to power in the first place.[49]

Wauchope secretly cabled Colonial Secretary William Ormsby-Gore, advising the appointment of a royal commission, the British Empire's highest form of public inquiry. Its members would examine not just the disturbances' origins but be granted wide terms of reference to prevent similar disorders in the future. The Cabinet agreed, but on condition that any such commission wait until order was restored, lest it be perceived as submission to violence.[50]

Across the country Arab stores were shuttered, transportation halted, and children kept home from class. When a Jerusalem merchant refused to close his shop, the city's national committee sent boys to dump sewage on his head. Arabs were instructed to swap the Ottoman fez, or *tarboush*, for the *keffiyeh*, the villagers' black-and-white-checkered headdress, and women to cover their faces. Armenians and other Christians were not exempt, and donned the Muslim peasant garb (some with evident embarrassment) for the first time.

It was the finest hour for Grand Mufti Hajj Amin al-Husseini. For the first time, all the major Palestinian-Arab players had joined the AHC's call for a strike, granting him virtually unchallenged authority. For a moment it seemed he had almost matched the unity of the Zionist leadership under Weizmann and Ben-Gurion.

Some Arabs tried bucking the trend. Farmers were loath to let crops go untended. Many of those employed by the government feared staying home meant losing their jobs.

In Haifa, Mayor Hassan Shukri had been touting the value of Jewish immigration since the start of the Mandate, opening municipal tenders to Jews and making Hebrew an official language for city documents. On May 11, after a show of solidarity with Jews who had been forced to flee Arab neighborhoods, a bomb went off next to his home. It would not be the last attempt on his life.[51]

The pressure to conform was growing irrepressible. Each day that the strike persisted, the self-segregation between Arab and Jew seemed to grow.

Ben-Gurion sensed an opportunity. He had spent years promoting separate, self-sufficient Jewish agricultural and industrial sectors that would be freed from a dependence on less-expensive Arab labor. When Arab workers at Jaffa Port enlisted in the strike, his Jewish Agency seized the moment, petitioning the government to open a rival port at Tel Aviv's northern tip.

After several weeks' hesitation, authorities agreed on one condition: The Jews must fund their new port themselves. Four days later a Yugoslav-flagged ship laden with cement arrived at a hastily built jetty. The mayor of Tel Aviv led a ceremony on the beach. The dockworkers were almost all Jewish immigrants from Israel Hazan's Salonica.[52]

For the Jews the win was double. First, Palestine's prized citrus industry—by far its biggest export, in which Jews now controlled a majority—could continue to be transported unimpeded to Europe (the

Jewish workers dance *hora* at Tel Aviv's new port, May 1936 (CZA PHKH/1278374)

first shipment was a crate of Jaffa oranges to the short-reigned Edward VIII). But more important than export figures was symbolism: The Jews now possessed their very own gateway to the outside world. A Hebrew poet penned an ode:

Port of mine
And of the nation
See the wonder!
The sea's amazed
See a venture
Fresh as a newborn
A port is born
To a nation dazed[53]

Ben-Gurion extolled Tel Aviv Port as a second Balfour Declaration. It exemplified his dream of Hebrew labor, of Jewish autonomy on every front: political, cultural, and economic. In his diary, he wrote that nothing better typified the Yishuv's resourcefulness, particularly in this "hour of disturbances." In parentheses he added: "Or is it war?"[54]

Zionist leaders were facing mounting evidence that this was far more serious than the day- or weeklong "flash floods" of the 1920s. Still, they counseled patience. On the first Bloody Day in Jaffa, as reports of new attacks accumulated, they announced that the continued "self-control and restraint [*havlagah*] of the Hebrew public" would be imperative. Henceforth, *havlagah* was the leadership's preferred term for its stated policy of forbearance in responding to violence.

For Ben-Gurion the calculus was simple: The Jews were few and depended on Britain's goodwill for immigration and settlement. The British were strong, and if they came to see the Jews as reliable allies, they might not only adopt pro-Zionist positions but ultimately arm them to protect their own settlements and even, just maybe, to fight alongside them.[55]

Havlagah was becoming a tougher sell with each passing week. Twenty-one Jews were killed in the rebellion's first month and ten more in the second. In the second half of May in Jerusalem alone, gunmen killed three Jews in three separate incidents, as well as an Austrian Christian they mistook for a Jew, a British policeman in the Old City, and three Jews walking out of the Edison Cinema.

The last of these shook the Yishuv to its core. Haganah commanders demanding reprisal filed into Ben-Gurion's office, but he refused.

It later emerged that the Edison killer, a nineteen-year-old English teacher named Sami al-Ansari, was a cousin of Musa Alami.

"Who would have imagined that Palestine—weak, small, slight, meek, and mild—could do this?" wrote Alami's former tutor Khalil Sakakini. "I'm not among the revolutionaries, and there is nothing I hate more than when people turn to solve their problems through violence and force, but these are the results of injustice and he who sows also reaps. I ask God for a good outcome."[56]

Days later Alami received a call from Moshe Shertok. They met at Alami's home, but the host was downcast. He wondered if the Jews were truly interested in an agreement—they seemed to remember the Arabs' existence only when their security was in jeopardy, and just as quickly to forget them when it improved.

He had another complaint: Why were the Jews vilifying the mufti, and prevailing upon their British friends—in the high commissioner's palace and in Parliament—to do the same? Did they not realize that any potential accord would inevitably go through him? Did they truly believe he was so sinister? Alami maintained that Hajj Amin had undergone a tremendous change over the last few years; he was now more tolerant. "Perhaps the mufti is the incarnation of the devil," he said. "Maybe he is only acting, but he told me that he is opposed to violence."

Alami had one more score to settle: He had learned that the Zionists were insisting the Great Revolt was being financed by Mussolini's Italy. "As far as I'm concerned, it is permissible to accept money from abroad too, but I deny this is actually happening," he said. He begged him to stop this "nonsense" about Italian funding. The Arabs believe they are sacrificing their blood for a noble cause, he said, and there was no greater insult than suggesting they are dying for Fascist gold.[57]

As spring gave way to summer, militant activity shifted from the cities to the countryside, where the hilly terrain, lack of roads, and near-absence of government proved ideal for hit-and-run attacks. Newly formed armed bands, inspired by Qassam's model, assaulted signs of British rule: troops and police, telephone and electric lines, railways, and—at least twenty times—the oil pipeline to Iraq. Scattered Jewish farming cooperatives also came under fire. Centered in Samaria and the Galilee, the armed bands soon spread around the country.[58]

They were led by men like Abdel-Rahim al-Hajj Muhammad, who operated in the Nablus-Jenin-Tulkarem area that the British dubbed the Triangle of Terror and the Arabs, the Mountains of Fire. A widely respected former grain merchant from Tulkarem, Abdel-Rahim hailed from a long line of Arab warriors who had battled invading armies dating back to Napoleon.

Another, of less-sterling reputation, was Aref Abdel-Raziq. The Haganah's fledgling intelligence department described him as "short of stature, flashily dressed in a senior British officer's uniform. Cunning and clever, he knows how to read and write, and in flowery language too." Unlike the independent-minded Abdel-Rahim, Aref was unstinting in demonstrating his fealty to Hajj Amin.[59]

As attacks persisted—in June, Arabs killed nine Jews and British forces killed twenty-two Arabs—the government expanded emergency regulations to include collective fines for whole villages and cities, the forcible reopening of shops closed in the strike, and the demolition of suspected insurgents' homes. The new measures allowed for detention in internment camps for up to a year, and five years in prison for anyone found with unlicensed weapons. Acts of sabotage or firing at troops or police could lead to life imprisonment or the gallows.[60]

A British report recorded that troops entered one Ramallah-area village after the sabotage of nearby telephone lines. After searching for arms they dipped bedsheets into vats of olive oil and then dumped the barrels into the street. Lest their message was unclear, they slaughtered some of the villagers' chickens. Palestine's top military commander secretly acknowledged that under the pretext of searching for wanted men and arms, troops were actually employing "Turkish methods" that were "punitive" in nature. In Quleh, a village near Lydda, furniture was smashed, foodstuffs destroyed, and seventeen homes razed to the ground.[61]

Complaints piled up. "This is not an appeal for mercy, but for justice and right," said one open letter that summer. "We refuse to believe that honest Britishers do not exist in this country," but unless they resist their own government's "rotten" Zionist program, they would know no peace but would earn the wrath of a whole generation of Arabs.[62]

Around the same time dozens of prominent Jews received an open letter of their own, signed only by "An Arab." It said that since the British arrived eighteen years earlier, the Arabs have sought to defend their homeland—sometimes peacefully, sometimes violently—but to no avail. As to Zionist ambitions:

> *If you were not aggressive, stiffnecked and impudent, the Arabs would have treated you as they treat other European people with due respect. But you come here boldly and shamelessly and you insult us, your newspapers degrade us, you try to tread upon us, you look at us not as equals but as mean, base creatures. Is that the way of living with a noble nation?*

"Now is the end," the author declared. "This is our last chance."[63]

Assistant Superintendent Alan Sigrist's penchant for casual violence had made him a loathed figure. In late May, he and his officers raided the Jaffa office of *Al-Difa*, breaking one's staffer's nose with a truncheon and wounding dozens more. Once Sigrist beat an Arab police officer who refused to remove nails that militants had strewn on roads to pierce tires (patrol cars were eventually fitted with broom-heads on their front bumpers). Sigrist and his subordinates habitually haunted the warrens of Jerusalem's Old City, pushing residents aside and forcing them to salute in "humiliation operations."

On June 12 two men plotted to kill him. For one, the grievance was personal: Sigrist had roughed up and degraded him multiple times, once knocking off his tarboush and threatening to shoot him if he retrieved it. Now, the would-be assassin kept his Beretta under that same tarboush. Beside him, pistol in pocket, was Sami al-Ansari, the gunman from the Edison Theater and Musa Alami's cousin. As Sigrit's chauffeured car passed, they opened fire. The driver shot back, killing Ansari and wounding his co-conspirator.[64]

"Another hero fell yesterday in the field of honor," wrote Sakakini.

The *Filastin* front page carried his photo—handsome, well-dressed in a suit and tie—hailing him as a "martyr" alongside the late Sheikh Qassam.[65]

Sigrist was seriously wounded but survived. Within forty-eight hours the government struck back. Though the assassination attempt

Vlo. XX No. 109 - 3300

«السنة العشرون»

العدد ١٠٩ - ٣٣٠٠

الاشتراك

في يافا جنيه وربع في فلسطين وشرق الاردن جنيه ونصف وفي الخارج عشرة دولارات اميركية

الاعلانات

اجرة السطر ٥٠ ملا . الاعلانات الشهرية والسنوية يتفق عليها مع الادارة

مركز ادارة وتحرير الجريدة

العجمي (البوابة) تلفون ٩٤ صندوق البريد ٩٤

فلسطين

FALASTIN

جريدة ، يومية سياسية ، اخبارية ، ادبية ، مصورة

صاحب الجريدة

عيسى داود العيسى

محرر الجريدة

يوسف حنا

مدير ادارة الجريدة

داود بندلي العيسى

٩ جمادي الاولى سنة ١٣٥٥

Jaffa Monday 27 July 1936

يافا الاثنين في ٢٧ تموز سنة ١٩٣٦

فريق من الشهداء الابرار الذين قتلوا في الثورة الحالية في سبيل انقاذ وطنهم الذبيح

الشهيد المرحوم جميل عبد الرؤوف القرم من سكان حرم سيدنا علي وقد قتل برصاص الجند البريطاني في سبيل المحافظة على بلاده وانقاذها من شر الاستعمار

الشهيد الشيخ عبد الحفيظ بركات ابو الفيلات وقد استشهد في ٥ تموز الجاري برصاص الجند في جبال الخليل وكان رحمه الله يسير على منوال الشهيد القسام في الجهاد لخلاص بلاده من الاستعمار

الاستاذ سامي الانصاري وهو مدرس في مدرسة الرشيدية ومن خيرة الشباب الوطني استشهد في القدس برصاص البوليس الانكليزي وكان رحمه الله يلتهب وطنية وحماسة لانقاذ بلاده

الشهيد العظيم الشيخ عز الدين القسام زعيم عصبة المجاهدين التي اصطدمت مع رجال البوليس في يعبد وسقط زعيمها وثلاثة من اخوانه شهداء بالرصاص وقد كان عمل هذه العصبة اول مرحلة للثورة الوطنية الحاضرة

شهيد الخليل المرحوم محمود عبد الباسط التميمي الذي سقط صريع الغدر والخيانة برصاص اليهود في احد شوارع القدس بينما كان خارجا من بيته في الصباح الباكر

***Filastin*, July 27, 1936: Izz al-Din al-Qassam, center, and Sami al-Ansari, bottom left**
(NLI Jrayed Collection)

had been in Jerusalem, troops detonated more than 220 buildings in Old Jaffa, purportedly to improve sanitation but in fact as a security measure: Its winding alleys had proved too difficult to police. Some six thousand Arabs were left homeless, having been instructed by air-dropped leaflets to vacate their homes. The chief justice of Palestine was appalled. When he protested, he was relieved of his post.[66]

Meanwhile at his base on the Haram al-Sharif, Hajj Amin was growing impatient. In the revolt's early months, he had made himself head of the strike campaign but had generally refrained from militant rhetoric or endorsement of attacks. Friday sermons at mosques remained comparatively moderate.

Yet as summer set in, the mufti moved to own the violence as well. By June his offices were giving moral and monetary support to the fighters. Preachers and pressmen under his sway began appealing to Muslims' religious sensibilities, calling on them to back the Arab revolution and, better still, to enlist in it themselves. Imams amplified allegations of British desecrations of mosques and the Quran, and of the threat to Islam should the Zionist project prevail. The mufti's Supreme Muslim Council used religious judges to funnel money, arms, and intelligence to insurgents. The Haram was the hub of this new activity, where meetings were held, weapons stored, and perpetrators of violence granted sanctuary. The British dared not inflame Muslim resentment by entering the compound.[67]

Acts of bloodshed and sabotage reached an apex. A number of soldiers were killed while bathing near the Sea of Galilee, the armed bands making off with their rifles and Lewis machine guns. Jews were killed by snipers or waylaid on highways. In June alone, seventy-five thousand Jewish-owned trees were uprooted. Farmers in one cooperative in the Jezreel Valley awoke one morning to find fifty of their cattle slaughtered.[68]

The death toll of Arab collaborators—real, suspected, or falsely accused—was climbing too. Hebron's acting mayor was assassinated for his perceived willingness to work with Jews, and the head of Haifa's national committee suffered the same fate. So did Ahmed Naif, a police officer who had been pursuing Qassam's disciples. The mosques of Haifa all shut their doors rather than give him an Islamic burial—when a village cemetery finally agreed, police stationed a guard at the grave lest vandals unearth and mutilate his body.[69]

The British Empire was sorely overstretched. In March, Hitler again flouted the Versailles Treaty by sending army units into the Rhineland bordering France and the Low Countries. In May, Mussolini's Italy captured Addis Ababa, completing its conquest of Ethiopia and stoking British fears over the Suez Canal. In both cases, Whitehall lacked the resources to do more than lodge indignant complaints.

In Palestine, the government agreed in desperation to a step it had hitherto resisted: arming and training Jews for self-defense. It created the Jewish Supernumerary Police, called *notrim* ("watchmen") in Hebrew but more commonly known by the Arabic equivalent, *ghaffirs*. Initially a ragtag bunch of six hundred (they would grow fivefold in as many months), they carried aging hunting rifles or whatever other weapons were at hand. They sported tall Turkic sheepskin caps and later, broad-brimmed Australian-style bush hats with one side upturned. Nominally under British officers, the *notrim* were actually run by the Jewish Agency and above all the Haganah, even though the latter remained technically illicit.[70] Britain had birthed a Jewish armed force, and there would be no turning back.

On the night of August 22, Lewis Billig, a British-Jewish professor of Arabic literature at Hebrew University, was murdered at his desk. "The bullet, exploding with the force of a bomb, shattered the top of his head," the *Palestine Post* reported. "The manuscript he was preparing, a Concordance of Ancient Arabic Literature, and a large Arabic tome on which he was working, were spattered with blood." The obituary noted that he "probably did more for Arabic culture and advancement than any of the present Arab leaders."[71] He was thirty-nine.

"What an irony of fate, that this man should be chosen as the victim of the assassin's bullet," said Judah Magnes, a California-born Reform rabbi who was president of Hebrew University, at the funeral the next day. Magnes was an intimate friend of Musa Alami and linked to *Brit Shalom*, a small movement advocating a binational state, to which Billig had belonged.

"He devoted his talents to Arab science, to a comprehension of Islam," Magnes said in Hebrew. "This man had no foe or enemy in the world. He was a modest and retiring man of tender heart, ready to assist any in need, abjuring politics, and aspiring only to comprehend the soul of that religion, the lofty thoughts of the Islamic faith."[72]

That same morning some three hundred armed men, all veterans of the Ottoman or Iraqi armies, crossed the Jordan River into Palestine. At their head was a commander of unusual dash and magnetism, one destined for a place of honor in the Palestinian pantheon: Fawzi al-Qawuqji.

The fact that he was not Palestinian mattered for little. Born in Lebanon of Turkmen stock, he had first arrived in Palestine during the Great War, stationed in the Ottoman garrison village of Beersheba. His wartime acts of bravery—often fueled by champagne or rum-laced tea—earned him an Iron Cross from the Turks' German allies and the right to use the Turkish honorific "Bey."

Fawzi Bey cut a figure quite unlike the austere Sheikh Qassam. "Always smiling, never, never frowning," wrote Yusuf Hanna after meeting him. "More like a son of Europe than the East," recounted one of Fawzi's deputies, noting his light features and fondness for strong drink. An "Arab Irishman," recorded a British policeman, "with much of the Irishman's humor."[73]

His postwar career was that of an armed Arab journeyman. As the British took Palestine he fled to Damascus, joining Faisal's failed bid to drive out the French presence there. He then enlisted in the colonial French-Syrian army, commanding a cavalry squadron before quitting yet again to aid another, Druze-led rebellion against the French, even spearheading a brief uprising of his own in Hama. When that last revolt was crushed, Fawzi became a wanted man—he headed to the Hejaz to modernize the forces of a recently arrived conquering sheikh named Ibn Saud. Finding the desert monarch deaf to his counsel he decamped for Iraq, where the British had installed the ousted Faisal as emir.

Faisal envisioned a united Greater Syria confederated with Iraq under control of his own Hashemite dynasty. Fawzi shared that vision: He would rarely refer to "Palestine" per se, but rather "Southern Syria," or at most "Palestine, Southern Syria." That Syria-centric, pan-Arab outlook would put him squarely at odds with the grand mufti of Jerusalem.

Since the early 1920s the mufti had steadily abandoned any desire to see a Greater Syria led by the Hashemites or anyone else. His was by now a distinctly Palestinian nationalism, one with local enemies (the Jews and their British enablers) and a local leader (himself).

Still, Hajj Amin recognized Fawzi's undeniable competence—his combat experience outshone that of any of the other armed leaders. In late April 1936, just weeks into the Great Revolt, the mufti visited Baghdad. As his chauffeured vehicle circled the city, the two men reached an agreement: Fawzi would contribute men to the rebellion and aid Amin's AHC in confronting the British.

In subsequent weeks the veteran warrior activated his old networks: Iraqis, Syrians, and Druze from Lebanon. He stole British documents and uniforms from the Iraqi military academy, fraternizing—and drinking—with officers there to allay suspicions of his plans.[74]

The Iraqi volunteers trekked through the Syrian desert, picking up arms provided by sympathizers in Amman. The Syrians descended from Hama, Homs, and Damascus; the Druze from Mount Lebanon.

Days after crossing into Palestine, Fawzi Bey issued his first declaration in the local papers. It called on Arabs in Palestine and beyond to band together to expel the English and bring a halt to Jewish immigration. "The Arab nation is one," it said, and Palestine an indivisible part. He had arrived less than a week prior, but the statement presumptuously identified him as "Commander in Chief of the Arab Revolt of Southern Syria."

Basing himself in the so-called Triangle of Terror, he called a meeting in early September with leaders of the country's six largest armed bands. Fawzi asked them to pledge their loyalty and fold their men under his. They agreed. He split his forces into four units, according to origin: Syrians commanded by a Syrian, Iraqis by an Iraqi, Druze by a Druze, and Palestinians by a Palestinian.[75]

The very next morning, Fawzi threw his new squads into battle, deploying them on either side of two roads leading to Bal'a, a rebel-friendly village near Tulkarem. As an army convoy approached, the

Fawzi al-Qawuqji in Palestine, 1936 (Eltaher Collection)

fighters opened fire from north and south, killing a corporal. Troops split into two groups to give chase, but came under fire again from gunmen positioned on the second road. Recognizing it was a coordinated assault of unprecedented organization, the British called in reinforcements backed by tanks, artillery, and aircraft.

The battle lasted all day, with the rebels assisted by the women of Bal'a, who brought water and food as dusk fell. Machine-gunners on a nearby hilltop brought down two aircraft—hardly believing their achievement—and seized the planes' Bren guns. Nine of Fawzi's men had been killed.[76]

Before his arrival the revolt had been driven by the urban proletariat, then the rural peasants—virtually no members of notable families had taken up arms. For Palestine's middle- and upper-class Arabs, Fawzi's arrival gave the rebellion an air of respectability. In the weeks that followed he led two more significant battles, helping transform a disorderly outburst of random violence into a comparatively organized and deadly guerrilla uprising.

Poems were written in his honor, and children sold images of his visage.[77]

"His picture used to be in all the cafes, not the mufti's," reflected one British officer. "It was Fawzi who was hero of the Arabs."[78]

Three Kings from the East

Britain's tolerance for Hajj Amin was on the wane. The head of the police Criminal Investigations Department believed the Arab Higher Committee was paying the armed bands and pushing violent propaganda. Wauchope floated the idea of his deportation: "The mufti is no real leader," he cabled Colonial Secretary William Ormsby-Gore in late summer. The secretary shared that view: "I have a profound mistrust of the mufti and all his works. I believe him to be not only bitterly anti-Jewish but also anti-British and a rascal."[79]

In the meantime London took steps to restore order. In September it dispatched another division to Palestine, bringing its garrison to twenty thousand. It created a new officer position—General Officer Commanding, Palestine—and conferred it on John Dill, a celebrated general from the Great War. Dill begged the high commissioner to enact martial law and definitively quash the insurgency. Wauchope demurred, cleaving instead to a law-and-order campaign lest the government further embitter Arab hearts and minds. Police officers nicknamed him "Washout."[80]

Wauchope hoped the revolt would run itself out. And indeed, as the strike approached six months, the AHC found it needed relief. Arab citrus farmers were pressing it to end the stoppage before the fall harvest; the Arabs' moribund economy was becoming a liability to the mufti's leadership. Wishing to halt the work stoppage without losing face, Amin secretly appealed to a handful of Arab kings.

The monarchs obliged, and the royal courts of Saudi Arabia, Iraq, and Transjordan released a joint plea (in fact written by the mufti's AHC) for Palestine's Arabs to end the bloodshed and trust in British goodwill.[81]

It was the Arab states' first direct intervention in the Palestine problem. Hitherto Britain had resisted such efforts—the Mandate was its own, after all, and it saw itself accountable only to the League of Nations that had bestowed it. Nowhere in the Mandate's text was the wider Arab world given any role in Palestine's administration. Now Whitehall abandoned that principle, not in any deliberate, planned shift but the sort of ad hoc, stopgap policymaking for which Palestine was becoming notorious.[82]

In Geneva, the League deplored the reversal. In later decades Zionists would denigrate its successor body, the United Nations, as reflexively hostile to their interests. Not so in the mid-1930s—the chair of the League's Permanent Mandates Commission regretted that Britain's assent to Arab intervention had "completely transformed" a circumscribed conflict into one involving the entire region if not the world: "From that time forward, what could rightly be considered as a local problem had become the center of a vast international problem."[83]

Nevertheless the imperial objective had been reached. On October 12 the strike was declared over, and its concomitant violence and sabotage came to a stop. Peace having been restored, London would convene the proposed royal commission to get to the roots of a conflict that looked increasingly at risk of becoming a persistent, even permanent, source of strife in the Middle East.

The mufti's AHC secretly contacted rebel leaders:

> *Honored Brethren! Heroes! Our poor tongues cannot express the strength of our love and admiration and the exaltation concealed in our hearts for your self-sacrifice and your devoted war for religion, fatherland and all things Arab. . . . We stand now in a period of hope and expectation. If the Royal Commission comes and judges equitably and gives us all our rights, well and good. If not, the field of battle lies before us.*[84]

Days later, under pressure from Hajj Amin, Fawzi Bey announced he would be departing the country. General Dill wanted him killed, but Wauchope would not hear it—he had promised Arab leaders the army would neither disarm militants nor pursue their commanders. Some ten thousand admirers bid Fawzi farewell as he crossed to Transjordan, bound for Iraq.[85]

Fawzi ordered that no attacks be waged against Jews. Only if the British continue their unjust schemes for Palestine, he instructed, should the Arabs turn their guns on the Zionists. He penned a final, awkwardly translated manifesto:

> *Oh Britishers! I am enemy No. 1 of great despair to those who serve the Zionists, and friend No. 1 of great faithfulness to any just and honorable Englishman, who values Great Britain and her noble ally the Arab People. I beg you to shout in the faces of some of your politicians to give justice to the Palestinian Arabs and grant them their demands. You will find, then, on the part of this Arab people of glorious history, nothing but friendship, devotion and assistance, which you will never find among the Zionists.*[86]

Six months of disorder were over. Officials estimated the death toll at eighty Jews, twenty-eight Britons, and some two hundred Arabs, but acknowledged the Arab body count was likely closer to one thousand. The cost to Palestine taxpayers was at least 3.5 million pounds.

All the same, Arab Palestine basked in vindication. The strike and unrest had forced Britain to assemble a high-level commission with a broad remit to reconsider the country's future. Most of the rebels retained their arms and freedom. Victory seemed within reach.[87]

"The history of this revolution must be written," Sakakini wrote. "From now on, the name Palestine will not be mentioned without men bowing their heads in respect. As for the results of this revolution, suffice it to say this: Palestine was dead and she revived; she was lost and was found. Praise God."[88]

In Tel Aviv, Ben-Gurion upbraided his Mapai party comrades for dismissing the rebellion as mere mob brutality stirred up by the unscrupulous Hajj Amin. "The Arab fights in a way that cannot be ignored. He strikes, he is killed, he makes great sacrifices. I cannot remember a strike that lasted this long," he said.

> *There is a question at the center of the whole revolt, this Arab uprising: the question of aliyah [immigration]. The Arabs' war is against Hebrew immigration. Everything else is secondary or tertiary. . . . If we continue with large-scale immigration, the Jews will become a majority; the Arabs know this, and they battle against it with tremendous devotion.*

"It is inconceivable that a people would choose to become a minority," he continued, repeatedly invoking the word "people" (in Hebrew, *'am*), as if scolding colleagues who refused to see an Arab collective in Palestine.

And just as the Jews had scored many "triumphs" over those six months, he said, the opposing side had registered victories of its own. One was the conflict's regionalization—Palestine was now a pan-Arab issue, concerning the entire Middle East. Another was the elevation of the Palestine Arabs' self-confidence and self-respect, having "learned that they are able to fight."

He had no doubt over who had first sparked that transformation, that revolution in Arab perceptions: "It began with Izz al-Din al-Qassam."[89]

Chapter 3

The Two-State Solution

Musa Alami had spent nearly the entire six months of revolt in Europe. A day after the Bloody Day in Jaffa, he secured 100 days' leave on full pay for travel to Switzerland. Shortly thereafter, he took another 107 days' leave, again on full pay, then another 10. Permission came from the aptly named Harry Trusted, Palestine's chief justice, who presumed the trip was related to Alami's perennially failing health. He even threw in two first-class rail tickets to the port of departure on the Suez Canal.[1]

In early September he crossed from Switzerland into Italy. In a town on Lake Como, he proffered a letter from Hajj Amin to an envoy of Benito Mussolini. The mufti appealed for Italian aid, without which the Arab cause in Palestine might not last another two weeks. "Alami seems to me a very serious person," the *Duce*'s emissary recorded, noting that his decade-long career in the Mandate's justice system meant he aroused little British suspicion.

The visitor's request was precise: ten thousand rifles with one thousand cartridges each, five thousand grenades, twenty-five light machine guns and twelve heavy ones, and some mortars. And he wanted Italian help in sabotaging the pipeline carrying Iraqi oil to Haifa.[2]

The next day in Geneva, a courier gave Alami 13,000 pounds and promised another 75,000. Two weeks later he met Galeazzo Ciano, Mussolini's foreign minister and son-in-law, in Rome. They arranged an elaborate system involving double envelopes and a go-between at the American University of Beirut. Alami's codename was George, Ciano's was Charles, and Mussolini's was Charles's "father." Ten yards of silk was 10,000 pounds. Alami met the courier twice more over the coming months, accepting another 20,000 pounds—all told, worth 1.6 million pounds today.[3]

Three months earlier Alami had rebuked Moshe Shertok for suggesting the Arabs were Fascist-funded; now he was the mufti's point man for just such a scheme. It was a remarkable turnaround for a man universally hailed as a moderate.

However, Alami was not the first player in the Palestine drama to court Fascist support—twice in 1934 Mussolini had hosted Chaim Weizmann in Rome. The *Duce* was indifferent to Zionism but keen to erode British power in the Eastern Mediterranean; for Weizmann's part, he hoped to influence the League of Nations mandates commission, whose chairman was an Italian allied to the Fascist strongman.

At that time they had discussed a notion Weizmann had recently begun carefully and quietly airing: dividing the Holy Land into cantons, Jewish and Arab—perhaps even independent states.

Mussolini was not one for half-measures. "You must create a Jewish State. I have already spoken with the Arabs," he declared in typical staccato fashion. An accord could be reached, he believed, though the Jerusalem question posed problems: "The Arabs say the Jews must have their capital in Tel Aviv."

"The idea you have just raised is a great one," effused the Zionist leader, careful to portray the statehood idea as Mussolini's own. "When we reach the state of practicalities, can I count on your support?"

"Certainly," replied his host, praising him as "very wise."

"As we become stronger we shall be able to remember our friends," Weizmann said. "The Jews never forget their friends or their enemies." He asked if he and his wife might be honored with a signed photo (it still hangs in Weizmann's Rehovot residence). "Look after yourself. You look very tired. There is still need for you."[4]

That same year, the Revisionist youth movement opened a naval school in Rome. Jewish cadets collected scrap metal for the Italian arms industry and marched in solidarity during the Abyssinia invasion. The school even acquired its own training ship. When a Jewish cadet died in an accident, his Revisionist comrades held on an onboard funeral accompanied by a Roman—Fascist—salute.[5]

The Lords Set Sail

William Robert Wellesley Peel, 1st Earl Peel, cut a stately figure. Tall, with a handlebar mustache, he favored a top hat and tails—especially when touring the sultry Orient. His pedigree was similarly distinguished. His grandfather had founded the Conservative Party; his father was the first Speaker of the House of Commons to open the chamber to non-Christians and even atheists. Lord Peel himself had a formidable résumé, with a handful of Cabinet-level posts including secretary of state for India (twice). In late 1936 he was nearly seventy, his body stricken with cancer but his mind and manner full of vigor.

In summer 1936 Peel was appointed chair of the six-man Palestine Royal Commission. His deputy was Sir Horace Rumbold, 9th Baronet—a stout, monocled ex-ambassador to the Ottomans in their final years and the Nazis in their first, and among Whitehall's first diplomats to grasp the scope of Hitler's intentions. Completing the delegation were two bureaucrats named Morris—Morris Carter and Harold Morris, specialists in land and labor disputes, respectively—Laurie Hammond, a former provincial governor in India, and Reginald Coupland, a sinewy, pipe-smoking Oxford don with a specialty in colonial history and a partiality to bold ideas.[6]

On November 5, 1936, the commission set out for Marseilles to board the SS *Cathay*, bound for Port Said.[7]

That same day, Colonial Secretary Ormsby-Gore authorized a new six-month quota for immigrants to Palestine. The secretary had long been a sympathetic participant in the Zionist project: Two decades earlier he had even helped draft the Balfour Declaration. So solid was his commitment that rumor had it he had been a practicing Jew for decades.[8]

The new immigrant quota—1,800—was one-fifth the Jewish Agency's ask, but in Jerusalem the mufti smoldered. He insisted on a complete stoppage if the Arabs were to cooperate with Peel. As the delegates steamed across the Mediterranean, he declared that Palestine's Arabs would boycott.[9]

Arab leaders implored him to rethink. Emir Abdullah of Transjordan, elder brother of the late Faisal, complained that the mufti was shunting aside those who sought a genuine solution. Ibn Saud deemed the boycott "folly." The Nashashibi clan—the Husseinis' perennial foes—shared that assessment, as did Musa Alami, Yusuf Hanna, and even Fawzi Bey al-Qawuqji.[10]

Still, Hajj Amin was satisfied. His years of effort to make Palestine the center of Arab and Muslim attention were beginning to yield fruit, and within the country his leadership was effectively uncontested. Police investigators noted that he had created a climate in which an Arab appearing before Peel risked ostracism if not murder.[11]

Nonetheless, his time was short. Ormsby-Gore wrote Foreign Secretary Anthony Eden that the cleric was the "chief villain of the peace." Calm, he wrote, would best be served by the "early elimination of the mufti and the Seychelles are being got ready to welcome him and a few friends." These were dark days for the British Empire, he sighed: Mussolini was ensconced in East Africa, the Nazis had seized political control in the port of Danzig, and Franco appeared headed toward victory in Spain.

"What a bloody world!"[12]

On November 10 the commissioners disembarked in Egypt, and the next morning boarded a train following Britain's Great War tracks through Sinai and Gaza to Lydda and finally Jerusalem.[13]

Their home would be the King David, a sumptuous hotel built a few years prior by Jewish financiers in Cairo. But hearings were to be held at a nearby government building that until a year before had been the rival—Arab-owned—Palace Hotel.

The Palace had been Jerusalem's premier lodging, an arabesque jewel with a hulking foyer staircase and marble columns. Rooms boasted canopied four-poster beds and—the climax of luxury—bedside telephones. Financed by the mufti's Supreme Muslim Council, the Palace was a rare product of inter-communal cooperation, realized by a joint Jewish-Arab firm that had also constructed the city's towering YMCA. The architects included Weizmann's brother-in-law, as well as a Haganah commander who secretly carved weapons caches into the walls. Before the commission arrived, they had the hotel electrician install microphones in the chandelier above the witness stand.[14]

Hajj Amin, firm in his boycott, sent the lords a short welcome letter to "this holy Arab Land." He regretted that he could not extend them traditional Arab hospitality, but given Britain's broken promises and its efforts to "Judaize . . . this purely Arab Country," he had no choice. He again demanded a complete cessation of Jewish immigration, "fatal and prejudicial" as it was to Arab interests. Then and only then would he appear before their esteemed offices.[15]

At a grand event November 12, Wauchope and the commissioners officially inaugurated the proceedings.[16]

The star witness was Weizmann, head of the World Zionist Organization. Now in his sixties, he had made it his life's mission to explain—in the unmistakable Yiddish timbre of his native Russia—the Jewish people to the British and the British people to the Jews. He found greater success in the first objective than the second: Over three decades of Zionist activism he had become the favorite Jew of Britain's ruling class, among whom he counted many intimate friends.

A "brilliant talker with an unrivalled gift for lucid exposition," recalled a colonial administrator; Balfour's niece Baffy effused over his "great distinction of mind and profound natural modesty."[17]

Over the Peel Commission's two months in Palestine he testified five times—more than any other witness.[18]

Weizmann began with a stark overview of Europe's Jewish problem: "six million people pent up in places where they are not wanted, and for whom the world is divided into places where they cannot live, and places into which they may not enter." Germany had its book burnings and a raft of new laws limiting how Jews studied, worked, and married. Poland, Europe's largest Jewish community, remained battered by the global depression and was likewise shutting Jews out of education and the professions. In Bolshevik Russia, religious commitments were deemed subversive and Zionism a crime. America, the world's great sanctuary, had for over a decade boarded its doors almost completely. The commission's task was daunting, and came at as dark a time as any in Jewish history. "I pray it may be given to you to find a way out."[19]

Weizmann's remaining four testimonies were all given privately, and were correspondingly more candid. In these "in-camera" hearings, witnesses were instructed not to prepare written remarks—they, like the commissioners, operated on the premise that secret sessions would remain just that.

The Arabs were greedy, Weizmann suggested. They had gained three large kingdoms out of the Great War—Iraq, Saudi Arabia, and Transjordan—and still begrudged the Jews little Palestine. And their nationalism was a "crude imitation" of the European model, taking its guns and its rhetoric but bereft of spiritual and cultural content.

Lord Peel agreed: "No doubt the Arabs are a difficult people to deal with," he said, "not of the same caliber as the Jews, the same standard." He was not surprised Weizmann's people were impatient with them, but perhaps they were moving just a little too quickly, and "we have to go rather slow with them, have we not?"[20]

Yes, Weizmann conceded, "the Jew is argumentative; he never takes 'no' for an answer. If he is thrown out of the door he tries to come in through the window. He cannot afford to take 'no' for an answer. That is his trouble."

"The Arab, you see, has flowing robes; he bows gracefully," he continued. "The Jew has bad manners; he does not bow gracefully." The British were charmed by the Arabs' deferential languor—"picturesque inefficiency," he called it—but must not be deceived. "The Arab is a totalitarian."

"He does not like minorities?" pressed Professor Coupland.

"He does not. That is the whole of his history. I do not blame him. Such is the nature of the man."[21]

Hammond, the former governor in India, piped up: The Jews must take "the products of high civilization" and "superimpose them on this ignorant, prejudiced population of Arabs. It is a very, very difficult thing to do." Weizmann concurred: The impact of a "higher civilization" on a lower one always produces friction.[22]

In all his years in Palestine, Weizmann said, he could still not understand the Arabs' mentality. "I have tried, but I always go wrong."[23]

"I cannot count many friends among the Arabs," he admitted, while contending, unconvincingly, that the previous mufti—Amin's half-brother—had been "one of my best friends."[24]

Still, Weizmann insisted, the Jews had no desire to dominate Palestine, or to turn Arabs into proverbial hewers of wood. Asked three times if the Zionists aimed for a Jewish state, he replied each time that they did not. He instead proposed a system of parity, with equal representation for Arabs and Jews regardless of which was a majority now or later.

It was in Weizmann's fourth testimony, two days before Christmas, that the commissioners first hesitantly proposed the country's division: two cantons, Jewish and Arab, under continued British administration with mixed areas belonging to neither. Weizmann gave no definite reply, noting only the plan's drawbacks—it would mean cutting the country in two or even three; it would leave a quarter of Jews outside the Jewish enclave, which would anyway be a "little ghetto." Nevertheless he was keen to embody those qualities he believed the British prized: reasonableness, sensibility, compromise—if such a plan included continued immigration, he said, he would give it due consideration.[25]

The hearing dragged on for hours, and the stiff upper lip Weizmann had cultivated over three decades in Britain was beginning to curl. Europe's Jews need relief, he repeated. Six million needed a home. The riots were making a mockery of the British Empire—the Arab joke of the summer was that for every rebel killed by a bullet, two more died of laughter at British fecklessness.

"The underlying cause is that we exist, and the only question you have to answer is—have we a right to exist? If you answer that question positively, everything else flows from it," he remonstrated. "I have tried to cut out the core and tell you the truth. I have said all I have to say. I can add no more. I cannot plead harder than I have done. Here it is. Take it or leave it. I am sorry, My Lord, I have got so heated."

Lord Peel was forgiving. "We have, I am afraid, given you a very long day."[26]

A week into 1937, Weizmann met with the commission a final time. Professor Coupland now pitched an idea "a little more drastic" than before. The scheme, one of several the panel was weighing and which he raised merely "for the sake of argument . . . deserves to be called more than cantonization; it is really partition." It would "split Palestine into two halves, the plan being an independent Jewish State, as independent as Belgium . . . and the rest of Palestine, plus Transjordania, being an independent Arab state, as independent as Arabia. That is the ultimate idea."

It was a British official's first recorded mention of a two-state solution to the Palestine problem.

Again Weizmann was noncommittal. Again he warned of the consequences of "cutting the child in two," of the profound "administrative difficulties" and "high walls" it would require. "It will not be easy to carry my people," he warned, but if all sides agreed to such an offer and peace was in the offing, he reckoned that his people would at least consider such a program.[27]

The apparent prevarication was a bluff. Privately, Weizmann was elated.[28] He had been contemplating Palestine's division for several years, dating back to his initial feelers with Mussolini. In Professor Coupland, the panel's lone academic, he found a commissioner of like mind who could give the idea concrete form.

"Permit me not to give a definite answer now," Weizmann replied. "Let me think of it."[29]

THE MUFTI THINKS TWICE

Over six weeks the commission had summoned more than eighty witnesses—almost exactly split between Britons and Jews—but not a single Arab.[30] The Saudi, Iraqi, and Transjordanian kings pressed the mufti to change course; so did his Nashashibi rivals in Palestine. All feared that the panel, hearing mainly Jewish arguments, would draft a Zionist-slanted report with nary a nod to Arab apprehensions.

Just days before the commission was to leave Palestine, Hajj Amin canceled the boycott. Peel agreed to stay another week. *Filastin* blessed the turnaround as "wise."[31]

The first Arab to testify was Emir Abdullah, in Amman. It was the day after the secret session with Weizmann in which Professor Coupland first broached partition. Regally arrayed in white keffiyeh and black gown, the monarch's presence—as his ambitions—extended far beyond his sleepy desert realm.

The Balfour Declaration, he said, was "a birth certificate issued before the child was born," one that had armed the Zionists with "the spears of England . . . to stab the Arabs and so establish their alleged kingdom." In the Mandate's fourteen years, the Jews had threatened to grow to such numbers as had taken the Arabs fourteen centuries to reach. What right had Britain to convert one nation's homeland to that of another?

Even so, he said, what's done is done—the Jews who had already settled could stay but must never surpass a third of the population. Like his late brother Faisal, Abdullah appeared to tolerate Britain's pledge to the Jews so long as its promise of broader Arab independence—under his rule—was fulfilled. More than anything the emir's apparent pragmatism was self-interested: He wanted Palestine, or part of it, for his kingdom, and to one day reign over his brother's former dominion of Syria. A

Chaim Weizmann arrives to address the Royal Commission in Jerusalem, November 1936 (LOC M33-9233)

modest "tip" from the Jewish Agency (he had been receiving such subsidies for over a decade) helped ensure a comparatively moderate tone.[32]

In mid-January the commissioners met Hajj Amin. His appearance was short but sharp. The Mandate was illegitimate, he said, speaking through an interpreter (he had never learned English) in his usual hushed tones. In enshrining the Balfour Declaration, the Mandate contradicted the League of Nations Covenant's guarantees of self-determination. That same covenant held that any prior agreements made in contravention of the self-determination principle—such as, say, the declaration in question—were null and void.

"All this was done in consultation and agreement with the Jews on their own terms while the Arabs were never consulted."[33]

What's more, he added, Jewish nationalism imperiled Muslim holy sites. The Wall of Buraq—the Western Wall—was a "purely Muslim place" to which neither Jews nor any foreign power had "any connection or right or claim." Worse, he alleged, the Jews meant to rebuild the Temple on the ruins of the Dome of the Rock and Al-Aqsa Mosque.[34]

Given the Jews' undue influence in London, he said, Britain would let them do it:

> *My experience up till now shows that the Jews can do anything as far as Palestine is concerned . . . the people who have persuaded a great Government like Great Britain to destroy the integrity of an Arab people in order to replace it by their own can easily do that, especially when they become the majority in the country.*

"It is impossible to place two distinct peoples, who differ from each other in every sphere of their life, in one and the same country," he said. Creating a Jewish home in an "Arab ocean" has no historical precedent and would make the Holy Land a permanent backdrop for blood. He reiterated his core demands: terminating the Mandate, abandoning the national home, ceasing immigration, and banning land sales.

Questioned as to the fate of the four hundred thousand Jews already in Palestine, Amin was evasive, venturing only, "We must leave all this to the future." Pressed as to whether the country could assimilate them, his reply was brief.

"No."

In subsequent days more prominent Arabs delivered testimony similar to Amin's, berating Britain for the Mandate's intrinsic injustice. The head of the pan-Arab *Istiqlal* party said the Arabs could neither forsake "one meter" nor the country absorb one more immigrant. He refused to sit at the same table as Zionists, he said, or to touch Mandate stamps because alongside the word *Filastin* they bore the Hebrew letters *aleph* and *yod*, for *Eretz Israel.* Jamal Husseini, the mufti's cousin and political boss, bored the committee by repeating lengthy grievances it had already heard, and rankled it with his strident vow to starve with honor rather than settle for half a loaf.[35]

Foreign Secretary Eden commented that even if the Arab claims were reasonable, their "hectoring and threatening" tone left commissioners cold. Wauchope called the testimonies self-defeating and "crude"; he lamented that until recently many prominent Arabs had been moderate; now, led by the mufti, extremism was the rule. Musa Alami agreed: He was relieved the boycott was over, but the Arabs' appearances had been hastily prepared, aimed more at scoring points with the public than swaying the delegation.[36]

The Arabs' last witness was George Antonius. Far and away Arab Palestine's most eloquent spokesman, his testimony would be crucial to their case. But Lord Peel was anxious to leave Palestine. He gave him just two hours.[37]

Antonius protested that the government regarded Zionist and Arab nationalism in starkly different terms. To British officials, "a Zionist is a man who is perfectly all right and entitled to every kind of respect. An Arab nationalist is the devil incarnate, a revolutionary, he is spied upon, he is watched with suspicion."

The Arabs' opposition to Zionism was rooted neither in Jew hatred nor in an inability to compromise. Rather, their aspiration for independence was one on which they feel, rightly in his opinion, that no compromise was possible.

"The Arab mind throughout its history has been singularly free from any such thing as anti-Semitism which, as we all know, is a European and not an Arab invention," and "the greatest days of Jewish efflorescence have taken place when the Jews were under Muslim rule, whether in Baghdad, Cordova or Cairo."

No decent-minded person could view the treatment of Europe's Jews without abhorrence and contempt, he said. No such person would not want to do whatever possible to relieve their distress. "But what the Arabs say, and I say it with them, is this. If that relief is to be obtained only at the expense of inflicting corresponding distress on another people, the people of this country, then no it cannot be done."

The clock running out, Antonius hastened to his conclusion. A profound injustice had been committed against people whose "only crime has been that they are patriots who want to see their country develop and progress, who want to see their traditions installed and flourishing and who want to be able to govern themselves and live a life based on self-respect and dignity in their own country."

In his view the commission had a great opportunity. "That opportunity resolves itself into making efforts to remove a great injustice, and that alone, I think, is worth doing; it is perhaps the noblest task to which any man can apply himself."

"Thank you, Mr. Antonius," said Lord Peel, "for the very interesting statement you have made to us."[38]

ENTER: THE IRRIGATION EXPERT

Barely a week had passed since Coupland first mooted partition. Before joining the commission he had known little of Palestine, but as a historian he had studied partition plans for Ireland and India, and he was now convinced a similar model could work there too. But the commissioners were scheduled to leave the country within days, and if their final report were to even mention such a bold proposal, they would need to offer some details.[39]

In stepped a mid-level Palestine official, an irrigation specialist with a passion for statistics and a flair for maps. Douglas Gordon Harris had spent most of his career in India, but for the last year had been quietly working on a cantonization scheme for Palestine. In brief but detailed testimony, he laid it out.[40]

Harris had concluded that both cantonization and a Jewish-Arab federation were nonstarters, satisfying neither side. Instead, "if one were going to do anything in the nature of division, it would have to be on a much more far-reaching and drastic scale."

"May I produce a map," he said. "What I am visualizing is a State which would extend from somewhere near Majdal"—some Jews still knew it by its ancient name, Ashkelon—"up to Acre, and then across . . . the Plain of Jezreel, to near Beisan," which the Jews called Beth She'an. That Jewish state would include the strategic port of Haifa (perhaps with special rights reserved there for Britain), but all of the Galilee, overwhelmingly inhabited by Arabs, and the thinly settled southern desert would lie in the Arab state. His map showed the two states separated by a green line.

"Of course, under any arrangement of this kind, Jerusalem, Bethlehem and the vicinity would have to be excluded" from either polity, remaining instead a rump Mandate that included a corridor to the sea through Jaffa.[41]

Some 120,000 Arabs would be left in the Jewish state and a small number of Jews in the Arab one. That obstacle could be overcome by population transfer—Arabs could be resettled south of Majdal or north of Beisan—but if neither group wanted to move, that refusal would itself pose advantages: "If the Jews try to oppress the Arabs in the Jewish State there will be reprisals on the other side and the mere fact that reprisals are possible will probably keep them from being unduly oppressive."

Peel noted the "tremendous contrast" between the two prospective states, which he expected would operate "on a totally different scale of management and administration." Harris agreed, and said the Jewish state would be required to pay a substantial annual subvention to its Arab neighbor. By the same token, he expected the Jews to forge ties with the various neighboring Arab states, "who will be badly in need of their initiative and money."

Last was the question of arms. In the final plan, Coupland asked, would the Jews be an independent body that "could raise troops as they like?"

"Yes," Harris responded.

"A Jewish army?" Coupland pressed.

"Yes, I think so," said Harris, adding that he did not foresee "attacks in mass" on the prospective Hebrew state but rather the occasional minor raid.[42]

In barely five pages of testimony, a little-known irrigation engineer in the colonial service had delineated a plan for territorial division that the commission, steered by the eager Coupland, could embrace as its own.[43]

His session was one of over fifty held in secret—so secret that even the witness list was kept hidden. Transcripts of the hearings were recorded solely for the commissioners' use, and may well have been lost or destroyed had not the commission's secretary recognized their historical significance. Passing them to Whitehall for safekeeping, he scribbled that a few copies ought to be preserved, seeing as they chronicle "an important chapter in the history of Palestine and the Jewish people, and will, no doubt, be of considerable value to the historians of the remote future." (London quietly declassified them eight decades later, in 2017.)[44]

Following Harris's secret testimony (and a break for tea), it was the turn of Lewis Andrews, who had been his deputy in exploring cantonization schemes. Now Andrews was serving as the commission's liaison to the Arabs, and as such acted as an unofficial Arab spokesman. Coupland, leading the proceedings as usual, asked if he believed the Arabs would support partition.

"Moderate Arabs would," Andrews said. "In fact several Arabs have discussed it with me. Even the Mayor of Jerusalem has discussed it with me."

Andrews was speaking of Dr. Hussein Khalidi, a respected physician. He said Mayor Khalidi considered the Jews "a cancer in the body and the only way to make the body healthy is to cut the cancer out," limiting them to the lands they already possessed along the coast and in the Jezreel Valley.

Andrews insisted there was a "large body" of Arabs who would back such a plan but feared for their lives, just as Khalidi himself was too frightened to publicly air his proposal.[45]

But with Andrews's exceedingly brief testimony (it filled less than a page), Coupland had what he wanted. Here was a British official, knowledgeable in local affairs, confirming his belief—or at least hope—that a critical mass of moderate Arab opinion would accept Palestine's division into two states.[46]

In a subsequent secret session with Wauchope, Coupland said he had privately spoken with a senior Arab government official and a member of Jerusalem's Arab College, both of whom raised partition as a possible solution.[47] Coupland went so far as to say, "The Jews have not suggested this partition. It has come from an Arab source."[48]

They were the commissioners' final words in their final session in Palestine. Over the following days they made their respective exits from the country.

In Cairo they met to trade impressions. Peel said the national home's purpose had transformed since the Mandate's founding: From a cultural center, it was now expected to be a refuge for millions. Rumbold, his deputy, agreed: U.S. immigration limits and Hitler's ascent had changed everything, and the Arab claims for representative government were "very strong indeed." All of the commissioners present agreed that the aspirations of the Holy Land's two peoples were incompatible, and that satisfying them would ultimately require granting both greater autonomy.

Among them, Professor Coupland was keenest for bold, rapid strokes. When Peel warned of the difficulties they would encounter from world opinion, he countered that they themselves had acquired more knowledge than anyone back home, so why leave the big decisions to others? When Hammond noted they had taken little actual evidence on the specifics of division, Coupland retorted that he "did not attach great importance to evidence, so long as he himself was satisfied, and he had been fortified by the opinion of Mr. Harris and Mr. Andrews." Rumbold privately disparaged him as an "intriguing little professor" hatching brazen schemes with scant input from his colleagues.

Still, in the interest of unanimity, the commissioners resolved the report would speak in one voice, forthrightly laying out the problem's severity and the impossibility of solving it within the existing Mandate. They might therefore be compelled to recommend the most dramatic of the proposals brought before them.

They called it the "clean cut."[49]

Back in England, the commissioners called their final witnesses.

One was Jabotinsky, the Revisionist-Zionist leader whom the British had barred from Palestine seven years earlier. He echoed Weizmann: The source of the Jews' plight is being everywhere a minority, nowhere a majority. He too warned of their impending catastrophe: "We have got to save millions, many millions."

Where he differed was his prescription: a sovereign Jewish state, in maximal borders.

"The phenomenon called Zionism may include all kinds of dreams—a 'model community,' Hebrew culture, perhaps even a second edition of the Bible," he said, "but all this longing for wonderful toys of velvet and silver is nothing in comparison with that tangible momentum of irresistible distress and need by which we are propelled."

His stand on Arab nationalism differed starkly from Weizmann's—at once more empathetic and less accommodating.

"I have the profoundest feeling for the Arab case," he said, noting that tribunals rarely try cases in which justice is wholly on one side or the other. He understood that any people prefers to be a majority and not a minority. He put it plainly:

> *Palestine on both sides of the Jordan should hold the Arabs, their progeny and many millions of Jews. What I do not deny is that in that process the Arabs of Palestine will necessarily become a minority. . . . What I do deny is that that is a hardship. That is not a hardship on any race, any nation, possessing so many National States now and so many more National States in the future. One fraction, one branch of that race, and not a big one, will have to live in someone else's State.*

"Tell the Arabs the truth," he said, "and then you will see the Arab is reasonable, the Arab is clever, the Arab is just." But when asked if the government should seek consultation with the Arabs over Palestine's future, Jabotinsky's reply was brusque.

"None."

"None?"

"None." The Balfour Declaration was given to Jews, he argued, and the Mandate was drafted independently of the Arabs' attitude. If Britain no longer wished to pursue that Mandate, it should give it to some other power, but it must not pretend it was fulfilling its obligation.

"No, that cannot be done," he said. "That is not cricket."[50]

In Nablus, the *Istiqlal* activist Akram Zuaytir wrote that every Arab ought to read Jabotinsky's remarks. "This is true Zionism from the mouth of one of its leaders. Listen, listen to Jabotinsky!"[51]

Among the closing witnesses was Winston Churchill.

A staunch Zionist advocate in Parliament, Churchill had earned a reputation as something of a philo-Semite. Decades earlier he had written: "Some people like Jews and some do not; but no thoughtful man can doubt that they are beyond all question the most formidable and the most remarkable race which has ever appeared in the world."

> *We owe to the Jews in the Christian revelation a system of ethics which, even if it were entirely separated from the supernatural, would be incomparably the most precious possession of mankind, worth in fact the fruits of all other wisdom and learning put together. On that system and by that faith there has been built out of the wreck of the Roman Empire the whole of our existing civilization.*[52]

Churchill's Zionism was equally informed by a decades-long disdain for Islam. "No stronger retrograde force exists in the world," he had written in his twenties after his first foray in Muslim lands, helping quash a colonial revolt in Sudan.

> *How dreadful are the curses which Mohammedanism lays on its votaries! Besides the fanatical frenzy, which is as dangerous in a man*

> *as hydrophobia [rabies] in a dog, there is this fearful fatalistic apathy. The effects are apparent in many countries. Improvident habits, slovenly systems of agriculture, sluggish methods of commerce, and insecurity of property exist wherever the followers of the Prophet rule or live.*

"Individual Moslems may show splendid qualities," he allowed, but the "fact that in Mohammedan law every woman must belong to some man as his absolute property—either as a child, a wife, or a concubine—must delay the final extinction of slavery until the faith of Islam has ceased to be a great power among men."[53]

In mid-March 1937, Churchill met the commissioners for secret testimony. He was in characteristically combative form.

> *I insist upon loyalty and upon the good faith of England to the Jews, to which I attach the most enormous importance, because we gained great advantages in the War. We did not adopt Zionism entirely out of altruistic love for starting a Jewish colony: it was a matter of great importance to this country. It was a potent factor on public opinion in America and we are bound by honor, and I think upon the merits, to push this thing as far as we can.*

Keeping the Jews a minority, he said, would be contrary to the Balfour Declaration. One day, over generations or perhaps centuries, "there may be a great Palestinian State, in which a large majority of the inhabitants would be Jews . . . there might well be a great Jewish State there, numbered by millions, far exceeding the present inhabitants of the country and to cut them off from that would be wrong."[54]

In any case, he said, the Jews were the true natives of Palestine, a land that had held a larger population in Christ's day than at any time since the "great hordes of Islam" swept in and "smashed it all up."

Rumbold asked whether the Arabs had not once built a thriving civilization in Spain.

"I'm glad they were thrown out," Churchill growled. "It is a lower manifestation, the Arab." Palestine was at base a "question of which civilization you prefer."

Not that he reckoned the Jews blameless. They had failed to conciliate the Arabs—he expected they would have been cleverer than that—and ought to abandon their "foolish" Hebrew-only labor policy. Yet it was good for the world that Palestine be developed, and it was the Zionists alone who would do it.

He had "great regard" for Arabs, he swore, implausibly, but "where the Arab goes is often desert. . . . Why is there harsh injustice done if people come in and make a livelihood for more and make the desert into palm groves and orange groves? Why is it injustice because there is more work and wealth for everybody? There is no injustice. The injustice is when those who live in the country leave it to be a desert for thousands of years."

The central question was the numbers and speed at which Jews were arriving—if these were too high they could be eased, but "you must not give in to the furious outbreaks; you must quell them." And Britain must not be diverted from its basic purpose: settling as many Jews as possible without disturbing the country's economic life. If it cannot, it must give up the Mandate.

Churchill concluded with reference to an Ancient Greek fable. In it, a dog sleeps in a manger, or feeding trough, filled with hay. An ox approaches to feed, and the hound bares its teeth, keeping the animal from sustaining itself. The implicit analogy was clear: The Arabs were making inadequate use of the land, and the Jews needed it for their very survival.

> *I do not admit that the dog in the manger has the final right to the manger, even though he may have lain there for a very long time. I do not admit that right. I do not admit, for instance, that a great wrong has been done to the Red Indians of America, or the black people of Australia. I do not admit that a wrong has been done to those people by the fact that a stronger race, a higher grade race, or at any rate, a more world-wise race, to put it that way, has come in and taken their*

place. I do not admit it. . . . They had not the right nor had they the power.

Four days later Churchill wrote the commissioners seeking guarantees that his evidence would not appear in the final report. "You assured me that our conversation was confidential and private . . . there were a few references to nationalities which would not be suited to appear in a permanent record."[55]

An Irrepressible Conflict

George VI was crowned May 11, 1937, ending the crisis wrought by his elder brother's abdication six months prior. Letters from Palestine poured in. The National Committee of Ramle expressed its wish that his reign augur in an era of Arab "freedom and salvation." The chief rabbis of Jaffa and Tel Aviv proclaimed: "In your days may Judah be saved and Israel dwell in peace in their land!"[56]

Prime Minister Stanley Baldwin resigned, himself a casualty of the abdication crisis, and advised the new sovereign to replace him with the chancellor of the exchequer: Neville Chamberlain.

Weeks later the Liberal leader, Archibald Sinclair, hosted Weizmann and a handful of pro-Zionist politicians for dinner. The Peel report was almost ready, and rumors swirled that it would recommend the Mandate's termination and the cleavage of Palestine in two. Labour leader Clement Attlee told the dinner guests that ending the Mandate would be a blow to Britain, a triumph for Fascism, and an end to the "great experiment" of Zionism. It would be a concession to violence, and he wanted no part of it. Sinclair agreed.

Churchill fumed, holding forth for three hours in favor of Zionism and against the Chamberlain government. The new Cabinet members were "lily-livered rabbits." The proposed Jewish state was a mirage. As soon as the Arabs started trouble again, Whitehall would back down. The Jews had one choice: "Persevere, persevere, persevere!"

"You know, you are our master," he told Weizmann, "and yours, and yours," pointing to each party leader as if acting out an anti-Semite's fever dream of Jewish domination. "What you say goes. If you ask us to fight, we shall fight like tigers."

Weizmann relayed the events to Baffy Dugdale: Churchill was "in his most brilliant style, but very drunk."

For five months the commission drafted its report in strict secrecy—President Franklin Roosevelt was not shown its contents until the eve of publication. Weizmann seethed when denied an advance copy;[57] the Arabs never dreamed of asking for such a favor.

History would record it as the Peel report, but the four-hundred-page tome was more than anything the work of Professor Coupland.[58] It was a rare feat: a policy paper both pragmatic and elegant, meticulous, and readable.

On July 7 it went public.

> *An irrepressible conflict has arisen between two national communities within the narrow bounds of one small country. About 1,000,000 Arabs are in strife, open or latent, with some 400,000 Jews. There is no common ground between them. The Arab community is predominantly Asiatic in character, the Jewish community predominantly European. They differ in religion and in language. Their cultural and social life, their ways of thought and conduct, are as incompatible as their national aspirations.*

Its framing was tilted toward the Zionists, a result largely due to their vastly greater investment in preparation, testimony, and lobbying.

"Unquestionably," the report said, the Mandate's "primary purpose" had been to establish the Jewish national home. But that project rested on the hope that Arab enmity to Zionism would weaken with Jewish development of a "backward" country. It should have been obvious that "a very awkward situation" would arise if that basic assumption proved false.[59]

That awkward situation had now arisen. Zionist wealth and know-how had borne no conciliatory fruit. Poor and neglected though Palestine was, to the Arabs it was their home, the land where their forebears had lived and died. The report quoted an Arab witness: "You say my house has been enriched by the strangers who have entered it. But it is *my* house, and I did not invite the strangers in, or ask them to enrich it, and I do not care how poor or bare it is if only I am master in it."[60]

Hoping for the Arabs' acquiescence to Zionism was one thing; forcing it on them was something else, something contrary to the Mandate's spirit and moral basis. The national home "has been neither conditioned nor controlled by the Arabs of Palestine. It has been established directly against their will." From the outset it involved the "blank negation of the rights implied in the principle of national self-government."[61]

The report cast blame widely. The government had vested too much power in Hajj Amin al-Husseini, with his twin roles of grand mufti and chief of the Supreme Muslim Council. And the mufti's encouragement of the strike and failure to condemn terrorism meant he must bear a "full share of responsibility" for the carnage.[62]

The Zionists also did not escape reproach: "The Jews were fully entitled to enter the door forced open for them into Palestine. They did it with the sanction and encouragement of the League of Nations and the United States of America. But by doing it they have closed the other doors of the Arab world against them."

Zionism was "a purely Jewish ideal. The Arabs hardly come into the picture except when they force an entry with violence."[63] Some Jews acted as if "members of a superior race, destined before long to be masters of the country."

Yet if the commissioners believed otherwise, they scarcely showed it: Arabs were living in the past, separated "by centuries from the educated, resourceful, Western-minded" Jews. The latter were a "highly intelligent and enterprising race," the Arabs "on a different cultural level."[64]

Any attempt to combine "virtually two civilizations" into one system was bound to face hurdles, they wrote. But the recent disturbances had grown to an unprecedented scale—more enduring, more dispersed, and better organized—not riots but an "open rebellion," capturing the hearts and imagination of the entire Near East.[65]

The prognosis was bleak: "In these circumstances . . . we should be failing in our duty if we said anything to encourage a hopeful outlook for the future peace of Palestine under the existing system or anything akin to it. The optimism which naturally prevailed at the outset of the enterprise was chilled by the series of Arab outbreaks, but never extinguished. In each case it soon revived, and in each case it proved false."[66]

The commissioners rebuffed Arab demands to close Palestine's gates—facilitating Jewish immigration remained a binding international obligation. Nonetheless, they recommended capping quotas for new arrivals at twelve thousand annually for five years.[67]

That dramatic change—cutting Jewish immigration to one-fifth its 1935 figure—was the Great Arab Revolt's first major, incontestable achievement.

And yet, the report asserted, easing immigration would not treat the malady at its source. Bold measures were in order. Cantonization was inadequate, satisfying neither Arab nor Jew. Parity, as Weizmann advised, would only embitter the conflict, with two evenly matched fighters bloodying the other's nose indefinitely. No such palliatives would suffice: "They might reduce the inflammation and bring down the temperature, but they cannot cure the trouble. The disease is so deep-rooted that, in our firm conviction, the only hope of a cure lies in a surgical operation."

"Partition seems to offer at least a chance of ultimate peace," the commissioners wrote. "We can see none in any other plan."[68]

The guiding principle was that concentrations of Zionist-owned land should go to the Jews, most of the rest to the Arabs. For the former that meant an N-shaped swath starting just south of Tel Aviv and extending to Haifa, then southeast across the Jezreel Valley and due north again along the Jordan to the Galilee panhandle.

But although the Jews owned just 7 percent of Palestine's land, the plan gave them fully 20 percent of the country. And it went one better, granting them the overwhelmingly Arab Galilee for population growth and "colonization," based on religious-historical ties to Safed and Tiberias—though as mixed cities these would stay temporarily under Britain.

In line with the plan proffered by Harris, the irrigation engineer, the Crown would also retain Palestine's holiest terrain—Jerusalem and Bethlehem—with a passage to the sea just north of Jaffa (the city itself would join the Arab state). And as in Harris's plan, the Jewish state and Britain would pay regular subventions to the Arab state to compensate for reduced taxes now that the bulk of Palestine's economy would lie beyond its borders.[69]

The clean cut.

Commissioners hoped it would solve two festering world crises: that of Palestine and of Europe's harassed Jews. If the Arabs could help bring a "final solution" to the Continent's "Jewish problem" (the drafters could not have known the cruel irony of the wording), they would earn not just the Jews' gratitude but that of humanity. "Numberless men and women all over the world would feel a sense of deep relief if somehow an end could be put to strife and bloodshed in a thrice hallowed land."[70]

The next day His Majesty's Government endorsed the report's main principles. It noted that the proposed solution had significant merits:

> *The Arabs would obtain their national independence, and thus be enabled to co-operate on an equal footing with the Arabs of neighboring countries in the cause of Arab unity and progress. . . . It would convert the Jewish National Home into a Jewish State with full control over immigration. . . . The Jews would at last cease to live a "minority life," and the primary objective of Zionism would thus be attained . . . both peoples would obtain, in the words of the Commission, "the inestimable boon of peace."*[71]

The world's preeminent power now officially backed a two-state solution to the Jewish-Arab dispute over the Holy Land.

REVERBERATIONS

David Ben-Gurion hadn't slept in two weeks. His first impression, he wrote Shertok, was of "a political conquest and historic chance we have not had since our country was destroyed" two millennia before. "I see in the realization of this plan an almost decisive phase in the beginning of complete redemption, and an unrivaled lever for the gradual conquest of all of the Land of Israel."[72]

He had devoured the report, he effused, and found that it exceeded all of its predecessors in appreciating Zionism's achievements. It would be the Jewish declaration of independence, dwarfing even the Balfour

Declaration. Should partition be realized, the Jews must thank the mufti for prompting the commission in the first place.

"This means our control over the Land of Israel's sea, this is large-scale immigration. This is systematic settlement with government support," he wrote in his diary. "It is a Jewish army . . . a Jewish state. . . . It is succor to a persecuted nation, it is the beginning of redemption. . . . It seems to me this can't be other than a dream."[73]

Until the last minute he had not believed the Jews would get the Galilee. It would not be hard for the Arabs to prove it was "a great injustice," he conceded, but for the Yishuv it represented an act of courage and generosity. Still, two crucial objectives remained: the crown jewel that was Jerusalem, and the Negev desert, Palestine's one expanse of sparsely populated, virgin earth. "This is not a final agreement. We'll break these borders—and not necessarily at the tip of a sword."[74]

Scouring the report a second time, Ben-Gurion grew fixated on a passage he had missed at first reading. The document's final pages briefly proposed a population transfer similar to that between Greece and Turkey, brokered by the League of Nations, after the Great War. That exchange had drawn criticism at the time, but the commissioners noted approvingly that the "ulcer" of inter-ethnic tensions had been "clean cut out."[75]

Ben-Gurion thrilled at the prospect. Population transfer was more valuable even than additional territory. "It can give us something we never had, even when we were sovereign, even in the days of the First and Second Temples: The forced transfer of Arabs from the valleys offered to the Jewish state."[76]

"We get for the first time in our history a real Jewish state—an agricultural bloc of two million or more people, contiguous, densely populated, rooted in a land that is all its own," he wrote. "An opportunity of which we never dreamed, and couldn't dare dream except in our wildest imaginings."

The Jews had to cling to the transfer proposal as they had clung to the Balfour Declaration.

> *We must free ourselves from weakness of thought and will, and preconceived ideas that transfer cannot happen. I see . . . the enormous difficulty of an outside force uprooting some hundred-thousand Arabs from the villages from which they lived for centuries. Will England dare do this? She certainly will not if we do not want it, and if we don't push her with all the strength of our pressure and faith. . . . Any hesitation on our part over the necessity of this transfer, any doubt in the possibility of its realization, any hesitation on our part in its justice can cost us a historic chance that will not return.*[77]

"We could never allow ourselves to express such a thing, because we never wanted to disinherit the Arabs," he later wrote his son. "But since England is giving part of the land promised to us to the Arab state, it is only fair that the Arabs in our state be moved to the Arab part."[78]

Ben-Gurion was now categorically committed to partition. Like Weizmann though, he played coy, anxious that the Jews—especially those in the "diasporic hell"—would broadcast their joy too publicly. Partition had to appear as if forced on the Jews. To outsiders, therefore, he feigned disillusionment with the Empire, deploring both partition and continued British rule as equally dangerous. To close colleagues, however, he praised partition and urged the Mandate's continuation.[79]

Ben-Gurion expected that most influential Arabs would accept partition, however grudgingly. Some did, like Yusuf Hanna, Musa Alami, and the leaders of Syria's main nationalist movement, the National Bloc.[80]

Lebanon's President Émile Eddé, a Christian, feared Muslim domination of his own statelet and hoped a Jewish ally to its south would help safeguard its sovereignty. The day the report was released he was in Paris, where he met Weizmann and asked that the new state's first treaty of *bon voisinage* be with its northern neighbor. "Now that the Peel report is an official document," he gushed, raising a toast, "I have the honor of congratulating the first president of the future Jewish state!" The Maronite patriarch sent Weizmann a similar missive, but said Lebanon's Christians would suffer a "massacre" if those sentiments were to become known.[81]

Emir Abdullah of Transjordan, who stood to benefit politically and financially from partition, informed the British of his approval.[82]

Jerusalem ex-mayor Ragheb Nashashibi told the high commissioner he too backed partition, and quit Hajj Amin's Arab Higher Committee in a bid for London's good graces. The mayors of Jaffa, Nablus, Jenin, Tulkarem, and Haifa—all Nashashibi allies—followed his line.[83]

Yet within weeks, these erstwhile supporters reversed course. Abdullah denied ever endorsing partition and urgently sought rapprochement with the mufti. Nashashibi railed that the plan had legitimized even the Jews' most extreme claims, and that slicing little Palestine into three was inconceivable.

It was an abrupt turnaround. Abdullah had found himself alone among Arab leaders in publicly accepting partition, and had come to doubt Britain's commitment to the plan. Nashashibi fell in line amid mounting death threats and the murder of a string of his associates.[84]

Both had sullenly surrendered to the fact that the mufti remained the only man in Arab Palestine who mattered. And Amin was wasting little time not just in rejecting partition but in designating its proponents as traitors.

The report had caused him "profound grief and repugnance," he told Wauchope—Arabs would sooner die than submit to such an outrage. The commission had been swayed by "emotional and irrelevant" references to European Jews' plight. Such compassion, "praiseworthy in the abstract," had produced a bill that the Arabs could not and would not pay. The Jews, he said, were

> *a minority of intruders, who before the war had no great standing in this country, and whose political connections therewith had been severed for almost 2,000 years . . . such an attempt is without precedent in history, ancient or modern. . . . Palestine is still an Arab country, because the majority of its population is Arab, the majority of its property owners are Arabs, and because of its unbroken historical connection with the Arabs for over 1400 years.*

The borders were nonsensical, he said. The Jewish state would contain 225,000 Arabs—with another 100,000 in the British-controlled mixed cities—but the Arab state would include just 1,250 Jews. The proposed "population exchange" was therefore better called an expulsion. Subventions from the Jewish state would be a "degradation." The "surgical operation" would be fatal, as "an amputated limb dies even though the trunk with the vital organs may live." The whole project was "humiliating, impracticable and fraught with danger," and would rank among the catastrophes of Arab history.[85]

The mufti had now declared himself in diametric opposition to British Palestine policy. Rumors circulated of his impending arrest. In a hastily arranged meeting with the German consul, he asked for closer ties and louder opposition from the Reich to a Jewish state. The next day he moved into the Haram al-Sharif, where he was convinced no non-Muslim power would have the audacity to pursue him. He would not leave for five months.[86]

A TALE OF TWO SUMMITS

The twentieth Zionist Congress convened in Zurich in August 1937, exactly four decades since Theodor Herzl's first Congress in nearby Basel. "Today we conclude forty years of wandering in the desert," Chaim Weizmann told the audience. "Now we ask—is its end in sight?"

Weizmann was now a committed partitionist, but his movement was as fractious as ever. He too rejected Peel's specific borders as insufficient, he told delegates, but he begged them to at least accept the principle of partition as a legitimate one.[87]

He added a word on the Arabs for the record.

> *We know that the mufti and Qawuqji are not the Arab nation. . . . There is an Arab nation with a glorious past. To that nation we have stretched out our hand, and do so even now—but on one condition. Just as we wish them to overcome their crisis, and to revert to the great tradition of a mighty and civilized Arab people, so must they know that we have the right to build our home in Eretz Israel, harming no one, helping all. When they acknowledge this, we shall reach common ground.*[88]

Over the next two weeks some fifty speakers rose to applaud or decry partition; just over half spoke against it. Even within Ben-Gurion's Labor movement, a third of the delegates were opposed—the Jewish state, they said, was minute, indefensible. It left out Jerusalem, and what of the mixed cities? Besides, did anyone truly believe the English would carry it through? Golda Meyerson, a Labor delegate born in Kiev and raised in Milwaukee, was convinced they would never implement a program so certain to antagonize the Muslim world.

Weizmann and Ben-Gurion engineered a compromise: The Congress would neither accept nor refuse the Peel proposals. Instead it would reject the report's partition borders but pocket its grand prize—a Jewish state—and authorize the Zionist leaders to keep negotiating with Britain.[89]

The next month Hajj Amin convened a parallel summit in Bludan, a hilltop resort near Damascus. Four hundred prominent Arabs attended, representing almost every Arab country. As in Zurich, a single item filled the agenda: partition. But here the decision was never in doubt.

Palestine had been an Arab land for over a millennium, delegates affirmed. In the Great War the British had promised the Arabs independence, and they had shed their blood in pursuit of that purpose. Instead, however, the crown had cast in with the "cosmopolitan" Zionists, encouraging their "vainglory" and "cupidity." Britain must choose between friendship with one or the other—maintaining its Palestine policy could ultimately push the Arabs toward "other European powers" whose goals were "inimical" to its own.[90]

Attendees agreed that it was "the duty of Arabs and Muslims everywhere to fight as one man." Boycotting the Jewish national home was a pan-Arab obligation—anyone flouting it was himself a de facto "Zionist" to be shunned. Pamphlets circulated inveighing against the Jews, enemies of the faith and its Prophet, servants of Satan who even "prefer agnosticism to Islam." The conference concluded by asking God to grant victory in the Arab nation's "jihad" for independence and unity. It was for Hajj Amin another high-water mark in raising Palestine to the top of Arab and Muslim priorities.

Some participants felt the conference did not go far enough: They wanted an explicit commitment to relaunch acts of violence. Days later about a hundred of them met secretly in Damascus's medieval Sarouja market. They kept no records, but a spy posing as an ice-carrier relayed the proceedings to the local British consul.

Into the small hours they plotted the revolt's revival, including a systematic campaign of assault and intimidation against "treacherous" Arabs still on friendly terms with the British. Yacoub Ghussein, a member of the mufti's inner circle, appealed for money and arms, and read a letter from the exiled Fawzi Bey declaring that if partition went ahead, every Arab must shed his last drop of blood to thwart Palestine's dismemberment.[91]

The same day, Musa Alami was on Lake Lucerne accepting the final payment of Mussolini's pledge of seventy-five thousand pounds (four million pounds today). Chief Justice Trusted had granted him another three months' leave; Alami had told him he was off to the Karlsbad springs to "take a cure."[92]

Chapter 4

Black Sunday

Musa Alami owned farmland just south of Beisan, a mostly Arab town of four thousand at the junction of the Jezreel and Jordan Valleys. He had bought it from the government more than a decade before in a joint purchase with Jamal Husseini—his brother-in-law and the mufti's cousin and ally—and Tawfiq Canaan, a prominent physician and Arab nationalist. There they built a two-story fort-like farmhouse to house their caretaker, a black Bedouin named Namrud, and his four wives. Namrud planted cypress, orange, and grapefruit trees. The estate and its surroundings were called Zar'a.[1]

Alami and Jamal were close companions. One day, shortly before the rebellion erupted, they were chatting over coffee in the Jerusalem home their two families shared. Jamal had an idea: They could buy ships and export citrus to Europe during the winter months. Done right, the venture could make them a small fortune.

He could already imagine the vessels shuttling out of Jaffa Port: "One goes, one comes. One goes, one comes."

Jamal's daughter Serene remembered her uncle Musa as a brilliant pessimist. He could only laugh at his brother-in-law's flights of fancy, but in the end he assented.

Then came 1936. The Arab strike began; the economy collapsed. One after another, the unpicked juice-laden fruit dropped to the ground. Undaunted, Jamal turned to eggplants, which could at least go to local markets as long as exports were frozen. But the eggplants ripened and the strike persisted.

"Pickles!" Jamal declared one morning. "Eggplants make wonderful pickles."

They bought hundreds of tin cans and stored the produce in brine. Still the strike endured, now into its fourth month.

Never at a loss, Jamal proposed stockpiling the tins in the cool basement of their home. Alami protested: The cellar was full of copies of the Quran concordance that his father, the late mayor, had painstakingly compiled a half century before.

Yet there was no alternative, and space was cleared among the stacks of theological tracts for the vegetables to ferment.

As the rebellion raged, Alami thought of turning the basement into a shelter. Descending the stairs one day, he glimpsed a sight that left him cold. "There, swimming around in pickle juice like happy children in a pool were both the eggplants and his father's books," his niece recalled. "Later he understood that the tins had exploded and finally brought an end to all our dreams for Beisan."[2]

He resolved to sell the estate.

On August 28, 1936, the Jewish National Fund's leading land purchaser recorded his latest prospective deal in his diary. "The plot belongs to three of the leading Arabs opposed to Zionism," he wrote, listing Alami and his two co-owners. "They want to sell the land, but at a high price, and are now demanding more than before the disturbances."[3]

Musa Alami's secret dealings with Mussolini had undercut his own credentials as the Arab "moderate" so desperately sought by Britain and the Jews. Now he would sully his Arab-nationalist bona fides by committing the cardinal, but all too common, offense of quite literally ceding ground to Zionism.[4]

His choice was typical of Palestine's Arab elite. There was no notable family that had not sold land. Of the eight original members of the Arab Higher Committee, at least half had signed or brokered land deals. Jerusalem's former mayor Ragheb Nashashibi sold ground at Mount Scopus to Hebrew University. Alfred Rock, a Catholic from Jaffa, sold land south of that city that became Bat Yam. Awni Abdel Hadi of the hard-line *Istiqlal* party mediated the sale of virtually all of Wadi Hawarith, the basin along the central coast that the Jews called the Hefer Valley.[5]

In early June 1937, just before the Peel Commission released its report, Moshe Shertok visited the Beisan farmstead. It struck him as a "God-forsaken corner of the country, rife with dangers," from Bedouin raids to malaria. Nonetheless he insisted it must be settled: "If we drive in a stake at Zar'a, at the southern end of Beth She'an, it would be the strongest declaration of our claim to the whole area."[6]

The Zionists, after all, had already sunk roots across much of the Jezreel Valley and Galilee panhandle, and acquiring the Beisan plain would cement territorial contiguity in Palestine's north, ensuring it remained in Jewish hands in any future partition plan.[7]

Within weeks all was ready. Immigrants from Germany were chosen for the undertaking—the Hitler menace meant the Reich would soon surpass Poland as Zionism's leading source of immigrants.[8] Unlike most kibbutz settlers, however, these aspiring farmers were religiously observant. They suspected discrimination in the secular Zionist leaders' decision to dispatch them to a spot so perilous and remote.

In the early morning on the appointed day, June 30, 1937, an advance group of settlers arrived, Namrud served coffee, and, with a thumbprint on a piece of paper that he could not read, the deal was complete. Namrud's blockhouse became Zvi's Fortress, *Tirat Zvi*, named for a nineteenth-century German rabbi who had preached the Return to Zion.

One hundred people followed, with a half-dozen trucks, a tractor, and a plow in tow. They unloaded wood beams for huts and tents, installed a generator, and dug four zigzagging defensive trenches extending out from the fort. Two long iron fences were erected, a searchlight placed on the roof, and gravel added to the existing clay wall to make it bulletproof.[9]

Zvi's Fortress was the latest iteration of a new settlement campaign called Wall and Tower. An old Ottoman law, carried over by the British, held that any roofed structure constructed within a single day required no permit. Men and women would therefore set out before dawn to exploit the daylight, often accompanied by hundreds of farmers enlisted from neighboring settlements. Since the previous winter, the Zionist leadership had already set up eight "sunrise to sunset" settlements around the Jezreel Valley and the Sea of Galilee.

Women of Kibbutz Ein Hashofet undergo rifle training, circa 1938 (GPO D477-089)

Less than a week after Tirat Zvi's establishment, a group of Americans founded a kibbutz in the hills between Mount Carmel and Samaria that the Jews knew as the Heights of Manasseh and the Arabs as *Bilad al-Ruha*, the Land of Winds.

Dorothy Kahn, a *Palestine Post* reporter recently arrived in the country from Atlantic City, wrote, "It is strange to come into this remote, wild place, surrounded by the black tents of the Bedouin, and be greeted by lusty American slang and see young women from Detroit and Chicago walking around with rifles across their shoulders and cartridge belts around their waists." She compared the prefabricated shacks to Sears Roebuck homes, the fortified compounds to frontiersmen's barricades in the American West.

Louis Brandeis, a sitting U.S. Supreme Court justice, quietly donated fifty thousand dollars to the enterprise. The grateful settlers (with rather less discretion) named their homestead *Ein Hashofet*, Spring of the Judge.[10]

A Gift from Providence

In summer 1937 Lewis Yelland Andrews was promoted to district commissioner—governor, effectively—of Galilee.[11] The appointment was the work of Coupland, the "intriguing little professor" most responsible for Peel's partition plan. Dividing Palestine required a strong hand, and nowhere more than Galilee, which was to be transformed from an Arab agricultural bastion to the hinterland of the Jewish state. Coupland believed that Andrews—who had assured him that moderate Arabs would back partition—was the only official who would be "as firm with the Arabs as with the Jews."[12]

For two decades Palestine had been Andrews's life. An Australian, he had first arrived in the Great War, serving under Norman Bentwich in the Egyptian Camel Transport Corps and guiding the dromedaries from Sinai to Syria, leaving two fingers somewhere in the Holy Land en route.[13] After the armistice he returned to Palestine and joined the new Mandate administration. In the 1921 and 1929 riots he rescued Jews in Hadera.[14]

Wiry and garrulous, Andrews was typically found on horseback, his head wrapped in a white keffiyeh, and was likely the only Mandate official conversant in both local idioms. "Without a doubt one of Britain's most knowledgeable figures about the East, the Arabs, and their customs," noted a Jerusalem *oud* player in his diary, observing that he spoke Arabic "with the greatest fluency and on a high register."[15]

Some Arabs thought him a hopeless partisan. Zuaytir, the Nablus activist, dubbed him "famous for his cruelty and enmity toward the Arabs." Anwar Nusseibeh, a judge in Nazareth magistrate's court, recorded a similar impression.[16] Twice over the years Andrews had dodged assassination and now was attached a constable, Peter McEwan, as bodyguard.

A lifelong churchgoer, Andrews read the Bible daily and from youth knew Palestine's geography better than Australia's or Britain's. Shortly after the Great Revolt broke out, army engineers were set to demolish a domed structure near Bethlehem suspected of housing rebels. It was only Andrews's last-minute intervention that spared the edifice, Rachel's Tomb, from demolition.

On another occasion, while conversing with the founder of the new town of Netanya, he abruptly stood up. "We Christians believe the Messiah will come and redeem mankind only when a Jewish state is established," he announced. "I, who hoped all my life to be one of the helpers of this rebirth of the Jewish people, am fortunate to have this privilege."[17]

Now he was granted that chance. Of all the Empire's posts, Galilee was to be his bailiwick, Nazareth his home. The posting, just before his forty-first birthday, seemed a gift from Providence itself.

A few months earlier, William Denis Battershill had landed in Haifa Port, having been relocated from Cyprus to take the number-two position in Palestine. If his boss, High Commissioner Wauchope, favored top hats and tailcoats, Battershill's main distinguishing feature was his perfectly round glasses.

One of the first officials he met was Andrews, who showed him the Sea of Galilee. They shared the same age and the same Anglican outlook, but unlike the affable Australian, Battershill's faith was a private, English affair, emerging chiefly in correspondence with his mother, whom he wrote weekly back in Cornwall.

"My dearest mother," read his first letter, "I can easily see that I'm in for the devil of a ride. . . . It's all extremely odd out here."

"My dearest mother," he wrote the next week. "This place gets odder and odder as one learns things about it. I should think that it was absolutely *sui generis*."[18]

Battershill was working later than he ever had in comparatively placid Cyprus. "'He that watches over Israel shall neither slumber nor sleep,'" he wrote, quoting Scripture. "The Psalmist was about right!"

Nonetheless he insisted it was worth it: "I would not have missed this for anything."[19]

In August, Wauchope took an extended holiday in England.

"My dearest mother," Battershill wrote, "I should have to take charge for a couple of months. I do not mind in the least even though the responsibilities are heavy. . . . Things are reasonably quiet here and I hope they will remain so. But who can tell in this extraordinary country?"[20]

Andrews's birthday fell on a Sunday, and Constable McEwan drove him to Nazareth's Anglican church, where he was a warden, for evensong.

Andrews's deputy parked his car alongside them. As they walked toward the church, they spotted three men in keffiyehs and one in a tarboush. Something seemed off.[21]

"Run for your life!" Andrews bellowed.

The men began shooting. They hit the constable, who returned fire before losing consciousness. Andrews ran to the church and reached its steps when a shot to the jugular brought him down. The men pumped nine bullets into his body while his deputy lay on the ground, playing dead. Convinced all three were killed, the men scattered.[22]

The Arab Higher Committee issued a one-sentence condemnation that was carried in the Arab papers without comment. *Filastin* implored the authorities to show restraint.[23]

Andrews and McEwan were buried in a full military funeral at the Protestant Cemetery on Mount Zion. High-ranking Britons and Jews came out in force; Dr. Khalidi was the only Arab of note. Troops fired in the air, a trumpet sounded, and the Anglican bishop read Andrews's favorite Psalm. Bentwich praised his "courage, merriness, and resourcefulness." His coffin was draped in the Australian and British flags, but his headstone said he gave his life for Palestine. A colleague who saw his body said he was still smiling.[24]

Police dogs lost the killers' scent somewhere near the Muslim cemetery, but arrested one hundred people by the following morning. All were detained in the Ottoman prison at Acre.[25]

Some two dozen British troops and police had been killed in the revolt, but none had been senior government officials. And with Wauchope still in England shooting grouse, the task of restoring order fell to Battershill. The day after the murder he got a telegram from Colonial Secretary Ormsby-Gore: Britain must not stand meekly by as its representatives were liquidated.

There was no evidence tying Hajj Amin to the assassination. But Ormsby-Gore had already concluded he was Palestine's chief source of unrest, the foremost obstacle to partition, and generally a "black hearted villain." Six months prior, the king's Privy Council had granted the Mandatory government unfettered discretion to suppress "mutiny, rebellion, and riot." On that basis, the secretary authorized Battershill to get rid of the mufti.[26]

He needed no persuasion. The days since Andrews's murder had been the worst of Battershill's life, he scrawled in his diary—"a nightmare."[27]

On the first of October Battershill stripped Hajj Amin of his leadership of the Supreme Muslim Council and the Islamic endowment funds and declared the Arab Higher Committee illegal.

Arrest warrants were issued for AHC members.[28] Four who were outside Palestine were barred from returning; a fifth, the mufti's cousin Jamal, fled to Beirut. Within a day four more were placed on a ship bound for Seychelles, a British crown colony in the Indian Ocean. One was Dr. Khalidi, the same mayor that Andrews had sworn was both moderate and a backer of partition, and who had attended the dead man's funeral. Deputy Mayor Daniel Auster filled in, becoming the first Jew to oversee the holy city in two millennia.[29]

The mufti was a wanted man, but unlike his confederates was safely sheltered in his home on the Haram al-Sharif. For five months he had not left, protected by African guards and with little to do beyond gazing out his window overlooking the Western Wall.[30]

Twelve days later, dressed as a Bedouin, Hajj Amin descended the Haram wall before daybreak. Driven to Jaffa Port, he stepped into a rickety boat headed north to Syria.

French Mandate authorities apprehended him off the Lebanese coast. They were not particularly keen on his presence, but he was a political refugee and the other Arab states would not accept him. The prospect of irritating Britain was likewise tempting. They agreed he could stay under police protection, and he moved into a villa in a village north of Beirut. Palestine's Arab leadership was now in exile—it would not return for decades.[31]

Battershill ordered Musa Alami to pack his belongings and leave the country. He was being put on extended leave, pending forced retirement. A police profile suggested he had "interested himself in politics more than was proper in view of his Government appointment."[32] Stunned, Alami and his wife moved into a hotel in Beirut.

Judah Magnes, the Hebrew University president, fought to have him reinstated. "He is one of the cleanest and fairest men I have ever met," he wrote the Anglican bishop of Jerusalem. Could nothing be done "to retain his fine mind and pure character for the service of this country? There are all too few like him."[33]

Britain was in no mood for compromise. On October 14 rebels ambushed two buses outside Jerusalem. At the same time a dozen gunmen derailed a Haifa-to-Jaffa train, demanding to know if any Jews were on board (a single police officer fought them off, saving dozens of passengers). Later two constables were killed at Solomon's Pools near Bethlehem, and bombs were found in a Jerusalem cafe frequented by their comrades. Rebels sabotaged the oil pipeline from Iraq and struck the main airport at Lydda, burning down several of its buildings.

Battershill responded with twenty-three-hour curfews in towns near the attacks, authorizing collective fines and a wave of arrests. Troops detained a school headmaster, mid-lesson, in a village near Ramallah over suspicions he had planned the train derailment. A number of suspects' homes were summarily demolished.

There could be no doubt: The revolt had started anew.[34]

"Wauchope is a dear kindly little man," the colonial secretary wrote Neville Chamberlain, "admirable while the going's good but hardly the character to ride a storm." The "times are critical and menacing. . . . The moment is not one for half measures." Ministers agreed Wauchope's time as high commissioner was up.[35]

A new general took over Palestine Command: Archibald Wavell, who had lost an eye at Ypres and helped seize the Holy Land from the Turks. His first recommendation was to install military courts, separate from civil oversight and with no right of appeal. Carrying arms could now be punished by death.[36]

This time, Britain decided it would pacify Palestine at virtually any cost. It had not counted on terrorism coming from an entirely different source.

ONLY THUS

Uri Zvi Greenberg had recently returned to Palestine after a few years of Zionist activism in Warsaw. A writer, he had begun his career in Yiddish, the tongue of the Diaspora; now he favored Hebrew. He had started a socialist; now he was a Revisionist. Greenberg's time in Eastern Europe had convinced him Jewish life there was doomed.

Nazi Germany opened Buchenwald for political prisoners in summer 1937. In late autumn Josef Goebbels opened the exhibit "The Eternal Jew"—it drew four hundred thousand people in Munich before continuing to overflow crowds in Berlin and Vienna.[37]

Circumstances in Poland were scarcely more encouraging. The year 1937 brought seven thousand trials against Jews for "insulting the Polish nation," and 350 anti-Semitic assaults in August alone. At universities, nationalist student groups declared "Jewless" days, then weeks, and persuaded faculties to designate "ghetto benches" for their Jewish peers (many chose to stand instead). Quotas—first unofficial, then official—slashed Jewish matriculation by half. Marginalizing the Jews economically and encouraging their emigration became official government policy. Warsaw's ambassador in London pressed Britain to relinquish Palestine to the Zionists, as his own country desperately needed to offload its own Hebrew "surplus."[38]

Neighboring Romania was similarly committed to Zionism, and for similar motives. The year began with the Bucharest bar banning Jewish lawyers. "When a shoe hurts you remove it," the bar president said, encouraging Romanians to take out their "garbage" (by year's end he was named foreign minister). The prime minister's party emblem was a swastika, its platform almost entirely based on anti-Semitism. "The Jewish problem is an old one," he told an American reporter. "Briefly, we have far too many Jews." He demanded a "final solution" to that problem: a Jewish national home, "the further away the better."[39]

On that last point, Greenberg agreed: The Jews must leave Europe—now—and the Land of Israel was their irreplaceable haven. His 1937 Hebrew poem collection, *The Book of Denunciation and Faith*, railed against Britain and "Arab-Amalek," but most bitterly against Ben-Gurion's leftist Zionist leadership and its obstinate adherence to *havlagah*, self-restraint. He chastised those "who preach restraint over the bodies of 5696" (the Hebrew year ending in 1936), who "seek an ally in Arabia for David's throne."

> Blessed be the sadness that is the origin of rage
> And blessed be the rage whose visions and mind
> Move to action cruel and holy, as twins:
> Before them mountains will melt and chasms cover over.[40]

Such reveries were not his alone. Six years earlier, disaffected Haganah members had joined some Revisionist youth in forming the National Military Organization, or *Irgun Zvai Leumi*. It was a loose constellation, united primarily by ideological fealty to Jabotinsky, but its emblem bore a map of all of Palestine and Transjordan, overlain by an outstretched arm bearing a rifle and the words *Rak Kach*: "Only Thus."

In April 1937, a year into the revolt, half the splinter group returned to the Haganah. Jabotinsky, still barred by the British from Palestine, announced that those members who remained would henceforth fall under his own personal leadership.

"The idea and aim for which the Irgun was founded is that the Hebrew state cannot rise without resting on an independent military body," he said. "The question of *havlagah* will be decided by Ze'ev," he said, referring to himself by his Hebrew name. "My orders in the present conditions are: If riots renew, and show a propensity to attack Jews, *Do not restrain yourselves.*"[41]

That ardent rhetoric belied Jabotinsky's own ambivalence. On one hand he deemed reprisals justifiable in the face of persistent Arab attacks; on the other he was troubled by the inevitable civilian casualties such retribution would exact. He attempted to split the proverbial baby: He would authorize retaliation with a telegram signed "Mendelson" to Irgun commanders on the ground, but avoid any part in planning the details. Several times he sent telegrams bearing the secret word only to recall them shortly after.[42]

Irgun leaders in Palestine, like Jerusalem commander David Raziel, harbored no such qualms. Born in Lithuania, Raziel had been raised religious and studied math and science at university. But his passion lay in combat. He published the first-ever Hebrew pamphlets on drilling and firearms, typically under pen names like John of Gush Halav (a general in the Jewish revolt against Rome) and Son of Anat (she the Semitic war goddess).

On November 9 Arab gunmen killed five agricultural workers in a kibbutz near Jerusalem. Five days later, just before 7:00 a.m., a man named Ibrahim Karam of the village of Malha was guiding his donkey through Jerusalem's Rehavia neighborhood when he was shot dead and his brother Moussa seriously wounded. A half-hour later two Arab laborers from Beit Sahour were murdered in an ultra-Orthodox quarter near the Old City. And hours after that, a bus came under fire near Mahane Yehuda market, killing three passengers including two Christian women from Jaffa.

Ten Arab civilians were dead and at least as many wounded.

Raziel was triumphant, gloating that he had at last satisfied Jewish honor and struck fear into the Arabs. He exulted that he had broken the delusion of *havlagah*; the Yishuv must finally abandon its passivity in favor of "active defense."

"He who does not want to be defeated has no choice but to attack," he wrote. "The goal of every war is to break the enemy's will and impose the victor's."[43]

In his London exile, Jabotinsky equivocated. "No party was responsible" for the reprisals, he argued; blame instead lay with the government for failing to protect Jews, forcing them to seek justice themselves. Privately he was torn. He likely did not know about the planned attacks, and commanded that next time the Arabs be warned when a reprisal was being organized. Raziel balked: Perhaps the Jews ought also to hand out the assailants' names and addresses as well?[44]

Mainstream Zionism was appalled. The Jewish Agency complained that acts of terrorism diminished the Zionist struggle and blackened its name. An enraged Ben-Gurion told colleagues of an indigent vegetable seller who had been killed, "and the most atrocious thing was that Jewish children were dancing next to him."

Acting High Commissioner Battershill ordered two dozen Revisionists, including Jabotinsky's own son, detained at Acre prison.

The *Palestine Post* dubbed the events Black Sunday.

"The blood of the martyrs is the seed of Zionism. It is not the seed of savagery."[45]

Lebanon and Syria were now hubs of an emergent Palestinian exile community. Tens of thousands had fled the disorders since the year before, and Hajj Amin's Beirut headquarters became an obligatory stop for prominent refugees. In Damascus a new entity arose, the Central Committee for National Jihad in Palestine. Led by the Nablus intellectual Izzat Darwaza of the *Istiqlal* party, its stated purpose was to lead and coordinate the various armed factions waging the Great Revolt. In practice it was a waystation for the expatriate mufti's orders, delivered to diffuse and disparate rebel leaders in Palestine.

Things were moving fast. Through it all the Zionists' fast-maturing intelligence apparatus was listening in.[46]

The mufti was growing bitterly disappointed. Despite his labors to make Palestine the region's keystone cause, the Arab states had forsaken him. He would have preferred exile in Damascus, that fulcrum of Arab nationalism, to little Lebanon, but Syria's leaders were too busy negotiating their own independence from France to take notice of the Palestine struggle. Egypt was mired in internal affairs, loath to irk Britain lest it muddy its own path out of colonial rule. Iraq faced its own obstacles—not just the lingering English but mounting resentments between Sunnis, Shiites, and Kurds. If the Arabs could not unite over Palestine, he sighed, he would return to his native soil, turn himself in, and join his banished brethren in Seychelles.[47]

In Galilee the hunt continued for Lewis Andrews's assassin. The day before his death, police had warned him of intelligence that three men from Saffuriya, near Nazareth, had orders to eliminate him at any price.

Now officers had a suspect who matched their profile. A fellah and part-time fighter named Abu Rab told them he had been visited by a certain Abdullah Mohammed of Saffuriya, who told him that Andrews was an enemy of the people, determined to push through partition. This

Abdullah and two others were ready to take action, but they needed a fourth. "I got excited," Abu Rab told police. "I am a religious man and I thought that I would be doing a national service if I helped to kill Mr. Andrews."[48]

The investigation ultimately led to Farhan Sa'adi, a white-bearded seventy-five-year-old. The old sheikh had once been a Palestine policeman, but had quit to become deputy to the revered Izz al-Din al-Qassam. He called his group *Ikhwan al-Qassam*—Brothers of Qassam—and many Arabs reckoned him the fallen hero's heir. His fighters had been behind the murder of Israel Hazan, the Greek chicken merchant, the event that had catalyzed the Great Revolt. Farhan had played a title role in the rebellion ever since, suffering wounds at least twice.

At midnight one rainy Ramadan night, police and troops surrounded a village near Jenin and found the old man hiding in a grain bin. He became among the first suspects tried in military court—an Arab journalist marveled at his calm as the death sentence was pronounced. Three days later, at Acre prison, he was hanged.

"Since Qassam, I know of no hero's martyrdom that shook the nation like that of Farhan," wrote Akram Zuaytir, among the new Damascus exiles. "England, you villain!"[49]

Battershill wrote the Colonial Office:

> *There is no burking the fact that the situation is bad. . . . Assassinations or attempted assassinations occur daily, bomb throwing is comparatively common, acts of sabotage are frequent, armed gangs are loose in the country, reprisals by Jews on a large scale have begun . . . the Arab assassin is quite happy provided the man he kills is a Jew, no matter how insignificant. And the Jewish reprisals, as has been demonstrated recently, is satisfied if he kills a couple of Arab women.*

Battershill granted that the government's punitive measures were severe. "I frankly admit that they are most repressive, and I think they are as distasteful to the rest of the Service as they are to me." Nevertheless they appeared to get results. The very notion of military justice gave an impression of "something summary and drastic, and the recurring phrase 'the penalty of death' has an ominous ring."[50]

A Restless Destiny

George Antonius sat alone in an un-electrified cottage by a brook in an unmistakably Welsh hamlet by the name of Llanfrothen. The home was diminutive, but he had ensured there was space enough for his wife and daughter just in case they should decide to visit. "I am heartily sick of this life," he wrote his wife Katy. He had one desire: to finally complete the manuscript of his book *The Arab Awakening*.[51]

His timing was apt. Britain and the League of Nations were weighing Palestine's fate, war with Germany seemed progressively likelier, and the Holy Land's Jewish population had swollen to four hundred thousand, some 30 percent of Palestine's total. Zionism now had an adroit publicity apparatus and influential backers where it mattered: London and, increasingly, Washington. Champions of an Arab Palestine needed to counterpunch before it was too late.

Katy Nimr was born to Levantine nobility. Her father Faris was a Lebanese-Egyptian publisher who had founded the first Arabic newspapers promoting liberal-nationalist politics and popular science in Beirut and Cairo. Her mother was born in Alexandria to the daughter of the British consul, and also had French lineage. Educated in England, Katy was charming and chic, with upper-crust wit and Paris couture.

She declined her husband's invitation to the cabin, but mustered some words of encouragement. "I hope you'll be happy in it," she wrote from a Bavarian spa. "I hope you won't have to battle with lots of things (depression)—probably you'll find yourself happy to be quiet and alone."[52]

They shared much. Like him she was a Lebanese-Egyptian of Greek-Orthodox stock who had received top-flight British schooling. Like him she was a committed Arab nationalist, even as both favored writing in English and French—the languages of their copious correspondence—to Arabic. And like him, she was not conventionally attractive—sharing his undersized stature and oversized nose—but with bold green eyes and a gregarious demeanor that hid the gloom underneath.[53]

George Antonius (Public Domain)

Both were on patronage—he from his American plumbing baron and she from her father—allowing them a life of nannies and cooks, of dinner parties with pashas and dukes and assorted wits. Like Antonius's own mother, Katy was an accomplished hostess, decking their home at Karm al-Mufti with Central Asian rugs and her sister's impressionist paintings and making it a fixture for Jerusalem's Arab and British smart set.[54]

They traveled constantly—first-class, sometimes by air but typically sea. At times they journeyed together but more often apart: she to Alexandria, Athens, and Sofia; he to Damascus, London, and New York. Both seemed to be fleeing not only the other but themselves. Their marriage was stormy from the start, letters reveal, but in the early years at least, the good moments outbalanced the bad.

"I love you with all my heart," Antonius confided the year of their nuptials, and "I should not want any nicer lot than to get my own happiness by working for yours."

He called her "darling kitten." She addressed him more formally, but admiringly and affectionately, as "my G.A."

He craved "real peace of mind," he once wrote her from London to Paris. "I am born a person of extremes and of a mind that is fundamentally restive."[55]

"Perhaps," he ventured, "it was the mutual possession of a restless destiny which drew us together in the first place."[56]

Both tended to alternating fits of angst and ennui, even while leading lives out of reach to all but the world's luckiest.

Antonius once spent half an hour alone in the Oval Office with President Roosevelt, giddily reporting the meeting back to Katy: "I was taken in to the sanctum, and there had a half hour's tête-à-tête with one of the most charming men I have ever met. We talked about Arab affairs, and he seemed interested in what I had to say." But on the next page he rued the couple's growing estrangement—they had been married seven years but "don't seem to have learnt to know each other yet."[57]

Their letters were growing bilious. "It is curious you should chide me for not having shown you the newest chapters of my book," he wrote in spring 1937. "Because I have been making it a grievance against you that you never expressed the desire to see them, and felt hurt in consequence. Another sad example of the gap between us."[58]

By summer she was contemplating a separation. "I wonder if I do want to meet—you are one of those persons I'm very fond of but who don't give me the calm and peace I hanker for. It's our natures I expect. . . . I'm calmer and more at peace and so much more myself when I'm away from you."

One evening in Athens she went for a walk.

"I walked alone and looked at the sunset through the columns of the Temple of Poseidon down to the rocks and sea and the thought of how easy it would be—just one jump—one long moment of fear and pain and then all over. But I felt how Tutu hugged at my heart strings."[59]

Tutu was the nickname of their daughter Soraya, not yet ten.

Antonius was despondent. "It is tragic that two people who are apparently in their senses should continue for years to take such opposite views of the same thing and go on misunderstanding each other the way we do."[60]

A week later the Peel Commission published its report. Antonius had a friend mail it to the nearest post office, a mile from his cottage. He could hardly bear it: His marriage was disintegrating, and the report seemed to suggest that his life's work—explaining the Arabs and Palestine to the West—had accomplished precisely nothing.

The report was a "very imperfect piece of work," he wrote his employer in Washington, "full of errors and unwarranted assumptions." Its ecstatic reception in England—as a new "Book of Revelation"—he thought undeserved. And he was convinced its bottom-line recommendation, partition, was both unjust and impracticable.

Unjust, he wrote in the manuscript, because it placed the rival claimants to Palestine on the same footing, offering "the Jews a good deal more and the Arabs a good deal less than they possess or was promised to them." It made starkly different demands of each: "of the Arabs, the real and substantial sacrifice of something they own and want to keep; of the Zionists, the nominal sacrifice of something they do not own but want to have."[61]

And it was impracticable, he was convinced, because it rested on the expectation that the Arabs would renounce their own natural and political rights. The scheme assumed

> *that trade and good government can thrive in a small country not larger than Wales, after its dissection into some half-dozen entities made up of separate states, enclaves and corridors; and that a population of 600,000 settled people, deeply attached to their homes and their culture, would submit to either of the alternatives proposed for them by the Royal Commission: forcible eviction or subjection to a Jewish state to be established over their heads. It runs counter to the lessons of history, the requirements of geography, the natural play of economic forces, and the ordinary laws of human behavior.*

Antonius pronounced that the moral, political, and practical obstacles facing partition rendered it a nonstarter. Put simply, "it can never be carried into execution."[62]

Back at Whitehall, a formidable figure at the Foreign Office had reached the very same conclusion.

The Walkback

George Rendel was a two-decade veteran of His Majesty's Diplomatic Service. In the Great War's aftermath he had been among the first to reveal the Ottoman massacres and forced transfer of hundreds of thousands of Greek-speaking Christians in Anatolia.[63] In the early 1930s he was named head of the Foreign Office department for the Middle East and made his first visit to Palestine, then comparatively tranquil with Jewish immigration in the low thousands per year.

In the autumn of 1936 he had been key in enlisting the Arab kings to help bring the first, six-month phase of Palestine's Great Revolt to a close. That move drew the ire of Zionists in both Jerusalem and Westminster, but Rendel was unfazed. He had long found it peculiar, to say the least, that world Jewry was party to every policy discussion on Palestine while at the same time demanding the Arabs next door be excluded.

Early the next year Rendel and his wife traveled to the Arabian Peninsula as personal guests of Ibn Saud. Disembarking at Haifa, they traveled through the Jezreel Valley. It was stunning as ever, scarlet with early-blooming anemones, but another feature of the landscape troubled him. Zionist settlement had spiked since he last visited just a few years prior; the countryside was taking on a "brash modern look; while Jewish hiking-parties with stout young women from Central Europe in exiguous tight shorts made an odd contrast to the then still more numerous native Arabs, glaring suspiciously at these strange invaders."[64]

The Rendels continued to Syria, Iraq, Kuwait, Persia, Bahrain, and finally Saudi Arabia. In those days foreigners rarely made it to Riyadh: His wife Geraldine was the first Western woman to travel in the kingdom, to meet Ibn Saud in public, and to dine in his royal palace. The monarch gifted them Bedouin dress; they would wear it their whole stay. A keen photographer, Rendel snapped his wife lounging in a *dhow* boat in the Persian Gulf and lunching on the desert floor with the royal vizier.

He was particularly taken by Ibn Saud himself, judging him frank, brave, dignified, and (at six-foot-four) literally head and shoulders above the other rulers of the East. Rendel was persuaded: Britain's future lay with the king and with the Arab and Islamic civilization he embodied. Its endorsement of Zionism had been a profound blunder.[65]

"The Arabs outside Palestine have a quite special connexion with the Arabs in Palestine itself," he wrote upon returning, "The Arabs are a single race, occupying a vast area not naturally divided into clearly distinct territories." It defied reason that Arabs or indeed Muslims worldwide would remain indifferent to Palestine's fate.

In October 1937, five months after Peel had published his report, partition had become Crown policy. Rendel felt compelled to register his dissent.[66]

"I am more and more convinced that our present policy can only lead to disaster," he wrote colleagues.

> *The Arabs are not a mere handful of aborigines who can be disregarded by the "white colonizer." They do not represent a dying civilization. They have a latent force and vitality which is stirring into new activity. They have produced, and are still producing, great leaders, and are capable of patriotism, which it may be unwise to ignore and difficult to suppress . . . the ultimate importance of Arab patriotism and Moslem religious sentiment should not be underestimated.*

The entire Arab world had reacted violently to partition. "Are we not, then, by creating this little Jewish state, simply placing on the coast of Asia a kind of time-bomb, which must inevitably explode?"[67]

In later decades, Rendel's perspective would be known as "linkage"—the conviction that Palestine is central to the Arab and Islamic worlds, and that trouble there could mean trouble wherever Arabs and Muslims predominated. But in 1937 it was an unorthodox, nearly radical proposition; Britain ran Palestine policy through the Colonial Office, not as part of any wider regional strategy. Now, with Hitler and Mussolini ascendant and Palestine's neighbors moving toward independence, Rendel believed that paradigm was not just outdated but strategically calamitous. "It is a thankless task to prophesy disaster, but I have seldom seen a case where disaster is approaching more inexorably."[68]

He maintained the pressure over the following months. The Peel report's call for population transfer was particularly dangerous—he had not forgotten the Greek tragedy in Anatolia; he knew such mass removals were rarely "clean cuts." The report had to be binned, he argued, and the only feasible solution was keeping the Jews a perpetual minority, preferably under 40 percent.[69]

In Jerusalem, Acting High Commissioner Battershill thought otherwise. Yes, he acknowledged, virtually the only Arab leader backing partition was Emir Abdullah of Transjordan. But if Britain showed determination, the Arabs would acquiesce. "Fractious infants have to swallow unpalatable medicines. . . . The East does not understand compromise but merely accounts it as weakness."[70]

But Rendel's entreaties were winning over Foreign Secretary Anthony Eden, just forty and in his first Cabinet role. Rendel's memos soon became Eden's. A paper war ensued between Eden's Foreign Office and the Colonial Office led by Ormsby-Gore, the longtime Zionist ally who still clung to partition.[71]

Eden told the Cabinet that Palestine's Arabs uniformly opposed partition, and worse, so did the entire Arab world. Such a policy must not be pursued against the inhabitants' will—that was neither Balfour's intention nor Peel's—and it was imperative the Arabs be persuaded the Jews would never form a majority. The alternative was too grim to contemplate: earning the "permanent hostility" of the Arab and Muslim worlds.[72]

On December 8 the Cabinet convened in secret. Each minister received a stack of five memos: One from the colonial secretary pushing partition, another from the foreign secretary urging its reversal, then a rebuttal to that rebuttal and so on.

Neville Chamberlain opened the proceedings. Even more than Eden he was green, having occupied the prime minister's office for just half a year. Palestine was for him a footnote; his foreign agenda centered on conciliating the *Führer* and *Duce* to avoid another war. But as the meeting opened, he made clear he had adopted Eden's (that is, Rendel's) view: Palestine was key to the region, partition would likely antagonize the Arabs without even satisfying the Jews, and it would let Fascism expand its influence in the Levant by exploiting Arab outrage. Eden heartily agreed: Without the Palestine troubles, he could envision "the whole of the Middle East as being in a peaceful condition."

Still, Chamberlain cautioned that summarily announcing the abandonment of partition would look like capitulation to violence. If Britain were to renounce a two-state solution, it had to make a compelling case why.[73]

The Peel report had recommended sending a follow-up delegation, a so-called technical commission, to draw Palestine's new borders and address the manifold logistical issues that partition entailed. Half a year had passed and nothing had yet been done. The Cabinet was now ready to appoint just such a body, but its task would be not to prepare the ground for division but to decide whether to pursue it at all. All present understood the answer was expected to be "no."[74]

At Eden's insistence the statement on the technical commission's appointment made clear that "His Majesty's Government are in no sense committed" to partition, and that the new deputation would be reviewing the "practical possibilities" of any such scheme.[75]

Chaim Weizmann was downcast. Murmurs whirled that the Crown planned to kill partition, he wrote the Colonial Office on the last day of 1937, and was now making arrangements to give it a "decent burial." A permanent Jewish minority was out of the question: They were not returning to Zion to become "Arabs of the Mosaic faith, or to exchange their German or Polish ghetti for an Arab one."[76]

Days later the Colonial Office received another telegram. It came from Mohamed Ali Eltaher, a Palestinian journalist attempting to publish a book of images showing the devastation left by Old Jaffa's demolition, and of Arabs killed and wounded by British bullets. Authorities had seized the printing plates, but they could not keep him from the telegraph machine: "PALESTINE ARABS LEGAL OWNERS COUNTRY DETERMINED RESIST ANY ENCROACHMENT UNTIL DEATH."[77]

Chapter 5

Pray for the Peace of Jerusalem

"In common with the great majority of the British serving in Palestine at the time, in every capacity from private soldier upwards, I admired but found it very difficult to like the Jews."

Thus recollected one Palestine official, a fluent Arabic speaker based mainly in Gaza, many years after the fact.

"And again in common with most of my countrymen, I liked and sympathized with the Arabs but in general had less admiration for them."[1]

Diaries, memoirs, and correspondence from across the British service in Palestine reveal a strikingly broad consensus: affinity for the Arabs and their case, grudging admiration for the Zionists.

A junior army officer regarded the average Arab as "a rather lower form of human being, to be befriended and perhaps made fun of a little bit . . . but not taken a great deal of notice of." The Jews, he recalled, were inscrutable, distant. They rarely engaged the British unless they needed something, and friendships were few. Still, he added, soldiers "realized quite instinctively that these people came from a civilized race who had probably got a great deal more brains than we had."[2]

Some officers acknowledged an anti-Jewish prejudice: the "mild endemic antipathy towards Jews we had all grown up with . . . however unfair . . . of the 'usurer,' typified by Shylock."[3]

Many others spoke of manners. A police sergeant recorded approvingly that good manners "are almost a fetish with the Arabs. By comparison, the Jews are a boorish and ungracious race." The longtime governor of Jerusalem wished the Jews would "develop the virtues of tolerance and humility and shout, push and encroach less, and also look less upon everything that they had gained as their due."[4]

The notion of "charm" appears nearly as often.

"The Arab is an exceedingly charming fellow," Dorothy Kahn wrote. "The Jew usually is not charming at all." The Jew tends to feel perplexed, even suspicious of the Arab's charm, she supposed. The Arab feels insulted by the Jew's lack of it.

"I know of no synonym for this quality that usually accompanies the simplest Arab like an aura. . . . The daughter of the janitress of our office building has it. She is five years old. She lives in a tin hut behind the office. She has the bearing of a little princess and charm enough to subdue a tiger before his supper."

By contrast, she wrote, the Jew has had to fight and run. He has seen little reason to trust his fellow man. Back in Europe he knew not the broadness of field and sky but was penned up in dark places. And in the Promised Land, he has been too busy—scraping a livelihood in the city or coaxing the unyielding earth; above all, building a homeland—to cultivate something so seemingly superfluous as charm.[5]

"The cause for which the Arabs were fighting was, to us, understandable and just," remembered the Gaza official. "Their methods and the means they employed, particularly against unarmed and innocent Jews and frequently against their own people, were often barbaric and inexcusable; but as a general rule when admiration and liking are in conflict, the latter will prevail."[6]

The Jewish complaint, then, that the Palestine administration reflexively inclined toward the Arabs was not without foundation. But in the two decades since the British arrived in the country, the Jews had time and again enjoyed the good fortune of a single sympathetic official in a key position. Wauchope was one, as was the slain Lewis Andrews. At the dawn of 1938, it was Sir Charles Tegart.[7]

Born in Northern Ireland, the son of an Anglican priest, Tegart joined the Calcutta Police at age twenty and within a decade had risen to be its commissioner. Intensely private, he rarely allowed his photograph taken and never spoke to the press, but his ingenuity and firmness in quashing insurgency (he was an expert on Irish and Bengali militancy) and his perseverance through multiple assassination attempts had earned him a hero's reputation and a knighthood to boot.

One of Sir Charles's pastimes was touring Europe by car with his wife Kathleen (now styled Lady Tegart). In 1935 they visited a resort town in Germany's Black Forest and were greeted by banners barring non-Aryans and children raising Nazi salutes. Tegart was troubled, his sympathy kindled for Europe's beleaguered Jews.

In late 1937, with Palestine in its second round of open revolt, the Colonial Office asked him to take control of the police force there. He declined, claiming ignorance of the country and its warring tribes. London offered him a generous salary (intelligence reports said he would be targeted immediately upon arrival), with Lady Tegart getting two-thirds of his Indian pension if the posting proved to be his last.[8] Tegart agreed to serve in an advisory capacity. In Calcutta he boarded a ship bound for Egypt, then a train to Lydda.

The first days of 1938 saw the gala opening of the Palestine Archeological Museum, a wonder in white limestone designed by eminent British architects and funded by John D. Rockefeller Jr. Among the scheduled speakers was James Starkey, head of the dig at Lachish.

The Assyrians had sacked the city, southwest of Jerusalem, in the seventh century BC, immortalizing the conquest in the British Museum's famed Lachish Reliefs. Starkey's excavators had recently unearthed priceless Hebrew letters exchanged among the besieged forces. His team was mainly Arab, and he spoke their language capably.

Near Hebron, on the road to Jerusalem, armed men stopped Starkey's taxi. They ordered him out, told the Arab driver to proceed, and put several bullets in the Englishman's back. Some who knew Starkey believed that his full beard had led them to mistake him for a Jew.

Tegart set out with the governor of Jerusalem, following sniffer dogs. They drove for miles but found nothing but the dead man's body, his skull cracked in half. Flinders Petrie, the venerable Jerusalem-based Egyptologist who had trained Starkey, bemoaned the "brutal folly of gunmen destroying the friends of their country." Even the pro-mufti daily *Al-Difa* hailed him as a kind "gentleman" (it used the English word), a "beloved digger" whose end was "tragic."[9]

Shortly after, Tegart produced a twenty-eight-point plan for restoring peace to Palestine. He wanted more vehicles and more dogs. He wanted to convert the police into a paramilitary counterinsurgency force, to expand and improve its detective office, and to create interrogation rooms that he euphemistically called Arab Investigation Centers. And he wanted dozens of permanent, reinforced-concrete police forts at key points around the country and a fortified fence along its northern frontier.[10]

The fence plan encountered the most resistance; Palestine's budget-minders doubted its cost and efficacy. Undeterred, Tegart approached another quasi-governmental agency that he knew harbored no such reluctance. He called a meeting with David Hacohen, a former Ottoman army officer and head of the Histadrut construction arm.

Without preamble, Tegart made the situation plain: The security barrier would be built, and the Jews would do it.

They wasted no time. Zionist labor leaders recruited a thousand men for construction, and to ensure their safety the Haganah enlisted three hundred of its members as *notrim*—the government-armed Jewish police whose ranks were swelling by the month. And they ordered three thousand tons of barbed wire from Mussolini—a notable exercise in hypocrisy given the Jews' repeated complaints over the *Duce* cheering, arming, and funding the Arab rebellion. The barrier would descend six feet into the ground and rise equally high, with four interlocking coils of barbed wire. They promised Tegart it would be complete within three months.[11]

For its part, even as Britain retrenched from partition, even as it slowed Jewish immigration to a fraction of pre-revolt numbers, its dearth of resources and its fears over a coming European war meant it increasingly involved the Yishuv in Palestine's security. Building the barricade represented a coup for the Jews, their third great achievement during the disturbances after the launch of Tel Aviv Port and the creation of the *notrim*.

The project was called the Northern Fence, but everyone knew it as Tegart's Wall.

Not by Bread Alone

On a foggy, moonless night in late February 1938, gunfire awoke the pious farmers of Zvi's Fortress, Musa Alami's old homestead. Ten armed men had penetrated their barbed-wire enclosure, seizing one of the trenches and lobbing two hand grenades into the central courtyard. The grenades—Ottoman bombs with homemade, cigarette-lit fuses—failed to detonate, but another ten gunmen aimed at the searchlight atop the farmhouse, shattering it and leaving the settlers in the dark. Unable to signal for help, the Jews grabbed their weapons and rushed to their assigned positions.

They had expected an attack; theirs was the only Jewish settlement in the Beisan region, far from road and rail. And while the Arabs wielded German rifles left over from the Great War, the Zionists were now armed with the latest British weapons—which were legal—and a half-dozen grenades—which were not. The Jews' grenades, unlike the Arabs', functioned as designed.

The battle lasted just half an hour. The Arabs retreated, leaving at least four bodies behind; the Jews suffered no losses. The settlers had shown coolness under fire, a Haganah report found, praising their "economy of bullets." It would be the first and last time the new Jews of the Beth She'an Valley were tested, and soon five more settlements followed Zvi's Fortress, cornering Arab Beisan on all sides.[12]

High Commissioner Wauchope cabled the settlers congratulations on standing their ground. It was his last day on the job.[13]

"The difference between what we hoped for and what has been achieved is deeply discouraging," he told Palestine Broadcasting Service listeners in his farewell speech. He quoted Psalms: "Pray for the peace of Jerusalem: they shall prosper that love her."

Wauchope's replacement was Sir Harold MacMichael, hitherto governor in Dar es-Salaam.[14] The two were diametric opposites. Whereas the former cherished literary evenings washed down with choice wine and banter, MacMichael preferred to stay home with a suspense novel. He was, however, a competent administrator and, above all, unsentimental. And unlike all but a few members of the Palestine administration, he spoke fluently one of the country's non-English official languages. That

that language was Arabic gave Palestine's Arabs encouragement and its Jews pause.[15]

Both communities listened closely to his maiden broadcast, keen to gauge his sympathies. His first duty, MacMichael said, was "to maintain the authority of His Britannic Majesty and the firm establishment of law and order." That line pleased the Jews. Nevertheless, he said, Palestine's recent history had brought "the complete confounding of those who give to history a purely economic interpretation . . . it is still true that 'Man cannot live by bread alone.'" That pleased the Arabs.

A letter from Jerusalem's Arab Women's Committee prayed that "through His Excellency's wise judgment . . . the memory of the deplorable events which marred the recent history of the country will be wiped out." Greetings from the Yishuv hailed him, optimistically, as the same Michael whom the Book of Daniel names as a "great prince" sent to deliver Israel from its foes.[16]

In London, Chaim Weizmann's appointment book gave the impression he was already the reigning sovereign of the reconstituted Kingdom of Judah. Friday he was the guest of the Archbishop of Canterbury at Lambeth Palace, and Saturday of Lloyd George, prime minister during the Balfour Declaration, at his country home in Surrey. Professor Coupland, architect of Peel's partition plan, threw him a party in Oxford. There were conclaves at the War Office with its (Jewish) secretary, Leslie Hore-Belisha, and with General Robert Haining, the director of military intelligence newly tapped to take command of British forces in Palestine. And Weizmann had a first, extended meeting with the new foreign secretary, Lord Halifax (Eden having recently resigned to protest the government's appeasement of Fascism).[17] It was access unrivaled within the Zionist movement, and at a level the Arabs could contemplate only in their daydreams.

There was just one high official who had eluded him: Neville Chamberlain, who throughout his nine months as premier had resisted Weizmann's repeated entreaties to meet. Now he at last relented and invited the Zionist patriarch to Downing Street.[18]

They spoke for nearly an hour. The prime minister assured him that London remained committed to partition, the scheme on which

A study in contrast: High Commissioners Wauchope, left, and MacMichael (LOC M32-50403; M32-9649)

Weizmann still pinned his hopes of Jewish statehood. He seemed "unduly distressed," Chamberlain told him, and as they parted he again advised his guest to "not worry too much."[19]

The following day Hitler issued an ultimatum to Austria threatening invasion unless it joined the Reich. At dawn the next morning, German forces crossed the border unchallenged.

As onlookers jeered, Jews were ordered to their knees to scrub the sidewalks of Vienna. In a main square others were made to lie down and eat grass.[20]

Garden of Eden

Dr. Hussein Khalidi awoke in his bungalow after an anxious night.

It was spring 1938, the most glorious season in Palestine but the most stifling in his new domicile in Seychelles, closer to Jaipur than Jerusalem, the city he still nominally served as mayor.

"Now is the first day of our seventh month," he wrote in his diary. "It is hot, hot and maddeningly hot."

Khalidi hailed from one of Jerusalem's great families, tracing its line to Khalid Ibn al-Walid, a general serving the first Islamic caliphs in the conquest of the Levant. He attended British schools in Palestine and medical school at the Syrian Protestant College in Beirut (later renamed the American University), then served the Ottomans in the Great War but defected to join the revolt against the sultan for Arab independence. Since the start of the Mandate he had been Jerusalem's chief medical officer; his police file noted the wide respect he enjoyed among British colleagues, who found him "straight and reliable."

In 1934 Khalidi stood for mayor as an independent. Musa Alami arranged a meeting with the mufti, who gave his blessing for the candidacy, as did the city's Jews—the only issue, it seems, on which those two camps ever agreed. He won persuasively.[21]

During the Peel Commission's hearings, Professor Coupland had asked Lewis Andrews whether Khalidi was not an anti-Semite, given his seat on the mufti's Arab Higher Committee. "He is not a Jew-hater," Andrews said; "he is a moderate." But with Andrews's assassination nine months later, Khalidi became one of a handful of members of the now-banned AHC banished to the Indian Ocean.[22]

In his diary he wrote that the islands—a dumping ground for political prisoners since the Napoleonic era—seemed initially a "Garden of Eden." The deportees shared two hilltop cabins with spacious rooms, ocean views, and wide verandas—they were even provided a cook, maid, and gardener.[23] But then came the muggy winter monsoons, when breathing became nearly impossible, and now the sweltering dry season. His self-diagnosis was unequivocal: The climate was killing him.

He had been well-fed, even portly, upon arrival; now his cheekbones reappeared. Buzzing termites and scurrying rats kept him from sleep; he had the worst coughing fits of his life. And there was the mental and emotional strain: not just the prolonged absence of loved ones but the constant presence of guards, tight limits on his movements, and a prohibition on any unauthorized social interaction, however minor. Whenever the barber visited the bungalows, or when the deportees were escorted into town, chatter with locals was strictly *verboten*.[24]

He started keeping a journal shortly after arriving. There was, after all, little else to do. Mail was intermittent, books and newspapers scarce—it was months before a radio, then a *nargileh* water pipe could be procured. When shooting tooth pain required treatment (again, Khalidi faulted the climate), the choice was made easier by the lack of alternatives: He employed the services, he recorded with sardonic amusement, of "the only and best dentist in Seychelles."[25]

Then there was the news from home. It came in drabs, in weeks-old newspapers, Reuters telegrams, or through the heavy static of the BBC, the Palestine Broadcast Service, or the Arabic station Mussolini had set up in Bari.

It was over the radio that he learned in late 1937 of the murder of Avinoam Yellin, chief inspector for Jewish schools. A year earlier Yellin had eulogized Lewis Billig, with whom he had studied Arabic at Cambridge and had co-authored the standard Arabic textbook for Mandate schools and functionaries. Now both were dead and buried before their fortieth year, cut down by Arab gunmen.

"Poor Yellin I don't think he deserves it," Khalidi wrote. "He is one of the best Jews."[26]

From the radio he learned too about Starkey, the archaeologist. "It is a great pity this dastardly act took place, as it will not help the Arab case. . . . They must be damn fools those who did it."[27]

One spring evening, between coughing fits, he scribbled, "Things are again rather bad in Palestine. About 7 or 8 Jews were shot dead and wounded in various parts of the country. My God! Is there no end to all that misery?"[28]

Some days it was the Jews' turn, other days, the British or Arabs. Dr. Khalidi grieved for his city and his country.

He had no love lost for Hajj Amin. Khalidi disparaged the mufti's flight from Palestine as cowardly; he should have stayed in his sanctuary at the Haram al-Sharif or joined them in their tropical banishment.

It was five months before the mufti deigned to send a message to the deportees, rotting away physically and mentally for the sole reason of their membership in his Arab Higher Committee. Now in Beirut, he neglected even to consult them when issuing statements in the AHC's name. The deportees all agreed Amin "had played his role and proved unfit for leadership."[29]

"If the Mufti was a real leader," Khalidi wrote, he would refuse to return to Palestine, even if offered, until the exiles could return first. "When we meet again, I shall tell him what I think of him."[30]

Not that he opposed the Great Revolt. Yes, Khalidi's city had had a Jewish majority even before Balfour's accursed proclamation.[31] Yes, the Zionists had backed his mayoral candidacy. Yes, several colleagues at the AHC, and several of his predecessors as mayor, had sold land to the Jews—but he had not. If the Jews expected gratitude for recasting his patrimony into their national home, they would be disappointed.

One night the radio reported protesters in Algiers chanting "Down with the Jews!" Khalidi wrote approvingly: "We not only said 'Down with the Jews' but damn them. They are the cause of our exile. I doubt whether I can sit again with any of them."

"The Jews are all Bolsheviks," he recorded the following day, and having destroyed Russia, who knew if Palestine might be next.[32]

They had flooded the country in such numbers that even talk of keeping them a permanent minority was futile. The solution was simple: He was not "prepared to admit another single Jew."[33]

PARFAITE CONSIDÉRATION

In Palestine the Jews were planning their most brazen act of settlement yet. Peel's men had released their proposal the previous summer, but the Foreign Office was temporizing and the Zionists feared it would pare down their promised land or scrap the scheme altogether. Rumor was Galilee was on the chopping block. Its west and center were purely Arab, and its mukhtars and notables had made clear they—like nearly every other Arab leader in Palestine and outside it—flatly opposed partition.

"Galilee is in danger," Ben-Gurion told colleagues the first week of 1938. Land purchases had to be accelerated, but simply buying the plots was insufficient without facts on the ground. "We need to conquer the lands at once. Without conquest"—that is, settlement—"there is no value to purchase." The target was a rocky peak along the Lebanese frontier, one with meager agricultural potential and remote from any Jewish settlement.[34] But unlike the more than a dozen new settlements established since the start of the Arab uprising, this one had the explicit consent of a neighboring government.

Moshe Shertok, the Yishuv's de facto foreign minister, had met weeks earlier with Lebanon's prime minister. Khaireddin Ahdab was the country's first Muslim premier in a regime hitherto dominated by Christians, but he feared the ill effects of Hajj Amin's continued accommodation on the outskirts of Beirut. Meeting in the Jerusalem home of an influential member of the opposition Nashashibis, the prime minister grumbled that Amin was transforming Lebanon into a den of pan-Arab agitation and terrorism. He wanted money from the Jews and help in founding an anti-mufti newspaper. Above everything, he wanted the man out of his country.[35]

Shortly thereafter Shertok wrote Ahdab a letter. In French, he informed him that the Jews intended to settle a ridge near the border. Peace, friendship, and cooperation would guide the endeavor, with settlers specially chosen for fluency in the Arabs' language and customs. He asked only that Lebanon play its part in keeping its side secure.

Ahdab replied immediately: Lebanon would do its utmost, fostering the "best neighborly relations with the settlers" in a spirit of "*parfaite considération*."[36]

The landlords were a different matter. In the past, moneyed absentee owners had been only too keen to pocket the inflated prices the Jews were willing to render; over the preceding two decades, the Lebanese Sursock family had sold the Jews the entirety of *Marj Ibn 'Amer*, otherwise known as the Jezreel Valley. But the proverbial landscape had changed: Selling land was now deemed an unforgivable sin against the Arab nation, and the generous proceeds the transactions commanded could now come at the expense of an effendi's head. The Jewish National Fund therefore enlisted an official whose Italian name and passport offered no inkling he was a Jerusalem Jew dedicated to "redeeming" Hebrew earth.[37]

The settlement was to be called Hanita. The name came from a nearby ruin mentioned in the Talmud, but its resemblance to *hanit* ("spear") was fortuitous, for Hanita was to be the Jewish spearhead in Upper Galilee. The Haganah's official history book presents the mission to settle the site as a "military operation" led by a "conquest group."

The ascent began after midnight on March 21, 1938, just days after Hitler strode into Vienna. Departing its base camp near Haifa, the convoy numbered four hundred people, including one hundred *notrim* and nearly the same number of women. It included forty trucks and an equal contingent of donkeys loaded with wood planks, barbed wire, generators, and searchlights—everything required to raise a village within a day.

Within an hour the convoy reached the Arab city of Acre. A Haganah member from Chicago named Zvi Brenner recounted the city's residents gathering on their balconies in pajamas, watching the procession pass with a mix of confusion and resentment. The caravan proceeded north to Nahariya, the Jews' only landholding in all of western and central Galilee, then east along the just-paved frontier route. At daybreak they turned off-road for the arduous climb up the slope, following the pack animals.

On the hilltop they made camp, pitching tents and the barbed-wire fence, intoning odes to pioneering and labor. Two small Piper reconnaissance planes circled above—the complete fleet of the Yishuv's new air service *Aviron* ("Airplane")—lending the affair a mood of dreamlike jubilation. By dusk the roof and ramparts were in place, but the gravel to strengthen the wall was delayed and the barbed-wire perimeter unfinished. The exhausted settlers went to sleep, under orders not to light matches lest their precise location be known.

That night strong winds overturned a tent and someone briefly lit a flashlight. Shots were fired, then more, and still more, closer and closer—from two directions, then three. For more than an hour the defenders fired aimlessly into the black, until finally the gunmen withdrew across the border with their wounded. The assault had failed, but one settler was dead and one of the wounded would succumb within days. In the morning light the guards realized they had been shooting at a bonfire left as a decoy. The Haganah's static, stand-your-ground security doctrine was showing its limits.[38]

Shortly after, workmen clearing a road to the settlement again came under fire. It seemed an attack like any other—nearly two years of rebellion had rendered them almost routine. But then, Zvi Brenner recalled, "something unprecedented" happened. Two detachments of Jewish police appeared, sprinted across the border road and up the hillside on the attackers' two flanks as their comrades gave covering fire from below. Nearly encircled, the gunmen beat a hasty retreat.

The *notrim* looked indistinguishable from their comrades, but they were members of a new, illegal Haganah unit called the Field Squads. They were Zionism's first strike force, commanded by two young Haganah men from the Galilee farming villages: Yigal Allon, nineteen, and Moshe Dayan, twenty-two.[39]

The unit was the brainchild of Yitzhak Sadeh, a burly former wrestling champion of St. Petersburg who had led troops in the tsarist and Red

Moshe Dayan commands Jewish *notrim* settling Hanita, March 1938 (GPO D583-070)

armies and was among the only Zionist leaders with combat-command experience. Since the start of the Arab rebellion, when Sadeh had been a Haganah commander around Jerusalem, he had experimented with offensive measures—"leaving the fence," he called it—in stark violation of the official Zionist position of *havlagah*. He soon founded the Field Squads, named conspicuously after himself (Sadeh, his adopted Hebrew surname, means "field"), which by Hanita's founding numbered one thousand men.[40]

Before 1936 the Haganah had been among the Yishuv's least-developed institutions. Immigration, employment, settlement, and agriculture were the orders of the day, drawing the greater part of Zionist funds and attention.[41] In any case, authorities had been reluctant to provide the Jews training or firearms lest they appear partial in the Arab-Jewish quarrel.

Yet as the Great Revolt dragged on, that calculation was increasingly overtaken by events: The British had patently failed to secure the country, and were loath to recall troops and treasure from a Europe seemingly on the verge of war. Meanwhile, the Zionist leadership's self-restraint policy was bearing fruit, having reassured the government that tens of thousands of Jews with legal weapons might actually enhance, not diminish, prospects for peace in Palestine.

The British therefore facilitated the training and arming of Jews on a major scale. The several thousand *notrim* enlisted in 1936 grew to fifteen thousand within a year, each carrying a fully authorized rifle. Their instruction and weapons (and part of their salaries) came from the British, but at each and every step the Haganah wielded effective control.[42]

The Haganah was being transformed from a loose confederation of local night-watchmen to a unified, mobile, countrywide Jewish paramilitary, and one increasingly willing to pursue the enemy. *Havlagah* remained official policy—no innocents were to be targeted—but the defensive ethos centered on passive restraint was giving way to a more offensive, martial language in which words like "conquest" featured ever more prominently. The pedestal holding up the Hebrew settler, farmer, and worker now made room for the Hebrew fighter. By the dawn of

1938, the Haganah could boast of twenty-five thousand members, nearly one in five of whom was a woman.

Hanita was the central symbol of this new era. For the Zionists, it represented the synthesis of settlement and defense, the fusion of plowshare and sword. Ten settlers died in its first months, but at no point did they consider vacating the site. Hanita exemplified the maxim that a settlement, once created, was not to be abandoned.[43]

"In Hanita, the Wall and Tower method reached its peak," the Haganah history book relates. "Here the Haganah grew wings. Here the Haganah left its walls and positions, and could no longer return to its old methods and tactics. Here the Field Squads took shape. . . . Here the Haganah transformed from a defensive militia into the seed of an army of conquest and defense."[44]

That new spirit helped salve the Jews' sense of helplessness, but it did little to quell acts of violence.

In late March armed Arabs ambushed a vehicle on the new highway between Acre and Safed.[45] They killed six people, including a father and his twelve-year-old son, and an elderly woman and her daughter, the latter slashed with a knife. The U.S. consul in Jerusalem wrote that the scene was "reminiscent of the ravages of North American Indians." Within days it was the turn of the Spring of the Judge commune (the consul dubbed it "Kibbutz America"), with one of the Detroiters and a Canadian dead. And on Passover, gunmen attacked a car leaving Hanita, killing three.[46]

The Hebrew papers demanded action. *Haaretz* enjoined the government to cut the gangs' ties to the "hive of banditry" that was the mufti's Beirut headquarters and his henchmen in Damascus. *Hayarden*, the organ of the Revisionists, went one further, urging the creation of a full-fledged Jewish military force: "We could change the situation once and for all."[47]

In April, Britain's latest commission of inquiry set sail. Its remit was to operationalize the Peel report's partition recommendation, but with "full liberty to suggest modifications."[48] Yet the delegation's very composition seemed to bespeak lack of commitment. Whereas Peel was a member of the House of Lords who had held Cabinet posts, the men tasked with executing his proposals were mid-level bureaucrats, mostly from the Indian civil service, like its chairman John Woodhead.

Arabs, Jews, and Britons alike suspected these latest emissaries from London were merely play-acting, that the Foreign Office had prevailed over the pro-partition Colonial Office, steering Chamberlain's Cabinet away from the two-state solution. If anything, it seemed the Foreign Office had set up the Woodhead Commission to fail.[49]

Nonetheless, as before, the Jews prepared their opening statements, statistical charts, and policy papers, appealing yet again to British justice and fair play. As before, the Arabs planned to boycott. Shops closed in Palestine's Arab towns. "Everybody is dead against partition," wrote Dr. Khalidi, marveling at the "unity of front."[50]

Even as the mufti languished in exile, his ability to project power remained undiminished. From his Lebanese villa he exhorted the Arab masses to hit the streets—Cairo, Beirut, Damascus, and Baghdad all witnessed such displays—and wage a second general strike in Palestine. He made known that he judged cooperation with the new commission to be treason. No one doubted his ability to enforce his will from across the frontier.

Posters appeared under the name of his Arab Higher Committee instructing rebels to "kill every Arab who communicates with the commission in any form." Blacklists of "traitors" were posted in Haifa mosques. Hassan Sidqi Dajani, the Cambridge-educated Jerusalem vice-mayor, had planned to testify but thought twice after receiving a note from Amin's circles advising he bring a burial shroud.[51]

Upon their arrival the commissioners began dutifully touring the country, first to the Arab city of Jericho and the Jewish-owned Dead Sea Works at Sodom, then to Jaffa and Tel Aviv and dinner with Transjordan's Emir Abdullah in Jerusalem.[52]

Abdullah was the only Arab representative to risk the mufti's wrath by engaging the delegation. He submitted a twelve-point proposal in which Palestine and Transjordan would unite into one Arab kingdom (his), and where Jews would enjoy self-government and representation according to their numbers. Inside their designated districts, the latter could buy land and enjoy "reasonable" immigration. Within a decade, Britain would leave.

News of the emir's offer inflamed Arab Palestine—he had acted unilaterally, and his program implied acceptance of de facto partition. Abdullah was for his part unapologetic, writing one critic that "the Arabs are as prodigal in selling their land as they are useless in wailing and weeping."[53]

His righteous pique was less than fully sincere. Abdullah's peculiar circumstances meant he alone among Arab leaders still favored some version of Peel's plan, even if he could not say so publicly. His desert kingdom was short on money, resources, and inhabitants, let alone scientists or barons of finance and industry. For over a decade he had received payments from the Jewish Agency to keep his head above the sand. Expanding his dominion to lands west of the Jordan—a portion of them, or better yet, all—would give him a maritime outlet, custody of the holy sites, and vastly augmented international clout.

The emir's dissimulation was matched by that of Yusuf Hanna, himself a supporter of Abdullah and the anti-mufti opposition. His paper *Filastin* railed daily against Zionism and imperialism; upon Woodhead's arrival it likened Britain to a "mill ass who goes round and round but arrives at no destination." But in communication with the *New York Times'* Joseph Levy, he struck a franker and more hard-headed note, one he accentuated in capital letters:

> *Any Arab would openly admit in private how much plenty and progress the Jews have brought him and his country in the course of their building up a national home. . . . The people of Transjordan have not been dreaming of being annexed to Palestine for the purpose of being attached to Nablus, Beersheba and Hebron, but have been dreaming of being attached to THAT PIECE OF EUROPE THAT HAS BEEN SO SUDDENLY ESTABLISHED IN PALESTINE.*[54]

A Privilege to Die

Betar was the Revisionist movement's youth wing, named for a Jerusalem-area fortress where ancient Jewish rebels made their last stand against Rome. The name doubled as a Hebrew acronym for the Union of Joseph Trumpeldor, the one-armed warrior whose 1920 death at Arab hands in uppermost Galilee had made him Zionism's first martyr icon. Betar's members drilled in military uniforms, dreamed of a Jewish state on both sides of the Jordan, and revered their leader, Vladimir Ze'ev Jabotinsky.

The group was strong in Eastern Europe—Poland accounted for more than half of its seventy thousand members—but in Palestine its influence paled compared to that of the Labor-Zionist establishment led by Ben-Gurion. Increasingly, Betar's relatively small presence in Palestine was turning into the breeding ground for the Irgun, the burgeoning militant group behind Black Sunday.[55]

Shalom Tabacznik was a twenty-four-year-old new immigrant from a poor, traditional family in Poland that had lost its breadwinner some years before. He had arrived in Palestine illegally (Revisionists complained that the Jewish Agency habitually denied them immigration certificates) and was living near Safed in Rosh Pina, an old Zionist farming settlement where a seed of Betar devotees had taken root.

In Palestine he took to calling himself Shlomo Ben-Yosef. Perhaps the patronymic rang more biblical than his exilic surname; perhaps too the Hebrew name of King Solomon—builder of Israel's Temple, expander of her borders—seemed more appealing than the meek and mild Shalom of his birth.

By day the Betaris labored in the olive and tobacco rows. By night they stood watch. Like many Revisionists, Ben-Yosef grew exasperated as the Zionist upper echelon held fast to *havlagah* even as attacks continued unabated into spring 1938. One victim of that year's Passover ambush at Hanita was a friend who had been a Betar leader in Berlin.

On April 21, 1938, the day the Woodhead Commission embarked for Palestine, Ben-Yosef and two Betar friends—Avraham Schein, eighteen, and Shalom Zuravin, twenty-three—plotted their revenge. At the foot of Mount Canaan, on the same road the Arabs had struck weeks earlier, they prepared to target a bus departing the village that they believed had produced the assailants, Ja'ouna.

The younger two opened fire with pistols and Ben-Yosef hurled a grenade. It was an amateur affair: The gunshots missed and the grenade declined to explode. The bus continued on its way, its passengers frightened but unharmed. Police found the three Jews hiding with their weapons in a cowshed, took them for questioning, and detained them at Acre prison.

"Jewish Gang Caught in Safed," reported *Al-Difa*.[56]

The trial began a month later in Haifa, at one of the military courts established after Andrews's assassination. The suspects faced charges that under the latest emergency laws were capital offenses: illegal possession and discharge of weapons with the intent to kill or harm.

Nearly a thousand Arabs had been arrested and prosecuted for similar violations since the start of the revolt. Three had been hanged thus far (another three were executed years earlier after the Hebron massacre of 1929). Yet throughout the Mandate the authorities had never taken a Jewish life. A Jewish policeman, also a Betar member, had fired at an Arab bus five months earlier, killing a young boy, but his capital punishment was quickly commuted to a life sentence (he would ultimately serve just six years).[57]

"Ropes are made for Arab necks only," lamented Khalidi in his island exile.[58]

The military trial was a Babel of tongues. The defense team were prominent Tel Aviv lawyers, one originally from Montreal and the other, fluent in Palestine's three official languages, who insisted on serving as his own translator. One constable called to the witness stand spoke with a North of England accent so robust that his own countrymen struggled to follow. Zuravin's father testified in Yiddish that his son was mentally ill; three medical specialists corroborated that assessment in German. The two older suspects knew no English and sat through the interminable sessions puzzled and bored.[59]

After eleven days, the courtroom filled to capacity for the verdict. Zuravin was ruled not guilty on all counts due to insanity, and ordered into custody as a "criminal lunatic" until he could be institutionalized. The other two were cleared of the charge of throwing bombs with intention

From right: Ben-Yosef, Zuravin, Schein, and their defense attorneys (JI 7405)

to cause injury or death, but found guilty of carrying and discharging firearms.

Half an hour later came the sentences.

"The Court sentences Abraham Schein to be hanged by the neck until he is dead. The Court sentences Shlomo Ben-Yosef to be hanged by the neck until he is dead."

Silence filled the hall as the verdict was translated into the various languages. Schein's sister began sobbing.

"They had been calm throughout the whole trial, almost indifferent, and not even the horror of the gallows moved them from their apathy," wrote a sympathetic observer from the public gallery. "The streets were crowded with Arabs of all shapes, sizes, and classes. They were waiting for a verdict to recompense them for the Arabs that the same Court had hanged. They had to have a verdict, they were eager, hungry for it—and they got it."[60]

Appeals for mercy flooded into London from Jewish groups in Europe and America, from the chief rabbis of Palestine and the British

Empire, from churches and Anglican bishops. The *Guardian* of Manchester, long sympathetic to Zionist aspirations, ran an editorial pleading for clemency.[61]

Yishuv leaders depicted the incident as a youthful excess, a regrettable lapse in judgment after two years of Jewish bloodletting and restraint. No one was killed or even hurt, they argued, and the punishment grievously outweighed the crime.

Weizmann cabled Malcolm MacDonald, the new colonial secretary, but to no effect—the power to pardon anyone sentenced under military law rested with General Haining, the new head of Palestine Command. A birth certificate mailed from Poland convinced the general that the youngest suspect, Schein, was a minor (decades later the document was revealed as a forgery). On Ben-Yosef's sentence, however, he would not budge.[62]

Nor would Ben-Yosef. He ruled out any notion of rescue attempts, or even of suicide. Instead, he would show the world that Jews did not fear death.

He jotted messages on his cell wall, on scraps of paper, and in letters. In Yiddish, he wrote his mother and siblings in the old country. He begged them to either forget him or be proud—he had accepted his fate "with honor and a happy heart."[63]

The night before the scheduled execution he penned a letter to his old Betar companions in Poland. In vivid but imperfect Hebrew, he wrote, "Friends, tomorrow I am going to die by hanging, and is there another man happier than I?"

His death should serve as a "sign for war" of national liberation: "I am going to die with the complete confidence that the state of the Jews will rise despite all of the obstacles. . . . Long live Ze'ev Jabotinsky! Long live the state of the Jews in its historic borders! Long live the fighting Hebrew youth!" (At the bottom was an apology for typographic errors: "I still haven't managed to learn our language.")

Ben-Yosef's final communication was to Jabotinsky. "Sir, I have the great honor of informing you that tomorrow I will be fulfilling my holy and final task as a Betar recruit in the Land of Israel," he wrote. He urged his mentor not to worry; he knew he cared for his children like a father, but the natural course of events could not be averted. "I promise, as my last vow, that I will go to the gallows as a Betari, with my head high, and will die with your name, so dear to me, on my lips."[64]

It would be days or weeks until the letter reached Jabotinsky, but since the verdict he had been working relentlessly to stay the execution. He had written the colonial secretary three times—each with increasing urgency—and on June 28, the day before the sentence was to be carried out, they met. MacDonald stood firm: Haining had made his decision, and it was one he agreed with. Letting the condemned man live would be an incentive to other Jews bent on revenge, he said, and it was not Ben-Yosef's life alone that hung in the balance.

"Then my case is lost," said Jabotinsky.

"I am afraid it is," he replied.[65]

Through the night Jabotinsky frantically searched for a legal precedent allowing the appeal of a ruling handed down by a military court. He had heard of one such case from the Boer War, but frenzied scouring in the House of Commons library turned up nothing. A Jewish member of the Irish parliament told him of a similar instance in Ireland, and around 3:00 a.m. Jabotinsky located the case by candlelight in the High Court archive. But MacDonald could not be located and it was already daylight in Palestine.[66]

The deed was scheduled for 8:00 a.m. That morning the high commissioner's office in Jerusalem received a telegram from Ben-Yosef's widowed mother asking to see her son and bless him one last time. But the commissioner was not in, and had made clear he would not be intervening in military prerogatives.[67]

Ben-Yosef awoke early, had a cup of tea, and recited a few psalms with a Jewish prison guard. At 7:00 a.m. he brushed his hair and teeth.

At the appointed hour, as he was led to the gallows, he sang the Betar anthem and "Hatikvah" as other inmates joined in. As the hood fell over his eyes, he bellowed the words he had vowed would be his last: "Long live Jabotinsky!"

In London, the Revisionist leader's wife saw him cry for the first time.[68]

Dr. Khalidi heard the news on the radio and recorded it in his diary.

"At last and at least one Jew was hanged."[69]

The execution of Shlomo Ben-Yosef, the first Jew put to death in Palestine since antiquity, stunned world Jewry. Marchers in Tel Aviv brawled with police, with dozens treated for head wounds and a curfew declared on the city. *Haaretz* called him a *kadosh*, a saint. In Warsaw tens of thousands packed synagogues and fasted; stones burst the window of Britain's ambassador in Riga.[70]

Irgun commanders in Palestine met the next day. One faction insisted a campaign be launched against the British; another believed the hanging had finally exposed the bankruptcy of *havlagah*, that the hour was ripe for an unrestrained war against the Arabs. "We must create a situation," said one of them, "whereby killing an Arab is like killing a rat, where Arabs are dirt, thereby showing that we and not they are the power to be reckoned with." The second faction won the day.

"Acts of retaliation will show the British government and the world that the Yishuv is a fighting force," promised a placard posted by the Irgun leadership. "Acts of retaliation will break Arab terror!"

Jabotinsky had already laid the foundation for the new phase. Hours before Ben-Yosef's execution, he telegraphed his nephew, an Irgun activist in Haifa. "If final, invest heavily," he wrote, signing off as "Mendelson."[71]

The Irgun men in Palestine needed little encouragement—they shared none of his ambivalence over reprisals; if anything, his vacillation was risking them shaking off his control entirely.[72]

Within days Jiryis Hanna Zahran, a Christian from Nazareth, was abducted from his taxi in Haifa and hanged in a shack outside the city. An Arab bus in Jerusalem's Mahane Yehuda quarter was firebombed, killing four; another man was shot to death at Carmel Market on the Tel Aviv–Jaffa seam.

Haganah intelligence found that far from cowing the Arabs into submission, Jewish terrorism was pushing moderates toward the rebels and making them likelier to join their ranks.[73]

The day of the market blast, four moshav members were killed near Tulkarem. Shortly after, a shop owner and his son were shot dead in

Jerusalem's Jewish Quarter. A bomb hurled from a train in Tel Aviv killed a young woman at a kiosk on Herzl Street.

Ninety minutes after the last incident, a man dressed as an Arab porter entered the Arab vegetable market next to Haifa Port bearing two milk jugs. Each had false bottoms concealing time-fused landmines and thousands of iron rivets. The first bomb exploded, then minutes later the second, which according to an official Irgun history "was no less lethal than its predecessor, and brought the general panic to its peak."

Twenty-one Arabs were killed and more than one hundred wounded. "It took more than two hours to bring the dead and wounded from the market to hospital," the history boasted.[74]

Tovia Dounie, a prominent real-estate developer, sped over in his car. A three-decade resident of Palestine, he and his partners—a Jew and a Christian Arab—had built some of Jerusalem's most iconic buildings: the towering YMCA, the Palace Hotel where the Peel Commission had convened, and even Karm al-Mufti where George Antonius now lived.

One of the injured was police officer Musa Khamis. Bystanders tried to evacuate him in Dounie's car, but someone yelled that the bomber was inside, and shots were fired. Dounie "slumped at the wheel of his automobile, a bullet in his heart," the *New York Times* reported. He was one of six Jews killed in the general bedlam that followed the bombing.

Dounie was also the brother-in-law of Chaim Weizmann. Zionism's elder statesman pleaded that no one seek revenge. The colonial secretary sent him a handwritten note that he was "horrified."[75]

The next week removed any doubt that the violence had reached a new pitch, one that made the previous year's Black Sunday seem almost muted by comparison.

An Indian Muslim visitor was shot dead on the new coastal road linking Tel Aviv and Haifa. In Jerusalem, two bombs within as many days killed five Arabs and wounded dozens. Gunmen killed two Jewish police and a female settler next to Binyamina. Alexander Zaid, a celebrated founder of some of Palestine's first Jewish self-defense groups, was killed in the Jezreel Valley, then another five Jews in nearly the same spot. A bomb in a Jerusalem market left ten Arabs dead—half of them women, one with her young son—and thirty injured. A car bomb in Tel Aviv wounded two dozen Jews.[76]

In a macabre denouement, at the same ill-omened vegetable market in Haifa, a sixty-five-pound landmine in a pickle container killed fifty-three Arabs and wounded nearly as many. The U.S. consul wrote of a "shambles of dismembered corpses of human beings, donkeys and horses." The Irgun history book called it a "blood-harvest hitherto unknown since the start of the 1936 events, one which sent impressive reverberations throughout the world." The former put the body count at fifty-three; the latter swore it was seventy.[77] Either way, it was the most wretched day yet in Palestine's two-year agony.

Lists of the dead filled the columns of *Al-Difa*: Abed Mustafa of Haifa . . . Muhammad Malhas of Nablus . . . Ali Hussein Jarar of Gaza. Four were women and at least one a child. The wounded were listed by hospital: Abu Muhammad Hejazi of Safed was in the German-Templar

Mourners peer into a Jerusalem morgue after an Irgun bombing, July 1938 (LOC M33-9749)

hospital, Boutros Jiryis of Lebanon in the government one. The paper also named the two Jews killed in reprisals in the bomb's aftermath: Moshe Mizrahi and Dov Ben-Moshe.[78]

July 1938 saw sixty Jews killed across the country—by far their bloodiest month since the uprising began. But the monthly toll for Arabs was over one hundred. For the first time since the Great Revolt began, for the first time in Palestine's history, Jews were killing more Arabs than the reverse.[79]

In his island exile Dr. Khalidi deplored the "butchery" of attack and counterattack. "The place is simply an inferno." The Arabic press pondered why Britain did not seem unduly troubled by Arab bodies: "Nobody tries to explain anything. Not even one member of Parliament asks a single question." The fissure separating Jew and Arab since 1936 was growing into an unbridgeable chasm: Arab bus drivers started avoiding Jewish settlements, and Arab postmen steered clear of Tel Aviv unless provided armed guards.[80]

Jabotinsky was stunned—the lynching and the market explosions struck him as particularly barbarous—but in his ambiguity and double-speak over reprisals he bore no small responsibility for the grisly turn of events.[81] Many others across the Yishuv argued the bloodshed could not be the work of Jews.

Ben-Gurion demurred. "Poor peasants went to their city to sell the fruits of their labor—straight, honest people. And here come masses of Jews and kill them. What is the Arab to think? Does it not immediately create dozens, hundreds of new terrorists?"[82]

He had opposed hanging Ben-Yosef: The young man's deed had caused no death or injury, and turning him into a martyr would lead other Jewish youth to acts of "madness." Nonetheless, he knew Ben-Yosef was not alone.

"There is a Nazi party in Israel," he said.[83]

Lawlessness Was the Law

Al-Bassa was a mixed Christian-Muslim hamlet of 2,423 souls perched beside Palestine's border with Lebanon. It had two churches, a mosque, several coffeehouses, and Galilee's only Christian high school. Its farmers mainly grew olives, but also citrus, bananas, pomegranates, apples, and figs.[84]

Spring and summer 1938 brought new neighbors. Tegart's Wall arose along the frontier, as did a hulking police stronghold—among the first of dozens of "Tegart Forts" that would dot the terrain—and Hanita, the Jews' new border outpost, just down the road.[85]

One night in early September an army truck drove over a mine near al-Bassa, killing an officer and three soldiers with the Royal Ulster Rifles. There was no evidence implicating anyone from the village, but the battalion commander had warned local mukhtars that any hostile activity would draw punitive measures against whatever locale was closest to the act.

The next morning, according to a contemporary Arabic account, troops arrived in al-Bassa, shot four people, and, beating residents with rifle butts, began searching and looting homes. They took one hundred people to an army camp nearby, where another four men were undressed and forced to kneel on *sabr*—prickly pear—and beaten "without mercy or pity" until "flesh flew from their bodies" and they fainted. In the meantime soldiers set about destroying the hamlet.

One officer said he would never forget "the Rolls-Royce armored cars of the 11th Hussars peppering Bassa with machine-gun fire, and this went on for about twenty minutes. And then we went in and I remember we had lighted braziers"—metal boxes filled with charcoal—"and we set the houses on fire and we burnt the village to the ground."

In the aftermath, the Ulsters and some Royal Engineers gathered at least twenty men of al-Bassa and herded them onto a bus. A policeman recalled:

> *Villagers who panicked and tried to escape were shot. The driver of the bus was forced to drive along the road, over a land mine buried by the soldiers . . . it completely destroyed the bus, scattering the maimed and mutilated bodies of the men on board everywhere. The villagers were then forced to dig a pit, collect the bodies, and throw them unceremoniously into it.*

Shortly thereafter, the 8th Infantry Division received a new commander from England: Bernard Montgomery. According to one account, Monty told a subordinate, referring to al-Bassa, to "just go a wee bit easier in the future."[86]

It was hardly the only allegation of excess and abuse committed by British forces.

The Anglican archdeacon of Jerusalem protested that police had slapped his servant across the cheek until his mouth filled with blood. The manager of the city's Arab Bank said troops shot his brother point-blank, and produced an autopsy note by three doctors (two Arabs and a Jew) confirming the cause of death: "a hard body . . . driven through the different organs with great force, such as the bullet of a firearm."[87]

Village residents were routinely placed in open-air cages while their homes were searched. In one notorious incident in spring 1939, at Halhul near Hebron, troops set up two outdoor wire enclosures: one with ample shade, food, and water, and the other exposed to the withering sun. Access to the "good" cage depended on surrendering a firearm. The unfortunates in the bad cage were each given less than a pint of drinking water per day. According to Arab complaints to the League of Nations: "They buried their faces in the cool earth" against the heat, and "drank their urine under inhuman beating." After reportedly being left in such conditions for over a week, at least eight people died.[88]

When rail lines were sabotaged, men would be seized from nearby villages—or from cages like those at Halhul—and seated in a wheeled platform placed in front of the engine car. The governor of Jerusalem explained the brutally simple logic that if any mines were laid on the tracks, "they would get blown up first." Using Arabs as "minesweepers" was common enough to prompt daylong strikes in Haifa and Acre.[89]

Upon receiving one of the innumerable petitions filed by Frances Newton—a missionary living on Mount Carmel and a tireless critic of the administration—one senior Colonial Office official wrote that "rough play" was both expected and justified, at least to a point:

> *In the conditions of "sub-war" which we now see in Palestine there is bound to be a good deal of rough play by troops and police and (though*

> *this could hardly be admitted in public) it is justifiable up to a point as a means of convincing the inhabitants that terrorism and the shielding of terrorists do not pay.*[90]

From spring 1938, house demolitions became commonplace; sometimes dozens of homes were razed in a village on a single day. General Haining assured the Cabinet the practice was confined to the homes of militant leaders, or those where arms or ambushes had originated. He admitted, though, that there were conditions in which assigning collective responsibility was appropriate, as when an attack could be linked to a certain village but not any one individual. The "critics fail to realize," he said, that collective punishment was "fully recognized and understood by the Palestinian Arab."[91]

"After 1936 the British established a systematic, systemic, officially sanctioned policy of destruction, punishment, reprisal and brutality that fractured and impoverished the Palestinian population," argues Matthew Hughes, the historian who has most thoroughly examined the legal questions surrounding Britain's counterinsurgency campaign in Palestine. British law—and, once the revolt erupted, Palestine-specific emergency regulations—gave troops and commanders wide discretion, and from late 1937 or early 1938 the country was under de facto martial law.

"Lawlessness *was* the law," Hughes writes, and most of the repression inflicted was permitted according to the legal letter. "The British had to balance what was lawful, what was morally right, and what worked, and these were not compatible."

Other twentieth-century great powers faced with similar insurgencies responded with far more severe, less-discriminating violence, he notes. "This does not excuse British abuses in Palestine but it provides some comparative context. Put simply, in Palestine the British were often brutal but they rarely committed atrocities . . . the awfulness was less awful."[92]

A former private deployed to the Holy Land with the Manchester Regiment put it this way:

> *Soldiers don't go into battle with any hate or anything like that. They go in there because they've been trained to do a certain thing and that's to kill. A butcher's job is to chop meat up; a milkman's job is to deliver milk. A soldier's job is to kill, or at least to kill and try not to be killed himself. No, there was no hatred at all. The only hatred was when you "got" one in your company, when you knew someone who had been killed. . . . We knew that if they [themselves] hadn't killed them, their friends or their brothers had. So as far as we were concerned they were rubbish, they were dead.*[93]

A Palestine Police ditty expressed a similar sentiment, delivered in light verse:

> There's Christian, Jew an' Arab in this ruddy 'Oly Land,
> As matey as a bunch o' rattlesnakes;
> But if you'd give us coppers just a day or two's free hand,
> We guarantee we'd give the lot the shakes.
> Now there's Hussein el Mohammed and Moses Moshewix;
> Plus Parliamentary members safe in Tooting;
> What's mucking up the country with their rotten politics,
> And leaving British coppers to the shooting . . .
> Our brothers in the Army, they know the game as well,
> And don't do all their fighting by the book;
> So, it's: "Use your boots and butts, boys, go down and give 'em hell,
> They've knifed a British copper in the *souk*."[94]

Chapter 6

Lawrence of Judea

David Ben-Gurion was a hard-headed, pragmatic man with minimal need for human contact. Of that archetypically Jewish quality—a sense of humor—he had little. Weizmann once called him "humorless, morally stunted"; Golda Meyerson, a decades-long colleague, never heard him make a joke. But he possessed a brain of extraordinary discipline and analytical capacity. "When I come to a concrete question—what to do today, tomorrow—I become like a calculator," he said to party comrades. A childhood doctor once told his parents that his uncommonly large head portended untold talents.[1]

An unflagging note-taker and diary-writer, his millions of recorded words are models of clarity and concision. Impromptu remarks barely differed from prepared ones, typified by numbered priorities and countless lists. He had the singular ability to immerse himself in minutiae (there was always some committee meeting of the Jewish Agency, Mapai party, or Histadrut, and he headed all three) without losing focus on strategic objectives. A police intelligence report concluded that he was the only one among the Zionist leaders with a definite plan.[2]

And unlike so many of his peers, he had no difficulty seeing a situation from the perspective of another: a Briton's, for instance, or an Arab's.

"I want you to see things for a moment with Arab eyes," he told colleagues early in the revolt. "They—the Arabs—see everything differently, exactly the opposite of what we see. It doesn't matter whether or not their view is correct; that is simply how they see things."[3]

"No one would have thought the disturbances would last this long," he said in the bloodstained summer of 1938, "that the Arabs would show such great strength and that we too would show such tremendous ability to withstand. The final question is: Whose nerves and self-control will last longer."

> *Let us not delude ourselves: We are facing not terror but war. This is a national war the Arabs have declared upon us. Terror is just one of its means. . . . This is the active resistance of the Arabs of the Land of Israel to the plunder of their homeland by the Jews—that is how the Arabs see things, and that is why they fight. . . . When a nation fights the expropriation of its country it does not get tired so easily.*

The Jews faced not an uprising of hundreds of armed men, or even of thousands, but of the entire Arab people, he said. They should expect years of armed conflict; they should assume the war against them will grow fiercer. It might even last centuries.

> *This blood-war is just one manifestation of the conflict. The Arab-Jewish fight is fundamentally political, and on the political level it is as if we are the aggressors and the Arabs the defenders. . . . In the political battle, they have the advantage: the soil, villages, mountains, and roads are in their hands. The country is in their hands—because they inhabit it. And we, we just want to come and take hold of it—as they see it—we want to take the land from their hands, while we are still outside it.*

"There are *two peoples*" in Palestine, he declared, drawing out the words for emphasis, and "our enterprise is aimed at turning this land into a Jewish one."[4]

Ben-Gurion prided himself on turning adversity into opportunity, and in the Arab Revolt he perceived an unprecedented opening to realize two central Zionist aims.

The first was to make permanent the economic separation in place since 1936. Only a self-sufficient Jewish economy—one not dependent on Arab work but able to feed, house, and employ itself—could lay the foundation for the future Jewish state. From there sprang his insistence on "Hebrew labor," and his euphoria at the construction of the Tel Aviv Port.

The second was building a Jewish defense force that could withstand Arab hostilities without dependence on the British—indeed, one that could hold its own if ever the Crown relinquished the Holy Land. It was that motive that underlay his *havlagah* policy. Indiscriminate violence could sabotage the Jews' advances during the disturbances—advances that had only been possible with government consent.[5]

"Over this time we have made gains in our defense system that it would have been difficult even to dream of. From a method of passive defense we are moving more and more to active defense," he enthused. More Jews were now under arms in Palestine than British troops and police combined. "With the help of the government, we have created a kind of Jewish army, an army of thousands."[6]

As he spoke, delegates from thirty-odd nations met in Evian, on Lake Geneva, to discuss the plight of persecuted minorities in Hitler's Reich. The conference was the work of President Roosevelt, motivated as much by genuine sympathy as a bid to divert attention from immigration quotas, widely backed in Congress, that had kept America's gates mostly shut for well over a decade.

Over nine days, one representative after another rose to explain why his country could accept no Jews. France said its immigrant population had reached "saturation point." Four Latin American states said they could not tolerate the burden of absorbing any refugees at all, let alone "traders or intellectuals." The expansive British Empire was said to be at full occupancy—the head of its delegation said a few hundred Jews might be settled in Kenya or Northern Rhodesia, though even there British settlers were adamantly opposed. Only the Dominican Republic, run by a coercive military regime keen to "whiten" its populace, was ready to admit Jews as farmworkers. Meyerson, the emissary from the Yishuv, was not allowed to speak. As the conference concluded she told reporters, "There is only one thing I hope to see before I die, and that is that my people should not need expressions of sympathy any more."[7]

Yet Ben-Gurion was relieved. He had privately warned of the "damage, danger, and disaster" that could befall the Zionist endeavor if foreign countries took in the Jews *en masse*, thereby removing Palestine from the agenda in resolving the Jewish predicament. Again he was trying to leverage misfortune into opportunity: Yes, he wanted the Nazi menace destroyed, but as long as it existed, he wanted to utilize it for the good of Zionism.

"If I knew that it was possible to save all the children in Germany by transporting them to England, but only half of them by transporting to Palestine, I would choose the second," he said later that year, "because we face not only the reckoning of those children, but the historical reckoning of the Jewish people." Like every Jew, he hoped to save each member of his tormented people wherever possible, but "nothing takes precedence over saving the Hebrew nation in its land."

Hitler, who had welcomed Evian as a chance to cleanse his realm of its rejected subjects, drew his own conclusion from the summit's failure: The forced, large-scale emigration of Jews was impossible if almost no country was willing to accept them. Another solution would need to be found.[8]

The Logic of Facts

Nine months after fleeing the Haram al-Sharif to his Lebanese aerie, Hajj Amin al-Husseini was in buoyant spirits. The word Palestine had scarcely been uttered at Evian, and back home speculation simmered that the Woodhead Commission, tasked with implementing Peel's partition plan, was mulling abandoning it entirely. The mufti was sanguine that Britain would finally scrap its disastrous Jewish national home policy. Perhaps it would even set Palestine on course toward independence like its Arab brethren, paving his own return to his beloved land of birth.

In the meantime, His Majesty's Government was united in its judgment of his role in the carnage. The colonial secretary wrote Prime Minister Chamberlain that there was no question who lay behind so much of the bloodshed that was "disgracing the Arab cause." The Palestine Police believed he kept "the entire rebel movement" under his thumb. So did MI5: "The mufti controls the movement along its main path, and is explicitly obeyed in all leading issues."[9]

In later years the U.S. State Department compiled its own confidential profile of the man: "The names of Machiavelli, Richelieu, and Metternich come to mind to describe him, yet none of these apply."

> *Vigorous, erect, and proud, like a number of Palestinian Arabs he has pink-white skin and blue eyes. His hair and beard . . . foxy red. . . . Part of his charm lies in his deep Oriental courtesy: he sees a visitor not only to the door, but to the gate as well, and speeds him on his way with blessings.*

"The Mufti, in spite of his genteel charm, is ruthless toward his opponents," it said, and his "mystical devotion" to the Arab cause is "indivisibly bound up with his personal and family aggrandizement." For their part, "the Zionists consider him slightly worse than Mephistopheles."[10]

Hajj Amin was canny enough to leave no paper trail. Instead, oral instructions traveled from his villa to confidants among the Palestinian exiles in Damascus, and from there to rebel leaders on the ground. His message was consistent: Low-level violence was insufficient. A gently boiling pot barely disturbs the cook. The tempo of operations needed to rise, against Jews, Britons, and Arabs deemed personal and national obstacles. "Keep firm and show no sign of relaxation," went a typical missive, "the turning point in the struggle is at hand and success will only be attained by a firm stand."[11]

Musa Alami kept in regular touch with the mufti (he was living just ten miles away in Beirut's Hotel St. Georges), but his disposition was of a different world. Reserved and cerebral, Alami lacked the magnetism to rally the Arabs against the Zionist threat.

His niece recalled that her Uncle Musa was not inordinately fond of Hajj Amin, but believed only he could lead Palestine's Arabs at that time. Alami once told an associate there was only one man able to recruit thousands of Palestinians to the national cause, and it was not himself. The mufti's "style and policy were totally alien to him," the associate remembered, "but he never came out against him."[12] These were abnormal times calling for extraordinary measures. If Alami had any misgivings over the mufti's leadership, never during the Arab rebellion did he publicly break with him.

George Antonius was another matter. A writer and an aesthete, he had the Romantic's weakness for the zealot. Freya Stark, the Arabist and adventurer, suspected that the fugitive mufti had bewitched him "as securely as ever a siren did her mariner, leading him through his slippery realms with sealed eyes so that George . . . would talk to me without a flicker about the Mufti's 'singlehearted goodness.'"[13]

Antonius had met with the mufti regularly in the days before each was forced to quit Palestine the year before—the former fearing Britain's military censor, and the latter, its handcuffs. Often they lingered for an hour or more, with Antonius doing the talking and Hajj Amin simply listening. Amin was, after all, his landlord, and was keen to hear his thinking on the affairs of the day.[14] Now both were exiles: Antonius in Egypt, the mufti in Lebanon. They joined tens of thousands of Palestinian Arabs, preponderantly of the elite, who had fled the tumult to neighboring countries.[15]

In Alexandria then Cairo, Antonius threw himself into finishing his manuscript. These were the most troubled years of his troubled life, and writing gave him purpose amid his shattered family life—he was now separated from his mercurial wife Katy and seldom saw their daughter Tutu.

Writing diverted him from the alarming specter of Europe again dragging the world into war. It averted his attention from his angst over Palestine's fate, his disillusion with the British who had educated him and with the Arabs whose cause he was toiling to put into words. Above all it distracted him from the unending bloodbath of Arabs, Jews, and Britons dying at each other's hands, and of the mounting reports of Arabs murdering Arabs.

By summer he had nearly completed *The Arab Awakening*. Having filled a 350-page canvass covering a century of Arab history, he dedicated its final section to Palestine, "the most notorious and least successful of all the mandatory ventures."

He hoped his treatise would be widely read in the West (it would be published in Britain first, then America), and seems to have specially crafted it for empathy—an implicit counter to the charge of Arab intransigence as embodied by the mufti. Here was none of the denial of Jewish history or peoplehood, none of the Judeophobic tropes that colored the arguments of Hajj Amin. Before he, the most eloquent voice for Arab nationalism, condemned the Zionist project, he would pay it due respect.

He wrote, "The motives animating Zionism sprang from a humane concern over the precarious position of the Jews," who for two millennia "had maintained a distant but living connection with the Holy Land, which stands out as an impressive and moving example of faith and devotion."[16]

"The manifold proofs of public spirit and of capacity to endure hardships and face danger in the building up of the national home are there to testify to the devotion with which a large section of the Jewish people cherish the Zionist ideal."[17]

Zionist claims, he conceded, rested not just on ancient bonds but on more recent wartime diplomacy: "It is manifest that the Allies did get the benefit of important Jewish services which, but for the Balfour Declaration, would probably not have been forthcoming; the contention of the Zionists that they had a claim on the gratitude of the Allies is justified." The promise embodied in the Balfour Declaration had been approved by the Allied powers and the United States and therefore enjoyed the "sanction of a wide international recognition."[18]

"The motive was altogether humanitarian and generous," he repeated, "but whether the remedy proposed was a wise one is open to question."

"The unfortunate thing for Zionism—and herein lies the tragedy of the Palestine problem—is that Great Britain's promise lacks real validity," he wrote, "because she had previously committed herself to recognizing Arab independence in Palestine."[19]

The book would reveal, for the first time, the text of the 1915–1916 wartime correspondence between Britain's high commissioner in Egypt, Henry McMahon, and Hussein, *sherif* of Mecca, promising the Arabs independence if they rose up against the Ottomans.[20] Two decades on, Britain still maintained that McMahon had excluded Palestine from that pledge; Antonius was convinced that once published, *The Arab Awakening* would reveal the full scope of the deception.

Turning to the Mandate itself, Antonius repudiated the notion that either Britain or the Jews had brought a windfall to Palestine's Arabs. He maintained that beyond the enrichment of some landowners and middlemen, the Arabs' economic position, particularly that of the rural majority, was no better or worse than it had been for generations.

Lastly he came to the Arab Revolt.

"The fact must be faced that the violence of the Arabs is the inevitable corollary of the moral violence done to them, and that it is not likely to cease, whatever the brutality of the repression, unless the moral violence itself were to cease."

> *The moving spirits in the revolt are not the nationalist leaders, most of whom are now in exile, but men of the working and agricultural classes who are risking their lives in what they believe to be the only way left to them of saving their homes and their villages. . . . The rebel chiefs lay the blame for the present plight of the peasantry on those Arab landowners who have sold their land. . . . The fact that some of those landowners have served on national Arab bodies makes them only more odious.*

As his exposition came to a close, Antonius finally abandoned the pretense of disinterested historian. It was a crucial moment in the Arab national struggle, and as its foremost champion he would make his position plain:

> *There is no room for a second nation in a country which is already inhabited, and inhabited by a people whose national consciousness is fully awakened, and whose affection for their homes and countryside is obviously unconquerable. . . . There seems to be no valid reason why Palestine should not be constituted into an independent Arab state in which as many Jews as the country can hold without prejudice to its political and economic freedom would live in peace. . . . It would protect the natural rights of the Arabs in Palestine and satisfy their*

> *legitimate national aspirations. It would enable the Jews to have a national home in the spiritual and cultural sense, in which Jewish values could flourish and the Jewish genius have the freest play to seek inspiration in the land of its ancient connection.*

He acknowledged that Jewish existence in Europe had become untenable, but insisted the cure need not and could not be found in Palestine. It was for countries that prided themselves on their humanity to revise their own pitiful performances at Evian and "consent to some of the sacrifices which Arab Palestine has been bullied into making on a scale that has taxed her capacity." To force that burden on Palestine was "a miserable evasion of the duty that lies upon the whole of the civilized world. It is also morally outrageous. No code of morals can justify the persecution of one people in an attempt to relieve the persecution of another."

The "logic of facts is inexorable," he wrote in the book's final words, "no room can be made in Palestine for a second nation except by dislodging or exterminating the nation in possession."[21]

Army of Zion

The Holy Land has lured eccentrics for centuries, but in Palestine's modern history one stands alone. Orde Wingate would contribute more than any figure outside the Yishuv to the creation of Jewish military power, and almost single-handedly foreshadow the future phenomenon of militant Christian Zionism. Fundamentalist, individualist, Arabist, and Zionist, he was a distant cousin of T. E. Lawrence (whom he thought a charlatan) and would earn the epithet (which he loathed) of Lawrence of Judea.[22]

Wingate's upbringing foretold his fate: For several generations his family had cultivated the traditions of Bible and sword. His grandfather, a shipping heir, had undergone a religious awakening after his wife's premature death and devoted the rest of his life to converting the Jews to Christ. Wingate's father, a colonel in India's Northwest Frontier, joined the Plymouth Brethren, an austere non-conformist sect, and worked to bring the fervently Islamic Pashtuns to the Gospel—at forty-six he married a considerably younger woman from another Brethren family.

Orde, their first son, grew up with six siblings in a large Victorian house in a market town south of London. A sister described their father as "the most unhappy, the most lonely creature" she had ever known. He often beat his children, and as eldest, "Ordey" bore the brunt. The home was never heated; in winter they had only overcoats and visions of hellfire ("the perpetual fear of damnation," she remembered) to keep warm. On Sundays they wore black, with mornings taken up by religious devotions and afternoons by Bible study. A "temple of gloom," said a brother, "the most poisonous and repressive religious atmosphere that it is possible to conceive."

At the elite Charterhouse school Wingate went mostly unnoticed. One remembered him as a "little rat-like fellow"; another, as a "small uncommunicative untidy little scalliwag with a stooping gait." Yet even if the boy resented his father (he left no recollections this way or that), the patriarch's sober piety had sunk in his bones. At free time, when the others rushed to soccer or cricket, Orde could reliably be found in chapel at prayer. On one occasion, when a schoolmate told him his parents were taking him to a Sunday concert, he reacted in horror: "If you go you will bring your soul into danger of hell-fire!" On another, someone pointed out a small, pale, and generally unremarkable boy whom he said was Jewish. "How extraordinary!" Wingate marveled, "There is somebody who is a descendant of David!"

He stayed true to the family's martial tradition as well. His father's cousin was General Reginald Wingate, formerly commander of British forces in the Hejaz and governor in Sudan and Egypt. Wingate idolized his "Cousin Rex," and was seized by a powerful prophecy (they visited him regularly throughout his life) that a second world war was imminent. He enlisted in officer's school, earned a commission at an artillery base near Stonehenge, and passed the time undramatically in hunting, horsemanship, and prodigious reading. Inspired by his Cousin Rex, he learned Arabic at London's School of Oriental Studies and sought a posting in Sudan, where the family name was already famous.

In that languid corner of Empire his tasks were few (combating elephant poaching consumed much of his time). He studied Arabic intensively and was certified as a translator. After six years he used his final paid leave to explore the Great Sand Sea straddling Egypt and Libya in search of a lost oasis that according to Arab lore was home to great treasure and thousands of fluttering birds. On the return voyage he met an uncommonly pretty girl of just sixteen, barely half his age. In 1935 they wed in a small service in Chelsea to the sound of Bunyan's "To Be a Pilgrim" and Blake's "Jerusalem."[23]

Never an exceptional student, he was denied a spot in the Staff College. Instead, in autumn 1936 he was posted as an intelligence officer in Palestine, where at least his Arabic could be put to use in controlling the nascent rebellion.

As someone comfortable in the Arabs' language and culture, it would have raised no eyebrows had he displayed the pro-Arab sentiments of so many Palestine officials. Instead, in his first months there he was struck most by the achievements of Zionism.[24]

"It is amazing what the Jews have done and are doing in this country," Wingate wrote his mother shortly after arrival, quoting Isaiah: "The desert really begins to blossom like the rose."[25]

"I am not ignorant of Arabic or the Arabs, not prejudiced either for or against them," he wrote Cousin Rex, but officials were "to a man, anti-Jew and pro-Arab. . . . They hate the Jew and like the Arab who, although he shoots at them, toadies to them and takes care to flatter their sense of importance."[26]

He was learning Hebrew, and reported to his mother that he was speaking it haltingly with his Jewish servant. His Arabic still remained far superior, and he signed off in that language (which his mother could not read): "*Allah yibarik fiki*"—God bless you.[27]

Wingate's world was utterly shaped by the Bible, whose battles and miracles were for him not distant legends but recent events. Still, he had until then met few Jews outside of its pages (the pallid classmate was a rare exception). In Palestine the first prominent Zionist he chanced upon was David Hacohen of the Histadrut, at a makeshift military headquarters in a Haifa hotel. They were perfect strangers, but Wingate—his deep-set, unsmiling blue eyes all flame—launched into a sermon.

"I am a Zionist with my whole heart . . . I count it a privilege to help you in your struggle, and I shall devote the best years of my life to this."

Taken aback, Hacohen asked what books he had read on the topic. "There is only one important book on the subject, the Bible, and I've read it thoroughly," Wingate replied. He had read the entire Quran in Arabic and found nothing but florid verbiage. There could be no comparison between it and the eternal truth of Hebrew Scripture, nor any choice between a national movement inspired by one text and by the other.

Hacohen recorded Wingate's words to this effect:

> *I have been a great reader of the Old Testament, the eternal Book of Books, the sublime creation of the Jewish people and the everlasting witness to its life in this country. It is thanks to this Book that you have survived to this day. . . . Mankind's right to continued existence is dependent upon its living in accord with the moral principles of this Book. Whoever raises his hand against you and the rebuilding of your land and nation must be fought. . . . But the fight is yours, and mine is only the privilege of helping you. Please, open the hearts of the Jews living in this country to me.*[28]

Soon Wingate made the acquaintance of Chaim Weizmann. He was awestruck (a "prince in Israel," "more than a king"), wrote him gushing letters—"I have learned about 1000 *milim Ivrit*!" (Hebrew words)—and registered his pleasure at reading the Old Testament in the original.[29]

His surviving notebooks include vocabulary lists in Hebrew and transliterated English, evidence of the same rigorous self-education he had devoted to Arabic in Sudan.

"*Briyut*: Health."

"*Sakana*: Danger."

After Peel proposed partition, Wingate sent Weizmann an unsolicited memorandum on the army that should defend the future Jewish state: It ought to be based at the strategic port city of Haifa, and given the Jews' manpower shortage it must enlist "the full womanpower of the nation." He even gave it a name: the Jewish State Defense Force, or JSDF.[30]

His superiors would have soon aborted these freelance initiatives had Wingate not focused his formidably analytical brain on a problem

Orde Wingate, from an anonymous SNS member's album (Bitmuna Collection)

causing them unending grief: the rebels' relentless sabotage of the Iraq Petroleum Company pipeline.

The gunmen's method was as simple as it was effective. Nearly every night, somewhere along its route through the Galilee, they dug a few feet into the ground to expose the pipe. Placing a lit rag underneath, they retreated a safe distance and pierced it with a few bullet holes, sending the flaming fuel shooting into the night sky.

"Well, they've lit the menorah again," the Jews would mutter.

For the British Empire it was no mere inconvenience: The conduit served its entire Mediterranean fleet from its terminus at Haifa.[31] Amid the rumblings of world war, even unconventional schemes from the most unorthodox of characters were given a hearing.

In June 1938 Wingate proposed the creation of a unit expressly designed for movement at night, when the armed bands were most active and the army typically slept. No Arab police would be allowed—they were too sympathetic to the rebels—and most British servicemen lacked sufficient knowledge of the physical, human, and linguistic terrain. His solution was to enlist carefully chosen Jewish policemen, *notrim*, intimately familiar with the Galilee.[32]

Using the Jews, he wrote, would bring other benefits. The men could be housed, fed, and supplied for cheap, and secrecy would be maintained: "A Jewish Colony is at present the only place in Palestine where one can discuss operations with the certainty that everything will remain as secret as the grave."

Reducing noise was fundamental. Communication, if necessary, would be by whisper, and smoking would be banned as it could produce coughs (and embers visible even after dark). "Complete silence is the rule in all cases. . . . When in doubt, DON'T FIRE is always the rule." Each group would be expected to march at least fifteen miles nightly. They were to be called the Special Night Squads, or SNS.[33]

Gideon was Wingate's biblical ideal. The Book of Judges says the warrior-prophet gathered a select group of fighters at the Jezreel Valley spring of Ein Harod to face the Midianites, an oppressive "Ishmaelite" tribe of "children of the East." Gideon divided his men into three companies and, striking at night, shocked and scattered the invaders' camp with a blow of shofars.

Wingate likewise envisioned a handpicked cluster of night fighters split into three squads. His plan to obtain shofars came to nothing (junior officers were puzzled at the request for "chauffeurs"), as did an attempt to rename the unit Gideon Force. But he was allowed to set up his headquarters at the same ancient spring, now home to Kibbutz Ein Harod. The commune's cobblers fashioned rubber boot soles from tires for silent movement, and its metalworkers whetted bayonet blades to mortal sharpness.[34]

Chaim Sturman was Ein Harod's mukhtar (both Arabs and Jews used the Arabic word), and impressed Wingate as the exemplary candidate for the squads. A decades-long Galilee resident, Sturman was on close terms with his Arab neighbors, who called him *sheikh al-mashayekh*—the Jews' sheikh of sheikhs. He had won them over with his quiet dignity and the respect he showed even the least among them, free of conceit, flattery, or ulterior motive. With the revolt's outbreak and the increasing self-segregation of Jews and Arabs, he worried he was losing his Arabic entirely. As for English he knew little, but Wingate wasn't bothered. "Sturman's silence is better than other people's talk," he would say.

Sturman was among a number of prominent Jews initially skeptical of the SNS, fearing their methods could seed decades of Arab enmity.[35] Those misgivings grew quieter, however, once Wingate's irregular methods started yielding irrefutable results.

In one early mission, a mixed Jewish-British squad spotted fighters approaching the oil pipeline, allowed them to puncture it, then opened fire by the light of the blaze, leaving multiple casualties. In another, a force fifty strong—all in kibbutz attire of khaki shorts and blue shirts—marched twelve miles over craggy terrain to reach a Bedouin border village deemed responsible for attacks on Hanita. They surprised an armed band, killing its leader and compelling the local mukhtar to send the settlers a message of peace. General Haining, Palestine's topmost brass, conveyed to Wingate that he was "much impressed."[36]

Thus encouraged, Wingate expanded his ambitions. In July he set his sights on Daburiya, a village at the foot of Mount Tabor where he believed rebels were spending the night. It would be the biggest

SNS operation yet, involving all three squads: thirty British troops and fifty-five Jewish police in all.

Three trucks, driving without lights and without stopping, each dropped off a squad on a different side of the village. But things quickly went awry. The squad approaching from the south got lost in the dark. The one coming from the east moved too early, prematurely reaching the threshing house at the village outskirts, trading fire with gunmen and waking all to their presence. Heavy fire and grenades rained down from the flat mud roofs and the squadsmen responded in kind. Rebels fell to the ground one after another, and so did one of the squad leaders' valets, who in combat doubled as grenadier. Comrades wrapped him in white blankets that locals had left behind, and cloaked themselves with the blankets against the night cold. Wingate summoned a car and carried the wounded man to it, then gathered the remaining troops to chase the rebels up the mount.[37]

A bulky Ulsterman in the column's rear carried one of the squads' two Lewis machine guns. Up ahead, wrapped in blankets, Wingate's men cut silhouettes of billowing keffiyehs, and as they climbed Tabor, the gunner opened fire. Bullets ricocheting off the ground struck Wingate five times in the arms and legs. Two other Britons and a Jew were also wounded—the latter, badly, in the torso, and was soon dead.[38]

Wingate sat on the threshing floor. A squad leader, Rex King-Clark, wrote that he looked "white as a sheet . . . sitting there, in the hay, covered in blood, giving orders in English and Hebrew quite calmly." He refused evacuation, and instead went searching for some Jewish squad members still missing. They reconvened at Ein Harod and "had breakfast there with the dead Jew laid out beside the breakfast table, with his boot sticking out from under the blanket." The wounded valet died days later.

"Rather disastrous," concluded King-Clark.[39]

At Sarafand military hospital near Ramle, the new patient was anything but. Days after the battle, Wingate dictated a memo listing the squads' achievements: five major battles against bands 50 to 160 strong. At least 60 rebels were killed and twice as many injured, with 23 corpses brought back as receipts ("I have little faith in claims not so supported").[40]

After barely two restless weeks he released himself from treatment. He wrote his mother that his injuries were mere flesh wounds, that he had been lucky to avoid infection: "I must have pure blood or something." He thanked her for her prayers, "which I value as you know."[41]

With Wingate back the squads went from success to success. General Haining effused that the night missions were proceeding "magnificently," with the SNS leader showing enterprise and courage and his Jewish police-turned-troops doing "excellent work." The whole outfit was a "great tribute to the initiative and ingenuity of all concerned." At his recommendation, Wingate received the Distinguished Service Order, the army's second-highest decoration.[42]

In early autumn Wingate planned an elaborate foray at Khirbet Lidd, near Afula in the heart of the Jezreel. After midnight the entire SNS force, split into five, formed a circle half a mile wide around the village. Wingate's squad deployed among the Bedouin tents beside the hamlet, the men lying on their backs until sunrise. At first light, a kibbutz truck dropped off what looked like agricultural workers in blue shirts—SNS members dangled as bait. The ruse worked and the rebels came into the open.[43]

King-Clark then witnessed an extraordinary spectacle: "An Arab on horseback, his keffiyeh headdress pluming out behind him, galloped dramatically out of the tent and away from us across the plain." Two hundred yards out, the horseman came under machine-gun fire from a squad stationed to the east. "The Arab reined his horse dramatically on to its hind legs, turned it and galloped back towards the village, disappearing from our sight."

Pursuing him into the village, the men saw a fighter duck behind a low wall. King-Clark made a bayonet motion to one of the Jews. "I remember his eyes widening as he pointed to his fixed bayonet. I nodded vigorously, he took off and we watched." A minute later he returned, his "bayonet blooded to the hilt, his eyes wide with the shock of what he had just done."[44]

The rebels, now outnumbered and surrounded, dashed between one squad and another vainly seeking an escape route. Fourteen were killed, their bodies collected as per Wingate's custom. On closer inspection, one was identified as Sheikh Taha, a Bedouin who was deputy leader of an armed group that had bedeviled Jewish farms for months. He was the horse rider they had seen earlier.

The sheikh was dressed in a khaki Palestine Police uniform with black riding boots, silver spurs, a stolen British rifle, and papers revealing the movements of Yusuf Abu Dorra, an armed leader notorious for his cruelty to perceived foes, not least among the Arabs themselves. In the dead man's pocket was a tiny, handwritten leather-bound Quran.

"I'm afraid it hadn't been much help to him," observed King-Clark, but he had been a "gallant enemy and a fine horseman." Another squad leader put it more crudely: The rebels "looked magnificent with their rifles strapped on their back and their cloaks flying and horses galloping . . . it seemed a bloody shame to kill them."[45]

For the SNS, the mission was an unqualified success. On their return, Wingate allowed them, for the first time, to stop for an early morning drink in Afula.[46]

Wingate was proving—to the British and the Zionists themselves—that in Palestine were Jews who could fight if given the training and the chance. He had raised the Haganah's initial, hesitant offensive operations under the Field Squads to a new pitch, and with a competence and professionalism it could not otherwise have attained.[47] The Haganah, once merely tolerated by the British, was now being legitimized and coached by the world's premier armed power. The success of the SNS was an unmistakable milestone in the Zionists' steady march since spring 1936 toward becoming a formidable and lethal military force.

But Wingate was not done. He next convened the first-ever course to enlist Jews in the army as non-commissioned officers. The "Jewish sergeants' course" was fully sanctioned by military headquarters, but the one hundred candidates were all carefully chosen by the Haganah. Wingate had no doubt he was constructing a command echelon that would lead the Jews in the wars yet to come: against Hitler, the Arabs, or even his own British Army.[48]

On the course's second day, Wingate was mid-lecture when someone burst in. A car of Haganah leaders, scouting the Beth She'an Valley for the next Wall and Tower site, had hit a mine. Three people were dead, including Wingate's friend Chaim Sturman.[49]

Wingate fell silent, then with a scream ordered his troops into their vehicles. In Beisan, a suspected rebel hub, he told them to round up anyone with a weapon and shoot anyone trying to escape. Zvi Brenner remembered how they "began to beat and trample anyone in our path. Wingate himself went out of control, entering stores and destroying whatever was in them. An hour later we returned."

According to Brenner, Wingate later felt remorse over the outburst, in which according to some accounts innocent bystanders were killed. He subsequently treated his men to a typically lengthy lecture on the morality and efficacy of collective punishment. Wingate believed in collective retribution as a deterrent against villages aiding and abetting rebels, but he also tended to view the entire Arab nation in Palestine as a single recalcitrant village. It was "a rebellion by 1,000,000 people," he wrote—"the whole Arab population [is] against us."[50]

Militarily, his record spoke for itself. Pipeline disruptions fell 50 percent in the squads' first three months, and in the second half of 1938 the SNS accounted for nearly one-fifth of all rebels killed and weapons seized. For a lightly armed unit, active in limited space and time, and never numbering more than 150, the figures are staggering.[51]

Yet it was a record hardly beyond reproach.[52] Squadsmen recalled him once responding to pipeline sabotage by ordering troops to open villagers' mouths and stuff them with the oily soil; on another occasion he made them run five or ten miles. A staff officer said he ordered some seventy homes demolished in a village that had fired on troops. One of Wingate's squad commanders shot dead an Arab on a bicycle, and ordered several village residents executed when they failed to hand over rifles. Wingate's slain friend Sturman had objected to such punitive measures as equally immoral and counterproductive.[53]

"Odd." "Loner." "Dirty." "Brave." "Effective." "Extraordinary." "Genius." "Ruthless." These are the words that emerge and reemerge in testimonies of those who served with or knew Wingate.[54] Half a dozen Zionists and several army subordinates all settled on the same description: "Fanatic."[55]

His three squad leaders were likewise of one opinion: little affection for the man but much esteem.

"He was mad in all sorts of ways," said one of them. Once, at an officers' cocktail party aboard a ship, "he arrived, filthy as usual, with a sack of grenades over his shoulder."

"Good God," gasped the assembled brass. But feathers unruffled once the man's identity became known: "Oh, you must know—that's Wingate."[56]

He ate onions like apples and received guests in the nude, but behind the quirks lay a seriousness that was deadly in more than the figurative sense. Brenner said he never saw Wingate laugh. Like Ben-Gurion—that other humorless, dispassionate man of fixed vision—his gaze was set on the realization of the Jewish national project in its fullest political and military terms.

He made that ambition explicit in his welcome address to the Jewish sergeants' course, which he insisted on making in his determined but imperfect Hebrew. With characteristic directness he declared what even few Jews dared say aloud.

"We are establishing here the foundation for the army of Zion."[57]

Two Weeks in September

September 12 was the closing day of the annual Nuremberg Rally, and the theme for 1938 was "Greater Germany." Ever since annexing Austria six months prior, Adolf Hitler had fulminated over the Sudetenland, a ring of border territory in Czechoslovakia inhabited by several million ethnic Germans. It was necessary and just that they come home to the Reich, he proclaimed, vowing that the Sudetenland was his last territorial objective in Europe.

"The poor Arabs of Palestine may be unarmed and without help," he told the crowd of nearly a million, "but the Sudeten Germans are neither."[58]

The day after, Chamberlain asked Hitler for a meeting. Later that week they met for the first time at the latter's Bavarian retreat, then the following week at a hotel near Bonn. With each passing day the Nazi leader feigned greater fury at the Sudeten Germans' ostensible plight, and each day heightened his demands in accordance. On September 30, Chamberlain, with delegates from France and Fascist Italy, ceded Hitler the Sudetenland at the *Führerbau*, his stark, neoclassical headquarters in Munich.

Chamberlain's gambit was lauded in the United Kingdom and across Europe. Even opponents of appeasement held their tongues or offered grudging congratulations amid the outpouring of relief that war had been averted. Dugdale heard from a Cabinet member that Churchill himself had grasped Chamberlain's hand outside the House of Commons, remarking, "By God, you are lucky."[59]

In Palestine reactions were ambivalent. The mufti's devotees were heartened by London's capitulation; *Filastin* doubted whether Hitler cared a straw about Arab rights. Many of Palestine's Jews received the news with a flash of relief, followed quickly by foreboding.[60]

Such was the reaction of Ben-Gurion. Feeding the Nazi tiger had staved off world war, and "one cannot but be happy that a catastrophe"—a *shoah*—"has been avoided." But Britain and the Western democracies had sacrificed the Czechs, a small and courageous nation, in the interest of expediency. He was haunted by the prospect that the Yishuv would be next.[61]

TVERYA AND TABARIYA

Herod Antipas—son of Herod the Temple-builder and Roman client ruler of Galilee—built Tiberias as his lakeside capital in the first decades of the Common Era. He named it for Tiberius, Rome's dour second emperor, whose edicts included expelling the Jews from the eternal city for over-avid proselytizing. Over the next millennium, with Jerusalem razed and the Jews reduced to a mere remnant in the Promised Land, Tiberias served as their political and religious fulcrum. It was in *Tverya* that the elders of the Sanhedrin convened, where scholars wrote much of the Talmud, and where great sages like Akiva and Maimonides lie buried.

In the 1740s Zaher al-Omar, a local Bedouin chieftain, ruled from *Tabariya*, enjoying de facto Arab autonomy within the Ottoman Empire. It was there he erected a resplendent Great Mosque, black-basalt-walled and white-domed, with *ablaq* arches of alternating dark and light stones à la Mamluk. For economic reasons he encouraged the settlement of Jews. By the late nineteenth century, those Jews—Mizrahi and Ashkenazi alike, united in their piety—had regained the city's majority for the first time since antiquity. Early in the British Mandate, Zaki al-Hadif, a local son and native Arabic speaker, was elected to the mayorship with Arab backing, becoming the first Jewish mayor in modern Palestine.

In 1938, al-Hadif's city was home to ten thousand souls: six thousand Jews, most of the rest Muslims, and some Christians.[62] An army company was garrisoned at the lavish Feingold Hotel, in the new Jewish quarter of Kiryat Shmuel, on the hill northwest of the Old City.

October 2—two days after the Munich agreement and two days before Yom Kippur—was a Sunday. Per weekly habit, the troops filled the hotel's cinema and the officers decamped to a cafe on the Sea of Galilee.

At 9:00 p.m., three groups of armed men walked south toward the city along the waterside road. A whistle gave the signal: Two groups crossed into the Old City and the third to Kiryat Shmuel.[63]

An Arabic poster plastered across Palestine and its neighbors narrated a heroic chronicle of the fighters' "conquest of Tiberias." Three hundred fully armed *mujahideen* blocked all roads into the city, cut communication lines, and entered from three directions. They saluted the Arab flag—the black, green, and red flown in the Great Revolt against the Turks—and hailed the mufti, the late Sheikh Qassam, and the Seychelles deportees before three times intoning "*Allahu Akbar*!" There followed a valiant battle, as the warriors' bullets "pierced the windows of the Jewish homes. . . . The *mujahideen*, having cleared the inhabitants, set the magistrate's court and government building aflame, and also the Jewish stores and Zionist trading houses."

Some seventy Jews were killed, it said without elaboration.[64]

The truth was that the whole affair was of far smaller proportions. The fighters numbered about one hundred—those who entered Kiryat Shmuel were just a few dozen, armed mainly with daggers and matchboxes. The number of dead was considerably less than described.

Yet their deaths were more intimate and crueler. Rachel Mizrahi and her five children were stabbed repeatedly, their house set on fire. Yehoshua Ben-Arieh and his wife and two sons were killed in the same way, as were the three Leimer daughters staying at their home at the time. So too were Menachem "Max" Kotin of New York—the revolt's first American victim—and his wife Masha. The synagogue was set alight with the beadle still inside. Only four of the seventeen Jews killed in their homes were shot; the rest were burned or stabbed to death. Ten were children.[65]

The high commissioner telegrammed the colonial secretary the gruesome contours of "this brutal and disgusting massacre."[66]

The assault lasted some forty minutes. Some witnesses said the assailants broke into a restaurant and fed themselves a meal; others said they danced an impromptu *dabke* on the street.[67] What was beyond dispute was the systematic planning and execution of their operation and the almost complete absence of any British or Jewish resistance.[68] The suspected commander, Abu Ibrahim *al-Kabir* (the Great), even sat on the Central Committee for National Jihad, the Damascus-based rebel headquarters run by the mufti's votaries.[69]

To the *Palestine Post* the lesson was manifest: Consigning the Jews to minority status in an Arab state would be a death sentence. "The dastardly nightmare of the Tiberias slaughter has brought home afresh, to Jews near and far, a grim lesson which no sane man can expect them to ignore."

Three weeks later Mayor al-Hadif was leaving his office near the Great Mosque when three men shot him in the back. Within days he too was dead and buried. The assassination appeared to teach a second "grim lesson": The new Palestine that was emerging would have no room for a man like him, as Jewish as he was Arab. One nation was destined to dominate the other—the only question was which would be which.[70]

THE MUFTI SMILES

Rebel authority was at its apex. High Commissioner MacMichael wrote that 1938 had become "the worst year in the history of the country since the war," with the preceding month "in every way, the worst since the disturbances broke out." Palestine was now in "open rebellion . . . a national revolt involving all classes of the Arab community," with armed bands more respected and feared than the government. Beersheba, Gaza, and

Jericho were now rebel-controlled, and Jaffa was a "hotbed of terrorism," worse than any other town. Militants even temporarily gained control of predominantly Christian Bethlehem, roaming freely and burning government buildings. One official conceded that large areas of the country should now be regarded as rebel territory.[71]

"The Mufti Smiles," ran an *Evening Standard* headline beside an image of the beaming cleric. "In his village hideout in Lebanon the Uncrowned King of Palestine may count himself the most successful rebel against British authority for more than a century."[72]

The ubiquitous keffiyeh symbolized the new reality. The insurgency was steadily dooming the tarboush as respectable Arab headgear. To wear it was to link oneself to the landed (often, land-selling) urban establishment, and not the fighters, overwhelmingly of peasant origin, doing the killing and dying. Over one week in late summer 1938, by order of the insurgents, virtually the entire Arab male population—from soda vendors to supreme court justices—donned keffiyehs to help them evade detection.

Arab armed groups, bolstered by villagers enlisted as reinforcements, 1938 (Eltaher Collection)

Khalil Totah, principal of the American Quaker school in Ramallah, likened the checkered scarf to the liberty caps that French aristocrats were compelled to wear during the Revolution. He wrote the U.S. consul, noting that "the rebels have made a grand sweep in the direction of democracy. The fellahin do not conceal their delight at seeing their 'uppers,' the effendis, come down a peg and look like them."[73]

The bands also pressed the populace to cut all contact with the Mandatory courts. Instead, they inaugurated their own justice system, with four tiers of courts leading all the way back to the mufti's circles in Damascus. Penalties ranged from fines to lashes, exile, and even death.

Rebels commandeered supplies from villagers and stole typewriters from British offices. Haining reported on one such tribunal in Galilee "complete with its banner and documents; and a court of justice with wig, warders and witnesses. . . . They were conducting continuous and largely successful propaganda to show that their courts are more just, and above all more speedy, than the King's courts."[74]

In one instance armed men seized a Jewish engineer named Yehoshua Dafna along the coastal road, summarily tried him, and sentenced him to die. But the court allowed him to appeal, and after a new trial lasting five days, spared his life on the basis "that many trustworthy Arab witnesses have testified in favor of the accused, and considering that the man has not admitted to affiliation with the Zionist idea which we hate and loathe, and considering the fact that a death sentence would be catastrophic for his family and young children."

The court gave the anxious engineer five Palestinian liras, dressed him in Arab clothes, and returned him to the place of his abduction "so that it will be known in public that the Arabs perform lofty deeds in all they do."

The courts tended to operate under one of the handful of rebel leaders claiming to be the revolt's "commander-in-chief."[75] The two principal contenders for that mantle were particularly bitter rivals.

One was Abdel-Rahim al-Hajj Muhammad. Throughout the rebellion he had shown himself generally incorruptible, mostly abjuring intra-Arab score-settling and defying orders from the mufti's camp for extortion or execution. Even the British reluctantly admitted his mettle:

General Haining called him the "most patriotic and sincere" of the rebel leaders; the official history of the Palestine Police judged him the finest fighter since Fawzi Bey: "deeply religious . . . and devoted wholeheartedly to the Arab cause."[76]

The second, Aref Abdel-Raziq, hailed from the same part of Palestine but set an altogether different example. A mufti loyalist, he was according to Haining the exiled cleric's "principal agent in maintaining the terrorist grip." Forced contributions from villagers tended to wind up in his pocket, and internal communications show him ordering underlings to "finish up traitors who are dissenters to the nation." Abdel-Rahim complained sharply over the injustice of Aref's methods and the dangers they posed to the Arab revolution.[77]

In September 1938 those rival claimants and a number of other commanders met at Deir Ghassaneh, near Ramallah, to forge a unified front. The result was the "Bureau of the Arab Revolt," a joint military command under the two challengers' rotating control, all under the ostensible authority of the mufti's men in Syria.[78]

Nonetheless the rebel bands continued to operate with relative autonomy. Lacking a strict hierarchy, they seemed to move as if by instinct, filling the vacuum wherever the British army was over-exerted or under-resourced.

In the days surrounding the Tiberias attack, hundreds of insurgents made their way into Palestine's crown jewel: the Old City of Jerusalem. They closed its gates, set fire to the police station, and flew the Arab flag over Damascus Gate. For five days the Old City was theirs. The Great Revolt had registered its grandest, most symbolic military feat yet.

"There is nothing more lovely to the soul or dearer to the heart than the sight of the revolutionaries, the freedom fighters, and the volunteers entering holy Al-Aqsa Mosque fully armed and cheering," wrote one fighter who had served under Qassam. "The occupation of Jerusalem sent a profound and joyful echo through the Arab communities, which had placed such great hopes in Palestine's liberation."[79]

And yet the British had been making preparations of their own. Ending the Munich standoff and lifting war's shadow from Europe, even temporarily, had freed up gravely needed manpower for Palestine.

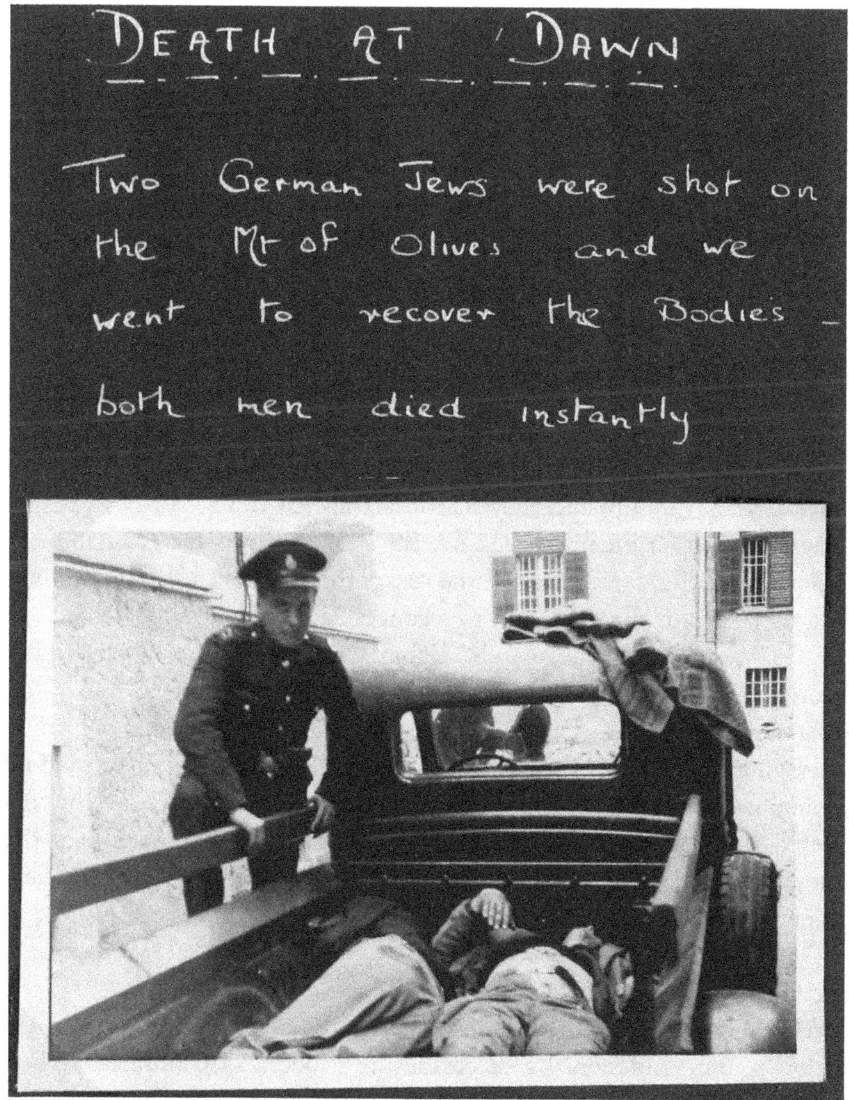

"Death at Dawn": Jewish murder victims in Jerusalem, probably 1938, from a Palestine policeman's album (NLI TMA 5589)

The War Office approved two full divisions—up to thirty thousand men. Within days the first units were shipped to Haifa and put directly to work.[80]

The latest siege of Jerusalem (history had seen two dozen before) began before daybreak on October 19. British forces deployed atop David's Citadel and the Rockefeller Museum. Two battalions, shod in tennis shoes for silence, readied outside the walls. One burst through Jaffa Gate from the west, another through Zion and Dung Gates from the south. Soldiers drew a north–south cordon along *Al-Wad* ("Valley") Street bisecting the Old City, cutting off the Muslim Quarter from the others. Combing the quarter's alleys, they walked residents ahead of them as human shields to deter snipers. The rebels fled beyond the walls or to the Haram al-Sharif, which troops still dared not enter or fire on.

It was all over within days, and with comparatively little loss of life. The Old City pacified, Tommies handed out thousands of bread loaves.

British battalions had put the rebels on the run for the first time in memory. By month's end they had reestablished control in Jaffa, whose Jews returned for the first time since the Bloody Day two and a half years prior. General Haining praised the recapture of these cities as a promising first salvo in the campaign to reconquer Palestine itself.[81]

In Westminster, meanwhile, Cabinet ministers were of one mind. Lord Halifax, the foreign secretary, spoke for all of them in remarking that at rock bottom, Palestine's troubles were political and not military, and no amount of blunt force could relieve them for long. A dual policy was in order, he said. The government must give the newly bolstered armed forces free enough rein to quell the rebellion, while at the same time directing "every effort to keeping open hopes of a political appeasement."[82]

RE-PEEL

Well over a year had passed since the Peel Commission made its partition recommendation. Its successor, the Woodhead Commission, had already spent three months in Palestine and interviewed more than fifty witnesses, both Britons and Jews. London's seemingly endless string of commissions provoked bemusement among Arabs and Jews alike—cynics labeled it "Re-Peel."[83]

Amid Hajj Amin's boycott, no Arabs came forward. Jerusalem Vice Mayor Hassan Sidqi Dajani, the mufti opponent who had once contemplated testifying, was found along the train tracks outside the city with two broken hands and two bullet holes in his forehead.[84]

The commissioners worked in strict secrecy, but as summer turned to autumn, whispers resurfaced that they planned to drastically alter the partition scheme, if not abandon it altogether, and to curtail or terminate Jewish immigration.[85]

"It appears likely that Woodhead Report will dispose of partition," the colonial secretary telegraphed Palestine in mid-October. It would strike a "death-blow" to partition, the chancellor of the exchequer told the Cabinet, venturing that once the Arabs saw the new policy, law and order might finally return.[86]

The report was due any day, but there was a new and unavoidable factor in Middle East geopolitics: the United States of America.

America's ambassador in London, the Boston financier Joseph Kennedy Sr., complained that the White House had been inundated with sixty-five thousand telegrams on Palestine. Western Union had only once before been so strained, he said, and it was over a U.S. Supreme Court seat. Kennedy, an inveterate Judeophobe, grumbled over the anti-Nazi ardor stoked by "the Jews, who dominate our press."[87]

Kennedy's opposite number, the British envoy to Washington, affirmed that nearly the entire American press corps objected to shuttering Palestine. "The New York press, as might be expected, appears to be solidly pro-Jewish," and even the *New York Times*—"Jewish owned but most Anglophil[e]"—editorialized against ending immigration. So did the *Washington Post*, which he added was similarly "Jewish-owned."

In any case, the trend extended beyond the Atlantic coast and beyond the Jews. Christian circles tended toward the same view, he wrote, and liberal ones were profoundly stirred by the Jews' maltreatment under Hitler. The telegrams to Roosevelt included twenty governors and senators, sixty members of Congress, and the postmaster, sheriff, and tax collector of Hawkinsville, Georgia. To prevent friction with Washington, the ambassador suggested delaying the document's release until after the November 8 midterm elections.[88]

And so it was: The Woodhead report saw light on November 9, 1938, at 4:00 p.m. GMT. As expected, its three-hundred-odd pages made for a dryer document than Peel's, and one less ambitious (or reckless, depending on perspective) in its aims. And as expected, its conclusions were those that partition opponents in Whitehall had worked assiduously to ensure that it would reach.[89]

The report presented three schemes. Plan A broadly followed the Royal Commission's lines, but was unanimously rejected by all four members. Such a plan, if it had any chance, rested on Peel's recommendation of population transfer, particularly from the Galilee heartland. London had already ruled out forced transfer a year earlier, and the new commission now deemed voluntary transfer a mirage: Arab farmers, it noted dryly, "have a deep attachment—shared by peasants all the world over—for their ancestral lands."[90]

In Plan B, the Jewish state was left without the hills in the Galilee's west and center where Arabs most heavily predominated. Nevertheless, those areas could not form part of the Arab state without endangering the security of the Jewish polity, and so were instead placed under permanent Mandate. One member preferred the plan, but three others overruled him, judging it "fundamentally wrong" that nearly one hundred thousand Arabs should be denied independence so as to secure that of the Jews.[91]

Finally, Plan C left the entire Galilee to the Mandate, granting the Jews a minuscule coastal state from Tel Aviv to Zichron Yaakov and a small southern enclave around Rehovot—less than five hundred square miles in all. The rest of Palestine (apart from Jerusalem, its environs, and the Negev, all of which stayed in the Mandate) would form the new Arab state.

The private papers of Charles Tegart, the security expert summoned from India, contain a sardonic sketch of his own proposed "Plan D": a corkboard of squares, triangles, and arches including a "Bedouin Legislative Council," "Communist Union," and "Preserve (for ex-members of commissions)." The central coast is marked, "This space free for advertising."[92]

Two commission members, including Woodhead himself, backed Plan C as the best partition plan they could devise (a third member found all three schemes so flawed he could not agree to any). Even that judgment, though, was half-hearted; they concluded that it too had so many problems that they could not in good faith recommend it. They had "no alternative but to report that we are unable to recommend boundaries . . . which will give a reasonable prospect of the eventual establishment of self-supporting Arab and Jewish States."[93]

The Chamberlain government said the commission had convinced it the political, administrative, and financial difficulties of partition were so formidable as to be insurmountable.

"It is clear that the surest foundation for peace and progress in Palestine would be an understanding between the Arabs and the Jews," it said, and invited representatives of Palestine's Arabs, of neighboring states, and of the Jewish Agency to a roundtable conference in London on future policy, "including the question of immigration." And it reserved the right to bar any leaders "responsible for the campaign of assassination and violence"—a conspicuous swipe at the mufti.[94]

The reference to immigration was an eleventh-hour addition. Days before the report's release, the Palestine high commissioner cabled Colonial Secretary MacDonald that immigration was "the whole crux of the matter and everything else is ancillary to it." Almost simultaneously, Britain's ambassador in Cairo communicated his own conviction, underlined for urgency, that no feasible policy was possible "*so long as immigration continues* . . . [the] Balfour declaration has been adequately implemented. We promised a national home not a national refuge for the Jews."[95]

It was a swift turnaround. Just weeks earlier MacDonald had told Arab leaders the Jews would never accept permanent minority status, that there could be no question of stopping immigration. Weizmann said the colonial secretary had promised him that rumors of abandoning Balfour's pledge were "nonsense."[96]

Re-Peel was looking more like Repeal, and many Arabs felt relief. The land would stay whole, and none of it would fall under Jewish domination. Moreover, the proposed London roundtable would be the first time the Arab states were recognized as official negotiators on Palestine. Despite Arab disappointment that immigration would continue, the conference would at least place the topic on the table. Many regarded these gains as themselves vindication of the Arab uprising and its sacrifices.[97]

The mufti took exception. His Arab Higher Committee blessed the conclusion that partition was unworkable, but regretted that it took imperial planners so long to alight upon a truth so "obvious from the very first day."

"All things based on wrong are wrong; and any future scheme to benefit the Jews at the expense of the Arabs will meet with the same fate," it said. The AHC did not recognize the legality of British obligations to the Jews, based as they were on "force and evil." The Arabs "alone are the owners of their country," and Jewish claims were predicated "on dreams and unsupported except by British bayonets."

As to the London summit, it said the Arabs "cannot regard the Jews as a party to the affair and will not enter into discussions with them as regards a solution." It wondered which Palestinian Arabs the authorities planned to invite if not the AHC, which enjoyed "the complete confidence of the Arab people," whom "no others" could possibly represent.[98] Officials privately acknowledged that the second claim was undeniably true: No one in Arab Palestine dared raise a hand without the mufti's assent. The only question was how much of that refusal stemmed from fear of the man and how much from favor.[99]

Dr. Khalidi confided to his diary that he was "furious" at Hajj Amin for speaking for the AHC members while they wasted away in their infernal Eden. The mufti was "putting on the same old disk again. . . . As if he was victorious and dictating terms to a defeated enemy—when instead Palestine is being overrun and screwed by dozens of British battalions arresting, hanging, routing and demolishing houses and the country is simply going to the dogs."[100]

But it was the Zionists who were most indignant over the Woodhead report. A "great blow, an immense encouragement to the Arabs," deplored Baffy Dugdale. It was "barefaced cynicism," rued Weizmann. The Jewish Agency said it could by no means serve as a basis for negotiations; the *Palestine Post* scorned its proposed statelet as a "concentration camp."[101]

Thirty minutes after the report's release, a German diplomat in Paris died from gunshot wounds inflicted by a Jewish teenager days earlier. Within hours Nazi stormtroopers and Hitler Youth were smashing, ransacking, and burning Jewish property across the Reich. More than 1,400 synagogues were damaged—some 250 destroyed completely—and 7,000 businesses. Thirty thousand Jews were detained and sent to Dachau, Sachsenhausen, and Buchenwald in the Nazis' first act of mass internment. Close to one hundred people were killed; hundreds more died later of injuries and of suicide.

The Nazis characterized the pogrom as a spontaneous popular outburst and dubbed it, euphemistically, Kristallnacht, the "Night of Broken Glass." They held the Jews themselves culpable and fined them one billion Reichsmark in damages.[102]

The diary of Ben-Gurion, compulsive note-taker, went blank for twelve days. Finally collecting himself, he called together his colleagues. The Jews stood before a war unlike any since the days of their revolt against Rome, he said. He was more convinced than ever that the people of Israel could no longer exist without the Land of Israel or outside of it. Mass immigration, legal or otherwise, was the only possible response.

"The month of November 1938 marks a new era, perhaps one never seen in the history of our people's torment. This is not merely organized destruction—systematic, physical elimination accompanied by the sadistic abuse of a community of 600,000 Jews—but a signal for the annihilation of the Jewish people the world over. I hope I am wrong. But I fear this is just the beginning."[103]

Chapter 7

The Burning Ground

THE ILLEGITIMATE SON OF A HIGHLANDS FARMHAND AND A MAID, Ramsay MacDonald rose to become Britain's first Labour prime minister. A fiery ideologue and orator, it was during his premiership that the Colonial Office sought to sharply curtail the Zionist experiment, in a White Paper following the 1929 Hebron riots.

At the time, furious Zionist lobbying against the retrenchment had centered on MacDonald's son Malcolm, then a newly minted backbench MP. The campaign ultimately succeeded—the prime minister overruled the planned changes in his famous letter to Weizmann—due in no small part to the younger MacDonald's efforts. He was on a first-name basis with Ben-Gurion, head of Labour's sister party in Palestine, and had, like so many colleagues, fallen under Chaim Weizmann's spell.

"I shall always watch developments there with sympathy," he had told Weizmann. "If I can be of any help at any time, you have only to let me know."[1]

In spring 1938 Chamberlain installed Malcolm MacDonald, just thirty-six, as secretary of state for the colonies, and as such the one man in the world most singly responsible for Palestine. The appointment prompted relief among the Holy Land's Jews, and head-shaking sighs among its Arabs.

"He is pro-Jew to his bones," scribbled Dr. Khalidi in his Seychelles diary, "and no improvement will be expected in Palestine during his term."[2]

Yet by year's end the Woodhead Commission had given voice to the Chamberlain government's unease over partition, and over the continued facilitation of the Zionist project itself. And though MacDonald was a Labourite and the prime minister a Tory, he was a faithful minister in a cross-party coalition for which appeasement was not yet a dirty word but stated policy, in both Europe and the Middle East.[3] In late November he rose to address Parliament.

MacDonald first saluted the British army. In recent weeks it had reoccupied Beersheba and Gaza, then Jericho—without even the benefits of trumpets as in the conquests of yore. Next he praised the Jewish national home. Its achievements had been "remarkable," turning wasteland to orchards, raising Tel Aviv from sand, building one of the few budget surpluses in a world still bruised by the Depression. The rampage that history would record as Kristallnacht was barely two weeks old, and "the tragedy of a people who have no country has never been so deep."

Now to the Arabs. "They can deny it as much as they like, but materially the Arabs in Palestine have gained very greatly from the Balfour Declaration," and modern health care and hygiene had granted life to infants who never would have drawn breath. But despite all that, he said, the Arabs continued to spurn such pragmatic considerations as vigorously and as completely as they had for two decades.

"The Arabs are afraid," he said. "They fear that it is going to be their fate in the land of their birth to be dominated by this energetic, new-coming people, dominated economically, politically, completely. If I were an Arab I would be alarmed."

The Palestine drama had two protagonists, he observed, and in the upcoming London conference, each would be allowed to argue for altering the Mandate to conform with their perception of both past pledges and present circumstances. If the two parties could not agree what that meant, His Majesty's Government would decide for them.[4]

MacDonald's principal point—that material gains were no replacement for self-determination—appears so self-evident to modern sensibilities as to verge on platitude. At the time, however, it was a sharp turn in the official discourse on Palestine.

It was the same logic Musa Alami had argued before Ben-Gurion under an ancient oak a few years prior. It was the argument George Antonius had unfolded so eloquently in his book. The speech was the "most conciliatory and understanding of Arab rights since the war," applauded Totah of the Ramallah Quaker school. "Government is showing a different attitude."[5]

That same day, Musa Alami was sipping tea at a hotel near Trafalgar Square when a man approached the table. He was an emissary from Mr.

Malcolm MacDonald, newly appointed colonial secretary, June 1938 (NPG x15374)

MacDonald, he said, and the secretary was very keen indeed that they should meet.

And so they did, the following morning, at MacDonald's office in Whitehall. Alami was in a pugnacious mood. His position had hardened since his exploratory meetings with Zionists in years past; he had come to doubt both their good faith and the value of Britain's word. He was gratified by the secretary's new tone in Parliament, but said it was regrettable the government had taken twenty years to recognize the Arabs had a case. He could not comprehend the value of the planned roundtable, or the insatiable English lust for commissions, committees, and conferences. Regardless, the figures of real influence were all outside Palestine: the Seychelles exiles and, whatever the authorities thought of him, the mufti—the one man in Arab Palestine whose word counted above all others'.

MacDonald was solicitous. He was, he said, still sympathetic to Zionist ideals, but at the same time genuinely hoped that the summit might allay Arab fears once and for all.

For the next two weeks they met almost daily. In due course they reached some preliminary understandings, and MacDonald agreed to provide Alami with a signed note laying them out. It said Britain would free the Seychelles exiles to attend the conference and even to confer with the mufti in Lebanon, and it hinted the Arabs would not be forced to negotiate directly with the Jews but only with their British hosts. And it expressed, for the first time, that London was willing to contemplate the eventual "independence of Palestine," implying that that independence could take many forms, including a sovereign Arab state with full control of immigration. The note amounted, in Alami's telling, to "just about all that the Arabs could hope for at that time."

By the time Alami reached the mufti's villa outside Beirut, the Seychelles men were already there, brimming with gratitude for his work in securing their freedom. As he read the note, translating each sentence to Arabic, "their eyes grew rounder and rounder, until at the end several of them jumped up and embraced me." Any thought of boycotting the conference was now abandoned—it seemed "half the battle for Palestine had been won in advance."[6]

Hajj Amin, however, remained barred from the summit. To save face, he announced he would serve as the Arab delegates' president, but "asking to be excused" would deputize his cousin and associate (and Alami's brother-in-law) Jamal Husseini. Dr. Khalidi, two more Seychelles deportees, and three others from the mufti's bloc rounded out the delegation.

Despite initial misgivings, Alami was himself persuaded to join. He telegraphed his close friend George Antonius, then on book tour in New York: "You are unanimously elected member secretary delegation please proceed London immediately."[7]

MacDonald was determined, despite the long odds that he himself admitted, that the conference yield some sort of agreement. He drafted a twenty-two-page memo for fellow members of the Chamberlain Cabinet, arguing that the time had come to "alter radically our outlook on the Palestine problem."

> *Hitherto British Governments and Parliaments have tended to be carried away, not simply by the tireless and clever propaganda of the Jews . . . but also by genuine enthusiasm for the conception of a new Jewish civilization in Palestine and by admiration for the astonishing achievements of Jewish money and settlers . . . I share that enthusiasm and that admiration. I do not write as an opponent of Zionism, but as a friend, and I say deliberately that we have paid too little heed to the rights of the Arabs of Palestine. We have been inclined to ignore them as a poor, weak people of whom we need not take very much notice.*[8]

He expected the Arab argument to pivot around the 1915–1916 McMahon-Hussein letters, thanks largely to the emphasis Antonius had given them in *The Arab Awakening* (the book was selling briskly ahead of the London conference—even Ben-Gurion bought a copy). Britain had long maintained that those letters' pledges of postwar Arab independence had excluded the Holy Land.[9] Yet MacDonald now wrote that Britain had been "rather confused about the whole business," and it was "a thousand pities that, perhaps owing to the exigencies of war," the correspondence had failed to make clear to the Arabs that "Palestine was not to be theirs."[10]

Now the cold reality was that the Empire stood at the ledge of another world war, and ensuring Arab and Muslim partnership was of paramount importance. The path to that cooperation lay in limiting immigration to assuage Arab fears of a Jewish majority, and announcing that Britain neither now nor in the future contemplated converting Palestine into a Jewish state. The Cabinet "should be prepared to go a long way to meet the Arab representatives. We should be prepared to go as far as we reasonably can."[11]

MacDonald envisioned the likeliest end result as neither a Jewish nor an Arab state, but a substantially modified Mandate with greater local representation and limits to land sales. On the knottiest question of all, immigration, he submitted two plans. One would let the Jews reach 40 percent—or at bare minimum, 35—at the end of a decade (they currently stood at 29 percent). The second was identical, save for an additional, crucial difference: After ten years "the Arabs would be given a veto" on any further Jewish immigration.

Chamberlain cheered the memo as "masterly."[12]

The air had palpably changed in the Arabs' favor. At Victoria Station, MacDonald received them in top hat; for the Jews, he donned a simple fedora.[13] The Arabs were feted at the Dorchester, the Savoy, the Ritz, and the Carlton; for the Jews more sensible accommodations sufficed. Women of London's smart set started sporting keffiyehs—Palestine's high commissioner received reports that they "found the sheikhs of the East fascinating while the Jews were merely ordinary and so boring."[14]

"The Arabs come to town," announced the *Evening Standard*. "Six successful rebels against British rule have arrived in London. Three of them speak perfect English. One is a Cambridge graduate, another a brilliant historian, a third an authority on health services," it reported (referring to Alami, Antonius, and Khalidi, respectively). Steeped in the "politics of the East," but trained in the manners of the West, they were the "brain trust" of the mufti, who had wrought terror in the Holy Land for nearly three years. "Yet they will be received in London not as criminals, nor even as suppliants. They come as victors. Mr. MacDonald proposes, but the Grand Mufti disposes."[15]

A Free Palestine

The London conference commenced February 7, 1939, at St. James's Palace, the red-brick Tudor edifice that was the royals' main London residence until replaced in the nineteenth century by the roomier Buckingham Palace just down The Mall. In the Picture Room, under vast portraits of dead monarchs dating to Henry VIII, Neville Chamberlain held court at the top table, flanked by his foreign and colonial secretaries. As the Arabs refused direct contact with the Jews, the prime minister was compelled to deliver nearly the identical, brief welcome speech twice.

"We all have a deep attachment, a special attachment, to Palestine," Chamberlain said. "You will be aware that my particular method of approach to peace is through understanding, and the first essential step to understanding is personal contact." Still, the demands on a premier's time meant that he would leave the heavy lifting to colleagues.[16] It was evident the conference would be MacDonald's.

Weizmann spoke first. In the name of the Jewish Agency delegation—one including not just representatives from Palestine but supporters from America, Britain, and Europe—he thanked the colonial secretary for his unfailing courtesy.

But once finished with pleasantries, Weizmann diverged sharply from his notes, launching into an impromptu discourse of the kind that appalled the more methodical Ben-Gurion but had always reliably, inexplicably bewitched the British.

He bemoaned Woodhead's unceremonious interment of Peel's partition plan, and with it, the possibility of Jewish control over immigration. The "fate of six million people" hung in the balance, he said, reiterating the figure he had stated before Peel. "Do you realize, Sir, that even if I were so bold as to ask for a very large figure of immigration—let me say 70,000–80,000 a year for the next five years—it would scarcely affect five percent of the people who are doomed to destruction, people like all of us here who sit in these magnificent surroundings, doomed to destruction!"

No "primitive country" in the world could absorb large numbers of Jews, he said. Even if it could, they would not show "the same fervor, the same apostolic devotion" anywhere but Palestine. "If Moses had chosen to bring us to America, our problem would have been easy, but he did not choose to do so, and he is not here to discuss it."

Weizmann's oration spread over two hours. He closed with an appeal to Britain's spiritual past and its imperial present:

> *I believe that you have become great because your work and your policy has been inspired by the Book which we have produced in Palestine. . . . From you, who have carried the ideals of justice, fairness, and good government into the remote corners of the globe, from you who have taken upon yourselves the white man's burden, I claim—and I believe I have the right to claim, with all respect and humility—that you should do justice to my people in this dark hour.*[17]

It was vintage Weizmann, and MacDonald was smitten, commending him for opening remarks so deftly interweaving reason and emotion. He had barely felt the time pass. "I do not know quite how our discussions are going to end in these next three weeks," he said, but he was certain they would be marked by the same frankness and sincerity they had always shown one another.[18]

MacDonald met the Arabs the next day. Nearly the entire delegation was present: eight Palestinians, along with representatives from five Arab states—Egypt, Iraq, Saudi Arabia, Transjordan, and Yemen—including three current or ex–prime ministers and a handful of princes. Most appeared in scarlet tarboush, but the Yemenis were turbaned and the Saudis arrayed in white headdress with black *aqal*.[19] Only Antonius—alert to his role as the Arabs' bridge to Britain—went bareheaded.

It was a distinguished assemblage, and reflected Whitehall's acquiescence to treating Palestine as a question for the entire Arab world, just as it was for global Jewry.

Jamal Husseini, the mufti's handpicked proxy as delegation president, made the opening statement. "The Arabs believe that their case was one of self-evident justice. It rests on the natural right of a people to remain in undisturbed possession of their country." That case "had nothing in common with anti-Semitism. It was not inspired by any hostility to the British people or to any other people. It was the case of a population, by nature peaceful and hospitable, trying to preserve the integrity of their country and to prevent the land to which they were deeply attached from being forcibly converted into a national home for another people."

The Arabs had been promised Palestine in the McMahon-Hussein letters, he maintained, and had never accepted the later contraventions of that pledge: the Balfour Declaration and the Mandate. He recapitulated their core demands: abandoning the Jewish national home, ceasing all Jewish immigration and land sales, and finally terminating the Mandate and replacing it with an independent Arab state.

With that, Jamal concluded the Arabs' opening remarks. MacDonald thanked him for a "very concise and clear statement." He would, if there was no objection, relay its contents to the Jews.

"As a matter of fact," Jamal replied, "we would like to ignore the existence of the other Conference as far as possible."

Antonius interjected, with perceptible embarrassment: "I think what our President meant was that we did not see the necessity of conferring with the Jewish delegation on the subject of our statement, because we consider that this is a statement made to you and to nobody else."[20]

A starker contrast could not have been drawn between the two parties' mastery of diplomacy than their respective opening gambits. Alami was exasperated: The Arabs, on their most favorable terrain in decades, were parading internal differences and niggling over minutiae. Even as the conference got underway, disputes persisted over their delegation's roster, with the mufti rejecting anyone from the Nashashibis' opposition camp.[21] For a national movement endeavoring to prove its ripeness for independence, the imagery was suboptimal.

In his weekly letter to his two unmarried sisters, Chamberlain wrote that the Arabs' opening salvo was "so completely intransigent & shows such an extremist spirit that I doubt the possibility of an agreement. In that case we shall just have to impose the settlement we have worked out ourselves."[22]

Still the talks went on. At one session Iraq's Prime Minister Nuri Said conveyed his deep regret that the conference was meeting "when world Jewry was suffering such an unparalleled misfortune. It was particularly unfortunate that at such a time the Arabs should feel compelled to resist the free entry of Jews into Palestine."

Islam had always guaranteed the position of the Jews, he said, and had given them shelter in ages when Christendom had cast them out. So it was in his own country, a former British mandate that six years before had struck its own independence treaty with the Crown. The abuses of Europe must not be a pretext for denying that same justice to Palestine, he said. "The Conference had aroused expectations which could not be allowed to fail."

In a triumph for Antonius, MacDonald agreed to create a British-Arab subcommittee to examine the McMahon-Hussein letters so central to the Arab case.[23]

A week into the summit, MacDonald dropped his bomb on the Zionists. It was not a concrete proposal but a mere "suggestion": soothing Arab fears by limiting immigration to keep the Jews below a certain rate of the populace. After ten years, no further immigrants would be allowed without Arab consent. Land sales would also be restricted. An independent state might eventually arise, neither Arab nor Jewish, with a parity agreement between the two.

The Jews were dumbfounded. Weizmann said it was inconceivable.[24]

To MacDonald's chagrin, the Arabs were likewise unimpressed. Jamal Husseini said Arabs and Jews had lived peaceably in Palestine for centuries until the British invasion, and under Arab independence their existence there would be far better than it was in Europe. Did he expect the country's majority to celebrate the humiliation of being relegated to the same level as the interlopers? It was out of the question.[25]

Chamberlain wrote his sisters: "I see no light. The Jews as far as I can judge are behaving admirably [and] most reasonable & pathetically patient in the face of brutal realities. The Arabs on the other hand are intransigent, unfair, prejudiced and unreliable."

Yet those same "brutal realities" appear to have left the prime minister untroubled. In the same letter he wrote, "I myself am going about with a lighter heart than I have had for many a long day. All the information I get seems to point in the direction of peace." The Fascist powers "had good cause to ask for consideration of their grievances, and if they had asked nicely after I appeared on the scene they might already have got some satisfaction." He and his wife Anne had dined at the German embassy "in an atmosphere of great cordiality," and "all of Italy was rejoicing" over his recent jaunt to Mussolini's Rome. He was "very hopeful about Spain," where the leftist elected government was on the brink of capitulation. He hoped to "get this surrender arranged, as clearly that is the best order . . . I think we ought to be able to establish excellent relations with Franco."

Events were "moving in the direction I want" and "if I am given three or four more years I believe I really might retire with a quiet mind."[26]

Two weeks passed before MacDonald could coax the Arabs—though not the Palestinians—to meet their opposite number. They agreed on condition that the talks remain unofficial: They would be speaking not with the Jewish Agency but with a collection of prominent figures linked to the Palestine question, all of whom happened to be Jews.

Egypt's delegate Ali Maher Pasha—chief adviser to King Farouk and formerly prime minister—said his country's Jews were his brothers. They had been his neighbors all his life, and were handsomely represented in the economy and the royal court. As to Palestine, the Arabs were, despite everything, willing to accept the four hundred thousand who were already settled there. The task before them was not re-litigating Palestine's past but determining its future. As ever, that question hinged on immigration.

Ben-Gurion said the Jews' position in Palestine was different from in Egypt—it was "their country," and they were in it by right.

Maher interrupted: What did he mean, "their own country"?

Ben-Gurion began to expound: For three millennia . . .

Maher again: Perhaps the Arabs would now claim Spain?

Afterward Ben-Gurion and Shertok approached Nuri Said and the Iraqis. They conversed together in Turkish, as in the old days before the war. The atmosphere was cordial, Shertok recorded, but it produced nothing.[27]

Over the coming days MacDonald's proposals grew ever farther-reaching, each time in favor of the Arabs.[28] Parity was off the table, and annual immigration quotas slashed. Ministers had originally authorized him to bring the Jews to 35 or 40 percent (meaning 150,000 to 300,000 more immigrants total) over ten years. Yet he was finding it "absolutely impossible" to get the Arab states—let alone the Palestinians, who "had proved very difficult"—anywhere near those figures.[29]

At last, in the waning days of February, he revealed his proposals.

The ultimate objective was to terminate the Mandate in favor of an independent Palestine state. Until then, and once calm was restored, the people of Palestine would play a steadily larger role in government. Jews would be kept to one-third of the population at most, meaning no more than seventy-five thousand of them could enter—and not over ten years but five. After that, any further immigration would rest on Arab consent.[30]

The Egyptian press got wind of the plan, inflated it further, and reported that the Arabs stood on the very doorstep of independence. All weekend, crowds across Palestine took to the streets, cheering Chamberlain and Hajj Amin and lifting policemen on their shoulders. Bonfires lit up Nablus; Nazareth called a public holiday.

Zionist reaction ranged from despondency to rage. The Jewish delegates considered walking out—Stephen Wise, the Reform rabbi who headed their American cohort, perceived Munich being replayed with the Jews in place of the Czechs.[31] In Palestine the Irgun launched grisly outrages in four cities at once.[32]

As the talks reconvened in early March, Jamal Husseini thanked the government for recognizing the justice of Arab demands. Yet merely promising steps toward independence was insufficient. The Arabs had been deceived too many times. They needed concrete commitments, and above all a timetable for independence.[33]

MacDonald replied that he was making very significant concessions. In due course "a free Palestine" would arise. Yet the Jews required guarantees—they were not an ordinary but an "extraordinary" minority, one needing extraordinary safeguards.[34]

Jamal proceeded: The Jews were "aggressive by nature," and if anyone needed protection it was the Arabs themselves. All would be well if Britain "ceased to treat the Jews as spoiled children. . . . Even God had failed to satisfy them, and how could Mr. MacDonald or Mr. Chamberlain?" The Palestinian delegates had enunciated their principles and would not move "one inch."[35]

MacDonald induced the Arab states to meet with the Jews one last time. Ali Maher addressed them in hushed tones. He "appreciated and respected the Zionist ideal for the reconstruction of their National Home," and if Palestine had been vacant, his and other Arab governments would have welcomed a Jewish state and been "glad to cooperate" with it. He commended the Jews' "perseverance and ability," but begged them to recognize realities. If they would slow their advance by suspending or at least reducing immigration, peace might be secured. Later, in a better atmosphere, they might be able to advance further—not by force, but with Arab goodwill.

Weizmann was reassured. He said he had never, in the twenty years since his desert encounter with Emir Faisal, heard such conciliatory words from an Arab of influence. From this starting point they could talk. For his part, if slowing the pace could foster quiet and compromise, he was amenable.

Enter David Ben-Gurion. He was "sorry to disturb the rejoicing," but he could see no common ground on that basis. Weizmann had rightly spoken of mutual concessions, but an immigration slowdown was a one-sided compromise and therefore impossible. They should not be discussing a slowing-down but a speeding-up, perhaps even a doubling. An aggravated MacDonald rebuked him coldly.[36]

Meanwhile the British-Arab subcommittee scrutinizing the McMahon-Hussein letters was winding up its work. In yet another blow to the Zionists, its members agreed that their report would affirm that the Arab interpretation of the correspondence had "greater force than has appeared hitherto," and that Palestine's exclusion from the area of Arab independence was not made "so specific and unmistakable" as previously thought.[37]

In Cabinet, MacDonald told ministers the proceedings were reaching "the end of their tether." Foreign Secretary Halifax favored the Arab veto as an incentive toward cooperation. "Hitherto the Jews had not made any attempt to work with the Arabs," he said. With "some reluctance," Chamberlain too endorsed MacDonald's general plan. He would have liked "to have done rather more for the Jews, who might be considered to have been rather roughly treated" in light of "the various expectations held out to them in previous years."[38]

Weizmann requested a final private audience with the prime minister and took a final walk, in his words, down "the *via dolorosa* to Downing Street." He knew it was all over, he said. He had come to take his leave. Chamberlain said he admired the Jews' courage—he wished it could be otherwise, but his advisors had presented arguments that were simply incontestable.

Weizmann likened him to a marble statue. "He was bent on appeasement of the Arabs and nothing could change his course."[39]

Early the next morning seven German army corps moved unopposed into the Czech heartland. It was a flagrant breach of the Munich pact, and of Hitler's repeated avowals that he wished merely to unite the Germans, not to subjugate their neighbors. At 9:30 a.m. his troops entered Prague.

Half an hour later Chamberlain convened his weekly Cabinet meeting. Czechoslovakia was first on the agenda. Next was Italy—would the *Duce* endorse Hitler's latest aggression?—and then Franco's most recent offensive in Spain. MacDonald's Palestine proposal was relegated to fifth. He told ministers these were great advances in recognizing the "rights and position of the Arabs," and assured them they were "fair, just and right." The Cabinet approved.[40]

Presenting his plan to the Arabs that afternoon, MacDonald again found them less than impressed. Antonius dismissed the notion of a state defined as neither Arab nor Jewish: Any democracy, if not forced to uphold special privileges for specific constituencies, "was bound to take on the color of the majority."

Alami felt likewise misled, even betrayed. Their earlier, face-to-face meetings had led him to believe that an Arab state—and an end to

Jewish immigration—was in the offing. Now he had come to doubt Britain would ever honor its promised Arab veto on that immigration, and was alarmed that MacDonald had balanced it with a *Jewish* veto on declaring Palestine's independence if the Jews felt their rights were being infringed. This "double veto" scheme, he feared, would incentivize the Zionists to withhold cooperation and do whatever possible to postpone independence.[41]

But Dr. Khalidi sensed that the climate had changed. Quiet for most of the proceedings, he now spoke up: After the "transitional period," would Britain's obligation to the Jewish national home be at an end?

MacDonald replied in the affirmative.

"Was it intended that there should be not one single immigrant more after the 75,000?"

In "no circumstances would a single Jew over and above that figure be admitted," MacDonald confirmed. "This was a revolutionary change in British policy, a reversal of policy on the most important question," he said. "The Jews would now not be able to count on British support in the matter which was most important to them."

"It was the view of His Majesty's Government that this should have the effect of making the Jews anxious at last to get co-operation with the Arab majority," MacDonald added. He "wished to emphasize the magnitude of the change involved in the British proposals on immigration. The Jews had certainly recognized this."[42]

So they had. When MacDonald presented them the plan that evening, Weizmann and Ben-Gurion declined to attend, sending Shertok, the Yishuv's "foreign minister," instead.

MacDonald read out the text, but Shertok stayed silent. After some time the colonial and foreign secretaries rose from their seats and, per custom, went through to the next room for tea.

"Are we going to the Last Supper?" Shertok asked. MacDonald missed the allusion, saying only that he hoped they could dine together again soon.

Shertok tried again. When some classical musicians began playing in the palace courtyard, he asked if it was a funeral march for the Jews.

This time the secretary had a ready reply. "Your funeral? It is my funeral."[43]

The rejection filled all of one sentence. "The Jewish Delegation, having carefully considered the proposals communicated to them by His Majesty's Government on March 15th, 1939, regret that they are unable to accept them as a basis for agreement, and decide, accordingly, to dissolve."[44]

Jamal Husseini spoke the final word for the Arabs. The plan was open to serious objection, both in terms of justice and practicability. The transition period to end the Mandate had no time limit, thereby allowing and even encouraging the minority to delay independence by withholding cooperation. Restricting land sales was insufficient—a full ban was required. He was gratified that the government had at last recognized that Jewish immigration must end, but insisted that step could not wait. The current Jewish population was simply "larger than the country can support."[45]

Yusuf Hanna surveyed the scene from Jaffa. "The Jews may have a case, and a strong one too, but their case is one based on humanity and official documents and promises," he wrote Joseph Levy. All of these were "nonsensical considerations in a period of crude realism."

The Arabs, by contrast, had a "natural case"—a people, living on its land, that wished to rule itself. And though he yearned for Arab independence, Hanna feared Palestine's leaders were not up to the task. The Nashashibi opposition lacked competence and integrity, and he was disgusted by the intransigence, intolerance, and ruthlessness of the mufti's coterie.

"There is not an Arab who wants to see himself ruled by the Jews, but there is not also an Arab with sense who wants to see himself ruled by assassins."[46]

THE BIG THREE

Abdel-Rahim al-Hajj Muhammad was in Damascus. He had made the perilous crossing from Palestine to meet the mufti acolytes who ran the rebellion nerve center they called the Central Committee for National

Jihad. His purpose was not to refill his dwindling coffers or to restock on arms or ammunition, but to issue his own ultimatum. Arabs were murdering Arabs at alarming rates. Without assurances against further assassinations, he told them, he would quit the battlefield.

"I am afraid that our cause will fail since every one of us is trying to work independently," Abdel-Rahim wrote another rebel commander. "I am most anxious because our work has become for personal interests."[47]

Several months earlier Fakhri Nashashibi, a young effendi in the anti-mufti opposition, had published an open letter. Titled "A Voice from the Tombs of Arab Palestine," it held Hajj Amin responsible for the deaths of thousands of fellow Arabs. Among the Arabs were deep reservoirs of resentment against the mufti, the manifesto insisted, but anyone who dared raise his voice was killed, cowed into praise, or compelled to flee the country.

He too, he said, had received countless death threats. Hosting the foreign press in Jerusalem, he pointedly refused to don a keffiyeh but sported the Ottoman-era tarboush. "One day every Arab in Palestine will be able to speak freely, but not if the Mufti is allowed to return!"[48]

The British doubted Nashashibi's virtue, suspecting his high-flown oratory owed more to personal and familial ambition than the redemption of Palestine. They reckoned that he and his uncle Ragheb—the family patriarch and ex-mayor of Jerusalem—lacked both scruples and influence, and were probably subsidized by the Jews.[49]

Those intuitions, particularly the last one, were sound. Ragheb had previously asked Ben-Gurion for money to fight the mufti in the press and in the hills, but the Yishuv leader had rebuffed him as unreliable.[50] Now the Zionists decided to gamble on the younger Fakhri (despite deeming him "rash, frivolous, and sometimes a womanizer and a drinker"), hoping to capitalize on growing disillusionment with the rebellion and to cultivate a homegrown counterweight to Hajj Amin. They sent him several crates of weapons through a Haganah man of Sephardic roots who had been a college mate in Beirut.

The armed units that the Nashashibis called the "peace bands" soon earned the cautious backing of the military. Several thousand *fellaheen* attended a parley at Yatta, near Hebron, where Fakhri declaimed

Abdel-Rahim al-Hajj Muhammad (marked by an X) with comrades near Tulkarem, 1938 (Eltaher Collection)

jeremiads against the mufti in classical Arabic that the rural folk struggled to understand, while British officers nodded along and added a few words on law and order.

The stated aim of the Nashashibi bands was to restore calm to Arab villages ravaged by gunmen. But more often than not, they seemed driven chiefly by the thirst for retribution against political and family adversaries. It was not just Amin's men, it soon emerged, who perceived the Arab Revolt as an opportunity for settling blood debts.[51]

It was one such "peace band" that in late March 1939, in a joint effort with Zionist intelligence and British troops, located Abdel-Rahim at the village of Sanur, in Samaria. There he met his end, shot through the heart by British bullets, along with his lieutenant.

Shops across the country shuttered in mourning.

"I saw with my own eyes a big officer taking his handkerchief out of his pocket and cover Abdel-Rahim's face with it," said one farmer. It may have been Geoffrey Morton, police chief of nearby Jenin, who remembered: "He was a man of comparatively high principles who sincerely believed in the cause for which he was fighting. He had his own code of honor, and as far as lay in his power he made his many followers adhere to it."

Like a proud hunter, Morton basked in Britain's mounting results in bringing the Arab uprising to ground: "Nothing succeeds like success."

Two weeks later Abdel-Rahim's arch-foe Aref Abdel-Raziq surrendered to the French at Palestine's boundary with Syria. Hounded by British forces, he had not eaten in days and was, per official reports, "in a state of complete physical collapse."[52]

Yusuf Abu Dorra was the last of the armed leaders whom senior officers called the Big Three. "A black-bearded, undersized little man in the middle forties," in Morton's description, "he was a vicious and unscrupulous killer who showed no mercy to man, woman or child."

The previous summer, at the revolt's peak, Abu Dorra could boast several hundred men at his command. Since then, authorities had placed a handsome bounty on his head and twice nearly nabbed him. As the dragnet grew wider, he fled across the river to the dry wilds of Transjordan.

In late July 1939 Abu Dorra fell into a British ambush. In his kit soldiers found a general's uniform, complete with red cuffs and epaulets. Crowds cheered him as he was led back across the Jordan for trial, but his defeat seemed to embody that of the uprising itself, mortally weakened not just by army maneuvers but Arab infighting, imprisonment, exile, and sheer exhaustion.[53]

In Haifa, another diminutive commander with visions of a generalship—Bernard Montgomery—wrote a comrade back home.

"The rebellion out here as an organized movement is *smashed*; you can go from one end of Palestine to the other looking for a fight and you can't get one; it is very difficult to find Arabs to kill; they have had the stuffing knocked right out of them."[54]

The Great Revolt had exacted a withering toll on Palestine. About 500 Jews had been killed and some 1,000 wounded. British troops and police suffered around 250 fatalities in their ranks. But the most onerous price of all was paid by the Arabs themselves: At least 5,000—perhaps more than 8,000—were dead, of whom at least 1,500 likely fell at Arab hands. More than 20,000 were seriously wounded.[55]

At least 7,500 Arab-owned firearms, 1,200 bombs and grenades, and 165,000 rounds of ammunition had been confiscated. Perhaps one in every five Muslim men had been detained.[56] As many as 2,000 homes were demolished.[57]

Forty thousand people had fled the country—as many as twenty-five thousand sought refuge in Beirut alone—disproportionately representing the political, commercial, and landed elite.[58]

The Arab economy was crippled. Crops had dried up as landowners fled and peasants were required to provision, feed, and fund thousands of armed men. Thousands of Arabs lost government jobs due to reduced public revenues and doubts over their allegiance. In the towns, the Arab boycott of Jewish businesses and buyers, which continued informally throughout the revolt, slashed Arab income. Half of all cargo that once passed through the port at Jaffa was now diverted to the Jews' port at Tel Aviv.[59]

Forcing the British retreat from the Balfour Declaration was the Arab uprising's singular, undeniable achievement. But the political, social, military, and economic fabric of Arab Palestine was savagely, irreparably torn.

More than one hundred Arabs were hanged for offenses committed during the revolt. Abu Dorra would be among the last of them, sentenced for the murder of a village mukhtar—just one, per Morton, "of his many brutal crimes."

On the appointed day he grasped the officer's hands warmly with both of his own and blessed him. "*As-salaamu aleikum, Morton Effendi!*"

The police chief recalled how he climbed the gallows: hands bound, gait steady, head upright, a smile on his face.

"In the few short years of his reign of power he had been a ruthless killer, but he died like a man."[60]

Denouement

News of MacDonald's proposals at St. James's had done much to sap the waning vigor of the revolt. He was hopeful that an official policy statement, a White Paper, would do the rest.

But there were still the Jews to worry about. The colonial secretary told ministers that his solution, "while pacifying the Arabs, might drive the Palestinian Jews into revolt," having "dashed to the ground" their hopes of many years. It was true, he admitted, that if not for the pressures of impending war, he would not have agreed to certain concessions of which he was not "convinced on merits." Yet he was persuaded that the planned White Paper was "wise and just in essentials. It was high time for us to set a limit to the more extravagant interpretations of the Balfour Declaration."[61]

To balm the wound, he urged that Britain consider immediately opening part or all of an imperial colony for Jewish settlement, or even a sovereign Jewish state. Ministers deemed British Guiana, on South America's Atlantic coast, the most promising available site. They had dispatched an Anglo-American fact-finding commission there a few months prior, and were relieved to learn that its initial report had not dismissed the proposition entirely. MacDonald advised that the Cabinet release the Guiana report ahead of the White Paper. Chamberlain concurred.[62]

MacDonald next invited Chaim Weizmann to his Essex country house for tea. The grizzled Zionist grudgingly accepted.

Their meeting proved deeply distressing for both. Weizmann fulminated that his host, who for years had professed his friendship, was now abandoning the Jews to their assassins—Hitler at least showed his contempt openly rather than couch it in tortuous legalities. The younger man tried to muster reassurances on possibilities outside Palestine, but his mere mention of "Guiana" met a contemptuous sweep of the hand. The "most unpleasant afternoon of my life," Weizmann told Wingate's mother-in-law, now a trusted pen pal; he had never spoken so rudely to any man.[63]

MacDonald's recollection was comparably distasteful. His father—an early sympathizer with Labor-Zionism—had recently died, and he had always venerated the man. Now Weizmann thundered that the ex-premier "must be turning in his grave" at his son's breach of faith.

"It was the cruelest thing that has ever been said to me—and it was spoken by one of the kindliest of men," MacDonald said. "I realized then that he had come to hate and despise me . . . I absolutely respected him for hating me and never lost my admiration for him. But it was very sad."[64]

On May 17, 1939, the Chamberlain Cabinet approved the Palestine Statement of Policy for publication at 7:00 p.m. that evening.[65]

Better known as the MacDonald White Paper, its text mostly mirrored the secretary's proposals at the London conference. Like him, it heaped praise on the national home, which had won the "admiration of the world" and brought "pride to the Jewish people." It leveled "unqualified condemnation" at the "methods employed by Arab terrorists against fellow-Arabs and Jews alike," but warned that fear of indefinite Jewish immigration risked sowing a perpetual and "fatal enmity" between the two peoples that called Palestine home.

The statement announced unequivocally that it was not government policy that Palestine should become a Jewish state. Instead, the Mandate would be replaced within ten years by neither an explicitly Arab nor Jewish state but an independent "Palestine state," accompanied by a treaty protecting the Crown's strategic interests. Until then the country would move toward significantly greater local involvement in governance, and toward restrictions against land sales.

As to immigration, the government could not accept the Arab demand for a total stoppage, which would prove ruinous to Palestine's economy, Jewish and Arab alike. And it could not ignore the predicament of Europe's Jews, which Palestine "can and should make a further contribution" to alleviating.

Immigration, however, would no longer be open-ended. Rather, for the next five years it would be limited to the total figure stated at St. James's—seventy-five thousand—and thereafter, only with the agreement of all sides. Without that consent, His Majesty's Government would "not be justified in facilitating, nor will they be under any obligation to facilitate, the further development of the Jewish National Home by immigration regardless of the wishes of the Arab population."[66]

Lastly, on one key point the White Paper differed from MacDonald's offer in London: In place of his earlier "double veto" formula, the Arab veto now stood alone.[67]

"It is as bad as we thought," wailed Dugdale. The Jewish Agency called it a rank betrayal, a "surrender to Arab terrorism," and a "cruel blow" delivered in their hour of greatest need. Jewish mobs in Jerusalem

Tel Aviv residents watch police chase Jews protesting the White Paper, May 1939
(GPO D836-050)

bombed the immigration office. In Tel Aviv they ransacked the district office, hurling its furniture into the street and setting it on fire. A Jew with a Mauser semi-automatic shot dead a constable named Lawrence. Ben-Gurion condemned the deed but warned General Haining that the British were witnessing the "beginning of Jewish resistance."[68]

In America, reactions were only marginally more favorable. Roosevelt wrote his secretary of state of having read the document "with a good deal of dismay . . . it is something that we cannot give approval to by the United States." The *New York Times* editorialized that it would "not satisfy the Arab extremists, although it goes far toward meeting Arab demands. Still less will it satisfy the Zionists, whose essential claim it denies by making the Jews a permanent minority in the homeland they have colonized with heroic enthusiasm and extraordinary success."[69]

In his home outside Beirut, Hajj Amin al-Husseini convened members of the AHC. For several weeks they held daylong meetings, broken up only by generous lunches served at the mufti's table. Izzat Tannous, a doctor of Christian origin who lived in Jerusalem's Talbiya quarter, headed the Arabs' public-relations office in London. He recalled the scene:

> *The morale was high and the expectation for a brighter future was higher. . . . But this sweet dream did not last long. The discussion became more strained as some of us began to realize that Hajj Amin was not in favor of accepting the White Paper. . . . The remaining fourteen members were not only strongly in its favor, but were determined to put an end to the negative policy the Arab leadership had been adopting heretofore. . . . Consequently, the sole concern of the Committee was now concentrated on convincing Hajj Amin that his negative stand was extremely detrimental to the Arab cause and was serving, unintentionally, the Zionist cause.*

The White Paper was filled with loopholes and ambiguities, the mufti told them, its transition period was too long, and its reference to the "special position" that the future state would have to grant the Jewish national home was an insult.[70]

The real reason for his foot-dragging, however, likely lay elsewhere: the continued British refusal to allow him a triumphant homecoming to Palestine.[71]

The White Paper faced one more hurdle before it could become Crown policy: Parliament. It was treacherous terrain for MacDonald, who complained that Westminster was captured by a "considerable balance of prejudice in favor of the Jewish case." Before addressing the Commons he allowed himself a rare cigarette.[72]

"I wish with all my heart that Palestine were an empty land so that its bounds were the only limits set to the remarkable creative work of these devoted people rebuilding a National Home," he said. But Palestine never was, alas, vacant, and when the British arrived two decades prior, it was already home to some six hundred thousand souls "whose ancestors had been in undisturbed occupation of the country for countless generations."

Since then, swelling Arab anxieties over Zionism had exploded into three years of "grimly sustained revolt," planting hatred that threatened to become "a permanent source of friction and strife" throughout the Middle East.

As to the existing national home, he was not concerned: It would not be weak or vulnerable as critics contended, but was now a confident, disciplined community whose economic clout alone had made it "unconquerable." He was convinced his program would let each of Palestine's twin societies continue to develop, but with neither subordinating the other.

The next day it was Winston Churchill's turn. At sixty-four he was enjoying a professional rebirth, emerging from a decade in the political wilderness to become the most tireless and searing critic of Chamberlain's appeasement schemes.

"I was from the beginning a sincere advocate of the Balfour Declaration," he said. That proclamation was not "an ill-considered, sentimental act," but one made with the greatest deliberation and, he hastened to add, warmly endorsed at the time by Chamberlain himself. In limiting immigration, the current proposal referred liberally to his own White Paper, issued while colonial secretary in 1922, which set "economic absorptive capacity" as the measure for fixing Palestine's immigration quotas. He now stated for the record that the "main purpose . . . the whole tenor" of his earlier paper had been to safeguard the "paramount pledge and obligation" of facilitating the Jewish national home.

There was much to object to in the new White Paper, he said, but he would limit himself to a single point: the Arab veto. "Now, there is the breach; there is the violation of the pledge; there is the abandonment of the Balfour Declaration; there is the end of the vision, of the hope, of the dream."

It was strange indeed, he said, for Britain to turn away from Palestine when "the local disorders have been largely mastered. It is stranger still that we should turn away when the great experiment and bright dream, the historic dream, has proved its power to succeed."[73]

The Labour-led opposition uniformly opposed the new policy. MP Tom Williams said it abrogated Balfour's "whole object and purpose"; Herbert Morrison said a future Labour government would not necessarily honor the "evil" decree. When the ballot was taken, all 159 opposition MPs voted against. They were joined by 20 Tories, and another 110 abstained.[74] The measure passed, but with an unsettlingly slim majority of 89 compared to the usual 250 in a chamber dominated by Chamberlain's own Conservatives.[75]

Years later, MacDonald acknowledged the motives that underlay his White Paper. "The Jews would be on our side in any case in the struggle against Hitler," he said. "Would the independent Arab nations adopt the same attitude?" If the Arab states opposed Britain, "we would probably lose the war and the Jews would lose the National Home. There may have been an element of cynicism in all this . . . but it was an attempt to . . . look far ahead."[76]

In the *Filastin* newsroom, Yusuf Hanna marveled at the change. "Who among the Arabs ever dreamt to get so much?" he wrote in a letter. "Immigration finished. Sale of lands finished. Dangers of Jewish predominance and such nonsense finished." The force of arms had been necessary at first, three years earlier, "when the nation was slumbering" and the Arab states shut their eyes to Palestine. Now, he considered it "a crime against this beloved country that I should use my pen anymore for any further troubles." Nine Arabs out of ten welcomed the White Paper, he reckoned, and anyone rejecting it must be "an Arab ass or an Arab traitor."[77]

Others agreed. The Nashashibi opposition privately commended the new policy as a "good augury" that had earned their "almost unanimous welcome." Antonius judged it a reasonable basis for discussion, a "startling advance" from earlier plans.[78] Rebel leaders in Damascus said the same, castigating Hajj Amin for having "desecrated the holy rebellion" for his own selfish aims. The fighter-chronicler Subhi Yasin wrote that there was "not even one loyal and perceptive Arab who did not approve of the White Paper."[79]

Yet on May 30, a week after Parliament gave its blessing, the mufti's Arab Higher Committee announced its formal rejection.

"The National Home has always been the fundamental cause of the calamities, rebellions, bloodshed and general destruction which Palestine has suffered," it said. The Arabs appreciated the government's newfound understanding on immigration, but could see no reason for not ceasing it immediately. The contention that such a step would be unjust to the Jews was absurd: The national home was itself built on injustice, and they could not see "how an unjust cause can invoke justice." Any further bloodshed would, "before God, history and humanity," fall on Britain's head.

"The Arab people have expressed their will and said their word in a loud and decisive manner, and they are certain that with God's assistance they will reach the desired goal: PALESTINE SHALL BE INDEPENDENT WITHIN AN ARAB FEDERATION AND SHALL REMAIN FOREVER ARAB."[80]

Rachel Loves Her People

The mainstream Zionist leaders had announced their complete and categorical repudiation of the White Paper. The Irgun had its own way of demonstrating objection, both to the new policy and to those very same leaders. The month following the White Paper was marked by attacks targeting civilians almost every day.

One morning some Irgun men stole a car belonging to Weizmann's brother, drove to Haifa's Lower City, and shot down three Arabs. On another occasion they went to a village called Biyar Ades, which they believed was billeting armed bands, but finding none they murdered four women and a man in their homes, staking the Zionist banner in the ground as they left.

At Jerusalem's Rex Cinema, a screening of *Tarzan's Revenge* was shattered by twin booms, later traced to candy boxes in the mezzanine. Eighteen people were wounded, mostly Arabs and, in the group's words, Jews "who found it appropriate to spend their time in an Arab cinema." And in the city's Russian Compound quarter, a young veiled woman speaking Arabic and carrying a fruit basket was found to be hiding a powerful time bomb. At trial she refused to testify but gave her first name as Rachel and her last as *Ohevet-Ami*—"Love-My-People."

Finally, at the long-suffering vegetable market in Haifa, a donkey-borne bomb produced a blast heard fifteen miles up the coast in Acre. Of the twenty or more people killed, half were women and children.

In the three years of the revolt, Irgun attacks had killed at least 250 Arabs and wounded hundreds more.[81]

From Jerusalem, High Commissioner MacMichael cabled that the latest murder campaign "came at a most untimely juncture," just when moderate Arab opinion was gaining influence in the White Paper's wake. "Unquestionably the Jews as a whole are genuine in their condemnation of these outrages, both on tactical and moral grounds, but they would do well, if ever they hope for Arab goodwill, to take strong steps . . . the Yishuv, for all their well-known discipline and organization and their glib lip service to the cause of decency, *do* nothing to put a stop to the campaign."[82]

He had discounted the degree to which the White Paper had pushed the Zionist establishment closer to the Revisionists' frame of mind. The Haganah had recently launched its own secret "special operations" branch, answering straight to Ben-Gurion, where members put into practice the knowledge they had gained in Sadeh's Field Squads and Wingate's SNS.

When a Jewish train conductor was slain near Haifa Bay, the special operations unit converged on Balad al-Sheikh, where Haganah intelligence had learned a wanted armed-band leader was lodging with his lieutenants. As Ben-Gurion told colleagues: "Once the names were known, the guys went into the village one night and brought out the people according to a list they had. They found five people and they shot them."

It was, according to his description, a pinpoint retaliation of the kind the Haganah had never waged before. But there were others in the group who saw the apparently loosened terms of engagement as license to slake their own appetites for vengeance. When a kibbutz member was killed beside the Sea of Galilee, the head of one such "special" unit brought his men to the village of Lubya, shot through the windows of a home chosen at random, and tossed in a grenade, killing three.[83]

"Creatures who slaughter women and children in cold blood . . . create a kind of horror, and cooperation with their kith and kin becomes repugnant," wrote MacMichael. He only hoped the Jews' "acute perception of which side their bread is buttered may enable the forces of moderation to win through."[84]

We Shall Meet Again

The White Paper did not resolve Britain's Palestine predicament, but it did postpone its reckoning. That, after all, was the objective: providing the diplomatic backing that, combined with military force and the Arabs' own dissension, would bring the Great Revolt to a close before the start of a world war. For it was now evident to everyone—even to Neville Chamberlain himself—that a global confrontation was inevitable. The only question was when.

Orde Wingate was recalled to England—General Haining had decided that his fervid Zionism was rendering his service "nugatory and embarrassing." Before departing the Promised Land, Wingate jotted down a note. Headlined "*Prophecy*," it predicted, "Hitler conquest of Poland in late summer or early autumn brings down govt's of Chamberlain and Daladier"—the British and French premiers at Munich—"replacing them by administrations who will reverse the policy in Palestine."

On the ship out of Haifa he penned a characteristically exhaustive and unbidden memo on Palestine's place in the coming war. His urgent advice: reverse the White Paper, withdraw the troops, raise a Jewish army, and let it secure the country. At Gibraltar he handed the paper to General Edmund Ironside, newly named the army's top commander in the Middle East.

Ironside, who had recently visited Palestine, was noncommittal: "I must confess that I have been a little frightened of the strength and sincerity of Zionism. To see Jews in such numbers is somewhat terrifying."[85]

Bernard Montgomery was likewise recalled to lead a division. "I shall be sorry to leave Palestine in many ways as I have enjoyed the 'war' out here," he wrote. "But I feel there is a sterner task awaiting me at home."

Monty summoned his junior officers. "When you get done, have a jolly good leave, then get down very quickly to learning how to fight Germans. You won't have much time."[86]

Planners at Whitehall hoped that the mufti, despite having snubbed the White Paper, would announce that the Arab world's interests lay with the democracies. They would be disappointed. Yusuf Hanna tried to explain the unexpectedly fulsome support found among certain Palestinian Arabs for the Reich:

> *When the Arabs were, in their opinion, oppressed by England for the sake of the Jews, Hitler was persecuting the Jews and defying the Great Empire. What the Arabs could not do for themselves, Hitler was doing for them. This is the psychology of the public. . . . In their present frame of mind, the Arabs believe they are weak and are badly treated by the powerful England. . . . The Arabs' love of Hitler is only based on this conception.*[87]

Among the Jews, Ben-Gurion had adopted a new credo: "We are faced, in the age of Hitler, with the necessity of *combative Zionism*." That meant renewed investment in the Haganah, rapid expansion of settlements—seven arose in a single day—and prodigious immigration, whether legal or not.

"The war now is over the Jews who are not in the Land," he said. "An immigration war."

Ben-Gurion had begun to despair of the British. He could see their imperial sun setting and another one rising across the ocean. "There is one man who can save us, and that's President Roosevelt."

"War is coming," he wrote Weizmann. "Terrible tragedies are on our doorstep."[88]

On August 16, 1939, 1,500 Jews from thirty-five countries converged on Geneva's opulent *Grand Théâtre*—a few miles from the League of Nations and a short boat ride from Evian—for the biennial Zionist Congress.

Weizmann led the proceedings. He felt a sense "of unreality and irrelevance," of being subsumed by two shadows simultaneously: the

White Paper on Palestine and an approaching world war threatening untold destruction.

Three days in, the first waves of German troops massed near the Polish border. Three days after that came the staggering revelation of Germany's nonaggression treaty with the Soviet Union. The pact's secret clause, dividing the land between the two countries among themselves, would not be known for years, but the agreement itself was enough to sow terror. There was now no major obstacle to Hitler's conquest of Eastern Europe, home to the majority of the world's Jews.

Weizmann moved quickly to wrap up the Congress, addressing it for the last time on the night of August 24.

"Beyond the heavy clouds amassing over the future, with a heavy heart, I take leave of my friends," he said. "I have but one wish: that we get to see each other again in life, and if so, to continue our work, and perhaps light will again shine from the darkness."

To the representatives from the Yishuv, he tried to summon words of encouragement: "Your position is precarious, but behind you stand the Jews of the world."

To those from Eastern Europe, he said in Yiddish that he prayed to God their fate would not be like that of their German brethren. "My heart is overflowing. I can say only this. . . . Our nation is eternal and our land everlasting. We will work, fight and live, until the days of calamity are passed. See you in peace."

Many in the audience wept. "Never shall I go through a more moving scene," wrote Dugdale. On the platform, Weizmann embraced the other delegates "as if he would never let them go."

Most of the Eastern European Jews were never seen again.[89]

For it was exactly a week later that a German battleship opened fire before dawn at a Polish naval base, and two thousand planes and tanks poured over the border with a million and a half troops loyal to Hitler. Two days later Britain and France declared war, and the world hurled headlong into the inferno.

Epilogue

The Revolt Rages On

THREE-QUARTERS OF A CENTURY ON, THE ENORMITY OF THE CRIMES perpetrated by Nazi Germany and its collaborators continues to strain human comprehension. Entire extended families and even whole towns were machine-gunned in open pits or gassed and incinerated in a system of industrialized slaughter melding astounding cruelty with unparalleled efficiency. In Hungary, Czechoslovakia, Lithuania, and Latvia, just three in ten Jews survived the onslaught. In Germany, two in ten. In Poland, Europe's largest Jewish community, one in ten remained alive at war's end.[1]

Among the Jews of Palestine, hardly a soul was untouched. The wife and son of Israel Hazan—the poultry merchant whose murder heralded the Great Revolt—were gassed at Auschwitz along with 95 percent of Salonica's Jews. The mother of the hanged Shlomo Ben-Yosef was among the twenty-five thousand Jews of Lutsk executed in the woods outside town.[2] Uri Zvi Greenberg, the poet-militant, never again saw his parents or siblings, nor did Menachem Begin, who arrived in wartime Palestine in a Polish army uniform but soon rose to lead the Irgun.

David Ben-Gurion emerged with his family comparatively intact—over the years he had managed to bring most of his kin to Palestine. A favorite niece, Sheindele, was his only close relation crushed under the Nazi juggernaut.

Still, he never quite forgave the British for abandoning Zionism, and for the White Paper that had all but bolted Palestine's gates through the six black years of war. Had Peel's 1937 partition plan gone through, he later argued, "the six million Jews in Europe would not have been exterminated. Most of them would have been alive in Palestine."

It is a damning allegation, but ultimately unpersuasive. Palestine of the late 1930s and early 1940s was unequipped to absorb millions of immigrants at once—much less so the sliver of the country that Peel had offered the Zionists. Be that as it may, Golda Meir's claim that "hundreds of thousands of Jews—perhaps many more" could have been saved is far more difficult to deny.[3]

Arthur Koestler, the prolific and eccentric Hungarian-born British-Jewish author, is best remembered for his great novel of totalitarianism, *Darkness at Noon*. But he also spent several of the interwar years in Palestine and penned a now-forgotten work of fiction, *Thieves in the Night*, set during the Great Revolt.

In yet another book, a keenly observed history of the Mandate, he affirmed "Britain's undeniable guilt in barring the Jewish escape road to Palestine," but ascribed it mainly to a "lack of imagination—the inability of the British mind to conceive that Hitler's atrocious threats against the Jews were meant in earnest. The fear of impending massacres was shrugged off as Jewish hysteria."

While not absolving Britain, Koestler put the decision in context. Compared to the other great powers—German madness, Soviet collaboration with that madness, American hand-washing of the whole European problem—the White Paper appears more a "sin of omission than a calculated one." That policy, he concluded, "cannot be measured by absolute ethical standards; it must be judged against the background of the moral depravity of Europe at the time."[4]

To Koestler's analysis must also be added a certain ambient anti-Semitism among British officialdom. This assessment, sent by Palestine High Commissioner MacMichael to the Colonial Office early in the war, was unusually frank but otherwise not atypical:

> *The Jews seem to me to be making a capital error in trying, with all the concomitant offensiveness which has led other people throughout the course of history to indulge in periodic pogroms at their expense, to assert their nationhood and particularize their territorial claims*

> *without regard to the rights of any other body or soul. Things will be vastly eased if and when, after the war, some alternate home can be found for those who do not want to remain packed like sardines in Palestine.*[5]

In an unpublished memoir, Malcolm MacDonald claimed he had drafted certain portions of the White Paper with tears in his eyes. And yet, he wrote, the British "could not let emotion rule" but had to act out of "absolute, unsentimental and, some people would say, even cynical realism."

In his account, after seeking out the best possible advice, especially from the Foreign Office and military chiefs, he determined Britain simply could not risk turning the Arab, and potentially Muslim, world against it on the eve of war:

> *After all, they were the experts. And who was I, a young man of 37, to tell them all that they were wrong, even if I was colonial secretary? The only point over which I criticize myself is that perhaps I should have held out for a higher figure of Jewish immigration. I have sometimes felt conscience-stricken. But, honestly, I did my darnedest. . . . If Britain lost and Hitler won, there would be no National Home. The Jews would be killed or expelled from Palestine, just as they had been 2,000 years earlier.*

At the back of his mind, MacDonald said, was the notion that if Britain won the war, he "could give the Zionists a better deal. It would have meant abandoning the White Paper, yes, another change of policy, but that's nothing new, is it?"

"From the Zionists' point of view they were right to oppose me, but I was not a Jew or a Zionist and my first thoughts had to be for Britain and the cause of democracy in general," he said. "I'm not saying that the White Paper was right. All I'm saying is that this was the reason for it and I'm damned if I can see what else could have been done."[6]

The historical literature on the Holocaust is prodigious. Not quite as expansive, but nonetheless well-chronicled, is Hajj Amin al-Husseini's wartime record.

Escaping Lebanon dressed as a woman, the mufti took refuge in Iraq, where he backed a pro-Axis coup before again fleeing British clutches (Churchill, now prime minister, favored his assassination). From there he made his way to Mussolini's Italy and finally the Third Reich.[7]

In Berlin he met with Hitler, who assured him that after conquering Europe, Germany's objective in the Middle East would be "solely the destruction of the Jewish element residing in the Arab sphere under the protection of British power."

And he met Heinrich Himmler, the second-most powerful Nazi after the *Führer*. "Himmler had tremendous importance in Germany," Hajj Amin later recounted matter-of-factly in his Arabic memoir, as "Reichsminister of the Interior, commander-general of the famous SS force, and head of public security matters and the Gestapo . . . I met Himmler repeatedly and liked his cleverness, resourcefulness, and knowledge."

The mufti worked doggedly to preclude any Jewish refugees from reaching Palestine. In summer 1943 he urged Hungary to send its Jews where they could remain "under active control, for example, in Poland, in order thereby to protect oneself from their menace." Shortly thereafter he came to know with certainty that the Nazis had already killed three million Jews, because—his memoirs state plainly—Himmler told him so.[8]

He was useful to the Nazis above all as a propagandist to and recruiter in the Arab and Islamic lands. He helped Himmler enlist two divisions of Bosnian Muslims for the Waffen-SS, and was a fixture of Nazi radio broadcasts in Arabic.

"If, by misfortune, England is victorious, the Jews will dominate the world," went one typical broadcast. "If, God forbid, America and her Allies are victorious . . . the Arabs will never rise again."[9]

In another he warned that Jewish "character traits make them incapable of keeping faith with anyone or of mixing with any other nation; they live, rather, as parasites among the peoples, suck their blood, steal their property, pervert their morals, and yet demand the same rights that the native inhabitants enjoy." Muslims' goal must be to drive all Jews from Arab and Muslim countries, he said—that was the sole path to salvation, and the example set by the Prophet himself.

"The mufti's anti-Semitism and collaboration with the Nazis is beyond all serious question," asserts Gilbert Achcar, a Lebanese scholar, in *The Arabs and the Holocaust*.

Yet in those same memoirs Hajj Amin worked to recast that collaboration as directed not against Jews but against Zionism alone. "In Germany I labored to offer whatever modest help I could for our Palestinian cause . . . because I was certain, and still am, that if Germany and the Axis had been victorious, no trace of the Zionists would have remained in Palestine and the Arab lands."[10]

George Antonius died suddenly, mid-war, in Jerusalem. He was just fifty. His final months and days had found him "bewildered and ill," in the words of his American ex-employer, having recently lost his job and received divorce papers from his estranged wife. Despite his book's success, he had no will, no assets, and nothing at all to leave his young daughter.

"Antonius died at the moment when he was most needed," wrote the scholar and activist Albert Hourani, "at the moment for which his whole life had been a preparation."

He was buried in the Orthodox cemetery on Mount Zion. His gravestone bore a single line of old Arabic poetry taken from the title page of *The Arab Awakening*: "Arise, ye Arabs, and awake!"

Epigraph had become epitaph.

Musa Alami was among the pallbearers. He consoled himself with the conviction that his friend's book would outlast its author as an enduring contribution to the struggle for an Arab Palestine. With Antonius silenced, Alami was now the principal English voice in that struggle, now entering its most critical period.

He recognized the war had changed everything. Emerging details of the depth of Nazi savagery had augmented international—and, crucially, American—backing for Zionism and rendered the mufti a diplomatic pariah. Shortly after the war Alami told a British official, speaking of

Hajj Amin, that London had "probably made a mistake not pushing him out altogether."[11]

And yet, right or wrong, for much of the Arab public in Palestine the mufti remained the preeminent embodiment of their national movement. Alami, whether out of national solidarity or fear for his life, never dared air his deepening disillusionment with the man.[12]

"Where is the White Paper?" Alami sighed in the war's aftermath. "Dare we dream of getting it back?"[13]

The postwar years found him a busy man, and in 1945 he was named the Palestinian delegate to the nascent Arab League. Painfully aware of the Arabs' handicaps in public relations, he spearheaded the League's public-diplomacy office in London, and in Washington and New York. The latter had recently been designated the cradle of the newborn United Nations.

He induced the Arab League to open a fund to improve cultivation, hygiene, literacy, and medicine in Palestine's rural villages, and to buoy small farmers lest they sell their land in despair to the Jews. The initiative was modeled on the Jewish National Fund—virtually alone among members of the Palestinian-Arab elite, Alami was willing to learn from the self-evident achievements of their Zionist adversary. Still, despite the fund's lofty aims, cash was slow in coming: Only Iraq delivered on its pledge of 250,000 pounds.[14]

Exhausted post-war Britain was losing its grip on Palestine. Even before the armistice, the feared result of the White Paper had come to pass: Palestine's Arab Revolt had been replaced by a Jewish one. The new rebellion was led first by the Irgun and its splinter, the Freedom Fighters of Israel (known by its Hebrew acronym, *Lehi*), then joined after the peace by the Haganah. The last of these had worked closely with Britain during the war, but was now scandalized that Palestine remained mostly locked even as survivors languished in DP camps and London's avowedly pro-Zionist Labour party had returned to power.

When the new U.S. president, Harry Truman, requested the United Kingdom let one hundred thousand survivors into Palestine, Britain asked that America finally help bear the impossibly heavy cross the Holy Land had become. The result, reflecting Washington's increasing centrality on the Palestine question, was dubbed the Anglo-American Committee of Inquiry.

That commission's report—recommending Jewish and Arab provinces under continued British trusteeship—was ultimately dismissed by both warring parties, and an exasperated Britain referred the whole bloody business to the UN.

"With the accumulation of defeats under Husseini's disastrous leadership," writes Achcar of the mufti, "the only path still open to the Palestinians, if they were to avoid the catastrophe, the Nakba, was to shake off the political influence of this disreputable individual once and for all. . . . This was not the path taken."[15]

In spring 1947 the UN convened its Special Committee on Palestine. Again, at the mufti's insistence, the Arabs of Palestine boycotted. Alami, testifying in an unofficial capacity, warned that any territorial concessions to Zionism would plunge the region into war: "A manifest injustice does not become just merely because the United Nations may for reasons of its own decide to espouse it."[16]

In September the committee recommended partition, embracing the spirit and central recommendation of the Peel plan a decade earlier, but with certain territorial and other modifications.[17]

On the 29th of November the UN General Assembly approved the scheme.

The next day an Arab-Jewish civil war erupted in earnest. Fawzi Bey—the journeyman hero of the Great Revolt—reappeared to lead militias in Samaria and Galilee, and in the initial months the initiative lay with the Arabs. But in April 1948, as the announced British withdrawal neared, the Haganah took the offensive. Within weeks, major Arab or mixed cities fell one after another—Tiberias, Haifa, Jaffa, Safed, Beisan. The civil war for Palestine came to an abrupt finish, and the Jews had emerged victorious.

On the afternoon of May 14, hours before the Mandate was set to expire, Ben-Gurion announced the advent of the State of Israel.

The armies of Transjordan, Egypt, Syria, and Lebanon invaded the next morning; contingents from Iraq and Saudi Arabia would follow. The Palestinians having failed, the Arab states would now try to redeem something of Arab honor and, if possible, seize portions of Palestine for themselves.

The war's second phase, pitting Israel and the Arab states, began with bitter and brutal combat and heavy casualties on both sides. Yet by the first UN-mediated truce, a month into hostilities, the emergent Jewish state had absorbed the four-pronged attack, stabilized its initially precarious position, and massively augmented its forces and arms. When fighting resumed that summer, the Israelis had the initiative. War with the Arab armies would stretch into the following year, but they would keep that initiative throughout, conquering lands far beyond their UN-approved borders.

Libraries worth of books have examined the 1947–1949 war, the triumph of Jewish Israel, and the destruction and dispersion of most of Arab Palestine. The particulars of that confrontation—above all, the reasons for a refugee exodus that would reach seven hundred thousand—are hotly disputed and mostly beyond the scope of this book.[18]

What is relevant here, yet generally overlooked, is the reality that the Arabs of Palestine had effectively already lost the war, and with it most of the country, a decade in advance.

The Great Revolt that had preceded the Second World War had left Palestine's Arabs mortally wounded for the decisive contest with Zionism that awaited after the peace. Tens of thousands were dead, imprisoned, or in exile. The political, business, and landed elite were profoundly divided; internecine feuding had riven virtually every town and village. The economy was in ruins, but worse, so too was national morale.

"The contrast with Zionist society was stark," writes the Israeli historian Benny Morris. "No national collective was more self-reliant or motivated . . . the Yishuv was probably one of the most politically conscious, committed and well-organized communities in the world."

The Jews, despite the undeniable price in blood, had skillfully turned the rebellion to their advantage. Over three years they had not abandoned a single settlement—on the contrary, their Wall and Tower campaign had left some sixty new ones at key strategic points. The Arab economic boycott had directly served Ben-Gurion's goal of creating separate, self-sufficient Jewish farming and industrial sectors. A Zionist metal and arms industry had emerged, producing mines and grenades and soon progressing to mortars and bombs.[19]

The Haganah had been massively trained and armed by the world's preeminent military. Wingate did not live to see his hoped-for "Jewish State Defense Force"—his brief life ended in a wartime plane crash in the Burmese jungle—but in men like Moshe Dayan and Yigal Allon he had created the leadership cadre of the Israel Defense Forces.[20]

For the Jews, perhaps the greatest shift was psychological: They had withstood a powerful, sustained assault and lived to tell about it. One book on Zionist leaders' thinking in this era is aptly titled *Abandonment of Illusions*. The belief that material gains would bring Arab consent now looked naive and, worse, dangerous. Instead, by the end of the revolt and the start of the world war, much of Palestine's Jewish mainstream had accepted the fact that the country's fate would ultimately be determined, and maintained, by force.[21]

"By 1939, the Yishuv had achieved the demographic weight, control of strategic areas of land, and much of the weaponry and military organization that would be needed as a springboard for taking over the country within less than a decade," writes the Palestinian-American historian Rashid Khalidi.

Khalidi argues that the Palestinian catastrophe of 1947–1949 was predicated on a series of previous failures: "a deeply divided leadership, exceedingly limited finances, no centrally organized military forces or centralized administrative organs, and no reliable allies. They faced a Jewish society in Palestine which, although small relative to theirs, was politically unified, had centralized para-state institutions, and was exceedingly well led and extremely highly motivated."

For Palestinians, he maintains, the *Nakba*—the "catastrophe" of their military drubbing, dispossession, and dispersal—was all but a foregone conclusion. For them, the terrible events that bookended the year 1948 "were no more than a postlude, a tragic epilogue to the shattering defeat of 1936–39."[22]

LESSONS LEARNED

The Palestine war found Musa Alami at his winter home in Jericho. Shortly after the armistice, in mid-1949, he published a short, somber essay in Arabic, then English. "The Lesson of Palestine" was one of the very first works published on the war and remains, decades later, unique among Arab accounts for its candor and self-criticism in considering the sources of the debacle.[23]

"The Arabs were faced by a challenge, the first since their liberation from foreign rule; and they did not meet it," he wrote. "During the course of the struggle we had an opportunity to finish with Zionism and its dangers altogether, but we did not take it."

The Jews, he wrote, were highly organized, wholly focused on success. The Arabs "thought that victory would come from shouting," and relied on the kind of improvised guerrilla warfare that had typified the earlier revolt.

The "biggest political failure we recorded was our inability to create some kind of real unity among ourselves in the face of a united enemy, at a most critical moment, in an historical and decisive struggle, with disaster facing us."

The fate of the refugees left him devastated: "If ultimately the Palestinians evacuated their country, it was not out of cowardice, but because they had lost all confidence in the existing system of defense. . . . Moreover, they had before them the specter of Deir Yassin, with all its brutality."

At least one hundred people were killed at Deir Yassin when the Irgun and Lehi, with assistance from the Haganah, conquered the Jerusalem-area village in April 1948. The proportion of the dead who were civilians remains in dispute, but at least 11 members of one family, including women and small children, were deliberately executed. Reports of mass rape—propagated by Dr. Khalidi himself but ultimately unfounded—helped turn what was a moderate trickle of refugees into a gushing stream.[24]

Palestine's Arab neighbors did not escape censure: "It is shameful the Arab governments should prevent the Arab refugees from working in their countries and shut the doors in their faces and imprison them in camps."

Still, he saw the defeat as symptomatic of deeper deficiencies. "The Lesson of Palestine" closed with a call for the "complete modernization in every aspect of Arab life and thought"—political, economic, scientific, and social. Freedom of expression, a social safety net, and equal treatment for women would be the necessary first steps.

> *I have a deep-rooted belief in the Arab nation and its great capacities. The disaster has shaken us profoundly, and wounded us deeply, and opened the door to a great danger. If the shock wakes us up, brings us together, and impels us to a new life from which we can derive strength, the wound will heal, the danger will be averted, and Palestine will be recovered. And the misfortunes will be a blessing.*
>
> *But if not, woe to the outcome.*[25]

Alami was a man with little left. Most of his properties were now in Israel, and Jericho was now in the portion of Palestine claimed by Transjordan (soon renamed Jordan) and rebranded as the West Bank. His wife Sa'adiya had run off with his younger personal assistant Wasfi Tal, later Jordan's prime minister. He had never had children.[26]

Instinctively he looked for ways to help the refugees. Like them he believed their exile was temporary—had not tens of thousands quit Palestine during the Great Revolt, only to return? Nonetheless he felt that in the meantime they needed something practical to do. Simply stewing in fruitless resentment would get them nowhere.

He had presciently stowed away the Iraqi money for the Arab League's stillborn agricultural initiative. Now, he convinced authorities in Amman to let him dig for water in the arid wastes between Jericho and the Jordan.

"I wore a big straw hat made by one of the refugees," he said. "The refugees going to and from the camps spread the story of the madman who was persisting in digging in the desert, and laughed because he was paying them good money for doing it . . . I am sure that all of the men were making fun of me."

Against all predictions they struck water deep within the earth. Gradually a farm sprang up, called the Arab Development Society, growing produce and grains at first, then some poultry and cattle.

Alongside the farm he built a small orphanage for the children of parents killed in the Palestine war. Demand far outstripped supply, but the 18 boys he took in grew steadily to 50, then 100, and finally 160. It was the unlikeliest outcome of a cruel and costly war: A man without children raising children without parents, together growing food in a land without water.

In its first two decades, more than six hundred orphans passed through the farm of the man they called Uncle Musa, gaining the social, agricultural, and vocational skills that would turn them from underfed, lost, and aggrieved castaways into human beings productively serving their own society. Aided by Ford Foundation grants, it signed a contract to provide fresh produce to ARAMCO, the Arabian-American Oil Company, in neighboring Saudi Arabia. Never before or since has the Palestinian tragedy produced a comparably edifying tale.

"He was sick, as he often was," writes Alami's biographer, "but his brain was working overtime on matters great and small, on ambitious plans for extension or development, on the smallest details of husbandry or of the boys' welfare."

The farm and the orphans gave his life purpose. He had lost nearly everything, but felt more fulfilled than at any time he could remember.

In June 1967 tanks returned to the West Bank. On the third day of what history would remember as the Six-Day War, IDF armored units rolled through the farm, destroying crop rows and dozens of wells. The alfalfa withered in the summer sun. Cows went unfed and unmilked; twenty thousand chickens died.[27]

David Ben-Gurion, ex–prime minister and octogenarian, was inundated with congratulatory telegrams from abroad: With astonishing speed, Israel had not just prevailed once again against the Arab armies massing against it, but had taken Jordan's West Bank, Syria's Golan Heights, and Egypt's Gaza Strip and Sinai Peninsula. Ben-Gurion's mind, however, was elsewhere. He was convinced the newly conquered territories were the bargaining chip his country needed, and had never before possessed, to reach a lasting peace. There was no time to waste.

"I was in a London hotel and a telephone rings saying, 'Tel Aviv calling,' and there was Mr. Ben-Gurion," Alami recalled in a recorded interview, likely the only one he ever gave.

"I have known Mr. Ben-Gurion for more than 40 years. I used to see him almost daily and to like, very much, Mr. Ben-Gurion because of his frankness. His frankness was sometimes *frightening*, when he would express his views about the destiny and the future of the Arabs. But although we disagreed, we always wanted to try and find common ground."[28]

This time, though, the line was poor. Ben-Gurion recounted their communication with a telling description: "He didn't hear me, although I heard him. Later on it got a little better and he heard me, but I didn't hear him."

He followed with a telegram:

> *There is now a unique chance to conclude peace between Israel and her neighbors. Your presence here is now vital. You are the man who more than any other can help to bring peace. I implore you to come home at once. Cable when you are coming and we will meet in Jerusalem or in Jericho as you like. Yours Bengurion.*[29]

But Alami could not return, for reasons both of practicality—the farm was now a closed military zone—and pride: He refused to return to the West Bank until its status was finalized. Through an intermediary he told Ben-Gurion he was keen to talk, but he would not be the first Arab to pay a visit to Israeli-held territory.[30] In the meantime he stayed in London, raising funds for the farm.

Two years passed. Ben-Gurion was visiting Britain, and upon arrival asked the Israeli ambassador to locate his old interlocutor. They met at Ben-Gurion's hotel, per the ambassador's notes, "with extraordinary warmth and friendliness, in an embrace."

Fully two decades had passed since they last saw each other, in the charged, fateful months in 1947 when the United Nations weighed

Palestine's future. Now, Alami said, he had a plan to move toward peace. It involved granting Palestinians the vote for their own representatives, perhaps under UN guardianship, followed by autonomy or unification with Jordan.

Ben-Gurion had not anticipated such a concrete proposal. He was now out of government, he said, but as "Alami's friend" he wished to hear more. They would meet several more times.[31]

Ben-Gurion's diary is silent on those encounters. Yet in Alami's account, the old Zionist revealed an unexpected and unprecedented determination to parlay Israel's victory into an accord: The Jewish state, he said, ought to relinquish all the conquered territories—with the exceptions of Jerusalem and the strategic Golan Heights—for peace.[32]

In a top-secret letter, Ben-Gurion reported the discussions to Israel's Foreign Ministry. Whether anyone in Jerusalem paid heed is unclear—his political career was nearly over, his influence substantially diminished, and his physical and mental health in manifest decline.

His talks with Alami in the mid-1930s had been Ben-Gurion's first attempt to find common ground with the Arabs of Palestine—now these would be his last.[33]

In 1970, in one of his first and only appearances on television (the medium had arrived in Israel just two years prior), Ben-Gurion was pressed on whether he had done enough to win Arab hearts and minds. He recounted a favorite anecdote from four decades earlier, when he met a certain Arab, "a very fair and honest man," who told him he would rather the land remain poor and desolate for a hundred years until the Arabs themselves could develop it.

"I understood him," he reminisced, smiling. "I said in my heart, 'If I were in his place, I would say the same.'"[34]

Soon thereafter came the 1973 Yom Kippur War, a surprise joint Arab assault that inflicted severe losses on Israel, exposing the first cracks in its ostensible invincibility. Weeks later Ben-Gurion suffered a brain hemorrhage in Tel Aviv and shortly after died; he was eighty-seven. Within six months, Hajj Amin al-Husseini breathed his last in Beirut.

Ben-Gurion had guided the Zionist movement to unimagined heights—his name graces Israel's main international airport and streets in almost every city and town. The mufti had been allowed into Jordanian-ruled East Jerusalem just once in his last four decades of life; no boulevards are named in his honor, no schools in refugee camps, no units of militant groups. This chieftain and icon of the Great Revolt was able to retain his leadership position even after brazen collaboration with the Nazis, but he could never recover the prestige he lost in the fiasco of 1948.

Achcar summarizes Hajj Amin's place in Palestinian collective memory with two words: "embarrassed silence."[35]

Musa Alami died in 1984 in Amman. As mourners brought his casket across the Jordan, IDF troops searched the coffin and body. He was buried in the city of his birth: Jerusalem.[36]

Tributes poured in.

"Almost alone among the defeated after the 1948 debacle he did something practical," wrote a British admirer, marveling how he had borne loss, dislocation, and occupation "with a dignity and patience that amazed me."[37]

His had been a long and eventful lifespan, but one also marred by loneliness, disillusion, and damaging mistakes. His prevarication in breaking with the mufti stands as the single most conspicuous failing of his life.

The two had been united in resistance to Zionism—Alami's role raising funds and arms for the revolt remained secret until after his death—but their respective worldviews, their core sensibilities, were a study in contrast. That incongruity grew sharper after 1948: Alami came to count many Israelis as friends and, after 1967, grew especially close with Ruth Dayan, a peace activist whose husband happened to be defense minister. Alami eventually recognized the mufti's fundamental extremism (as late as the 1970s, he feared he might have him killed), but by then it was far too late.

"Hajj Amin was his tragedy," said a close acquaintance.[38]

"Musa Alami had great personal charm," eulogized Eliahu Elath, Israel's first ambassador in Washington, an Arabist, and a close companion.

> *He was gifted with profound analytic ability and expressed his ideas clearly both to content and conclusions. He reacted very patiently to the ideas of others even when he disagreed with them. . . . He was careful not to show disrespect for the values cherished by his interlocutors or for the dignity of other people, including his opponents.*

"Alami was not a supporter of Zionism, nor sympathetic to the idea of the revival of the Jewish people in its ancient homeland," Elath wrote. "On the contrary, at various periods of his life he fought against Zionism, and endeavored to restrict the Jewish National Home's opportunities for growth and development. He and his forefathers were born in Palestine, and he desired to see it as an Arab country."

He had devoted his life and work to the Palestinian cause. Yet above even that, Elath wrote, he was a humanist who placed mankind at the center of his aspirations. "To be sure, more than once those principles

Alami in his final years (MECA Arab Development Society, GB165-0324 5/5/1-009)

were gravely tested. Though Alami did not always succeed in passing the test, his failures were never due to personal motives or interests."

Elath dedicated his tribute to the "Memory of a Seeker of Justice and Peace."[39]

The Flush of Victory, the Spirit of Defeat

One morning in December 1987 the driver of an IDF tank transporter lost control and slammed into a line of vans carrying Gazan laborers to Israel. Four people were killed. Rumors that the crash was deliberate, matched with decades of political grievances and economic woes, sent thousands to the streets burning tires and hurling Molotov cocktails. The first *Intifada*, or uprising, had begun.

Almost exactly half a century had passed since the original Palestine revolt, but parallels abounded.

In both, Palestinian leaders were caught unawares by the spontaneity and endurance of what was a popular, grassroots rebellion. Like the mufti, Palestine Liberation Organization chief Yasser Arafat scrambled to assert control over an outburst of rage that had sprung from below.

Like its predecessor, the Intifada was marked by strikes, civil disobedience, and sabotage: Shops were closed, taxes withheld, the Jewish economy boycotted, and crops and forests set ablaze. Again there were acts of violence against soldiers and civilians, though this time the weapon of choice was not typically the rifle but the stone. Arafat understood the power of imagery in the era of mass media: A paroxysm of wanton bloodshed would cast the Palestinians not as defiant victims of dispossession and occupation but as cruel, irrational terrorists. Over the Intifada's first three years, some sixty Israelis were killed—a painful blow, but just one-eighth the toll from the same span in the 1930s.[40]

The occupying power—this time, Israel—grasped it was facing a prolonged, nationwide insurrection on a scale not seen before. Again that power responded with large-scale troop deployments and massive force, invoking methods and emergency laws inherited from its imperial antecedent: Some one thousand homes were demolished and fourteen thousand people placed in administrative detention—that is, held without warrant or charge—often for six months or more.[41]

But as before, the Arabs' initial cohesion yielded to profound fissures: between town and country, rival clans, modernizer and traditionalist, Muslim and Christian. Again, within a few years the insurgency degenerated into internal strife—perhaps a third of the estimated 1,500 Palestinians killed had fallen victim to their own compatriots.[42]

The shock of the Intifada helped prod Israel into its first tentative talks with the Palestinians, culminating in the 1993 Oslo Accords with its onetime nemesis Arafat. As gaps remained on a host of core issues, the agreement was purposely left imprecise. Still, it did create a Palestinian Authority—dominated from the start by Arafat's Fatah faction—to begin exercising provisional self-government in Gaza and the West Bank. For the first time in memory, the promise of a conflict-ending deal appeared possible.

As before, however, extremists scrambled to subvert any such settlement. In Gaza the Muslim Brotherhood had birthed a new group, the Islamic Resistance Movement, commonly known by its Arabic acronym *Hamas*. Its armed wing carried the name of the original anti-imperialist, anti-Zionist, Islamist fighter-martyr of the mid-1930s: Izz al-Din al-Qassam. The Qassam Brigades' signature contribution to the hope-filled Oslo years was the suicide bomber and the homespun Qassam rocket.[43]

In 2000 the superpower—no longer the United Kingdom but the United States—convened the Camp David Summit, a St. James's Conference for a new era. As before, the gulf between the warring parties proved unbridgeable.

The collapse of the Oslo process was accompanied by a second, far bloodier Intifada. Civilians bore a heavier brunt than ever, accounting for two-thirds of the more than one thousand Israelis killed.[44] The charred skeleton of a civilian bus became the macabre emblem of the four-year convulsion of violence that would become known as the Al-Aqsa Intifada.

Once again, memories of the earliest revolt remained close at hand. One morning in early March 2002, a sniper took aim at a checkpoint in *Wadi al-Haramiya*, the "Valley of Thieves," between Ramallah and Nablus in the West Bank. Armed only with a World War II–era Mauser rifle, he methodically brought down ten Israelis, one by one.

"He is one of the old rebels, for this is their style," local elders proclaimed approvingly. "He is an old fighter who has stayed in hiding since 1939." When the perpetrator was identified as a Fatah gunman, the elders still favored the old story. "They needed heroes," argued Sonia Nimr—an activist and academic who served time in Israeli prison—"and the only ones they could think of were those rebels of the 1936–39 revolt."[45]

Within weeks Israel launched Operation Defensive Shield, its largest since the Six-Day War. Tanks besieged Arafat's Ramallah headquarters, housed in one of the Tegart Forts erected during the Great Revolt (dozens of others are used by Israeli forces).[46] Work began on a West Bank security barrier that in time would stretch hundreds of miles—a Tegart's Wall for a new set of threats. Troops imposed curfews, reoccupied Palestinian cities, and clashed with keffiyeh-clad militants in street battles recalling their British forerunners'.

The two prior rebellions had brought Palestinians tangible gains: In the 1930s, the White Paper; in the 1980s and 1990s, peace talks and greater autonomy. This time the devastation appeared pointless, almost nihilistic. Partisans of Hamas and Fatah came to see the other not as fellow countrymen but as sworn enemies to be destroyed. Of the approximately five thousand Palestinians killed in the Second Intifada—a figure matching the most common estimate from the Great Revolt—perhaps 12 percent were victims of infighting. For all the agony inflicted on Israelis, concludes Khalidi, "the biggest losers in every way were the Palestinians."[47]

The uprising "directed discontent not only at the Israeli occupation but also toward the inefficiency, corruption, and authoritarian rule of the Palestine Authority," add Kimmerling and Migdal. "Aiming the people's wrath both outward and inward, the Al-Aqsa Intifada was reminiscent of the Great Arab Revolt."[48]

The Second Intifada sputtered out in 2005, just as Israel withdrew from the Gaza Strip. Two years later the Hamas-Fatah schism reached its nadir as the Islamists took over the enclave, forcibly expelling their rivals. Subsequent years would see three major rounds of fighting with Israel, with airstrikes wreaking havoc on the territory and rocket salvos sowing dread and destruction as far as Tel Aviv and even Haifa.

In 2021 war broke out yet again, but this time hostilities extended to a new, twenty-first-century battleground: social media. Amid the mutual recriminations, timelines in both camps were atwitter with parallels from the past.

"The riots of the Arab enemy take us back many years to the Great Arab Revolt," posted a far-right Israeli lawmaker, berating the government as lax on terror just like its Mandate precursor.[49]

When Palestinians in Gaza, the West Bank, and Israel united in a daylong strike, their supporters reached for their own analogs from days gone by. "Tomorrow a general strike is declared across historic Palestine," a prominent Palestinian activist tweeted. "This is a historic moment. Last time this happened was on May 16, 1936. Exactly 85 years ago. . . . A legacy of resistance."[50]

And on October 7, 2023—50 years and a day since the Yom Kippur War, 100 years and a week since the Mandate's birth—the Qassam Brigades led a savage, sadistic onslaught across Israel's border, killing nearly 1,200 people and taking some 250 hostage. It was, by a vast margin, the bloodiest day in Israel's history.

The 1936 revolt was the "first true 'Intifada,'" Mustafa Kabha writes in a sprawling Arabic lexicon of that earlier rebellion's fighters and commanders. "Though it did not reach its goal of abolishing the Jewish national home and expelling the occupation, it marked the beginning of the Palestinian revolution that has not stopped blazing until the writing of these lines." The rebellion's symbols and slogans, he notes, are "a cornerstone of Palestinian national rhetoric to this very day."[51]

Indeed, folk songs and dance still celebrate the insurgents of old: "Raj'at al-Baroudeh"—"The Gun Has Returned"—remains a standard. A main street in a Palestinian area of the Jordanian capital was recently named after Abdel-Rahim al-Hajj Muhammad, the revolt's chief commander, and Tulkarem's Kadoorie technical university organized a major commemoration on the anniversary of his death.[52]

But in the arid Jordan Valley, east of Jericho, stands a monument of a different kind—not to militancy but pragmatism, resilience, and resolve. At the edge of the valley's lunar wastes, beside the checkpoint the locals call Musa Alami Crossing, appear suddenly the lush fields and orchards of the old man's agricultural project. Its *labneh* is still prized from Nablus to Amman, but beyond the cowsheds now stretch tens of thousands of acres of the valley's famed date palms and the glinting panels of a high-tech solar-power plant.[53]

Nearly nine decades earlier, Alami had sworn to Ben-Gurion that he would wait a century, if necessary, until the Arabs could build up their land themselves. Today his farm perseveres, obstinately thriving on the same once-parched patch of earth where, despite it all, a lonely man and his war orphans made the desert bloom.

In the interview recorded after the Six-Day War, he had reflected on prospects for peace.[54] Amid ample reasons for fatalism, then as now, a note of hope cuts through the temptation to despair. His message, addressed squarely to his Israeli neighbors, reverberates across the intervening decades. Were he alive today, it would likely sound much the same:

> *You are now in the flush of victory, and we remain under the spirit of being defeated and downtrodden. So both of us are under abnormal conditions; I consider you just as abnormal as we are. You are not considering the future—you are only considering the present. And we are not considering the distant future—only our present suffering. But I do believe, still now, that this country has the makings of peace.*

Notes

Introduction

1. This framing of the revolt as precursor and template for subsequent Arab-Israeli clashes is indebted to Kenneth W. Stein, "The Intifada and the 1936–39 Uprising: A Comparison," *Journal of Palestine Studies* 19, no. 4 (July 1, 1990): 64–66, passim.

2. "The first significant Arab attempt to gain mastery in Palestine came not in the late 1940s but in the late 1930s, and in many ways it is the most interesting," notes James P. Jankowski. "Only at this time . . . did Palestine assume its central position in Arab perceptions." Jankowski, "The Palestinian Arab Revolt of 1936–1939," *Muslim World* 63, no. 3 (July 1973): 220, 230.

3. Baruch Kimmerling and Joel S. Migdal write, "The revolt helped to create a nation—even while crippling its social and political basis." Kimmerling and Migdal, *The Palestinian People: A History* (Cambridge, MA: Harvard University Press, 2003), 102, 131. Per Ghassan Kanafani, a novelist and militant spokesman assassinated by Israel in 1972: "In the whole history of the Palestinian struggle the armed popular revolt was never closer to victory." Kanafani, *The 1936–39 Revolt in Palestine* (London: Tricontinental Society, 1972, 1980), 48.

4. Anita Shapira sees mainstream Zionism shifting in this era from a defensive to an offensive ethos: "The basic psychological and moral decision was made at the time of the Arab Rebellion." Shapira, *Land and Power: The Zionist Resort to Force, 1881–1948* (Oxford; New York: Oxford University Press, 1992), 219–22, 250–54, 270. On Zionist illusions see Yehoyada Haim, *Abandonment of Illusions: Zionist Political Attitudes Toward Palestinian Arab Nationalism, 1936–1939* (London; New York: Routledge, 1983), passim.

5. Matthew Hughes notes: "The literature—in Arabic, English and Hebrew—on the revolt is exiguous." Hughes, "The Banality of Brutality: British Armed Forces and the Repression of the Arab Revolt in Palestine, 1936–39," *English Historical Review* CXXIV, no. 507 (April 1, 2009): 315.

6. Ted Swedenburg, *Memories of Revolt: The 1936–1939 Rebellion and the Palestinian National Past* (Minneapolis: University of Minnesota Press, 1995), xxii. One book was published within a decade of the revolt: John Marlowe, *Rebellion in Palestine* (London: Cresset Press, 1946). Yet it was based on private experience and conversation, not historical documentation, which naturally remained classified.

7. Yuval Arnon-Ohanah, *Mered Arvi be-Eretz Israel 1936–1939* [The Arab Revolt in the Land of Israel, 1936–1939] (Jerusalem: Ariel, 2013). One other Hebrew work is, like Hughes's, a military-history study of the counterinsurgency: Yigal Eyal, *Ha-Intifada ha-Rishona: Dikui ha-Mered ha-Arvi al-Yede ha-Tsava ha-Briti be-Eretz-Yisrael, 1936–1939* [The "First Intifada": The Oppression (*sic*) of the Arab Revolt by the British Army, 1936–1939] (Tel Aviv: Maarachot, 1998).

8. Mustafa Kabha, "The Courts of the Palestinian Arab Revolt, 1936–39," in *Untold Histories of the Middle East*, ed. Amy Singer, Christoph K. Neumann, and Selçuk Akşin Somel (London; New York: Routledge, 2011), 197. Kabha has done more than anyone in recent years to close the gap in Arabic. In 2009 he co-authored the first significant Arabic work on the revolt: a one-thousand-page lexicon of combatants and commanders based on archival documents and oral testimony. Mustafa Kabha and Nimer Serhan, *Sijil al-Qadah wal-Thuwar wal-Mutatawi'in li-Thawrat 1936–1939* [Lexicon of Commanders, Rebels, and Volunteers of the 1936–1939 Revolt] (Kafr Qara, Israel: Dar Elhuda, 2009). One earlier book in Arabic is Subhi Yasin, *Thawrah al-Arabiyah al-Kubra* [The Great Arab Revolt] (Cairo, 1959). Swedenburg observes that Yasin is useful on certain details but otherwise "highly unreliable." Swedenburg, *Memories of Revolt*, 21, 215n36.

9. Matthew Hughes, *Britain's Pacification of Palestine: The British Army, the Colonial State, and the Arab Revolt, 1936–1939* (Cambridge: Cambridge University Press, 2019). Matthew Kraig Kelly, *The Crime of Nationalism: Britain, Palestine, and Nation-Building on the Fringe of Empire* (Oakland: University of California Press, 2017). At the time of this book's publication, Charles W. Anderson was also writing a history of the revolt "from below"; see Anderson, "State Formation from Below and the Great Revolt in Palestine," *Journal of Palestine Studies* 47, no. 1 (November 1, 2017): 50.

10. This is not to suggest there were not Jews hoping for eventual statehood or fearing mass killing in Europe, or that there were not Arabs who feared dispossession and eviction by Zionists, but that no one knew if, when, or how their fears would be realized. Most Palestine residents likely expected the Mandate to last at least several more decades.

11. The quote is from William Faulkner.

Chapter 1

1. Simon Sebag Montefiore, *Jerusalem: The Biography* (London: Weidenfeld & Nicolson, 2011), 305–6n, 370, 522n. Yehoshua Porath, *The Palestinian Arab National Movement*, vol. 2, *From Riots to Rebellion, 1929–1939* (London; New York: Routledge, 1977), 60. Geoffrey Furlonge, *Palestine Is My Country: The Story of Musa Alami* (New York: Praeger, 1969), 6–10.

2. Johann Büssow, *Hamidian Palestine: Politics and Society in the District of Jerusalem 1872–1908* (Leiden: Brill, 2011), 554. Montefiore, *Jerusalem*, 433–44.

3. Furlonge, *Palestine*, 33–34.

4. Eliahu Elath, "Conversations with Musa al-'Alami," *Jerusalem Quarterly* no. 41 (Winter 1987): 37. Furlonge, *Palestine*, 6–15, 33–34, 86.

5. The Zionist interlocutor was Victor Jacobson. Yaakov Sharett and Rina Sharett, eds., *Shoher Shalom: Hebetim u-Mabatim al Moshe Sharett* [A Statesman Assessed: Views and

Viewpoints About Moshe Sharett] (Tel Aviv: Moshe Sharett Heritage Institute, 2008), 536ff.

6. Philip Mattar, *The Mufti of Jerusalem* (New York: Columbia University Press, 1992), 6–8. Furlonge, *Palestine*, 6.

7. Kenneth Stein, *The Land Question in Palestine, 1917–1939* (Chapel Hill: University of North Carolina Press, 1984), 233. Tom Segev, *One Palestine, Complete* (New York: Henry Holt, 2001), 275.

8. Amin al-Husseini, *Mudhakkirat Al-Hajj Muhammad Amin al-Husayni* [The Memoirs of Hajj Amin al-Husseini], ed. Abd al-Karim al-Umar (Damascus: Al-Ahali, 1999), 10. See also "Haj Amin al-Husayni, the Mufti of Jerusalem," U.S. State Department confidential file, April 24, 1951, in CIA files on Husseini, vol. 4, no. 160, http://archive.org/details/HusseiniAminEl; Mattar, *Mufti of Jerusalem*, 8–15, 142.

9. The McMahon-Hussein correspondence would reemerge in the Palestine policy debates of 1938 and 1939, thanks in large part to the efforts of George Antonius. See Chapters 6 and 7.

10. Furlonge, *Palestine*, 38–47. Elath, "Conversations," 37.

11. For this period see for example Benny Morris, *Righteous Victims: A History of the Zionist-Arab Conflict, 1881–2001* (New York: Vintage, 2001), 68–72; Howard M. Sachar, *A History of Israel*, 3rd ed. (New York: Knopf, 2007), 94–111.

12. The motives behind the Declaration are both contested and beyond the scope of this book. One useful account, emphasizing Weizmann's role, is Jonathan Schneer, *The Balfour Declaration: The Origins of the Arab-Israeli Conflict* (New York: Random House, 2010), passim. Another, highlighting Britain's strategic interests, is Michael J. Cohen, "Centenary of the Balfour Declaration," in Cohen, *Britain's Hegemony in Palestine and the Middle East, 1917–56: Changing Strategic Imperatives* (London; Portland, OR: Vallentine Mitchell, 2017), 7–20. See also Benny Morris, "Mandate Palestine in Perspective," *Bustan: The Middle East Book Review* 5, no. 2 (January 1, 2014): 142–43.

13. In 1937 Lloyd George gave private testimony on the Declaration's motives, stressing the wartime propaganda effect on Russian and American Jews. See Oren Kessler, "'A dangerous people to quarrel with': Lloyd George's Secret Testimony to the Peel Commission Revealed," *Fathom*, July 2020. His remarks are echoed in the secret memo "The Origins of the Balfour Declaration," Foreign Office Research Department, November 6, 1944, TNA FO 492/18.

14. W. F. Stirling, *Safety Last* (London: Hollis and Carter, 1953), 118–19. Ronald Storrs, *Memoirs* (New York: Putnam, 1937), 439. For Weizmann's own account see Chaim Weizmann, *Trial and Error: The Autobiography of Chaim Weizmann* (New York: Schocken, 1966), chap. 14–18.

15. Morris, *Righteous Victims*, 76, 90. See also Yasin, *Thawrah*, 11, 15.

16. Furlonge, *Palestine*, 67.

17. On the Faisal-Weizmann agreement and its attendant controversy, see Ali A. Allawi, *Faisal I of Iraq* (New Haven: Yale University Press, 2014), 116–18, 186–89; Oren Kessler, "Book Review: 'Faisal I of Iraq,'" *Wall Street Journal*, April 14, 2014. See also Michael J. Cohen, "Colonial Intrigue in the Middle East: The Faysal—[Lawrence]—Weizmann

Agreement, January 1919," in *The British Mandate in Palestine: A Centenary Volume, 1920–2020*, ed. Cohen (London; New York: Routledge, 2020), 13–28.

18. Cited in "Cmd. 5479: Report of the Palestine Royal Commission" (His Majesty's Stationery Office, 1937), 24.

19. For a useful description of Zionist pre-state political bodies, see Kelly, *Crime of Nationalism*, 188n15.

20. Colin Shindler, *The Triumph of Military Zionism: Nationalism and the Origins of the Israeli Right* (London: I.B. Tauris, 2006), 21. The Palestine Arab Congress, which met several times through the 1920s, was unrecognized but tolerated by British authorities.

21. Elath, "Conversations," 38, 68. Furlonge, *Palestine*, 73, 78.

22. Gawain Bell, *Shadows on the Sand* (London: C. Hurst, 1983), 97.

23. Khalil Sakakini, *Kadha Ana ya Dunya* [Such Am I, O World] (Beirut: Al-Ittihad, 1982), 193–94. Segev, *One Palestine*, 127–28.

24. *The Times*, April 8, 1920. Mattar, *Mufti of Jerusalem*, 17. Yasin, *Thawrah*, 16. Segev, *One Palestine*, 135–39. Yehuda Taggar, *The Mufti of Jerusalem and Palestine: Arab Politics, 1930–1937* (New York: Garland, 1986), 16. Hajj Amin al-Husseini called the 1920 events the "First Jerusalem Revolt"; see *Mudhakkirat*, 12.

25. Kessler, "Faisal I." Morris, *Righteous Victims*, 77.

26. Segev writes, "The British acted on the basis of the same consideration that led them to issue the Balfour Declaration: they wanted to prevent the country from being given to the French and they submitted to Zionist pressure." Segev, *One Palestine*, 142.

27. On Churchill and Transjordan see Morris, *Righteous Victims*, 99–100.

28. For a more detailed account see Oren Kessler, "The 1921 Jaffa Riots 100 Years On: Mandatory Palestine's First 'Mass Casualty' Attack," *Times of Israel*, May 1, 2021, https://www.timesofisrael.com/1921-jaffa-riots-100-years-on-mandatory-palestines-1st-mass-casualty-event.

29. Yehuda Slutsky, *Sefer Toldot ha-Haganah* [The Haganah History Book], vol. 2 (Tel Aviv: Maarachot, 1963), 80–81. "Cmd. 1540: Reports of the Commission of Inquiry with Correspondence Relating Thereto" (His Majesty's Stationery Office, 1921), 22, 27, 46. Michael J. Cohen, *Britain's Moment in Palestine: Retrospect and Perspectives, 1917–1948* (London; New York: Routledge, 2014), 86. Yasin, *Thawrah*, 16–17.

30. Slutsky, *Sefer Toldot*, 2:103–4, 1110.

31. Ari Shavit, *My Promised Land: The Triumph and Tragedy of Israel* (New York: Spiegel & Grau, 2015), 73.

32. "Cmd. 1540," 54–55. "Cmd. 1700: Correspondence with the Palestine Arab Delegation and the Zionist Organization" (His Majesty's Stationery Office, June 1922), passim. See also Kessler, "1921 Jaffa Riots."

33. Joseph B. Schechtman, *Rebel and Statesman: The Jabotinsky Story—The Early Years* (New York: Yoseloff, 1956), 25–44. See also Oren Kessler, "Scion of Zion," *Foreign Policy*, May 3, 2012, http://foreignpolicy.com/2012/05/03/scion-of-zion.

34. Samuel's memoirs make no mention of Hajj Amin, or of his selection as mufti and head of the Supreme Muslim Council. Samuel's son Edwin called those decisions among his father's "bad political mistakes," as Amin "turned out to be an implacable enemy not only of Zionism but also of Britain." Herbert Louis Samuel, *Memoirs of Viscount Samuel*

(London: Cresset Press, 1945), 157–59, 167. Edwin Samuel, *A Lifetime in Jerusalem: The Memoirs of the Second Viscount Samuel* (London: Vallentine Mitchell, 1970), 17–18.

35. Oren Kessler, "Herbert Samuel's secret 1937 testimony on the infamous mufti of Jerusalem revealed," *Times of Israel*, August 19, 2023, https://www.timesofisrael.com/uk-reveals-herbert-samuels-secret-1937-testimony-on-the-infamous-mufti-of-jerusalem. See also Bernard Wasserstein, *Herbert Samuel: A Political Life* (Oxford: Clarendon Press, 1992), 266. "Like Neville Chamberlain's . . . misplaced trust in Hitler, Samuel's faith in the Mufti was a profound error of personal and political judgment."

36. Alami agreed with the decision against an Arab Agency: Whatever its merits, the proposal would have put the Arabs on the same level as the "intruders." Furlonge, *Palestine*, 86–87.

37. "Moussa Eff. Alami," ISA M-758/25.

38. Furlonge, *Palestine*, 77, 87, 94–95.

39. Figures based on *Census of Palestine 1931* (Alexandria: Palestine Government, 1933). See also "Cmd. 5479," 279ff; Segev, *One Palestine*, 273–83. The calm was due partly to Palestine's late-1920s economic woes—in 1928, for example, more Jews emigrated than immigrated.

40. Hillel Halkin, *Jabotinsky: A Life* (New Haven; London: Yale University Press, 2014), 141. Vladimir Jabotinsky, "The Iron Wall," November 4, 1923, JI. Morris, *Righteous Victims*, 108, 112–13. See also Kessler, "Scion of Zion."

41. "Moussa Eff. Alami," ISA M-758/25.

42. "Cmd. 3530: Report of the Commission of the Palestine Disturbances of August 1929" (His Majesty's Stationery Office, 1929), 31. Mattar, *Mufti of Jerusalem*, 34–41. Segev, *One Palestine*, 307.

43. "Cmd. 3530," 50–54. Cohen, *Britain's Moment*, 216.

44. Gudrun Krämer, *A History of Palestine: From the Ottoman Conquest to the Founding of the State of Israel* (Princeton: Princeton University Press, 2011), 230. Mattar, *Mufti of Jerusalem*, 46. "Cmd. 3530," 54–57.

45. Hillel Cohen, *Year Zero of the Arab-Israeli Conflict 1929* (Waltham, MA: Brandeis University Press, 2015), 89–90. "Cmd. 3530," 56–57.

46. "Cmd. 3530," 61. Edward Keith-Roach, *Pasha of Jerusalem: Memoirs of a District Commissioner under the British Mandate*, ed. Paul Eedle (London; New York: Radcliffe Press, 1994), 122–23. "Arabs Opened Attack after Noon Prayers," *New York Times*, August 25, 1929. Krämer, *History of Palestine*, 231.

47. More specifically, fifty-nine people were killed and eight more died over the following days and weeks of wounds sustained that day. Joseph Levy, "12 Americans Killed by Arabs in Hebron," "Moslems in Open Revolt," and "Troops Seize Arab Chiefs at Gates of Jerusalem," *New York Times*, August 26, 29, and 30, 1929. "Eye Witnesses Describe Horrors of the Moslem Arabs' Attacks at Hebron," *JTA*, September 1, 1929. Bruce Hoffman, *Anonymous Soldiers: The Struggle for Israel, 1917–1947* (New York: Knopf, 2015), 30–32. Cohen, *Year Zero*, xxi. Segev, *One Palestine*, 320. Yasin, *Thawrah*, 17–18.

48. "Arabs in Hebron who Saved or Assisted Jews" and "List of Arabs of Hebron Who Behaved Well Towards Jews" (both undated), CZA S25/3409–5/6. *Megillat Hebron (The Hebron Scroll)*, https://hebron1929.info/Hebronletter.html. Hoffman, *Anonymous Soldiers*, 32.

49. The Arab death toll was estimated at 116. Two Jews, Simha Hinkis and Yosef Urfali, were sentenced to death (later commuted) for murdering Arab civilians. See Cohen, *Year Zero*, 24–25, 45–46.

50. "1,000 Sign Up Here to Fight the Arabs," and "Hoover Message of Sympathy Read at Garden; Urges Generous Relief for Palestine Victims," *New York Times*, August 29 and 30, 1929.

51. "British are Urged to Quit Palestine," "British to Uphold Prestige in East," and "2,000 Tribesmen Menace Jerusalem," *New York Times*, August 27 and 28, 1929. Hoffman, *Anonymous Soldiers*, 32–34. Morris, *Righteous Victims*, 114.

52. "Cmd. 3530," 185–89, 499, 527.

53. "Cmd. 3530," 108–10. On Jabotinsky's banishment and his own meager attempts to reverse it, see Halkin, *Jabotinsky*, 168–70.

54. "Cmd. 3530," 50, 63, 74, 82, 152–61. On the mufti's responsibility see also Bernard Wasserstein, *The British in Palestine: The Mandatory Government and the Arab-Jewish Conflict 1917–1929* (Hoboken, NJ: Blackwell, 1991), 230–34. Per Wasserstein: "The precise nature of the Mufti's role in the riots remains obscure" but there is "little doubt that the key . . . was the Mufti's year-long campaign" rousing Muslims against the alleged threat to holy places.

55. "Cmd. 3686: Palestine: Report on Immigration, Land Settlement and Development" (His Majesty's Stationery Office, 1930), passim.

56. On the complex forces behind the MacDonald Letter—including the government's economic woes and fear of American-Zionist hostility—see Michael J. Cohen, "The Strange Case of the Palestine White Paper, 1930," in Cohen, *Britain's Hegemony*, 81–106.

57. "Prime Minister's Letter," HC Deb, February 13, 1931, vol. 248, col. 751–57.

58. Donald Lankiewicz, "Mein Kampf in America: How Adolf Hitler Came to Be Published in the United States," *Printing History* 20 (July 2016): 5. Sachar, *History of Israel*, 109.

59. Adolf Hitler, *Mein Kampf* (New York: Reynal & Hitchcock, 1941), 84, 984. Dugdale's abridged 1933 edition included the first quote but not the second.

60. Francis R. Nicosia, *Nazi Germany and the Arab World* (Cambridge: Cambridge University Press, 2014), 72. Tom Segev, *The Seventh Million: The Israelis and the Holocaust* (New York: Henry Holt, 2000), 15, 21. Porath, *Palestinian Arab*, 76.

61. Nicosia, *Nazi Germany*, 72.

62. Lankiewicz, "Mein Kampf," 12–16.

63. "Haavara Winds Up Reich-Palestine Transfer Operations; Handled $35,000,000 in 6 Years," *JTA*, September 10, 1939. Segev, *Seventh Million*, 24.

64. Hitler, *Mein Kampf*, 447–48.

65. Lt. Gen. John Evetts, commander of British troops in Palestine from 1935 to 1937, later said of Wauchope: "A very nice little man, but I always thought he was trying to back both those horses: Arabs, Jews, Arabs, Jews, Arabs, Jews. He couldn't make up his mind which to back. In any case he shouldn't have backed either as high commissioner." "Evetts, John Fullerton," IWMSA 4451/2. Elath, "Conversations," 45–47. Weizmann, *Trial and Error*, 335.

66. Hanna to Levy, December 1935, ISA P-695/5. Hanna, born in Egypt to Syrian parents, joined the paper in 1931 and soon became acting editor and columnist. He is often confused with Yusuf Hanna al-'Isa of Jaffa, one of the paper's founders. See Mustafa Kabha, *The Palestinian Press as Shaper of Public Opinion 1929–1939* (London: Vallentine Mitchell, 2007), 7, 65n6, 272. On Levy see Jerold S. Auerbach, *Print to Fit: The New York Times, Zionism and Israel, 1896–2016* (Boston: Academic Studies Press, 2019), chap. 2.

67. "Moussa Eff. Alami," ISA M-758/25. Furlonge, *Palestine*, 98.

68. Elath, "Conversations," 45–46.

69. Furlonge, *Palestine*, 98–100. Elath, "Conversations," 47.

70. W. F. Abboushi, "The Road to Rebellion: Arab Palestine in the 1930's," *Journal of Palestine Studies* 6, no. 3 (Spring 1977): 26. "Cmd. 5479," 279.

71. Porath, *Palestinian Arab*, 43–45.

72. Ian Black, *Enemies and Neighbors: Arabs and Jews in Palestine and Israel, 1917–2017* (New York: Atlantic Monthly, 2017), 68. Porath, *Palestinian Arab*, 44. Yasin, *Thawrah*, 18–19.

73. Elath, "Conversations," 52. Hoffman, *Anonymous Soldiers*, 44.

74. Taggar, *Mufti of Jerusalem*, 169.

75. "Moussa Eff. Alami," ISA M-758/25. In her memoir, Alami's niece revealed that for decades he had suffered from diabetes. See Serene Husseini Shahid, *Jerusalem Memories*, ed. Jean Makdisi Said (Beirut: Naufal, 1999), 223.

76. Furlonge, *Palestine*, 100–102. Philip Mattar, *Encyclopedia of the Palestinians* (New York: Infobase, 2005), 17.

77. "Arab Named Gov't Advocate for Palestine," *JTA*, February 28, 1934.

78. Shabtai Teveth, *Ben-Gurion and the Palestinian Arabs* (New York: Oxford University Press, 1985), 5–7, 22.

79. Teveth, *Palestinian Arabs*, 101–3, 118–19. On Ben-Gurion's rapid attainment of Ottoman Turkish and faltering attempts at Arabic, see Shabtai Teveth, *Ben-Gurion: The Burning Ground, 1886–1948* (Boston: Houghton Mifflin, 1987), 67–69, 76–82.

80. David Ben-Gurion, *My Talks with Arab Leaders*, ed. Misha Louvish, trans. Aryeh Rubinstein (New York: Third Press, 1973), 15. Ben-Gurion to Weizmann, August 5, 1934, and to Louis Brandeis, December 6, 1940, BGA.

81. Black, *Enemies and Neighbors*, 70. By the mid-1930s Ben-Gurion would be named Jewish Agency chairman, and Shertok would remain sole director of the political department.

82. Neil Caplan, *Futile Diplomacy*, vol. 2, *Arab-Zionist Negotiations and the End of the Mandate* (London; New York: Routledge, 2015), 189–92. Teveth, *Burning Ground*, 133.

83. Ben-Gurion, *My Talks*, 15–17. Teveth, *Palestinian Arabs*, 132–34.

84. Ben-Gurion diary, September 4, 1934. BGA. Ben-Gurion, *My Talks*, 15. Teveth, *Palestinian Arabs*, 132–34.

85. Furlonge, *Palestine*, 103. Alami made similar comments on Ben-Gurion to Shertok. See Shertok to Mapai Central Committee, June 21, 1936, LPA 2–23–1936-13.

86. Handwritten notes between Ben-Gurion and Alami, in "Arab individuals," BGA STA file 871, 69ff.

87. In talks with Alami, Ben-Gurion spoke specifically about a "Jewish state"; in the later note to Judah Magnes he spoke merely of a "state of *Eretz-Israel.*" Ben-Gurion diary, September 4 and September 7, 1934, BGA. Ben-Gurion, *My Talks*, 24–34. Teveth, *Palestinian Arabs*, 137–42. Segev, *One Palestine*, 375.

88. Ben-Gurion was characteristically prescient: Israel's Jewish population is predicted to reach eight million by 2024. Ben-Gurion, *My Talks*, 35–39. David Ben-Gurion, *Zichronot* [Memoirs], 6 vols. (Tel Aviv: Am Oved, 1971–1987), 3:253, 3:283. Teveth, *Palestinian Arabs*, 142–46. A more skeptical account of the encounter (in which Ben-Gurion's outrage was mere "face saving") is in Teveth, *Burning Ground*, 490.

89. Ben-Gurion diary, June 11, 1969, BGA. Ben-Gurion, *My Talks*, 40. Teveth, *Palestinian Arabs*, 147–48, 197. Ben-Gurion later recounted these talks in his 1937 Peel Commission private testimony (see Chapter 3).

Chapter 2

1. Shai Lachman, "Arab Rebellion and Terrorism in Palestine, 1929–1939: The Case of Qassam and his Movement," in *Zionism and Arabism in Palestine and Israel*, ed. Elie Kedourie and Sylvia G. Haim (London; New York: Routledge, 2015), 59–62. On the question of Rida, Abduh, and other Islamic modernists' influence on Qassam, see also Mark Sanagan, "Teacher, Preacher, Soldier, Martyr: Rethinking 'Izz al-Din al-Qassam," *Die Welt des Islams* 53, no. 3–4 (2013): 326–28.

2. Abdullah Schleifer, "The Life and Thought of 'Izz-Id-Din Al-Qassam," *Islamic Quarterly* 23, no. 2 (1979): 63.

3. Ibid., 65. Kedourie and Haim, *Zionism and Arabism*, 59–60. Yasin, *Thawrah*, 19–20.

4. Ted Swedenburg, "Al-Qassam Remembered," *Alif: Journal of Comparative Poetics*, no. 7 (Spring 1987): 17. Sonia Nimr, "The Arab Revolt of 1936–1939 in Palestine: A Study Based on Oral Sources" (PhD diss., University of Exeter, 1990), 66–67. Basheer M. Nafi, "Shaykh Izz al-Din al-Qassam: A Reformist and a Rebel Leader," *Journal of Islamic Studies* 8, no. 2 (February 1, 1997): 194–95. Kabha, *Palestinian Press*, 169.

5. For differing accounts of Qassam's knowledge of and participation in these attacks, see Kedourie and Haim, *Zionism and Arabism*, 64–66; Porath, *Palestinian Arab*, 134–35; Yasin, *Thawrah*, 26. *Mashayekh* could also be translated as "elders."

6. In 1918 Jews made up just one-eighth of Haifa's population, and four years later their share had doubled; they were likely a majority by 1938 at the latest. Maya Seikaly, *Haifa: Transformation of an Arab Society 1918–1939* (London: I.B. Tauris, 2002), xvii–xix, 47–51, 240ff. Tamir Goren, "The Judaization of Haifa at the Time of the Arab Revolt," *Middle Eastern Studies* 40, no. 4 (July 2004): 141. Cohen, *Britain's Moment*, 262n17.

7. Mahmoud Yazbak, "From Poverty to Revolt: Economic Factors in the Outbreak of the 1936 Rebellion in Palestine," *Middle Eastern Studies* 36, no. 3 (July 2000): 106–7.

8. Schleifer, "Life and Thought," 63–71, 75.

9. "Cmd. 5479," 279–80. Sachar, *History of Israel*, 189; Krämer, *History of Palestine*, 240, 264; Kedourie and Haim, *Zionism and Arabism*, 53, 67–68; Abboushi, "Road to Rebellion," 28–29; Stein, *Land Question in Palestine*, 182.

10. Cohen, *Britain's Moment*, 245–48.

11. *Al-Difa*, September 30, 1935. Kedourie and Haim, *Zionism and Arabism*, 68–69.

12. Hathorn Hall to MacDonald, October 22, 1935, TNA CO 733/278/13. See also Kedourie and Haim, *Zionism and Arabism*, 69–70. *Thawrat Filastin Ama 1936* [The Palestine Revolt 1936] (Jaffa: Matba'at al-Jamia al-Islamiya, 1936), 24–26.

13. Rosenfeld's murder appears to have been a spontaneous act, neither planned nor instructed by Qassam. See Sanagan, "Teacher, Preacher," 345. Kedourie and Haim, *Zionism and Arabism*, 71. Porath, *Palestinian Arab*, 136.

14. A British constable, R. C. Mott, was also killed. Sanagan, "Teacher, Preacher," 347. Yasin, *Thawrah*, 29–30.

15. *Al-Difa*, November 20, 1935. *Filastin*, November 22 and 24, 1935. In private, Yusuf Hanna, a Christian, wrote, "Terrorism is rooted in Islam," and denounced Qassam as "the first terrorist." See Hanna to Levy, November 28, 1935, ISA P-695/5, and May 28, 1937, ISA P-695/6.

16. Ben-Gurion to Mapai Central Committee, December 2, 1935, LPA 2–3–1929-22. See also Ben-Gurion to Mapai Central Committee, September 29, 1936, LPA 2–023–1936-14; and July 6, 1938, LPA 2–23–1938-20. Ben-Gurion, *Zichronot*, 2:531. Teveth, *Palestinian Arabs*, 151.

17. "Palestine," HC Deb, March 24, 1936, vol. 310, col. 1079, 1083, 1094–95, 1103–4, 1113–16, 1123–26, 1147–48. "Palestine," HL Deb, February 26, 1936, vol. 99, col. 753, 766, 790.

18. The legislative council was to be half Arab, one-quarter Jewish, and one-quarter British and "others." A number of prominent Arabs backed the idea, even with reservations, but the mufti called it a "dish mixed with poison" unless it stopped land sales and immigration completely. See Abboushi, "Road to Rebellion," 30–33; Elath, "Conversations," 41–47; Zvi Elpeleg, ed., *Through the Eyes of the Mufti: The Essays of Haj Amin*, trans. Rachel Kessel (London; Portland, OR, 2009), 39, 41.

19. Rami Hazan (Israel Hazan's grandson) to the author, August 16 and October 3, 2017. "Zvi Dannenberg," Israel Ministry of Defense, https://www.izkor.gov.il.

20. *Palestine Post*, *Filastin*, and *Al-Difa*, April 17, 1936.

21. "The robbery and murder on the Nur Shams-Anabta road," April 1936, HA 8/36/26. Recollection by Yehoshua Nafkhi, the third man in the car, in Alexander Zauber, *Dam Kedoshim be-Afar ha-Kvish* [Blood of Martyrs on the Dirt Road] (Tel Aviv: Sefer, 1936), 12–15. Akram Zuaytir, *Yawmiyat Akram Zuaytir* [Diaries of Akram Zuaytir] (Beirut: Institute for Palestine Studies, 1980), 53–54.

22. Ofer Aderet, "The Intifada That Raged More Than 10 Years Before Israel Was Established," *Haaretz*, April 16, 2016.

23. "Nablus Bandits Seen as Izz ed Din's Followers," and "The Desert vs Civilization," *Palestine Post*, April 17 and 24, 1936. *Do'ar Hayom*, April 17, 1936.

24. The shooters appear to have been members of the Irgun (on the group, see Chapter 4). Slutsky, *Sefer Toldot*, 2:631–32, 657. Bracha Habas, *Me'ora'ot Tartzav* [The 1936 Events] (Tel Aviv: Davar, 1937), 420. Zuaytir, *Yawmiyat*, 55.

25. "The disturbances and their development," April 1936, HA 8/36/427–430. Habas, *Me'ora'ot*, 421–22. Slutsky, *Sefer Toldot*, 2:632–33, 1192.

26. The government's version of events is "Col. 129: Report by His Majesty's Government [. . .] to the Council of the League of Nations on the Administration of Palestine and Trans-Jordan for the Year 1936" (His Majesty's Stationery Office, 1937), 7. The Jewish Agency's is in Weizmann to Wauchope, July 18, 1937, WA.

27. "Disturbances and their development," HA 8/36/431–432. Habas, *Me'ora'ot*, 424–25. Slutsky, *Sefer Toldot*, 2:632–33. Ben-Gurion, *Zichronot*, 3:122. "Col. 129," 7. Weizmann to Wauchope, July 18, 1937, WA. See also Kelly, *Crime of Nationalism*, 11–12.

28. "Robbery and murder," HA 8/36/27–33. "Disturbances and their development," HA 8/36/433–435. "Col. 129," 7. Weizmann to Wauchope, July 18, 1937, WA. Joseph Levy, "11 Killed, 50 Hurt in Palestine Riots," *New York Times*, April 20, 1936. *Al-Liwa* and *Al-Difa*, April 20, 1936. *Filastin*, April 21, 1936. Kelly, *Crime of Nationalism*, 11–12.

29. "Disturbances and their development," HA 8/36/441–444. Habas, *Me'ora'ot*, 4, 14–18, 637. Bichutsky's killer was sentenced to fifteen years' hard labor; *Haaretz*, June 10, 1936.

30. "Robbery and murder," HA 8/36/27, 33–36; "Disturbances and their development," HA 8/36/438, 442–444. Yosef Lieberman, a carter, was also apparently killed near the police station in Ajami, though the manner, time, and location were never precisely determined. Habas, *Me'ora'ot*, 4–5, 17–19, 638–40. "Shambadal, David," The Haganah—Official Site, http://irgon-haagana.co.il.

31. Slutsky, *Sefer Toldot*, 2:634. Habas, *Me'ora'ot*, 4–6, 14–16, 19–22.

32. "Robbery and murder," HA 8/36/37, 436. "Col. 129," 7. *Al-Difa*, April 20, 1936. *Filastin*, April 21, 1936. Weizmann called the charges of Jews stoning cars "utterly unsubstantiated"; Weizmann to Wauchope, July 18, 1937, WA.

33. Hauranis appear to have taken a lead role in the violence from the start. "Robbery and murder," HA 8/36/26–32; "Disturbances and their development," HA 8/36/434–444. Joseph Levy, "11 Killed, 50 Hurt in Palestine Riots," and "Deaths Rise to 20 in Palestine Riots," *New York Times*, April 20 and 21, 1936. Krämer, *History of Palestine*, 277.

34. Witnesses spoke of "hundreds" of Arabs throwing stones at vehicles on the road to Jerusalem. The wives of two senior British officials were seriously wounded. Tamir Goren, "The Destruction of Old Jaffa in 1936 and the Question of the Arab Refugees," *Middle Eastern Studies* 55, no. 6 (November 2, 2019): 1007. *Filastin*, April 21, 1936. Habas, *Me'ora'ot*, 10. Levy, "11 Killed, 50 Hurt in Palestine Riots."

35. *Al-Difa*, April 20, 1936. *Filastin*, April 21, 1936. Zuaytir, *Yawmiyat*, 64–65, 68–69. "Palestine: The Disturbances of 1936 Statistical Tables" (Jerusalem: Jewish Agency for Palestine, December 1936).

36. "Disturbances and their development," HA 8/36/442–443. Habas, *Me'ora'ot*, 4, 19–20. 640. The victims' names were Yosef Haim Zelikov and Shemayahu Kramer.

37. *Davar*, April 20, 1936. Yasin, *Thawrah*, 30–31. "Jaffa's Shame," *Palestine Post*, April 20, 1936.

38. *Al-Difa*, *Filastin*, and *Al-Jamia al-Islamiya*, April 20, 1936. *Davar*, April 21, 1936.

39. "Col. 129," 9–10. Abboushi, "Road to Rebellion," 36–37. Official Communiques, April 19–21, 1936, ISA M-567/3.

40. "Although the situation is now quiet," the *New York Times* reported, "no one can foretell what tomorrow will bring." Levy, "11 killed, 50 Hurt in Palestine Riots." Albert Viton, "Why Arabs Kill Jews," *The Nation*, June 3, 1936.

41. Trial notes for Levinson-Marsum murders, ISA P-197/18. Also "Robbery and murder," HA 8/36/37, "Disturbances and their development," HA 8/36/442–443; Habas, *Me'ora'ot*, 9, 641. "2 More Jews Die of Riot Wounds; 10 Wounded in New Jaffa Attacks," and "18 Jews, 12 Arabs Dead in 4 Days of Palestine Riots; Strike Spreads," JTA, April 22 and 23, 1936. The recent arrivals were Tuvia Prusak and Daniel Cohen.

42. "Robbery and murder," HA 8/36/37, "Disturbances and their development," HA 8/36/442–444. Habas, *Me'ora'ot*, 4–12, 20, 642. Their names were Simha Siman-Tov, Shalom Haddad (from wounds sustained the first day), and Yitzhak Zeitlin. Israel later renamed King George Street as Jerusalem Boulevard.

43. "Highwayman's Second Victim Dead," *Palestine Post*, April 21, 1936.

44. "Col. 129," 9–10. One of the Arabs killed the second day was named as Abd al-Laqa; reports differ as to the others. *Al-Difa* and *Al-Liwa*, April 21, 1936.

45. Susan Silsby Boyle, *Betrayal of Palestine: The Story of George Antonius* (Boulder, CO: Westview, 2001), 24–25, 85–86, 102–3, 127–28, 136–46. Fouad Ajami, *The Dream Palace of the Arabs: A Generation's Odyssey* (New York: Vintage, 1999), 17–18. Forster to Antonius, January 28, 1917, ISA P-1053/11. For Crane's report and related primary sources, see "King-Crane Commission Digital Collection," Oberlin College Archives, https://www2.oberlin.edu/library/digital/king-crane/.

46. George Antonius, *The Arab Awakening* (New York: Lippincott, 1939), 54–55, 79–91, 107–21, 164–83, 237–42, 276–78, 413–27, passim.

47. The proposed fate of other areas, including Galilee, is unclear in this plan. Ben-Gurion, *My Talks*, 42–44, 49–62. Ben-Gurion, *Zichronot*, 1:3, 130–31, 232–33, 254. Ben-Gurion briefly mentioned these meetings in his Peel Commission private testimony (see Chapter 3).

48. Wauchope was skeptical of the talks' value, suggesting Antonius had little direct political influence. Shertok believed even an "intellectual" agreement was worthwhile; see Moshe Sharett, *Yoman Medini* [Political Diary], vol. 1 (Tel Aviv: Am Oved, 1968), May 22, 1936. Shabtai Teveth depicts the talks as a mere "academic exercise" for both sides; see Teveth, *Burning Ground*, 538–40, and *Palestinian Arabs*, 159–67, 192–93. See also Michael J. Cohen, "Secret Diplomacy and Rebellion in Palestine, 1936–1939," *International Journal of Middle Eastern Studies* 8, no. 3 (July 1977): 380–85.

49. Zuaytir, *Yawmiyat*, 61–67, 76–82. "Cmd. 5479," 96–97. Yasin, *Thawrah*, 31. *Al-Liwa* and *Al-Difa*, April 20, 1936. Arnon-Ohanah, *Mered Arvi*, 34. Porath, *Palestinian Arab*, 169–70. Mattar, *Mufti of Jerusalem*, 147.

50. Wauchope to Ormsby-Gore, May 8, 1936, TNA CAB 24/262. Porath, *Palestinian Arab*, 220–21.

51. Hillel Cohen, *Army of Shadows: Palestinian Collaboration with Zionism, 1917–1948*, trans. Haim Watzman (Berkeley: University of California Press, 2008), 15–17, 99–112, 109. Fadi Eyadat, "Haifa Honors First Mayor's Legacy of Coexistence," *Haaretz*, February 18, 2010. Police investigators' report (likely 1937), MECA Tegart Papers 1/3c/111ff. For punishment of "traitors" see also Yasin, *Thawrah*, 37–38.

52. *Davar*, April 22, 1936. Porath, *Palestinian Arab*, 175–76.

53. Kenneth Stein, "Palestine's Rural Economy, 1917–1939," *Studies in Zionism* 8, no. 1 (1987): 45. Arnon-Ohanah, *Mered Arvi*, 255. In Avigdor Hameiri, ed., *Shirat ha-Damim; Kovetz Shirim mi-Tovei Meshorerenu al Me'ore'ot 5696* [Poem of Blood: A Collection from

Our Best Poets on the Events of 5696] (Tel Aviv: Sifrut La'am, 1936), 32. Translation is the author's.

54. The port represented the beginning of a "Jewish sea," he said; without the Jews, Jaffa Port was "fated to be destroyed." Ben-Gurion, *Zichronot*, 3:343. Ben-Gurion to Mapai Central Committee, September 29, 1936, LPA 2–023–1936-14. Teveth, *Burning Ground*, 547–48. Ben-Gurion diary, July 11, 1936, BGA.

55. On *havlagah*: Slutsky, *Sefer Toldot*, 2:833–46; Ian Black, *Zionism and the Arabs, 1936–1939* (London; New York: Routledge, 1978, 2015), 365–380; Meir Chazan, "The Dispute in Mapai over 'Self-Restraint' and 'Purity of Arms' During the Arab Revolt," *Jewish Social Studies: History, Culture, Society* 15, no. 3 (Spring/Summer 2009): 92–93. See also "*Havlagah*," BGA STA file 57, passim.

56. Sakakini, *Kadha Ana ya Dunya*, 286–87. Sakakini, who knew the perpetrator, rejoiced in Ansari's act: "There is no heroism like this, except the heroism of Sheikh al-Qassam." See Segev, *One Palestine*, 365–66. For the police investigation into the incident, see MECA Tegart Papers 1/3c, 37ff.

57. Sharett, *Yoman Medini*, vol. 1, June 21, 1936. Shertok undated memo, CZA S25/3435. Ben-Gurion, *My Talks*, 55, 85–91. Caplan, *Futile Diplomacy*, 213–15.

58. Porath, *Palestinian Arab*, 184ff.

59. Hala Sakakini, *Jerusalem and I: A Personal Record* (Amman: Economic Press, 1990), 58. Kedourie and Haim, *Zionism and Arabism*, 74. For a fuller biography of Abdel-Rahim, see Sonia Nimr, "A Nation in a Hero: Abdul Rahim Hajj Mohammad and the Arab Revolt," in *Struggle and Survival in Palestine/Israel*, ed. Mark LeVine and Gershon Shafir (Berkeley: University of California Press, 2012), 144ff. Ezra Danin, ed., *Teudot u-Demuyot mi-Ginze ha-Kenufyot ha-Arviyot bi-Me'ore'ot 1936–1939* [Documents and Portraits from the Arab Gangs' Archives in the Arab Revolt in Palestine 1936–1939], 2nd ed. (Jerusalem: Magnes Press, 1981), 30–48, 91–104. On Abdel-Rahim and Abdel-Raziq see Chapters 6 and 7.

60. Collective fines were imposed on Nablus, Acre, Safed, and Lydda in June, and Jaffa in August. "Col. 129," 10–11. Abboushi, "Road to Rebellion," 36. Martin Gilbert, *Atlas of the Arab-Israeli Conflict*, 6th ed. (New York: Oxford University Press, 1993), 20.

61. Dispatch by Air Vice-Marshal Peirse, October 15, 1936, TNA CO 733/317. See also Matthew Kelly, "The Revolt of 1936: A Revision," *Journal of Palestine Studies* 44, no. 2 (2015): 32–34; Hughes, *Britain's Pacification of Palestine*, 190–92; Arnon-Ohanah, *Mered Arvi*, 65–67; *Al-Liwa*, June 13 and 14, 1936.

62. "An Appeal to Conscientious Britishers," July 15, 1936, HA 8/39–120.

63. "An Open Letter to the Jews," June 18, 1936, HA 8/38–284.

64. Matthew Hughes, "Assassination in Jerusalem: Bahjat Abu Gharbiyah and Sami Al-Ansari's Shooting of British Assistant Superintendent Alan Sigrist 12th June 1936," *Jerusalem Quarterly* 44 (2010): 6–10. Yasin, *Thawrah*, 171. *Filastin*, June 20, 1936.

65. Sakakini, *Kadha Ana ya Dunya*, 286–87. Zuaytir, *Yawmiyat*, 171. *Filastin*, June 20 and July 27, 1936. See also Sandy Sufian, "Anatomy of the 1936–1939 Revolt: Images of the Body in Political Cartoons of Mandatory Palestine," *Journal of Palestine Studies* 37, no. 2 (Winter 2008): 32–34.

66. Michael F. J. McDonnell and R. J. Manning, "The Town Planning of Jaffa 1936: Judgments," in *From Haven to Conquest*, ed. Walid Khalidi (Beirut: Institute for Palestine Studies, 1971), 343–51. Yasin, *Thawrah*, 199–200. *Al-Difa*, June 17 and 18, 1936; *Filastin*, June 25 and 28, 1936. Compensation was ultimately offered; see "Emergency Regulations (Compensation for Jaffa Demolitions), 1936," *Palestine Gazette*, no. 627, supp. 2; Goren, "Destruction of Old Jaffa," 1008. An image of Old Jaffa's demolition appears on the cover of this book.

67. Porath, *Palestinian Arab*, 193–95. Mattar, *Mufti of Jerusalem*, 78–79.

68. "Col. 129," 16. Slutsky, *Sefer Toldot*, 2:656. Gilbert, *Atlas of the Arab-Israeli Conflict*, 20–21.

69. "Murder of Inspector Naif," *Palestine Post*, August 5, 1936. "Moslem Leader Slain in Arab Factional Fight," *JTA*, September 28, 1936. Cohen, *Army of Shadows*, 105–6. Arnon-Ohanah, *Mered Arvi*, 68. Kedourie and Haim, *Zionism and Arabism*, 79. A police investigators' report (likely from 1937) blamed armed leader Yusuf Abu Dorra; MECA Tegart Papers 1/3c/105ff.

70. Slutsky, *Sefer Toldot*, 2:881–93.

71. "Lewis Billig, Arabic Scholar Shot Dead While at Studies," and "Lewis Billig" (obituary), *Palestine Post*, August 23, 1936.

72. "To the neighboring nation that dwells with us in this land, he was a true man of peace," eulogized the German-Jewish orientalist S. D. Goitein. "I felt a glimmer of consolation in that he was killed in an instant, and didn't suffer as did many of our fallen brothers." "The Funeral" and "Tribute to Lewis Billig," *Palestine Post*, August 23, 1936.

73. Danin, *Teudot*, 1–5. Hanna to Levy, October (no date) 1936, ISA P-695/5. Roger Courtney, *Palestine Policeman* (London: Jenkins, 1939), 69.

74. Laila Parsons, *The Commander: Fawzi al-Qawuqji and the Fight for Arab Independence, 1914–1948* (New York: Hill and Wang, 2016), 21–25, 36, 93, 106–21, 266n. Laila Parsons, "Rebels Without Borders," in *The Routledge Handbook of the History of the Middle East Mandates*, ed. Cyrus Schayegh and Andrew Arsan (London; New York: Routledge, 2015), 398–404.

75. Akram Zuaytir, citing a *Haaretz* report, lists Fawzi's contingent as one hundred men, with the British fielding five hundred. Zuaytir, *Yawmiyat*, 54–56, 162–63, 167. Porath, *Palestinian Arab*, 189–90. Parsons, *Commander*, 125–26. Danin, *Teudot*, 2–3. Parsons, *Commander*, 118–22. Nimr, "Arab Revolt," 95–96. Zuaytir, *Yawmiyat*, 161–62.

76. The account of the Second Battalion, Royal Lincolnshire Regiment, says one plane landed safely. See *On Special Service in Malta and Palestine, 19th September 1935–20th December 1936* (Portsmouth: Navy, Army and Air Force Institutes, 1937). Rebels took the dead pilot's photos and money, but Fawzi later claimed he made sure they were returned to his widow: "I should be very relieved to know that the poor wife has received her husband's papers." Hanna to Levy, October 1936, ISA P-695/5.

77. Courtney, *Palestine Policeman*, 69. Parsons, *Commander*, 123. "Packer, Charles Ernest," IWMSA 4493/1. One salient exception to the reluctance of notables to join the revolt was Abdel-Qader Husseini, who led a band in the Jerusalem area.

78. "Gratton, John Stewart Sancroft," IWMSA 4506/2.

79. Some Arabs felt the same. Yusuf Hanna groused that he was immoral and corrupt, with nothing to match the Jews' scientific acumen beyond fatwas. Hanna to Levy, November 8, 1936, ISA P-695/5. Wauchope to Ormsby-Gore, August 20 and 22, 1936, TNA CAB 24/263/55, and September 12, 1936, CAB/264/29. Ormsby-Gore to Wauchope, September 1, 1936, CAB/23/85.

80. Hughes, *Britain's Pacification of Palestine*, 75.

81. The same day the AHC accepted the appeal and called to end the disorders and the strike. Husseini, *Mudhakkirat*, 26–27. Porath, *Palestinian Arab*, 212–15. Sakakini, *Kadha Ana ya Dunya*, 290.

82. Michael J. Cohen, "Origins of the Arab States' Involvement in Palestine," *Middle Eastern Studies* 19, no. 2 (April 1983): 244–52. Aaron S. Klieman, "The Arab States and Palestine," in Kedourie and Haim, *Zionism and Arabism*, 119–34. Porath, *Palestinian Arab*, 199–216. Ben-Gurion, *My Talks*, 104–21.

83. "League of Nations Permanent Mandates Commission Minutes [. . .] Devoted to Palestine," August 4, 1937. See also "Disturbances 1936–1939," BGA STA file 212, 43–57.

84. Morris, *Righteous Victims*, 135; Porath, *Palestinian Arab*, 215; Zuaytir, *Yawmiyat*, 211–12.

85. Other sources put the figure of admirers at five thousand or even fifteen thousand. See for example Royal Lincolnshire Regiment, *On Special Service*; Danin, *Teudot*, 7; Zuaytir, *Yawmiyat*, 221–22.

86. Parsons, *Commander*, 134, 139, 163.

87. Authorities had suspended Arabic newspapers thirty-four times and Hebrew ones thirteen times. "Col. 129," 19–20. "Cmd. 5479," 105–6. Sachar, 201. Kimmerling and Migdal, *Palestinian People*, 129. Boyle, *Betrayal of Palestine*, 24, 50–52. Antonius, *Arab Awakening*, 111–15, 152–58.

88. Sakakini, *Kadha Ana ya Dunya*, 290.

89. "The land promised to the Jews is not empty but one in which the Arabs have been settled for a long time—maybe not less time than the English have been settled in England," he said. Ben-Gurion to Mapai Central Committee, September 29, 1936, LPA 2-3-1929-22. See also similar remarks on July 6, 1938, LPA 2-23-1938-2; Segev, *One Palestine*, 370–71. On gaps between his and colleagues' views of the Palestinian-Arab national movement, see Haim, *Abandonment of Illusions*, 132–33, 137.

Chapter 3

1. "Moussa Eff. Alami," ISA M-758/25.

2. Luigi Goglia, "Il Mufti e Mussolini: alcuni documenti italiani sui rapporti tra nazionalismo palestinese e fascismo negli anni trenta," *Storia Contemporanea* 17, no. 6 (December 1986): 1220. Nir Arielli, "Italian Involvement in the Arab Revolt in Palestine," *British Journal of Middle Eastern Studies* 35, no. 2 (August 2008): 194–96. Nir Arielli, *Fascist Italy and the Middle East, 1933–1940* (New York: Palgrave Macmillan, 2013), 113.

3. Arielli, "Italian Involvement," 191–92; and *Fascist Italy*, 116. "Currency converter: 1270–2017," The National Archives, https://www.nationalarchives.gov.uk/currency-converter.

4. Note by Leo Kohn, February 23, 1934, WA 22–1725 (for Mussolini's portrait see WA 4–1725). Chaim Weizmann, *The Letters and Papers of Chaim Weizmann, Series B*, ed. Barnet Litvinoff, vol. 2 (New Brunswick, NJ; Jerusalem: Transaction Books; Israel Universities Press, 1983). Motti Golani, "The Meat and the Bones: Reassessing the Origins of the Partition of Mandate Palestine," in *Partitions: A Transnational History of Twentieth-Century Territorial Separatism*, ed. Arie Dubnov and Laura Robson (Stanford: Stanford University Press, 2019), 98. See also Norman Rose, *The Gentile Zionists: A Study in Anglo-Zionist Diplomacy, 1929–1939* (London: F. Cass, 1973), 102ff.

5. Eran Kaplan, *The Jewish Radical Right: Revisionist Zionism and Its Ideological Legacy* (Madison, WI: University of Wisconsin Press, 2005), 157.

6. Penny Sinanoglou, *Partitioning Palestine: British Policymaking at the End of Empire* (Chicago: University of Chicago Press, 2019), 31. For background on Coupland see Arie Dubnov, "The Architect of Two Partitions or a Federalist Daydreamer? The Curious Case of Reginald Coupland," in Dubnov and Robson, *Partitions*, 56ff; Monty Noam Penkower, *Palestine in Turmoil: The Struggle for Sovereignty, 1933–1939*, vol. 2 (New York: Touro College, 2014), chap. 6, passim.

7. "Cmd. 5479," ix.

8. Ormsby-Gore lodged Weizmann at his home while the Cabinet debated the Balfour Declaration. He was also the government's liaison to the 1918 Zionist Commission to Palestine. Scott Anderson presents his religious conversion as fact, a conclusion uncorroborated elsewhere. See Scott Anderson, *Lawrence in Arabia* (New York: Anchor, 2013), 254.

9. *Al-Liwa*, November 8, 1936. *Al-Difa*, November 11, 1936. Taggar, *Mufti of Jerusalem*, 423. Porath, *Palestinian Arab*, 221–23. Ben-Gurion also expected an immigration stoppage and was euphoric at the reversal; see his diary, November 5, 1936, BGA.

10. Cox to Moody, February 11, 1937, TNA CO 733/326/4. Hanna to Levy, December 19, 1936, and January 7, 1937, ISA P-695/5. Zuaytir, *Yawmiyat*, 239. Furlonge, *Palestine*, 110, 117. Taggar, *Mufti of Jerusalem*, 424–26. Elath, "Conversations," 54. Kabha, *Palestinian Press*, 237.

11. Husseini, *Mudhakkirat*, 17. Taggar, *Mufti of Jerusalem*, 418, 424.

12. Ormsby-Gore to Eden, October 1, 1936, TNA FO 954/12B/383.

13. "Cmd. 5479," ix. Sinanoglou, *Partitioning Palestine*, 65. "Royal Commission in Jerusalem," *The Times*, November 12, 1936.

14. Black, *Enemies and Neighbors*, 79. Ian Black and Benny Morris, *Israel's Secret Wars: A History of Israel's Intelligence Services* (New York: Grove Press, 2003), 12. Segev, *One Palestine*, 278–80. The Palace Hotel building is currently home to the Waldorf Astoria.

15. "Haj Amin's letter to Earl Peel" (likely November 1936), MECA Jerusalem and the East Mission Papers (JEM) 65/1.

16. "Col. 134: Palestine Royal Commission: Minutes of Evidence Heard at Public Sessions" (His Majesty's Stationery Office, 1937), iii–v.

17. Weizmann, *Letters*, series B, vol. 2, 283. Storrs, *Memoirs*, 439. Blanche E. C. Dugdale, *Baffy: The Diaries of Blanche Dugdale, 1936–1947*, ed. Norman Rose (London: Vallentine Mitchell, 1973, reissued 2021), 62.

18. Shertok testified five times in public and twice in private, though four of these were in tandem with other witnesses; Weizmann testified alone each time. "Col. 134," viii–ix.

19. "Col. 134," 30–39.

20. Weizmann, *Letters*, series B, vol. 2, 132–36, 150.

21. Ibid., 141, 192–93.

22. Ibid., 200.

23. Ibid., 162–68.

24. According to the minutes, Weizmann referred to the fallen Qassam as "Sheikh Kasr Abdin." It is unclear whether the error was his or the stenographer's. Ibid., 133, 143, 252.

25. Ibid., 175, 212–21, 236.

26. Ibid., 233–49. The final report quotes Weizmann's comment ("that we exist") anonymously; "Cmd. 5479," 110.

27. Weizmann, *Letters*, series B, vol. 2, 257ff. Most of the Zionist leadership thought Weizmann's testimony masterly. Ben-Gurion, a frequent Weizmann critic, praised his delivery but felt he displayed "irresponsibility" and over-eagerness to concede. See Ben-Gurion diary, December 9, 23, 24, and 30, 1936, BGA, and Teveth, *Burning Ground*, 574–82, 587–88.

28. Weizmann's secretary said that after the session he tearfully marveled that the long toil of his life had been crowned with success. Christopher Sykes, *Crossroads to Israel* (Bloomington: Indiana University Press, 1973), 153–67. Rose, *Gentile Zionists*, 123–45.

29. Weizmann, *Letters*, series B, vol. 2, 228, 259–64. For a skeptical take on Weizmann's years-long commitment to partition, see Teveth, *Burning Ground*, 587ff.

30. Laila Parsons, "The Secret Testimony of the Peel Commission (Part I): Underbelly of Empire," *Journal of Palestine Studies* 49, no. 1 (Autumn 2019): appendix, 1–4.

31. Taggar, *Mufti of Jerusalem*, 425–26. Yoav Gelber, *Jewish-Transjordanian Relations, 1921–48*. (London; Portland, OR: F. Cass, 1997), 95–98. *Filastin*, January 7, 1937.

32. "Cmd. 5479," xii. Hanna to Levy, December 19, 1936, ISA P-695/5, and to Mrs. Levy, January 18, 1937, P-695/6. Ben-Gurion diary, May 11, 1937, BGA. Gelber, *Jewish-Transjordanian Relations*, 92–93, 108–9. The emir received 3,700 pounds from Zionist leaders in the two years following the outbreak of riots; see Black, *Zionism and the Arabs*, 168. For Abdullah's written memo to the commission, see Hathorn Hall to Ormsby-Gore, March 4, 1937, TNA CO 733/344/11.

33. "Col. 134," 293–95. Sykes, *Crossroads to Israel*, 162–63. Zuaytir, *Yawmiyat*, 257ff.

34. AHC memorandum to Royal Commission, January 10, 1937, ISA P-3060/6.

35. "Col. 134," 296–98, 305–23.

36. Wauchope to Ormsby-Gore, December 15, 1936, and January 12, 1937, TNA CAB 24/267/1 and 24/267/31. Taggar, *Mufti of Jerusalem*, 428. Furlonge, *Palestine*, 110–11.

37. Peel's final report noted the complete monopoly the AHC enjoyed over Arab witnesses, and that all either represented the AHC or, like Antonius, testified with its assent. All "supported, in toto, the Arab Higher Committee's case." "Cmd. 5479," 132. Hussein Khalidi began his testimony saying, "I am a member of the Arab Higher Committee. I am the Mayor of Jerusalem," but emphasized he was speaking only in the former capacity." "Col. 134," 335.

38. "Col. 134," 358–67. Antonius testimony in "Abandoned documents, Government of Palestine," ISA P-3059/16. Antonius to Walter Rogers, February 16, 1937, ICWA. Zuaytir, *Yawmiyat*, 274–76. The final report cited the sentiment behind the "no decent-minded person" remark, attributing it to an "able exponent of the Arab case." See "Cmd. 5479," 395.

39. Dubnov and Robson, *Partitions*, 59, 68ff, 104ff. Sinanoglou, *Partitioning Palestine*, 112. Laila Parsons, "The Secret Testimony of the Peel Commission (Part II): Partition," *Journal of Palestine Studies* 49, no. 2 (winter 2020): 11–19.

40. Laila Parsons is the first scholar to analyze the committee's newly unclassified secret sessions, and to recognize Harris's pivotal role in formulating and endorsing a partition plan: Parsons, "Secret Testimony (Part I)," 11ff. Harris had worked under Archer Cust, formerly a senior Palestine official, who in 1935 wrote a detailed memo on cantonization. Harris's first line of testimony acknowledges Cust's plan as a basis for his own. For Cust see Sinanoglou, *Partitioning Palestine*, 53–64; Roza El-Eini, *Mandated Landscape: British Imperial Rule in Palestine, 1929–1948* (London; New York: Routledge, 2015), 317–24, 368–69, 535; Dubnov and Robson, *Partitions*, 74–76, 100–102; Chaim Weizmann, *The Letters and Papers of Chaim Weizmann, Series A*, ed. Barnet Litvinoff, vol. 17–19 (Jerusalem: Israel Universities Press, 1979), 261–62, 293–95.

41. Harris put Acre itself in the Arab state. Originally he proposed that that state also include Jaffa, connected to it by a corridor. But he agreed with Coupland's idea that the corridor could instead link the city to the Mandate enclave around Jerusalem.

42. "Palestine Royal Commission: Minutes of Evidence Heard at Secret Sessions," TNA FO 492/19, 440–43. Harris also suggested some Arab-owned lands in the Jewish state be exchanged for Jewish-owned lands in the Arab state of similar value.

43. The following day, Coupland met secretly with Weizmann at Moshav Nahalal, where the former's faith in partition cemented further. Sinanoglou, *Partitioning Palestine*, 110; Dubnov and Robson, *Partitions*, 103–5; Penkower, *Palestine in Turmoil*, 368–69; Sykes, *Crossroads to Israel*, 165–66. Coupland corresponded with Harris in April 1937, and much of the latter's text on partition appears in the commission's final report. Parsons, "Secret Testimony (Part II)," 15–17; El-Eini, *Mandated Landscape*, 318–24.

44. "Secret Sessions," TNA FO 492/19. Laila Parsons was alerted to the files' existence by Steven B. Wagner, who generously provided them to this author. See Parsons, "Secret Testimony (Part I)," 9–10, passim, and "Secret Testimony (Part II)," passim. A few Zionist leaders retained their secret testimonies, likely aided in transcription by the aforementioned hidden microphone; see Weizmann, *Letters*, series B, vol. 2, 126ff; Ben-Gurion, *Zichronot*, 4:8–18.

45. Andrews had likely presented Coupland this assessment in a prior, private conversation. Earlier that day, Coupland told Palestine Chief Secretary John Hathorn Hall: "One or two moderate Arabs have suggested" partition, and said the "mayor of Jerusalem . . . his group is interested." Hathorn Hall expressed surprise, predicting that beyond some allies of Abdullah, few Palestinian Arabs would accept division. "Secret Sessions," TNA FO 492/19, 431–32, 444. Yusuf Hanna attributed the "cancer" comments to "an Arab official, of the most refined type," who had told Peel: "We prefer collecting these cancers in one limb . . . and amputat[ing] that limb. No cantonization but amputation . . .

Jews living in our part should be exchanged with Arabs living in theirs." Hanna to Levy, January 11, 1937, ISA P-695/6.

46. Parsons considers it "extremely unlikely" Khalidi would have so confided in Andrews, noting that his memoir portrays the latter as deceitful; see Parsons, "Secret Testimony (Part II)," 13–14. But the memoir was written years later, after Israel's creation, when there would have been pressure to disavow a pro-Zionist partitionist like Andrews. Khalidi's more contemporaneous 1937–1939 diary contains no impressions, positive or negative, of Andrews. Khalidi, *Exiled from Jerusalem: The Diaries of Hussein Fakhri al-Khalidi*, ed. Rafiq Husseini (London: I.B. Tauris, 2020), passim.

47. Coupland left the supposed Arab backers of partition nameless, but Dr. Khalidi's brother Ahmad was the Arab College's principal, and three years earlier had published an anonymous proposal for a federation of cantons in *Filastin*. The plan was broadly rejected in the Arab press, and met mostly tempered interest from Britain and the Jews. See Caplan, *Futile Diplomacy*, 26–27, 196–98; Sinanoglou, *Partitioning Palestine*, 52–53.

48. "Secret Sessions," TNA FO 492/19, 455–56. Parsons calls this "one of the most obvious examples of Coupland's dishonesty and manipulation throughout the process." See Parsons, "Secret Testimony (Part II)," 15.

49. "Notes of Discussion at Helouan," January 21, 1937, TNA CO 733/346/19. Rumbold's remark, and the comment that he sacrificed his convictions "for the sake of unanimity," is in Sinanoglou, *Partitioning Palestine*, 112.

50. "Col. 134," 370–78.

51. Zuaytir, *Yawmiyat*, 279.

52. Martin Gilbert, *Churchill and the Jews* (London: Pocket, 2008), 38. For a more skeptical reading see Michael J. Cohen, "The Churchill-Gilbert Symbiosis: Myth and Reality, Martin Gilbert, Churchill and the Jews," *Modern Judaism* 28, no. 2 (April 2, 2008): 204–222, passim. Cohen believes Churchill committed to Zionism only in 1929, and that he was often motivated by pragmatism and politics, and sometimes tainted by anti-Semitism.

53. Weizmann recorded, with some understatement, that Churchill had "a low opinion of the Arab generally." Gilbert, *Churchill and the Jews*, 48, 53.

54. See Lloyd George's private testimony on the motives behind his ministry's issuance of the Balfour Declaration in Kessler, "'A dangerous people to quarrel with.'" The ex-premier solicited Weizmann's help in crafting his testimony, and the latter even coached him to say a Jewish state had been the ultimate goal. Weizmann to Lloyd George, March 11, 1937, WA 19–1969, and vice versa, April 12, 1937, WA 12–1975. Angela Clifford, ed., *Serfdom or Ethnic Cleansing?—Churchill's Evidence to the Peel Commission (1937)* (Belfast: Athol Books, 2003), 16, 19–21. Gilbert, *Churchill and the Jews*, 112–13.

55. Clifford, *Serfdom*, 20, 23–28, 34–35. The full testimony is in "Secret Sessions," TNA FO 492/19, 500–508.

56. Rabbis Amiel and Uziel to Wauchope on accession of George VI, December 15, 1936, ISA M-525/43. "Messages addressed to H.M. the King on the occasion of his Coronation," May 14, 1937, ISA M-526/22.

57. Weizmann, *Trial and Error*, 389–92.

58. In a 1950 letter to Weizmann, Coupland acknowledged authoring the first and third of the report's three parts ("The Problem" and "The Possibility of a Lasting Settlement"). Dubnov and Robson, *Partitions*, 104.

59. "Cmd. 5479," 41–42.

60. Ibid., 7, 127–31, 363.

61. Ibid., 42, 119–31, 263, 370.

62. Musa Alami also came in for censure, albeit implicit. Jewish witnesses had complained that Palestine's court system was biased toward Arabs, citing cases in which suspects of sabotage operations were wrongly acquitted. In response the report recommended that the job of senior government advocate—the very title Alami held—be filled by a British attorney. The fact that Alami had been on leave in Europe during those trials counted for little. Ibid., 167, 177–81. Furlonge, *Palestine*, 111–12.

63. "Cmd. 5479," 119, 124.

64. Ibid., 46, 52, 299.

65. Ibid., 104–5, 389.

66. Ibid., 373.

67. Ibid., 39–41, 306–7.

68. Ibid., 363–68, 375–79.

69. Ibid., 383–86. Harris feared the Arab state would be insolvent, wondering in 1938 whether it would exist at "subsistence or starvation level." See El-Eini, *Mandated Landscape*, 340; Krämer, *History of Palestine*, 281.

70. "Cmd. 5479," 395–96.

71. "Cmd. 5513: Statement of Policy by His Majesty's Government" (His Majesty's Stationery Office, 1937). See also Zuaytir, *Yawmiyat*, 294–95.

72. Ben-Gurion diary, July 3, 6, and 20, 1937, BGA. Itzhak Galnoor, *Partition of Palestine: Decision Crossroads in the Zionist Movement* (Albany: SUNY, 1995), 77. Ben-Gurion's January 7 public and private testimonies to the commission are in "Col. 134" and TNA FO 492/19, respectively; his handwritten presentation notes are in BGA STA file 52.

73. Ben-Gurion diary, July 3, 4, 6, and 9, 1937, BGA. See also Ben-Gurion's secret memo, "After a first reading," July 10, 1937, in "Partition: June-July 1937," BGA STA file 282, 150ff.

74. Ibid., July 7, 9, 19, and 27, 1937. Teveth, *Burning Ground*, 612–13. As early as February, Ben-Gurion thrilled at the prospect of a Jewish state, telling colleagues it must include all of Galilee and the Arava valley to the Red Sea. Ben-Gurion to Mapai Central Committee, February 5, 1937, LPA 2-023-1937-16. The inclusion of Galilee, like many of the recommendations, was due largely to Coupland. See El-Eini, *Mandated Landscape*, 324.

75. Ben-Gurion diary, July 27, 1937, BGA. "Cmd. 5479," 390–91. Rumbold had been ambassador in Constantinople at the time, and may have been responsible for this recommendation.

76. Ben-Gurion diary, July 12 and 23, 1937, BGA.

77. Ibid., July 12, 1937.

78. Ibid., July 27, 1937.

79. Ibid., July 7 and 15, 1937. Teveth, *Burning Ground*, 608–10. Ben-Gurion in *Daily Herald*, July 9, 1937. Weizmann also considered transfer "vital"; see Weizmann to Ormsby-Gore, July 14, 1937, WA.

80. Ben-Gurion diary, July 9 and 11, 1937, BGA. Hanna to Levy, May 28, 1937, ISA P-695/6. Krämer, *History of Palestine*, 284. Per Elath, Alami said both he and Antonius believed the plan should not be rejected out of hand; see Elath, "Conversations," 55.

81. Laura Zittrain Eisenberg, *My Enemy's Enemy: Lebanon in the Early Zionist Imagination, 1900–1948* (Wayne, MI: Wayne State University Press, 1994), 62–63, 100–101, 188n44. Kabha, *Palestinian Press*, 220. Black, *Zionism and the Arabs*, 269ff.

82. Gelber, *Jewish-Transjordanian Relations*, 112, 115; Dugdale, *Baffy*, 42. Abdullah's continued Zionist "subsidies" included five hundred pounds from the Jewish Agency and one thousand from the industrialist Pinhas Rutenberg.

83. Coupland to Ormsby-Gore, June 23, 1937, TNA CAB 24/270/11; Wauchope to Parkinson, July 10, 1937, CAB 24/270/38. Hanna to Levy, May 28, 1937, ISA P-695/5. See also Zvi Elpeleg, *The Grand Mufti: Haj Amin al-Hussaini, Founder of the Palestinian National Movement* (Portland, OR: Frank Cass, 1993), 46; Porath, *Palestinian Arab*, 229.

84. Nashashibi to Wauchope, July 21, 1937, ISA M-528/11. Gelber, *Jewish-Transjordanian Relations*, 117. Porath, *Palestinian Arab*, 229–30.

85. Included in Wauchope to Eden, September 9, 1937, ISA M-528/13.

86. Porath, *Palestinian Arab*, 235–36. Taggar, *Mufti of Jerusalem*, 451.

87. Galnoor, *Partition of Palestine*, 205.

88. Weizmann, *Letters*, series B, vol. 2, 283. His remarks were reproduced in the Histadrut's newly launched Arabic weekly; see *Haqiqat al-Amr*, August 11, 18, and 25, 1937.

89. Galnoor, *Partition of Palestine*, 175, 214–17, 221. Shabtai Teveth notes that opposition to partition ran deep across nearly all of the Zionist parties. Later, especially after the Holocaust, Golda Meir and many other anti-partitionists conceded they had erred. See Teveth, *Burning Ground*, 608, 614–17.

90. Elie Kedourie, "The Bludan Congress on Palestine, September 1937," *Middle Eastern Studies* 17, no. 1 (January 1981): 115–18. Zuaytir, *Yawmiyat*, 315. Husseini, *Mudhakkirat*, 35. Full speeches of the conference's leading speakers, including a letter by Hajj Amin, are in Fuad Khalil Mufarrij, ed. *Al-Mu'tamar al-Arabi al-Qawmi fi Buludan* [The Arab Nationalist Conference in Bludan] (Damascus: al-Maktab al-Arabi al-Qawmi, 1937), 49–54, passim.

91. Kedourie, "Bludan Congress," 107–11, 117–25. Five years later Ghussein would sell land in Wadi Hnein that would become part of Jewish Nes Ziona, and in Beit Hanun that would become Kibbutz Nir Am. See Stein, *Land Question in Palestine*, 70, 230.

92. Alami to Trusted, May 29, 1937, ISA M-758/25. See also Arielli, *Fascist Italy*, 116; Goglia, "Il Mufti e Mussolini," 1245. "Currency converter: 1270–2017," TNA.

Chapter 4

1. Shlomo Rosner, "Tirat Zvi: Yated rishona be-drom emek Beth-She'an" ("Tirat Zvi: First Stake in the South Beth She'an Valley") in *Yamei Homa u-Migdal 1936–1939* [Days of Wall and Tower 1936–1939], ed. Mordechai Naor (Jerusalem: Ben-Zvi Institute,

1987), 94–95, 101. Alami's niece claims the third owner was not Canaan but Shibli al-Jamal; Serene Husseini Shahid, *Jerusalem Memories*, ed. Jean Said Makdisi (Beirut: Naufal, 2000), 95–103.

2. Serene Shahid writes that Alami and Jamal "were great friends . . . but no two temperaments could have been more different." Shahid, *Jerusalem Memories*, 95–103.

3. On Alami's sale see Aryeh L. Avneri, *The Claim of Dispossession: Jewish Land-Settlement and the Arabs, 1878–1948* (London; New York: Routledge, 1984, 2017), 168, 232; Joseph Weitz, *Yomani ve-Igrotai la-Banim* [My Diary and Letters to the Boys], vol. 1 (Tel Aviv: Masada, 1965), 158; Ben-Gurion to Brandeis, December 6, 1940, BGA.

4. According to Elath, settlers arriving at Zar'a found a letter from Fawzi Qawuqji authorizing Alami to sell the land. See Elath, "Conversations," 56, and Penkower, *Palestine in Turmoil*, 319. Alami's biography makes no mention of the sale, nor does his niece's memoir. Years later he said he had given Dr. Canaan power of attorney and the latter made the decision. Avneri, *Claim of Dispossession*, 299n58.

5. Avneri, *Claim of Dispossession*, 224–33; Stein, *Land Question in Palestine*, 68–70, 229–38; Porath, *Palestinian Arab*, 86ff.

6. Sharett, *Yoman Medini*, vol. 1, June 5 and 7, 1937. See also Weizmann to Dugdale (April 4, 1938, WA) on the need to purchase "as much land as we can, particularly in both poles of the future Jewish State and in the Beisan area."

7. Slutsky, *Sefer Toldot*, 2:858–66. Herbert Samuel's son called the Beisan sales one of his father's "bad political mistakes: the grant of large tracts of valuable, well-watered land near Beisan to Arab squatters who promptly sold them to Jews." Samuel, *Lifetime in Jerusalem*, 17–18.

8. Germany overtook Poland as the top source of Jewish immigrants in 1938. *Palestine: Blue Book, 1938* (Jerusalem: Palestine Government, 1939), 342.

9. The Tirat Zvi settlers were not new arrivals but had waited seven years for their own plot. Naor, *Yamei Homa u-Migdal*, 96, 101–2.

10. Dorothy Kahn Bar-Adon, *Writing Palestine 1933–1950*, ed. Esther Carmel-Hakim and Nancy Rosenfeld (Brookline, MA: Academic Studies Press, 2017), 174–75. Louis D. Brandeis, *Letters of Louis D. Brandeis*, ed. Melvin I. Urofsky and David W. Levy, vol. 5 (Albany: SUNY Press, 1978), 618.

11. Galilee District was a new creation, carved from the Northern District in July 1937 after the Peel report's publication. Andrews's title was acting district commissioner; District Commissioner Edward Keith-Roach, who was relocated to Jerusalem later that year, bitterly opposed cantonization and partition. See Sinanoglou, *Partitioning Palestine*, 58–60.

12. Coupland to Ormsby-Gore, July 11, 1937, TNA CO 733/351/2. Quoted in Parsons, "Secret Testimony (Part II)," 16–17.

13. *Davar*, September 28, 1937.

14. Nadav Shragai, "Lewis Yelland Andrews, the Jews' Forgotten Friend," *Israel Hayom*, July 23, 2017.

15. Nevill Barbour, *Nisi Dominus: A Survey of the Palestine Problem* (Beirut: Institute for Palestine Studies, 1946, 1969), 188–89. Wasif Jawhariyyeh, *The Storyteller of Jerusalem: The Life and Times of Wasif Jawhariyyeh, 1904–1948*, ed. Salim Tamari and Issam Nassar,

trans. Nada Elzeer (Northampton, MA: Olive Branch Press, 2014), 222. Shragai, "Lewis Yelland Andrews."

16. Jawhariyyeh, *Storyteller of Jerusalem*, 222–23. Zuaytir, *Yawmiyat*, 211. Yasin, *Thawrah*, 96. Segev, *One Palestine*, 7.

17. Andrews had led efforts to drain the swamps around Netanya, facilitated the sale of government land to establish the town, and kept a home there. *Davar*, September 28, 1937. Shragai, "Lewis Yelland Andrews."

18. Battershill to mother, May 9 and 14, 1937, Battershill Papers, MSS. Brit. Emp. 467, box 4, WL.

19. Battershill to mother, June 13 and 23, July 1, 1937, Ibid.

20. Battershill to mother, August 23 and 31, 1937, Ibid.

21. Hoffman, *Anonymous Soldiers*, 65–66, Shragai, "Lewis Yelland Andrews."

22. Andrews's deputy, Christopher Pirie-Gordon, survived. Battershill to Wauchope, September 27, 1937, Battershill Papers, MSS. Brit. Emp. 467, box 10, WL. Hoffman, *Anonymous Soldiers*, 65–66. *Al-Difa* and *Al-Jamia al-Islamiya*, September 27, 1937. "Tinker, Edward Hayden," IWMSA 4492/3.

23. *Filastin*, September 29, 1937. *Davar*, September 28, 1937.

24. Funeral program, September 27, 1937, TNA CO 733/322/10. "Mr. Lewis Andrews—Prof. Bentwich's Tribute." *The Times*, September 29, 1937. Shragai, "Lewis Yelland Andrews." Keith-Roach, *Pasha of Jerusalem*, 190.

25. Battershill to Ormsby-Gore, October 14, 1937, TNA CO 733/332/10. Another hundred were arrested over subsequent days.

26. Battershill to Ormsby-Gore, September 27, 1937, TNA PREM 1/352, and September 29, 1937, TNA CO 733/332/11. "Palestine (Defence) Order in Council, 1937," *Palestine Gazette*, no. 675, March 24, 1937. Cabinet summary, September 29, 1937, TNA CAB 23/89/6. Taggar, *Mufti of Jerusalem*, 453; Cohen, *Britain's Moment*, 269.

27. Battershill diary, October 10, 1937, Battershill Papers, MSS. Brit. Emp. 467, box 12, WL.

28. Battershill to Ormsby-Gore, October 1, 1937, TNA CO 733/332/11. Husseini, *Mudhakkirat*, 29, 35–36. The same order banned the countrywide network of the AHC's "national committees."

29. Cabinet summary, September 29, 1937, TNA CAB/23/89/6. Porath, *Palestinian Arab*, 235–36. Taggar, *Mufti of Jerusalem*, 457. The AHC deportees were joined by Rashid al-Hajj Ibrahim, an *Istiqlali*. The mayor recounts his deportation in Khalidi, *Exiled from Jerusalem*, 9–21, 70. Less than a year later, his relative Mustafa Khalidi became mayor and Auster was again deputy.

30. "Mufti's pledge to Palestine Jews." *Daily Telegraph*, July 29, 1937. Arnon-Ohanah, *Mered Arvi*, 170–71.

31. Husseini tried to maintain his disguise, identifying himself to French authorities as "Muhammad al-Ja'afari," but to no avail. Various Foreign Office correspondence, October 1937, TNA FO 371/20816, 371/20817. Husseini, *Mudhakkirat*, 30–34; Zuaytir, *Yawmiyat*, 336–37; Taggar, *Mufti of Jerusalem*, 461; Mattar, *Mufti of Jerusalem*, 83.

32. Shahid, *Jerusalem Memories*, 123ff. Furlonge, *Palestine*, 112–13. "Moussa Eff. Alami," ISA M-758/25. "Who's Who of Palestine: Arab Politicians and Personalities," September 1944, TNA FO 492/27.

33. Magnes's esteem was mutual: Alami once confessed that no man, even among the Arabs, was closer to his heart. Magnes to Graham-Browne, December 17, 1937, MECA JEM 64/5. Sharett, *Yoman Medini*, vol. 1, June 21, 1936. Caplan, *Futile Diplomacy*, 83.

34. Battershill to Ormsby-Gore, October 23, 1937, TNA CO 935/21. Bernard Fergusson, *The Trumpet in the Hall 1930–1958* (London: Collins, 1970), 39–43. Hoffman, *Anonymous Soldiers*, 67. Zuaytir, *Yawmiyat*, 330–32.

35. Ormsby-Gore to Chamberlain, July 22, 1937, TNA PREM 1/352. Ormsby-Gore to Cabinet, October 8, 1937, TNA CAB 24/271/32. Porath, *Palestinian Arab*, 239.

36. Ormsby-Gore to Battershill, November 6, 1937, TNA FO 371/20820. Martin Kolinsky, "The Collapse and Restoration of Public Security," in *Britain and the Middle East in the 1930s: Security Problems, 1935–39*, ed. Michael J. Cohen and Martin Kolinsky (London: Palgrave Macmillan, 1992), 154.

37. "Timeline of Events," United States Holocaust Memorial Museum, www.ushmm.org/learn/timeline-of-events/1933-1938/.

38. Martin Gilbert, *The Routledge Atlas of the Holocaust* (London: Routledge, 2009), 8. *Foreign Relations of the United States (FRUS), 1937*, vol. 2 (Washington: Department of State, 1954), documents 402–25. Memo by George Rendel including note by Polish ambassador, November 4, 1936, TNA FO 371/20028. See also Jehuda Reinharz and Yaacov Shavit, *The Road to September 1939: Polish Jews, Zionists, and the Yishuv on the Eve of World War II* (Waltham, MA: Brandeis University Press, 2018), chap. 1, passim.

39. Memo by George Rendel, November 26, 1937, TNA FO 371/20821 (Poland and Romania were "anxious to be able freely to get rid of their Jews"). Dispatch, August 11, 1937, American Legation at Bucharest, NARA II. "Rumania: Bloodsucker of the villages," *TIME*, January 31, 1938. "Jews spurned in Rumania," *The Argus* (Melbourne), January 24, 1938.

40. Uri Zvi Greenberg, *Sefer ha-Kitrug veha-Emunah* [The Book of Denunciation and Faith] (Jerusalem: Sdan, 1937), 11–12, 103. Translations are the author's.

41. I. Alfassi, ed., *Irgun Zvai Leumi (National Military Organization): Collection of Archival Sources and Documents April 1937-April 1941*, vol. 1 (Tel Aviv: Jabotinsky Institute, 1990), 15, 132–33.

42. Joseph B. Schechtman, *Fighter and Prophet: The Jabotinsky Story—The Last Years, 1923–1940* (Silver Spring, MD: Eshel Books, 1986), 449–54. Colin Shindler, *The Rise of the Israeli Right: From Odessa to Hebron* (Cambridge University Press, 2015), 181, and *Triumph of Military Zionism*, 195.

43. The total of ten Arab fatalities includes three killed on November 11 and seven on Black Sunday itself. Battershill considered the attacks a direct response to the November 9 incident at Kiryat Anavim. Battershill to Ormsby-Gore, November 23, 1937, TNA CO 935/21. "2 Arabs Killed, 5 Wounded by Bomb in Jerusalem," and "Lifta Arab Found Dead in Jerusalem," *Palestine Post*, November 12, 1937. "Six Killed, Several Wounded in Jerusalem's Day of Terror," *Palestine Post*, November 15, 1937. Hoffman, *Anonymous*

Soldiers, 69–70. Shindler, *Rise of the Israeli Right*, 182–183, and *Triumph of Military Zionism*, 197.

44. *Zionews*, November 24, 1937, JI. Schechtman, *Fighter and Prophet*, 453. Slutsky, *Sefer Toldot*, 2:1060–62.

45. Ben-Gurion to Jewish Agency Executive, November 14, 1937, in "*Havlagah*," BGA STA file 57. Ben-Gurion to Mapai Central Committee, November 17, 1937, LPA 2–023–1937-17b. "Six Killed, Several Wounded in Jerusalem's Day of Terror," *Palestine Post*, November 15, 1937. *Haqiqat al-Amr*, November 17, 1937.

46. Hughes, *Britain's Pacification of Palestine*, 144, and (on Zionist intelligence) 151–53; Shahid, *Jerusalem Memories*, 123–24; Eisenberg, *My Enemy's Enemy*, 103–111; Michael J. Cohen, *Palestine, Retreat from the Mandate: The Making of British Policy, 1936–45* (New York: Holmes & Meier, 1978), 55–56; Porath, *Palestinian Arab*, 242–43. For a more skeptical stance on the mufti's control over rebel leaders, see Kedourie and Haim, *Zionism and Arabism*, 81–82.

47. Ormsby-Gore to Eden, November 11, 1937, TNA FO 371/20820.

48. Kedourie and Haim, *Zionism and Arabism*, 97n186. "Statement of Mohamed Naji Abu Rab (Abu Jab)," November 30, 1937, and "Terrorism—1936–1937," MECA Tegart Papers 1/3.

49. Farhan had also served under Fawzi al-Qawuqji during the latter's brief stint in Palestine. Battershill to Ormsby-Gore, November 23, 1937, TNA CO 935/21. Kedourie and Haim, *Zionism and Arabism*, 78–82; Kabha, *Palestinian Press*, 214–15; Zuaytir, *Yawmiyat*, 340–42.

50. Battershill to Ormsby-Gore, November 21 and 23, 1937, TNA CO 935/21, CAB 24/273/11. Kabha, *Palestinian Press*, 214; Cohen and Kolinsky, *Britain and the Middle East*, 154.

51. Antonius to Walter Rogers, August 3, 1937, ICWA. George to Katy Antonius, June 30, 1937, ISA P-1053/4.

52. Katy to George Antonius, July 21, 1937, ISA P-1053/4.

53. Katy Antonius acknowledges her "lack of Arabic" in a letter of October 28, 1938, ISA P-1053/8. See also Hadara Lazar, *Six Singular Figures: Jews and Arabs under the British Mandate*, trans. Sondra Silverston (Oakville, ON: Mosaic, 2016), 189–90.

54. Boyle, *Betrayal of Palestine*, 146.

55. George to Katy Antonius, November 27, 1927, ISA P-1053/12.

56. George to Katy Antonius, undated, ISA P-1053/12.

57. George to Katy Antonius, undated, ISA P-1053/8. See also Boyle, *Betrayal of Palestine*, 218.

58. George to Katy Antonius, April 4, 1937, ISA P-1053/4.

59. Katy to George Antonius, June 10, 1937, and undated letter, ISA P-1053/4. Lazar, *Six Singular Figures*, 207.

60. George to Katy Antonius, June 29, 1937, ISA P-1053/4.

61. Antonius to Walter Rogers, August 3, 1937, ICWA. Antonius, *Arab Awakening*, 399–405.

62. Antonius, *Arab Awakening*, 403–5. A year earlier Antonius had helped Alami draft a memo to Wauchope on behalf of Arab senior government officials addressing the

outbreak's causes and insisting on a halt to immigration. The memo appears in the Peel report as an appendix: "Cmd. 5479," 401–3.

63. Rendel memo, March 20, 1922, TNA FO 371/7876.

64. Elie Kedourie, "Great Britain and Palestine: The Turning Point," in Kedourie, *Islam in the Modern World* (New York: Holt, Rinehart and Winston, 1981), 113–14, 130–31. George Rendel, *The Sword and the Olive* (London: Wyman, 1957), 98–99.

65. Rendel, *Sword and the Olive*, 112–25. "Sir George Rendel Photo Gallery: Saudi Arabia, 1937," MECA, https://sant.ox.ac.uk/mec/mecaphotos-rendel.html. Kedourie, "Great Britain and Palestine," passim.

66. Rendel's campaign against partition began even before the Peel report. See Kedourie, "Great Britain and Palestine," 116, 145, 166, passim.

67. Minute by Rendel, October 14, 1937, TNA FO 371/20816.

68. Meeting summary by Rendel, October 30, 1937, TNA FO 371/20818.

69. Memo and Minute by Rendel, November 14 and 18, 1937, TNA FO 371/20820. Memo, December 10, 1937, FO 371/20822.

70. Battershill to Shuckburgh, November 17, 1937, TNA CO 733/354/1.

71. Ormsby-Gore to Cabinet, November 9, 1937, TNA CAB 24/272/15. Several relevant documents are in Aaron S. Klieman, ed., *A Return to Palliatives*, The Rise of Israel Series (Vol. 26) (New York: Garland, 1987), 1–84. See also Klieman, "The Divisiveness of Palestine: Foreign Office versus Colonial Office on the Issue of Partition, 1937," *Historical Journal* 22, no. 2 (1979): passim. The year before, Ben-Gurion had hailed Ormsby-Gore as "among the most ardent Zionists, a friend of the Jews." See his comments to Jewish Agency Executive, July 6, 1936.

72. Eden to Cabinet, November 19, 1937, TNA CAB 24/273/6. On Eden's deference to Rendel see also Kedourie, "Great Britain and Palestine," 113, 161, passim.

73. Cabinet summary, December 8, 1937, TNA CAB 23/90A/8.

74. Chamberlain and Eden in Cabinet summary, December 8, 1937, TNA CAB 23/90A/8. Ormsby-Gore to Cabinet, December 17, 1937, CAB 24/273/35.

75. Memo by Ormsby-Gore, December 17, 1937, TNA CAB 24/273/35. Ormsby-Gore to Wauchope, December 23, 1937, reprinted in "Cmd. 5634: Policy in Palestine" (His Majesty's Stationery Office, January 1938).

76. Weizmann to Shuckburgh and Weizmann to Ormsby-Gore, December 31, 1937, TNA PREM 1/352. Weizmann, *Trial and Error*, 394–96.

77. Telegram, Mohamed Ali Eltaher to Colonial Office, January 5, 1938, TNA CO 733/381/60. One of Eltaher's two pamphlets on the revolt escaped the censor: *'An Thawrat Filastin Sanat 1936: Wasf wa-Akhbar wa-Waqa'i wa-Watha'iq* [On the 1936 Palestine Uprising: Description, News, Facts, and Documents] (Cairo: al-Lajnah al-Filastiniya al-Arabiya, 1936).

Chapter 5

1. Bell, *Shadows on the Sand*, 95–96.

2. "Bredin, Humphrey Edgar Nicholson," IWMSA 4550/1–2. A fellow subaltern expressed similar sentiments: see "King-Clark, Robert," IWMSA 4486/3–6. Laila Parsons, referring to the Peel Commission testimonies, writes that for many British officials,

"Arabs were incompetent but lovable, whereas Jews were competent but unlovable"; Parsons, "Secret Testimony (Part I)," 13.

3. Robert King-Clark, *Free for a Blast* (London: Grenville Publishing, 1988), 152. Similar remarks are in "Grove, Michael Richard Leslie," IWMSA 4510/1.

4. Courtney, *Palestine Policeman*, 65–68. Keith-Roach, *Pasha of Jerusalem*, 150.

5. Kahn Bar-Adon, *Writing Palestine*, 152–58.

6. Bell, *Shadows on the Sand*, 96.

7. Ben-Gurion wrote his wife Paula on October 18, 1938: "There is just one man of high position who does not oppose us, and actually seeks our success, and it's Tegart." In "Tegart, Charles," BGA STA file 221.

8. Cahill, Richard. "Sir Charles Tegart: The 'Counterterrorism Expert' in Palestine." *Jerusalem Quarterly* 74 (Summer 2018): 57–61. Downie to Tegart, November 5, 1937, MECA Tegart Papers 4/4.

9. Keith-Roach, *Pasha of Jerusalem*, 192. Fergusson, *Trumpet in the Hall*, 47–48. *Haaretz*, *Palestine Post*, *Filastin*, and *Al-Difa*, January 11 and 12, 1938. The British suspected Hebron rebel leader Issa Battat; he was killed in May; see "Reported Entry of Arab Terrorist Chief Stirs Military Activity; Band Leader Slain," *JTA*, May 9, 1938. Yosef Garfinkel posits Starkey may have been killed in a land dispute; Garfinkel, "The Murder of James Leslie Starkey Near Lachish," *Palestine Exploration Quarterly*, 128, no. 2 (2016), 84–85, 99, 106, passim.

10. Cahill, "Counterterrorism Expert," 62–63; Hoffman, *Anonymous Soldiers*, 72–74; Eyal, *Ha-Intifada ha-Rishona*, 346–48; Gad Kroizer, "From Dowbiggin to Tegart," *Journal of Imperial and Commonwealth History* 32, no. 2 (2004), 123–29.

11. Tegart to Battershill, February 19, 1938, MECA Tegart Papers 3/2. Shmuel Stempler, "Ha-gader ba-tzafon" ("The Northern Fence"), in Naor, *Yamei Homa u-Migdal*, 158–60; Eyal, *Ha-Intifada ha-Rishona*, 348–51; Slutsky, *Sefer Toldot*, 2:903–7.

12. Slutsky, *Sefer Toldot*, 2:862–69, 1329–31.

13. As a parting gift, Wauchope asked for the lyrics and text to "Hatikvah" so it could be played for him at his English country home. Sharett, *Yoman Medini*, vol. 3, February 26 and March 2, 1938.

14. Fergusson, *Trumpet in the Hall*, 31–33. Colonial Office telegrams, November and December 1937, announcing MacMichael's candidacy and the king's approval, are in the MECA MacMichael Collection 1/3.

15. Tegart was appalled at the administration's paucity of local-language knowledge. See Naomi Shepherd, *Ploughing Sand: British Rule in Palestine, 1917–1948* (New Brunswick, NJ: Rutgers University Press, 2000), 32, 191, 206. On the stark differences between Wauchope and MacMichael, and Zionist distaste for the latter, see Hoffman, *Anonymous Soldiers*, 74–78; Slutsky, *Sefer Toldot*, 2:811.

16. "Speeches and broadcasts," MECA MacMichael Collection 1/6. MacMichael to Ormsby-Gore, March 22, 1938, TNA CO 935/21. Arab Women's Committee to MacMichael, March 23, 1938, CZA S25/22793. "Greetings to Sir Harold Alfred [MacMichael]," March 1938, ISA M-529/20.

17. "Dr. Weizmann's diary, London, February 17th, 1938 to March 16th, 1938," CZA S25/5476. Rose, *Gentile Zionists*, 155–59; Dugdale, *Baffy*, 84–88.

18. A handwritten note, apparently by Chamberlain, says there is "no longer any objection" to his hosting Weizmann. See Ormsby-Gore to Chamberlain, and Chamberlain's secretary (Cleverly?) to H. G. Creasy, January 27 and 29, 1938, TNA PREM 1/352. Eden had also refused to see Weizmann; Leo Amery chided him in October 1937: "It might be useful to the Foreign Secretary to meet the future President of the Jewish State!" TNA FO 954/19A/17–20.

19. Weizmann, *Letters*, series B, vol. 2, 302–4. Dugdale, *Baffy*, 87.

20. "Holocaust | Jewish Communities of Austria." ANU—Museum of the Jewish People, https://spotlight.anumuseum.org.il/austria/modern-era/holocaust/.

21. "Who's Who of Palestine," September 1944, TNA FO 492/27. Khalidi, *Exiled from Jerusalem*, x, 1–3. The same year the government had decided the mayorship must remain Arab, despite Jerusalem's Jewish majority (the city council was to be evenly split). The Jews had soured on mayor Ragheb Nashashibi over having joined a 1930 anti-Zionist delegation to London; the mufti backed Khalidi in a bid to sideline his Nashashibi rival. See Porath, *Palestinian Arab*, 62–63, 70, 77–78.

22. "Secret Sessions," TNA FO 492/19, 444–45. The other deportees included Fuad Saba, a publisher and one of two Christians on the AHC; Ahmad Hilmi Pasha of the *Istiqlal* party; and Yacoub Ghussein of the Palestine Youth Congress. Rashid al-Hajj Ibrahim, an *Istiqlali*, was also deported despite not being an AHC member.

23. Khalidi, *Exiled from Jerusalem*, 23–27, 38.

24. For Khalidi's ailments and other complaints in Seychelles, see Ibid., 61, 67, 148–49, 167, 179–80, 187, 194, 223. His and family members' correspondence, including a petition to George VI, show he had suffered from chronic asthma, throat issues, and high blood pressure even before deportation; TNA CO 733/369; ISA P-3049/8.

25. Khalidi, *Exiled from Jerusalem*, 145.

26. Ibid., 40–45, 109. Yellin was the son of the prominent educator David Yellin. His 1931 textbook, *An Arabic Reader* (commonly known as "Yellin-Billig") was reprinted in 1948 and 1963 with prefaces by the orientalist S. D. Goitein.

27. Ibid., 108–9.

28. Ibid., 148.

29. Ibid., x, 47, 71, 79, 108, 144, 276. Khalidi's file at the police criminal investigation department (CID) noted he was "not an extremist," and his deportation was prompted solely by his AHC membership; "Who's Who of Palestine," September 1944, TNA FO 492/27.

30. Khalidi, *Exiled from Jerusalem*, 47. He complained that the mufti treated the deportees as "a zero to the left," an Arabic phrase suggesting they were as irrelevant as a zero placed before another number.

31. Khalidi conceded in his Peel testimony that Jews were indeed a majority in his city. "Col. 134," 338. His testimony on self-government is cited (without naming him) in the committee's report: "Cmd. 5479," 108–9, 350–51.

32. Khalidi, *Exiled from Jerusalem*, 44–45.

33. Ibid., 308.

34. Ben-Gurion was growing increasingly involved in defense matters, becoming the Yishuv's de facto "defense minister" in this period. See Tom Segev, *A State at Any Cost: The*

Life of David Ben-Gurion, trans. Haim Watzman (New York: Farrar, Straus and Giroux, 2019), 276–77. Ben-Gurion to Mapai Central Committee, January 5, 1938, and Smaller Zionist Actions Committee, January 11, 1938; Shertok to Mapai Central Committee, March 14, 1938—all in "Land, 1920–1939," BGA STA file 193. Slutsky, *Sefer Toldot*, 2:851–52, 872–73.

35. Sharett, *Yoman Medini*, vol. 3, February 13, 1938. Ahdab was also the author of a scathing April 7, 1938, letter that Weizmann sent Ormsby-Gore from a "prominent Moslem personality in Lebanon" denouncing the mufti's activity; TNA PREM 1–352. He may have been in Jewish pay before taking office; see Cohen, *Army of Shadows*, 146, 293n7.

36. Ahdab's letter arrived in an envelope with the return address clearly marked "RÉPUBLIQUE LIBANAISE." Sharett to Ahdab and reply, March 16 and 18, 1938, CZA S25/5581 and S25/5588. Mordechai Naor, "Hanita, ha-he'ahzut ha-rishona ba-aretz" ("Hanita, the First Outpost in the Country") in Naor, *Yamei Homa u-Migdal*, 74. Also Eisenberg, *My Enemy's Enemy*, 110–11, 191–92.

37. The landowners—the elite Lebanese-Christian Tueni family—were told the Italian planned to build a monastery; once the ruse was exposed, his Lebanese guide paid with his life. Am-Ad, Karni, "Historical document from 1938 reveals: How the Hanita lands were bought from Lebanese residents" (Hebrew), *Yedioth Ahronoth*, August 13, 2018.

38. Naor, *Yamei Homa u-Migdal*, 75–78. Slutsky, *Sefer Toldot*, 2:873–80, 1331–32; Yosef Eshkol, *A Common Soldier: The Story of Zwi Brenner* (Tel Aviv: MOD Books, 1993), 72–73. Moshe Dayan, *Story of My Life* (New York: Morrow, 1976), 44–45. Shapira, *Land and Power*, 253.

39. Yigal Allon, *Shield of David: The Story of Israel's Armed Forces* (Lexington, MA: Plunkett Lane Press, 2019 [1970]), chap. 3. Slutsky, *Sefer Toldot*, 2:877–80, 1333; Eshkol, *Common Soldier*, 83–84; Dayan, *Story of My Life*, 44; Naor, *Yamei Homa u-Migdal*, 78–79.

40. The Field Squads grew out of the *notrim* patrol units (*nodedet* or *mishmar na*) that Sadeh had created in 1936–37 around Jerusalem. Sadeh, Allon (his surname at the time was Paicovich), and Dayan would play key roles in the Haganah's *Palmach* (literally, "strike force") throughout the 1940s. Slutsky, *Sefer Toldot*, 2:689–94, 900–903, 939–43, 1323–324; Shapira, *Land and Power*, 250.

41. Shapira, *Land and Power*, 212, 250.

42. Jews were also increasingly assuming command position: Eight hundred *notrim* became squad commanders in 1937 and 1938. Slutsky, *Sefer Toldot*, 2:737–39, 756–58, 881–903, 1014–20. *FRUS, 1938*, vol. 2, document 774.

43. For the Zionist shift from a defensive to offensive ethos, see Shapira, *Land and Power*, 237, 250–55, 269–70, passim. She writes that the revolt "was the time when Jewish youth in Palestine took up the task of fighting as the special and distinctive mission of the generation."

44. The book describes the chain of Tirat Zvi, Hanita, and Tegart's Wall as forming the "seed of the future 'People's Army.'" Slutsky, *Sefer Toldot*, 2:880, 907.

45. Ibid., 2:806–9. The road was one of dozens built from 1937 to improve security forces' access to Arab locales. See map in Steven B. Wagner, *Statecraft by Stealth: Secret Intelligence and British Rule in Palestine* (Ithaca: Cornell University Press, 2019), 210.

46. Wadsworth to Hull, April 16, 1938, NARA II 867N.4016/52. Slutsky, *Sefer Toldot*, 2:807–9.

47. MacMichael to Ormsby-Gore, April 14, 1938, TNA CO 935/21.

48. "Cmd. 5634," 3.

49. El-Eini, *Mandated Landscape*, 331–33. Cohen, *Retreat from the Mandate*, 38–49.

50. Khalidi, *Exiled from Jerusalem*, 157. On the Arab consensus against partition, see also Zuaytir, *Yawmiyat*, 370, 381–83; in Damascus, Zuaytir reported marches of tens of thousands.

51. Cohen, *Army of Shadows*, 127. Dajani had also planned to testify before Peel but relented after an assassination attempt was revealed; see Hanna to Levy, January 11, 1937, ISA P-695/6.

52. Wadsworth to Hull, May 1, 1938, NARA II 867N.01/1075.

53. The commission dismissed Abdullah's plan, saying it fell outside its terms of reference. Avi Shlaim, *Collusion across the Jordan: King Abdullah, the Zionist Movement, and the Partition of Palestine* (New York: Columbia University Press, 1988), 59–61; Gelber, *Jewish-Transjordanian Relations*, 133–35; Caplan, *Futile Diplomacy*, 238–39.

54. *Filastin*, quoted in Wadsworth to Hull, May 1, 1938, NARA II 867N.01/1075. The editor's comments were made the previous year, upon publication of the Peel report. See Hanna to Levy, July 8, 1937, ISA P-695/6. For his similar dissembling on Qassam, see Chapter 1.

55. On the nexus between Betar, the Irgun, and the New Zionist Organization—all headed by Jabotinsky—see Daniel Kupfert Heller, *Jabotinsky's Children: Polish Jews and the Rise of Right-Wing Zionism* (Princeton, NJ: Princeton University Press, 2017), 223ff; Shindler, *Triumph of Military Zionism*, 199ff.

56. "Three Jews detained with weapons," April 24, 1938, HA 8/32a/1. Shindler, *Triumph of Military Zionism*, 202–3, and *Rise of the Israeli Right*, 185. Schein appears to have been the instigator of the plot and to have recruited Ben-Yosef only when another candidate was reassigned. Monty Noam Penkower, "Shlomo Ben-Yosef: From a British Gallows to Israel's Pantheon to Obscurity," in Penkower, *Twentieth Century Jews: Forging Identity in the Land of Promise and in the Promised Land* (Boston: Academic Studies Press, 2010), 311–16, 349n14.

57. The shooter was Yehezkel Altman (later, Ben-Hur), the first Jew sentenced to death in Palestine. The sentence was commuted within a week. Shindler, *Triumph of Military Zionism*, 203; Slutsky, *Sefer Toldot*, 2:1058–59; Penkower, "Ben-Yosef," 315, 325. For execution statistics, see Khalidi, *From Haven to Conquest*, 846–47.

58. Khalidi, *Exiled from Jerusalem*, 117. Alec Kirkbride, who succeeded Andrews as Galilee district commissioner, recounts the grisly protocol of hangings in "Until You Are Dead," reproduced in Khalidi, *From Haven to Conquest*, 353–56.

59. Penkower, "Ben-Yosef," 319. The defense attorneys were Philip Joseph, brother of future Israeli minister Dov (Bernard) Yosef, who represented Schein and Zuravin, and Aharon Hoter-Yishay, who defended Ben-Yosef and would become Israel's first military advocate general.

60. Trial records by Kathy and Michael Kaplan, May-June 1938, JI K-16/1/20; see also "Newspaper Items," K-16/1/17. "2 condemned to die in Rosh Pinah trial," *Palestine Post*, June 6, 1938, and *Haaretz*, June 6, 1938.

61. "A case for clemency," *Manchester Guardian*, June 6, 1938. Editor William Crozier's lead article was prompted by a June 5, 1938, cable from Jabotinsky: JI A-28/2/1. See also Penkower, "Ben-Yosef," 322; Schechtman, *Fighter and Prophet*, 468–69. The *Guardian* had held a pro-Zionist line since 1916, when then-owner/editor C. P. Scott introduced Weizmann to Lloyd George; see Weizmann, *Trial and Error*, 190–92; Antonius, *Arab Awakening*, 259.

62. Correspondence on Ben-Yosef, TNA CO 733/379, including note, Haining to Henry, June 7, 1938. On June 24 MacDonald questioned whether the wait was necessary, scribbling, "I should have thought it was unnecessary to keep this unhappy youth in mental agony so long." See also Penkower, "Ben-Yosef," 323–27. For an Arab view on Haining, see Zuaytir, *Yawmiyat*, 370–71.

63. The Jabotinsky Institute has over a dozen handwritten notes and letters Ben-Yosef wrote in Acre prison; K-16/1–3, JI. See also Penkower, "Ben-Yosef," 323, 327–30; Heller, *Jabotinsky's Children*, 230.

64. Ben-Yosef files, JI K-16/1–3.

65. MacDonald note, TNA CO 733/379.

66. Schechtman, *Fighter and Prophet*, 469–71. Jews smashed windows at the British embassies in Lithuania and Latvia, where a stone crashed through the ambassador's study wrapped in a warning: "The Jewish people will never forget the blood of their brother." Charles Orde to Foreign Office, June 29, 1938, TNA CO 733/379.

67. MacMichael to MacDonald, July 26, 1938, TNA CO 733/379.

68. Penkower, "Ben-Yosef," 331–32. Schechtman, *Fighter and Prophet*, 468–71.

69. Khalidi, *Exiled from Jerusalem*, 204.

70. *Haaretz*, June 30, 1938. *Canadian Jewish Chronicle*, July 8, 1938. Telegram from Sir Charles Orde, June 29, 1938, TNA CO 733/379.

71. The "rat" remark came from Joseph Katzenelson; before he died eighteen months later, he asked to be buried beside Irgun bomber Yaakov Rass (see Note 78). David Niv, *Maarchot ha-Irgun ha-Tzvai ha-Leumi* [Battle for Freedom: The Irgun Zvai Leumi], vol. 2 (Tel Aviv: Klausner Institute, 1975), 71–72. Alfassi, *Irgun*, 31, 265–69. Hoffman, *Anonymous Soldiers*, 78–81.

72. Jabotinsky's doublespeak on reprisals could reach absurd lengths: In an August 1938 letter to Palestine Revisionists, he insisted there was "no link" ("*ein kesher ve-ein gesher*" in his colorful Hebrew) between his New Zionist Organization and "groups connected to Mr. Mendelson"—namely to himself. In Alfassi, *Irgun*, 37. See also Shindler, *Rise of the Israeli Right*, 181, 185–88; Heller, *Jabotinsky's Children*, 229–36.

73. Porath, *Palestinian Arab*, 238.

74. Niv, *Maarchot*, 77–80. MacMichael to MacDonald, September 13, 1938, CO 935/21. *Haaretz* and *Filastin*, July 5 and 7, 1938. Slutsky, *Sefer Toldot*, 2:811–13. "Taxi driver found hanged in shack," *Palestine Post*, July 7, 1938.

75. Weizmann wrote that Dounie's death had been "noble," as it had come while "assisting the enemy"; letter to family, July 8, 1938, WA 1–2078. MacDonald to Weizmann, July 7, 1938, WA 23–2077. *Haaretz*, *Davar*, *Palestine Post*, and *New York Times*, July 7, 1938.

76. Compensation request by Abed Shukri Al-Halawani, November 25, 1939, ISA P-297/13. MacMichael to MacDonald, September 13, 1938, CO 935/21. Slutsky, *Sefer Toldot*, 2:811–13. *Haaretz*, July 11, 12, 17, and 26, 1938.

77. Wadsworth to Hull, August 8, 1938, NARA II 867N.4016/61. Niv, *Maarchot*, 79–80.

78. MacMichael to MacDonald, September 13, 1938, CO 935/21. *Al-Difa* and *Haaretz*, July 26, 1938. The following day an even worse atrocity was thwarted when an explosive was found in a produce basket in Jerusalem's Old City. The suspected perpetrator, an Afghan-born Revisionist named Yaakov Rass (Raz), was stabbed multiple times and later expired. Some accounts say he died after removing his bandages in hospital lest he give incriminating information to investigators. The Irgun exalted Rass, who was also behind several of the prior attacks, as "the first martyr of the offensive actions . . . a redeemer of Hebrew blood, carrying the bomb for Ishmael." Niv, *Maarchot*, 87–89. Alfassi, *Irgun*, 138, 272–73. Slutsky, *Sefer Toldot*, 2:2:811–13, 1219.

79. Irgun figures claimed 140 Arabs were killed in July; on August 26 a massive bomb in Jaffa killed another 24 Arabs. Niv, *Maarchot*, 90–94. Wadsworth to Hull, July 22 and August 8, 1938, NARA II 867N.4016/60–61. MacMichael to MacDonald, September 13, 1938, CO 935/21. Slutsky, *Sefer Toldot*, 2:801.

80. MacMichael to MacDonald, September 13, 1938, CO 935/21. *Haaretz*, July 5 and 26, 1938. Khalidi, *Exiled from Jerusalem*, 206–8.

81. Slutsky, *Sefer Toldot*, 2:811; Shindler, *Rise of the Israeli Right*, 186.

82. Ben-Gurion to Histadrut Council, July 26, 1938, in BGA STA file 145.

83. Ben-Gurion even resigned (temporarily) from the Histadrut executive committee when it flew a black flag over its headquarters for Ben-Yosef. Ben-Gurion, *Zichronot*, 5:205–6, 220–23. Ben-Gurion to Mapai Council, July 6, 1938, LPA 2–23–1938-20. Slutsky, *Sefer Toldot*, 2:810–11. Hoffman, *Anonymous Soldiers*, 78.

84. *Census of Palestine 1931*, 99; *Village Statistics* (Jerusalem: Palestine Government, 1938), 5; *Village Statistics* (Jerusalem: Palestine Government, 1945), 4. Alan Allport, *Britain at Bay: The Epic Story of the Second World War, 1938–1941* (New York: Alfred A. Knopf, 2020), chap. 4.

85. On Tegart Forts see Richard Cahill, "The Tegart Police Fortresses in British Mandate Palestine: A Reconsideration of Their Strategic Location and Purpose," *Jerusalem Quarterly* 75 (Autumn 2018): 48–61.

86. According to another account, Monty answered complaints over al-Bassa by repeating, again and again, "I shall shoot them." Hughes, "Banality of Brutality," 338, and *Britain's Pacification of Palestine*, 330–34. Similar testimony on being forced to stand on prickly pear leaves is in Nimr, "Arab Revolt," 110.

87. "Correspondence re alleged brutality by British police & troops, 1936–1939," MECA JEM 65/5. Letter from Abdul Hamid Shoman, November 21, 1938, TNA CO 733/371.

88. Hughes, *Britain's Pacification of Palestine*, 337–41. Arab Center memo, June 1939, ISA P-361/4. Some accounts speak of separate cages for men and women; photos of such a division are in *Filastin al-Shahidah* [Palestine the Martyr] (Istanbul, 1939?), 52–53, 66ff. For MacMichael's response, blaming hot weather and advanced age, see his September 22, 1939, letter to MacDonald, TNA WO 32/4562.

89. Keith-Roach, *Pasha of Jerusalem*, 196. On minesweepers and British acts of brutality generally, see Jacob Norris, "Repression and Rebellion: Britain's Response to the Arab Revolt in Palestine of 1936–39," *Journal of Imperial and Commonwealth History* 36, no. 1 (March 2008): 34, passim. See also "Palestine excesses by British disclosed," *The Independent*, January 21, 1989.

90. Martin to Dawson, March 25, 1938, TNA CO 733/370. He added, "But there is a point where such behavior, if it results in grave loss or injury to innocent persons, may defeat its own ends by instilling in the minds of the inhabitants a sullen and bitter hatred of the Government and all its works."

91. Haining memo, "Hostile propaganda in Palestine," December 1, 1938, TNA WO 32/4562. Hughes, *Britain's Pacification of Palestine*, 177–93.

92. Hughes, "Banality of Brutality," 318, 349–54, and *Britain's Pacification of Palestine*, passim, especially chap. 5, 6, 8.

93. "Lane, Arthur," IWMSA 10295/3.

94. Courtney, *Palestine Policeman*, 241–43.

Chapter 6

1. Golda Meir, *My Life* (New York: Putnam, 1975), 154. Segev, *State at Any Cost*, 10. Teveth, *Burning Ground*, 3. Ben-Gurion to Mapai Council, September 12, 1936, LPA 2–023–1936-14. Weizmann's dim view of Ben-Gurion is reflected in his autobiography mentioning him just three times—the first is over 500 pages into the 589-page text. Weizmann, *Trial and Error*, 544. See also Norman Rose, *Chaim Weizmann: A Biography* (New York: Penguin Books, 1989), 378–79, 446–47, 456–59.

2. "Jewish notables whose names recur frequently in summaries," undated, MECA Tegart Papers 1/3b.

3. Teveth, *Palestinian Arabs*, 165.

4. Ben-Gurion to Mapai Council, July 6, 1938, LPA 2–23–1938-20, and to Histadrut Council, July 26, 1938, BGA STA file 145. "Plunder" and "expropriation" are this author's translations of "*gezel*"; "nation" and "people" are "*'am*"; "country" and "land" are "*aretz*."

5. Teveth, *Burning Ground*, 546–52, 601. Teveth presents a third objective, one that arguably overlaps with the first two: "laying the groundwork for the government of the state-to-be."

6. Ben-Gurion to Mapai Council, July 6, 1938, LPA 2–23–1938-20. As early as summer 1936 he had boasted of the Jews' new "little army": see Chazan, "Purity of Arms," 98, passim. On Jewish force numbers see Cohen, *Retreat from the Mandate*, 71; Eyal, *Ha-Intifada ha-Rishona*, 412; Hughes, *Britain's Pacification of Palestine*, 274–81.

7. Winterton to Cabinet, July 20, 1938, TNA CAB 23/94/6. Meir, *My Life*, 158–59; Sykes, *Crossroads to Israel*, 184–89; Penkower, *Palestine in Turmoil*, chap. 8 and 543–45; Francis R. Nicosia, *The Third Reich and the Palestine Question*, 2nd ed. (New Brunswick,

NJ: Transaction Publishers, 1999), 157–67. "Closed Borders: The International Conference on Refugees in Evian 1938," https://evian1938.de/en. For Arab reaction see Wadsworth to Hull, July 11, 1938, FDR PPF 601.

8. Ben-Gurion, *Zichronot*, 5:219–20. "Evian Conference," BGA STA file 84. Ben-Gurion to Jewish Agency Executive, December 11, 1938, BGA 226905. Segev, *State at Any Cost*, 280–83, and *One Palestine*, 392–96; Sykes, *Crossroads to Israel*, 188–89; Teveth, *Burning Ground*, 639.

9. "The Mufti: His aims, etc. and his opponents," May 2, 1938. Police excerpt, September 14, 1938. "The Mufti's organization in the Lebanon," October 7, 1938. "Palestine: The Mufti's policy," October 27, 1938. All in "Haj Amin el Husseini," Security Service personal file, TNA KV 2/2084. MacDonald to Chamberlain, August 19, 1938, TNA PREM 1–352.

10. "Haj Amin al-Husayni, the Mufti of Jerusalem," Biographic Sketch No. 60, April 24, 1951, NARA II, RG 263, vol. 4, file 61, https://archive.org/details/HusseiniAminEl.

11. "Palestine: Miscellaneous," July 21 and November 22, 1938, TNA KV 2/2084.

12. Quoted in Lazar, *Six Singular Figures*, 11, 23. See also Furlonge, *Palestine*, 117; Elath, "Conversations," 57, passim.

13. Stark is quoted in Martin Kramer's generally negative appraisal of Antonius's character and work: "Ambition, Arabism, and George Antonius," in *Arab Awakening & Islamic Revival: The Politics of Ideas in the Middle East* (Piscataway, NJ: Transaction Publishers, 2009), 118. Also in Lazar, *Six Singular Figures*, 200–201.

14. The mufti's memoirs refer to their "long and friendly acquaintance"; Husseini, *Mudhakkirat*, 64. Antonius to Rogers, February 11, 1938, ICWA. Dugdale, *Baffy*, 48; Lazar, *Six Singular Figures*, 200–201.

15. Arnon-Ohanah, *Mered Arvi*, 186. Matthew Hughes writes that forty thousand fled to Syria and Lebanon alone; see Hughes, *Britain's Pacification of Palestine*, 144.

16. Antonius, *Arab Awakening*, 386, 393–95.

17. Ibid., 411–12.

18. Ibid., 393–95, and for Antonius's account of the origins of the Balfour Declaration, 258–67. On "Jewish services" provided during the war, see Lloyd George's account in Kessler, "A dangerous people."

19. Antonius, *Arab Awakening*, 392–96.

20. Ibid., 164–83, 413–37.

21. Ibid., 406–12.

22. Christopher Sykes, *Orde Wingate, a Biography* (London: Collins, 1959), 133. On Lawrence see Wingate to Ironside, May 6, 1939, and reply, June 8, 1939, BL M2313.

23. Sykes, *Wingate*, 21–37, 51–81. Alice Ivy Hay, *There Was a Man of Genius: Letters to My Grandson Orde Jonathan Wingate* (London: Neville Spearman, 1963), 24–31. John Bierman and Colin Smith, *Fire in the Night: Wingate of Burma, Ethiopia, and Zion* (New York: Random House, 1999), 7–12. Trevor Royle, *Orde Wingate: A Man of Genius, 1903–1944* (Barnsley, South Yorkshire: Pen & Sword Military, 2010), 88–89.

24. Trevor Royle notes: "It has to be said that if Wingate had been friendly to the Arabs no one would have commented on it." Royle, *Man of Genius*, 94, 108.

25. Wingate to mother, October 14, 1936, Wingate Papers, BL Microfilm 2313.

26. Wingate to Reginald Wingate, January 12, 1937, BL M2313.

27. Wingate to mother, April 20, 1937, BL 2313.

28. Hacohen wrote, "He had fiery, searching, unsmiling eyes—extraordinary deep-set eyes that penetrated into your inner being." David Hacohen, *Time to Tell: An Israeli Life, 1898–1984* (New York: Cornwall Books, 1985), 53–54. Sykes, *Wingate*, 111–12.

29. Wingate to Weizmann, May 31, 1937, WA 20–1986. Sykes, *Wingate*, 173. Eshkol, *Common Soldier*, 194–96.

30. Hebrew notebook, March 1938, BL M2303. Wingate to Weizmann, August 1, 1937, WA 2–2003. A related memo, "Palestine Territorial Force," February 17, 1938, is in WA 17–2047.

31. Simon Anglim, *Orde Wingate: Unconventional Warrior: From the 1920s to the Twenty-First Century* (Barnsley, South Yorkshire: Pen & Sword Military, 2014), 67–69. Eshkol, *Common Soldier*, 141.

32. "Appreciation by Captain O.C. Wingate," June 5, 1938, and "Principles governing the employment of special night squads," June 10, 1938, BL M2313.

33. "Organization and training of Special Night Squads," August 3, 1938, BL M2313.

34. Judges, 6:1–8:24. In an August 2, 1938, letter to his mother, Wingate described living "on the site of Gideon's successful attack *on the Arabs*" (emphasis mine); BL M2313. Sykes, *Wingate*, 149, 171; Bierman and Smith, *Fire in the Night*, 91–95; Eshkol, *Common Soldier*, 151–52, 156; Royle, *Man of Genius*, 127; Robert King-Clark, *Free for a Blast* (London: Grenville Publishing, 1988), 171.

35. Sturman never joined the squads (he was already in his forties), but ultimately provided Wingate with informers on armed bands' movements. "Appreciation by Captain O.C. Wingate," June 5, 1938, BL M2313. Slutsky, *Sefer Toldot*, 2:870–72, 921–23, 1237; Sykes, *Wingate*, 168–69; Black, *Enemies and Neighbors*, chap. 5.

36. Wingate report, June 19, 1938; Dove to Wingate, June 28, 1938; Wingate to Evetts, January 31, 1939, BL M2313. Eshkol, *Common Soldier*, 102–7, 156–57; Slutsky, *Sefer Toldot*, 2:918–20. A list of every SNS operation is in Shlomi Chetrit, *Rishonim Leha'ez: Plugot ha-Layla ha-Meyuhadot shel Orde Wingate* [First to Dare: Orde Wingate's Special Night Squads] (Mikveh Israel: Yehuda Dekel Library, 2017), 118–21.

37. Wingate report, July 23, 1938, and letter to Evetts, January 31, 1939, BL M2313. Anglim, *Orde Wingate*, 79–80; Bierman and Smith, *Fire in the Night*, 100; Eshkol, *Common Soldier*, 158–60.

38. Wingate report, July 23, 1938, and letter to mother, August 2, 1938, BL M2313. Bierman and Smith, *Fire in the Night*, 101.

39. King-Clark, *Free for a Blast*, 189. "King-Clark, Robert," IWMSA 4486/5. See also Chetrit, *Rishonim Leha'ez*, 73–83.

40. "Note on the development of Special Night Squads," July 14, 1938, and letter to Evetts, January 31, 1939, BL M2313. His value to Zionism in this period is clear from Weizmann's July 18, 1938, letter (just twelve days after his brother-in-law's murder) reminding his sister, twice, to give Wingate blessings for a full recovery; WA 27–2082.

41. Wingate to mother, August 2, 1938, BL M2313.

42. Haining to Hore-Belisha, August 24, 1938, TNA WO 32/9497.

43. The village was also known as al-Awadin (today the site of Moshav Hayogev). Wingate report, September 4, 1938, and Wingate to Evetts, January 31, 1939, BL

M2313. Eshkol, *Common Soldier*, 162–66; King-Clark, *Free for a Blast*, 197–98; Bierman and Smith, *Fire in the Night*, 110–13.

44. King-Clark, *Free for a Blast*, 198–99. He said the Jewish policeman was "euphoric" at the battle's end, and showed the bloody bayonet around nearby Jewish villages; see "King-Clark," IWMSA 4486/5.

45. *Notrim* in Kibbutz Sarid killed three more rebels who had fled the battle. Wingate report, September 4, 1938, and Wingate to Evetts, January 31, 1939, BL M2313. King-Clark, *Free for a Blast*, 197–200; "King-Clark," IWMSA 4486/5; "Grove, Michael," IWMSA 4510/1. See also Chetrit, *Rishonim Leha'ez*, 85–93.

46. Eshkol, *Common Soldier*, 166. Yasin, *Thawrah*, 145–46.

47. Sadeh (see Chapter 5) had preceded Wingate's innovations and initially worked with him. Still, Sadeh and others conceded the latter brought unmatched competence and professionalism to the effort. Slutsky, *Sefer Toldot*, 2:919, 937; Allon, *Shield of David*, chap. 3; Dayan, *Story of My Life*, 46; Uri Ben-Eliezer, *The Making of Israeli Militarism* (Bloomington: Indiana University Press, 1998), 21–28.

48. Eshkol, *Common Soldier*, 188–90. Allon, *Shield of David*, chap. 3. Slutsky, *Sefer Toldot*, 2:929–32. See also Hughes, *Britain's Pacification of Palestine*, 274–88.

49. At Sturman's funeral Wingate laid a wreath with a banner reading: "In honor of a great Jew and a firm friend of the Arabs who murdered him." Chetrit, *Rishonim Leha'ez*, 44. Six other Jews were killed across the country the same day. *Haaretz*, *Filastin*, and *Palestine Post*, September 15, 1938.

50. Wingate report, July 23, 1938, and Wingate to Evetts, January 31, 1939, BL M2313. Eshkol, *Common Soldier*, 175–76; Bierman and Smith, *Fire in the Night*, 114–16. On collective punishment, see Hughes, *Britain's Pacification of Palestine*, 56–62, and Hughes, "Terror in Galilee: British-Jewish Collaboration and the Special Night Squads in Palestine during the Arab Revolt, 1938–39," *Journal of Imperial and Commonwealth History* 43, no. 4 (August 8, 2015): passim.

51. Wingate wrote that the SNS's gains were twenty-five times greater than usual for a unit its size; see "Palestine in Imperial Strategy," May 6, 1939, BL M2313. Dayan, *Story of My Life*, 47; Chetrit, *Rishonim Leha'ez*, 106–9; Bierman and Smith, *Fire in the Night*, 109.

52. Debate continues over Wingate's legacy, even within Israel, where he is widely admired. For two contrasting Israeli views see Segev, *One Palestine*, 429–32, and Michael Oren, "Orde Wingate: Friend Under Fire," *Azure* 10 (Winter 2001).

53. Eshkol, *Common Soldier*, 174; Chetrit, *Rishonim Leha'ez*, 118–21. On house demolitions see "Crew, Graeme Campbell Eley," IWMSA 6118–3. On forced running and atrocities, including executions, by squad commander Bredin, see Hughes, "Terror in Galilee," 595–601. According to Uri Ben-Eliezer, Wingate ordered "the killing of every Arab found in the vicinity" at Beisan. But his source is Sykes, who wrote of orders that "rebels" (not "Arabs") be "rounded up, and shot if they tried to escape." Ben-Eliezer also alleges that Wingate practiced decimation, but that too is sourced to Sykes, who wrote only that nine bodies were found at Daburiya. Ben-Eliezer, *Making of Israeli Militarism*, 26–27. Sykes, *Wingate*, 158, 169.

54. See for example "Grove," IWMSA 4510/3; "Bredin," IWMSA 4550/4–5; "Crew," IWMSA 6118–3; "King-Clark," IWMSA 4486/6; "Tinker," IWMSA 4492/2; "Dove, Arthur Julian Hadfield," IWMSA 4463/2. Dayan, *Story of My Life*, 47.

55. Weizmann, *Trial and Error*, 398. Dayan, *Story of My Life*, 46. Dugdale, *Baffy*, 80, 153. Allon, *Shield of David*, chap. 3. Hacohen, *Time to Tell*, 59. Sharett, *Yoman Medini*, vol. 3, June 6, 1937, and October 13, 1938. For army subordinates see "Bredin," IWMSA 4550/4; Bierman and Smith, *Fire in the Night*, 71.

56. "King-Clark," IWMSA 4486/6 ("I didn't particularly like him, but I admired him tremendously"). "Grove," IWMSA 4510/3 ("I didn't like him much, but by God was he efficient"). "Bredin," IWMSA 4550/4 ("My soldiers didn't like him, I don't think, but they had enormous respect for him"). See also Hacohen, *Time to Tell*, 58–59. The cocktail-party anecdote is Grove's.

57. David Ben-Gurion, "Britain's Contribution to Arming the Hagana" and "Our Friend: What Wingate Did for Us"—both in Khalidi, *From Haven to Conquest*, 371–74, 382–87. Other accounts have him saying, "Zionist army" or "Jewish army." Eshkol, Common Soldier, 111, 189; Slutsky, *Sefer Toldot*, 2:930, 1238; Allon, *Shield of David*, chap. 3; Bierman and Smith, *Fire in the Night*, 113.

58. That same night local pro-Nazi paramilitary assaulted dozens of Czechs and Jews throughout the Sudetenland. "Hitler Threatens Statesmen," *Palestine Post*, September 13, 1938. Shindler, *Triumph of Military Zionism*, 205. Ben-Gurion dismissed Hitler's "crocodile tears" for the Arabs; Segev, *State at Any Cost*, 277.

59. The source was Health Minister Walter Elliot; Dugdale also wrote of her own initial relief at the agreement. Dugdale, *Baffy*, 106–9.

60. The two-part Jewish reaction was partly due to the lag in learning the deal's details; see for example "Another Breathing Spell" and "Peace Without Honor," *Palestine Post*, September 29 and October 2, 1938. Hebrew and Arabic press reactions are from *Colonial Information Bulletin* (likely late October 1938), TNA CO 733/371. "British Setbacks Fan Arab Revolt," *New York Times*, October 16, 1938.

61. Ben-Gurion to Amos, Geula, and Emanuel Ben-Gurion, October 1, 1938, BGA. Segev (*State at Any Cost*, 282) incorrectly translates the word as "holocaust." Teveth, *Burning Ground*, 643–53. Dugdale, *Baffy*, 99.

62. *Village Statistics 1938*, 16. *Census of Palestine 1931*, 85.

63. Sharett, *Yoman Medini*, vol. 3, October 4 and 6, 1938. Slutsky, *Sefer Toldot*, 2:818–22. Akram Zuaytir, *Watha'iq al-Haraka al-Wataniyya al-Filastiniyya, 1918–1939* [Documents of the Palestinian National Movement, 1918–1939] (Beirut: Institute for Palestine Studies, 1979), 508.

64. The account is attributed to "Abu Omar" (Abd al-Rahman al-Salih), whose brother Muhammad ("Abu Khaled") was a rebel leader whom some sources say organized Andrews's murder. It appears in Slutsky, *Sefer Toldot*, 2:822, and Zuaytir, *Watha'iq*, 508. See also Yasin, *Thawrah*, 95. On the brothers see Danin, *Teudot*, 13, 35n69, 60n117; Porath, *Palestinian Arab*, 245.

65. The number of victims is often given as nineteen, but two of these were inexperienced *notrim* who mistook the assailants for British troops. "21 Jews Slain in Tiberias Massacre, Worst Since '29," *JTA*, and "Massacre in Tiberias Town," *Palestine Post*—both October 4, 1938. *FRUS, 1938*, vol. 2, document 775. Slutsky, *Sefer Toldot*, 2:820.

66. MacMichael to MacDonald, October 24, 1938, TNA CO 935/21. The government used similar language, describing the attack as "systematically organized and savagely executed"; see its 1938 report to the League of Nations (Col. 166), 15.

67. Impressions by *Va'ad Leumi* (Jewish National Council) delegate Moshe Ostrovsky are in "*Tverya*," *Ha-Tzofe*, October 9, 1938, and Ben-Zvi to Tegart, October 7, 1938, MECA Tegart Papers, box 2, file 4.

68. As the gunmen left the city, they met a combined SNS-*notrim* force, which killed at least six of them. Wingate's deputy Bredin later led a retaliatory operation in Hittin, likely accompanied by atrocities against civilians. See Hughes, "Terror in Galilee," 596–97. Eshkol, *Common Soldier*, 166–73. Sykes, *Wingate*, 178–81. Slutsky, *Sefer Toldot*, 2:818–23, 925–26. Wingate to Evetts, January 31, 1939, BL M2313.

69. On Abu Ibrahim (Khalil Muhammad Issa), see Kedourie and Haim, *Zionism and Arabism*, 66, 83, 91n71; Kelly, *Crime of Nationalism*, 144–45; Porath, *Palestinian Arab*, 242–43. Subhi Yasin, perhaps in error, attributes the attack to another rebel leader, Abu Ibrahim the Lesser; Yasin, *Thawrah*, 93–94.

70. "Under Arab 'Rule,'" *Palestine Post*, October 4, 1938. On Arab support for al-Hadif, see commemoration in *Davar*, November 29, 1938, and *Haaretz*, October 28, 30, and 31, 1938. Still, apparently out of fear of retribution, no Arabs appear to have attended the funeral.

71. MacMichael to MacDonald, September 2, TNA CAB 104/7, and October 24, 1938 and January 16, 1939, TNA CO 935/21. Haining to Hore-Belisha, November 30, 1938, TNA WO 32/9498. *FRUS, 1938*, vol. 2, documents 711 and 727.

72. *Evening Standard*, October 7, 1938.

73. Khalil Totah, *Turbulent Times in Palestine: The Diaries of Khalil Totah, 1886–1955*, ed. Thomas M. Ricks (Jerusalem; Ramallah: Institute for Palestine Studies, PASSIA, 2009), 33, 231. Wadsworth to Hull, September 15, 1938, NARA II 867N.4016/64. Swedenburg, *Memories of Revolt*, 30–37, 216n48.

74. Arnon-Ohana, *Mered Arvi*, 122–26; Shepherd, *Ploughing Sand*, 204; Anderson, "State Formation from Below," 45–48; Kelly, *Crime of Nationalism*, 127–31.

75. The courts were initially founded by Fawzi al-Qawuqji but significantly expanded in 1937 and especially during the revolt peak in 1938. On the case of Dafna, his reprieve by Abdel-Rahim, and rebel courts generally, see Kabha, "Courts," 198–211. Also Nimr, "Arab Revolt," 166–74.

76. Nimr, "Nation in a Hero," 144. Swedenburg, *Memories of Revolt*, 87, 94, 100. Edward Horne, *A Job Well Done (Being a History of the Palestine Police Force 1920–1948)* (Lewes, East Sussex: Book Guild, 2003), 224–25. Haining to Hore-Belisha, April 24, 1939, TNA WO 32/9499, and December 1, 1938, WO 32/4562. Ezra Danin was more skeptical, portraying him as barely literate and lacking scruples; see Danin, *Teudot*, 30–34.

77. CID report, September 1938, TNA CO 733/370. Haining memo, "Hostile propaganda in Palestine," December 1, 1938, TNA WO 32/4562. HA 8/1/8. Danin, *Teudot*, 35–48, 91–103. Ann Mosely Lesch, *Arab Politics in Palestine, 1917–1939: The Frustration of a Nationalist Movement* (Ithaca: Cornell University Press, 1979), 124–25.

78. A combined land and air operation targeting the parley killed the aforementioned Abu Khaled. On Deir Ghassaneh and the Bureau, see Nimr, "Arab Revolt," 131–32,

160–74, and "Nation in a Hero," 150; Hughes, *Britain's Pacification of Palestine*, 151–52; Arnon-Ohanah, *Mered Arvi*, 117–22, 130. Danin, *Teudot*, 22–23, 35n69, 82n166, 96n200.

79. Yasin, *Thawrah*, 195–96.

80. Haining to Hore-Belisha, November 30, 1938, TNA WO 32/9498. Hughes, *Britain's Pacification of Palestine*, 357–58; Slutsky, *Sefer Toldot*, 2:774; Eyal, *Ha-Intifada ha-Rishona*, 422, 600n66.

81. Nineteen Arabs were killed and one soldier in the Jerusalem operation; troops reconquered Beersheba, Jericho, and Gaza a month later. MacMichael to MacDonald, December 3 and 12, 1938, TNA CO 935/21. Haining to Hore-Belisha, April 24, 1939, TNA WO 32/9499. Eyal, *Ha-Intifada ha-Rishona*, 418–20; Slutsky, *Sefer Toldot*, 2:774–75; *FRUS, 1938*, vol. 2, document 757; Hughes, *Britain's Pacification of Palestine*, 112.

82. MacDonald to Battershill, October 10, 1938, and Cabinet minutes, October 13, 1938; TNA CAB 104/7.

83. A list of Jewish witnesses is in CZA S5/628, and some of their testimonies are in "Woodhead Commission," BGA STA file 71. The other testimonies, including British ones, appear to have been destroyed. On "Re-Peel" see Rose, *Gentile Zionists*, 154ff.

84. Dajani's murder was widely assumed to be the mufti's work, carried out by Aref Abdel-Raziq; see MacMichael to MacDonald, December 3, 1938, TNA CO 935/21. Hillel Cohen attributes it to al-Hajj Muhammad, while conceding the latter carried out comparatively few executions. See Cohen, *Army of Shadows*, 130–31, 289n46.

85. As early as May 1938, Weizmann was alarmed by rumors over the commission's purported plans; Weizmann, *Letters*, series A, vol. 18, 387–90. See also "The Road to Appeasement" letter collection in Weizmann, *Letters*, series B, vol. 2, 312–30.

86. MacDonald to Battershill, October 10, 1938, and Cabinet minutes, October 13, 1938; TNA CAB 104/7.

87. *FRUS, 1938*, documents 780, 785. Penkower, *Palestine in Turmoil*, 574, 596, 611n99. Kennedy called the pressure campaign "the most sustained and embarrassing agitation" that Roosevelt had faced since taking office. MacDonald memo, January 18, 1939, TNA CAB 24/282/4.

88. Lindsay to Halifax, October 14 and 18, 1938, TNA CO 733/369. Telegrammed pleas in FDR OF 700; OF 76c, box 6.

89. Useful accounts on the Woodhead Commission are in El-Eini, *Mandated Landscape*, 331–44; Cohen, *Retreat from the Mandate*, 38–49, 66–72; Penkower, *Palestine in Turmoil*, chap. 8 and 9, passim. On Whitehall's guidance against partition, see Teveth, *Burning Ground*, 635–36.

90. "Cmd. 5854: Palestine Partition Commission Report" (His Majesty's Stationery Office, 1938), 83. Peel's plan is examined throughout Chapters 4–10, with Chapter 8 devoted to the transfer question.

91. The majority report cites Haifa's mixed population among Plan B's "fatal" flaws. The lone dissenter in favor was Alison Russell, who thought Plan C offered too small a state to meet British obligations to the Jews. He regretted that Plan B also offered such a small state ("considerably smaller than . . . Norfolk") but saw no alternative; Ibid., 85–98, 249–62.

92. MECA Tegart Papers, box 2, file 3. Also in El-Eini, *Mandated Landscape*, 343, 544.

93. "Cmd. 5854," 13–14, 243–46. The majority report suggested a "modified form of partition, which we call economic federalism"—a customs union that would offer some autonomy to both peoples but fall short of sovereignty.

94. MacMichael privately conceded that though the mufti was barred, his "point of view would be considered"; letter to MacDonald, December 29, 1938, TNA CO 935/21. "Cmd. 5893: Palestine—Statement of Policy by His Majesty's Government in the United Kingdom" (His Majesty's Stationery Office, November 1938), 3–4. MacDonald doubted the conference would succeed; see cable to Lampson, October 28, 1938, TNA CO 733/386.

95. MacMichael to MacDonald, October 31, 1938; Lampson to MacDonald, October 30, 1938; MacDonald to Battershill et al., November 7, 1938—all in TNA CO 733/386/16. Lampson's senior adviser was Antonius's brother-in-law Walter Smart.

96. These were MacDonald's words as paraphrased by Weizmann. He said MacDonald told him he would "fight to the last ditch before placing us in a 'minority' position." Weizmann, *Letters*, series B, vol. 2, 324–25. Ben-Gurion diary, October 25, 1938, BGA. See also Penkower, *Palestine in Turmoil*, 566–73.

97. MacMichael to MacDonald, December 29, 1938, TNA CO 935/21. Robert L. Jarman, ed., *Political Diaries of the Arab World: Palestine & Jordan*, vol. 3 (Slough, Berkshire: Archive Editions, 2001), 394–95, 402–3.

98. "Statement by the Higher Arab Committee," November 16, 1938, TNA FO 684/11.

99. See for example Jarman, *Political Diaries*, 394–95, and MacMichael to MacDonald, February 27, 1939, TNA CO 935/22.

100. Khalidi was replaced as mayor by his relative Mustafa Khalidi in August; at the time of this entry he was on hunger strike. Khalidi, *Exiled from Jerusalem*, 237, 248–52, 261, 276, 282.

101. Weizmann, *Letters*, series B, vol. 2, 330. Dugdale, *Baffy*, 93, 99–101, 110–13. Teveth, *Burning Ground*, 634–38. MacMichael to MacDonald, December 29, 1938, TNA CO 935/21. *Palestine Post* and *JTA*, November 10, 1938.

102. "Kristallnacht," United States Holocaust Memorial Museum, https://encyclopedia.ushmm.org/content/en/article/kristallnacht.

103. Ben-Gurion to *Va'ad Leumi*, December 12, 1938, BGA STA file 866. Teveth, *Burning Ground*, 653.

Chapter 7

1. Malcolm MacDonald's biographer dubbed him "under Weizmann's charm . . . a willing target" in that period. Clyde Sanger, *Malcolm MacDonald: Bringing an End to Empire* (Montreal: McGill-Queen's University Press, 1995), 87–97. See also Weizmann, *Trial and Error*, 411–13.

2. MacDonald had also briefly served in the post in 1935. In 1938 Dugdale called his selection "the best appointment that could be made from the Jewish point of view."

Dugdale, *Baffy*, 90; Khalidi, *Exiled from Jerusalem*, 162; Sanger, *Malcolm MacDonald*, 96, 162; Segev, *One Palestine*, 336–40.

3. MacDonald represented National Labour, the breakaway Labour faction founded by his father, which since 1931 had joined with Conservatives and others in National Government coalitions. See Carly Beckerman, *Unexpected State: British Politics and the Creation of Israel* (Bloomington: Indiana University Press, 2020), 129.

4. See also Churchill's reply, which also noted Arab population growth in Palestine, but proposed limiting Jewish immigration below thirty-five thousand for ten years to keep the relative proportions stable. "Palestine," HC Deb, November 24, 1938, vol. 341, col. 1987ff.

5. Antonius correspondence, January-February and April 6, 1939, ICWA. Totah, *Turbulent Times*, 243. MacDonald's shift came as early as spring or summer 1938; see Nicholas Bethell, *The Palestine Triangle: The Struggle for the Holy Land, 1935–48* (New York: G. P. Putnam's Sons, 1979), 43–50.

6. Furlonge, *Palestine*, 118–22. MacDonald notes, November 25 and 28, 1938, TNA CAB 104/8. Nasser Eddin Nashashibi, *Jerusalem's Other Voice: Ragheb Nashashibi and Moderation in Palestinian Politics, 1920–1948* (Exeter, Devon: Ithaca Press, 1990), 166ff. See also Khalidi, *Exiled from Jerusalem*, 182, 282–84, 302; Bethell, *Palestine Triangle*, 51–52, 194.

7. Telegram, January 15, 1939, in "Abandoned documents, George Antonius archive," ISA P-341/22. Antonius to Rogers, January 20, 1939, ICWA. AHC statement, January 17, 1939, ISA P-353/50. MacMichael to MacDonald, February 27, 1939, TNA CO 935/22. Husseini, *Mudhakkirat*, 44–45. See also Boyle, *Betrayal of Palestine*, 5ff.

8. MacDonald memo, January 18, 1939, TNA CAB 24/282/4. See also Sanger, *Malcolm MacDonald*, 164–67. In November he had told the Cabinet: "The government had to choose between its commitments to the world of Jewry and its commitments to the world of Islam." In Martin Gilbert, "The Turning of Malcolm MacDonald," *The Guardian*, January 17, 1981.

9. For internal discussion of the correspondence during the Peel Commission, see TNA CO 733/244/22, FO 371/20029, FO 371/20810. McMahon himself reaffirmed the British position in a July 23, 1937 letter to *The Times*. Book receipt, Ben-Gurion diary, November 5, 1938, BGA.

10. MacDonald memo, loc. cit. In his own memo Halifax agreed that the British case had "points of serious weakness"; minutes, January 23, 1939, TNA CAB 24/282/19.

11. MacDonald memo, loc. cit., and minutes, January 18, 1939, TNA CAB 23/97/1.

12. Halifax and MacMichael broadly agreed with MacDonald, and were ready to limit immigration further still. MacDonald memo, loc. cit., and Halifax reply, January 23, TNA CAB 24/282/18; minutes, February 1, 1939, TNA CAB 23/97/3. Through Dugdale's friend Walter Elliot, now health minister, the Zionists knew the memo's outlines. Rose, *Gentile Zionists*, 181–82; Penkower, *Palestine in Turmoil*, 625.

13. Images, January 28 and February 7, 1939, via Alamy Stock Photo.

14. "Guests of Britain—in Gaol Island and De Luxe Hotel," *News Chronicle*, January 30, 1939. Hanna to Levy, February 16, 1939, ISA P-695/6. MacMichael to MacDonald, March 24, 1939, TNA FO 935/22. Khalidi, *Exiled from Jerusalem*, 312–14.

15. *Evening Standard*, February 1, 1939 (the paper failed to note that Antonius was also a Cambridge graduate).

16. Chamberlain sat directly opposite Weizmann, and MacDonald opposite Ben-Gurion. For Chamberlain's comments to the Arabs, see official notes, February 7, 1939, ISA P-360/16; to the Jews, see Ben-Gurion, *My Talks*, 199–201, and Downie's notes, February 7, 1939, WA 25–2123.

17. Weizmann, *Letters*, series B, 341ff. Also in Ben-Gurion, *My Talks*, 202ff. Weizmann's prepared notes, February 8, 1939, WA 2–2124.

18. Draft notes, February 8, 1939, in WA 1–2124. Largely reproduced in Ben-Gurion, *My Talks*, 214–17.

19. Ragheb Nashashibi, head of the anti-mufti Defense Party, was absent due to "ill health," though Amin's opposition to his participation was likely a factor as well. "Jew and Arab," *The Times*, February 8, 1939. See also Penkower, *Palestine in Turmoil*, 616, 626.

20. Notes, February 11, 1939, contained in "Abandoned Documents, Government of Palestine" in ISA P-360/16.

21. Furlonge, *Palestine*, 122–23. Nashashibi, *Jerusalem's Other Voice*, 154–60, 173. The mufti ultimately relented, and Ragheb Nashashibi and Yacoub Farraj attended. But per Dugdale, MacDonald pushed the Nashashibis not to attend, lest their presence cause the mufti's camp to withdraw; see Dugdale, *Baffy*, 122.

22. "The proceedings began with a complete disagreement among the Arabs themselves," Chamberlain lamented. Neville Chamberlain, *The Neville Chamberlain Diary Letters*, ed. Robert C. Self, vol. 4 (Aldershot, Hampshire; Burlington, VT: Ashgate, 2005), 381.

23. Notes, February 13 and 15, 1939, contained in ISA P-360/16. The Arabs on the subcommittee were advised by Michael McDonnell, ex–chief justice of Palestine, removed in 1936 for opposing the razing of Jaffa's Old City (see Chapter 2). Dugdale, *Baffy*, 123. Boyle, *Betrayal of Palestine*, 7ff. On the subcommittee see Elie Kedourie, *In the Anglo-Arab Labyrinth: The McMahon-Husayn Correspondence and Its Interpretations 1914–1939*, 2nd ed. (London; New York: Routledge, 2014), chap. 10, especially 299–308.

24. Ben-Gurion, *My Talks*, 240–47.

25. Notes, February 15, 1939, ISA P-360/16.

26. Chamberlain, *Diary Letters*, 380–85. MacDonald also bemoaned Arab "intransigence"; minutes, February 15 and 22, 1939, TNA CAB 23/97/7–8. But by early March, Halifax was calling the Jews "extremely unreasonable"; see Penkower, *Palestine in Turmoil*, 640.

27. Comparison of official minutes with Ben-Gurion and Shertok's diaries in Caplan, *Futile Diplomacy*, 240–51. Jewish "panel" minutes, February 27, 1939, WA 12–2132.

28. Dugdale wrote, "Malcolm is really impressed with the Arab case. A change has come over him since he met them." Dugdale, *Baffy*, 123. Ben-Gurion and Weizmann were similarly stunned by the turnaround; Jewish "panel" minutes, February 24, 1939, WA 15–2131.

29. From MacDonald's later remarks to the Cabinet in minutes, March 2 and 8, 1939, TNA CAB 23/97/9–10.

30. Norman Rose writes, "The weekend of 24–26 February was . . . the watershed of the conference." Rose, *Gentile Zionists*, 188. Minutes and Jewish delegation notes, February 27, 1939, WA 12–2132 and 13–2132.

31. Dugdale, *Baffy*, 126. Penkower, *Palestine in Turmoil*, 637.

32. Thirty-eight Arabs were killed and dozens wounded in the attacks of February 27, 1939, mostly in Haifa and Jerusalem. The group warned that if the Jews were left under Arab control, there would be "hundreds and thousands" more attacks to follow. MacMichael to MacDonald, March 24, 1939, TNA CO 935/22. "Ninety-One Arab Casualties," *Palestine Post*, February 28, 1939. Alfassi, *Irgun*, 217–18.

33. Notes, February 27 and March 1, 1939, ISA P-360/16.

34. Notes, March 2, 1939, ISA P-3048/22, and minutes, TNA CAB 23/97/9.

35. Notes, March 3, 6, and 7, 1939, ISA P-3048/22. MacDonald agreed that claiming more than their share was "in the nature of the Jewish people" due to their "minority complex." Weizmann learned of the remark and rebuked him; see Rose, *Gentile Zionists*, 193; Penkower, *Palestine in Turmoil*, 639. Also Boyle, *Betrayal of Palestine*, chap. 1.

36. Comparison of official minutes with Shertok's diary is in Caplan, *Futile Diplomacy*, 252–60. Ben-Gurion, *My Talks*, 261–63. Weizmann remembered Maher as "personally friendly" at St. James's; Weizmann, *Trial and Error*, 502. Dugdale, *Baffy*, 129. See also Cohen, *Retreat from the Mandate*, 79–81.

37. "Cmd. 5974: Report of Committee Set up to Consider Certain Correspondence between Sir Henry McMahon and the Sherif of Mecca in 1915 and 1916" (His Majesty's Stationery Office, March 1939), 10–11. Meetings with Arab delegation, February 11, 14, and 15, 1939, ISA P-360/16, and smaller Arab delegation, February 17, P-3048/17. Minutes, March 2, 1939, TNA CAB 23/97/9.

38. Chamberlain still hoped to raise the five-year quota to one hundred thousand. Minutes, March 2 and 8, 1939, TNA CAB 23/97/9–10. The government had also refused a Jewish request to allow ten thousand children into Palestine, but in late 1938 authorized their entry into Britain; see Minutes, December 14, 1938, TNA CAB 23/96/11. The first group of what would become known as the *Kindertransport* arrived that December.

39. Weizmann, *Trial and Error*, 504. Sharett, *Yoman Medini*, vol. 4, March 14, 1939. Conference summary, February-March 1939, WA 9–2130 and CZA S5/1040.

40. Minutes, March 15, 1939, TNA CAB 23/98/1. For other points, including greater local participation in various government councils, see Ben-Gurion, *My Talks*, 263–65; Cohen, *Retreat from the Mandate*, 82.

41. Notes, March 15 and 17, 1939, ISA P-3048/17. Bethell, *Palestine Triangle*, 65–66. Furlonge, *Palestine*, 124–26. Perhaps due to that sense of betrayal, Alami took a harder line against the proposals that became the White Paper than even Jamal Husseini, blasting Britain's "half-hearted measures" and "lack of courage." Khalidi, *Exiled from Jerusalem*, 321; MacDonald to Luke et al., Phipps to Luke, May 25–26, 1939, TNA CO 733/408/14–15.

42. Notes, March 15 and 17, 1939, ISA P-3048/17.

43. Shertok, *Yoman Medini*, vol. 4, March 15, 1939.

44. In a final meeting, Weizmann told the Jewish delegates that while their dreams had been "partly shattered," they would one day build them anew. The delegates, some

with tears in their eyes, sang "Hatikvah." Panel minutes, March 16, 1939, WA 5–2137A; conference summary, WA 9–2130. Ben-Gurion, *My Talks*, 265–66; Rose, *Gentile Zionists*, 195.

45. Notes, March 17, 1939, ISA P-3048/17. On February 16, Jamal Husseini "said that the Arabs did not wish to get rid of Jews, but that if the Jews wished to leave Palestine, so much the better"; ISA P-360/16. Shertok, *Yoman Medini*, vol. 4, February 5–6 and March 8, 1939. Caplan, *Futile Diplomacy*, 108, 318n125.

46. Hanna to Levy, various letters January to March 1939, ISA P-695/6. Per MacMichael, the new policy gave most Arabs "more than they had ever expected" and most Arab Christians (like Hanna) "more than they ever had wanted" (suggesting they preferred a continued Mandate). MacMichael to MacDonald, July 21, 1939, TNA CO 935/22.

47. Hanna to Levy, likely March 23, 1939, ISA P-695/6. Nimr, "A Nation in a Hero," 153. Some Israeli studies have been skeptical of Abdel-Rahim's reputation for integrity; see Danin, *Teudot*, 34, 40; Arnon-Ohanah, *Mered Arvi*, 161–62. On Central Committee links to armed groups, see also Nimr, "Arab Revolt," 131–32, 154–56.

48. Fakhri Nashashibi, *Sawt min Qubur Filastin al-Arabiya* [A Voice from the Tombs of Arab Palestine] (Jerusalem, 1938). "Arab challenge to Mufti," *The Times*, November 16, 1938. "The Tarboush Stands for Liberty," *Egyptian Gazette*, December 13, 1938.

49. Various files in TNA CO 733/386, including MacMichael to MacDonald, November 19, 1938.

50. Caplan, *Futile Diplomacy*, 318n126. Fakhri was paid by the industrialist Pinhas Rutenberg and kept him apprised of the Arabs' meetings at St. James's. Dugdale wrote that Fakhri was "earning his keep." Dugdale, *Baffy*, 119; Ben-Gurion, *Zichronot*, 6:363.

51. Cohen, *Army of Shadows*, 145–55; Hughes, *Britain's Pacification of Palestine*, 258–73; Porath, *Palestinian Arab*, 249–58. MacMichael to MacDonald, January 16, 1939, TNA CO 935/21. The peace bands' top field commander was Fakhri Abdel-Hadi, formerly Qawuqji's deputy. Both Fakhris would be assassinated by rivals within a few years.

52. Hanna mourned Abdel-Rahim as "the noblest among the rebel leaders." Abdel-Raziq soon fled Syria for Iraq and rejoined the mufti's circle. Hanna to Levy, March 23, 1939, ISA P-695/6. Geoffrey J. Morton, *Just the Job: Some Experiences of a Colonial Policeman* (London: Hodder & Stoughton, 1957), 65, 96–96. Porath, *Palestinian Arab*, 257. Cohen, *Army of Shadows*, 152, 160. Nimr, "A Nation in a Hero," 153ff, and "Arab Revolt," 210–16. Yasin, *Thawrah*, 156–58. Kelly, *Crime of Nationalism*, 159–60. Totah, *Turbulent Times*, 258–59. MacMichael to MacDonald, July 21, 1939, TNA CO 935/22. Haining to Hore-Belisha, July 30, 1939, TNA WO 32/9500.

53. Morton, *Just the Job*, 65, 76. "Secret: Note on the Leaders of Armed Gangs in Palestine," September 1938, TNA CO 733/370/9. "Arab Rebel Leader Captured," *Palestine Post*, July 26, 1939. Zuaytir, *Yawmiyat*, 438.

54. Nigel Hamilton, *Monty: The Making of a General, 1887–1942* (New York: McGraw-Hill, 1981), chap. 6, 307. See also Montgomery's demi-official correspondence, 1938–1939, TNA WO 216/111, and "Brief Notes on Palestine," July 21, 1939, WO 216/46.

55. *A Survey of Palestine*, vol. 1 (Jerusalem: Government of Palestine, 1946): 38–49. Slutsky, *Sefer Toldot*, 2:801. Khalidi, *From Haven to Conquest*, 846–49. Hughes, *Britain's*

Pacification of Palestine, 245–48, 375–84. Hillel Cohen believes Arab infighting has been overstated; see Cohen, *Army of Shadows*, 142–44.

56. *Survey of Palestine*, vol. 2, 59. See also Morris, *Righteous Victims*, 159.

57. The largest demolition campaign (an estimated four hundred buildings) was in Jenin following the August 1938 murder of Jenin's Assistant District Commissioner William Moffat. For a detailed tally see Shlomi Chetrit, "Ha-Milhama ha-Ktana be-Yoter: Ha-Ma'avak ha-Tzvai ha-Briti Neged ha-Mered ha-Arvi be-Eretz Yisrael, 1936–1939 [The Biggest Small War: The British Military Struggle against the Arab Revolt in Palestine, 1936–1939]" (PhD diss., Bar-Ilan University, 2020), 340–43.

58. See for example Arnon-Ohanah, *Mered Arvi*, 185–98.

59. See for example *Palestine Post* editor Gershon Agronsky's private report, "Palestine Arab Economy Undermined by Disturbances," January 20, 1939, CZA S25/10091. Hughes, *Britain's Pacification of Palestine*, 56ff, 129–46, 249–52.

60. Kabha writes that Abu Dorra was executed for the January 1939 assassination of not one but four mukhtars after his rebel court sentenced thirty-eight people to death in absentia. He was executed a year later. Morton, *Just the Job*, 85–86; Kabha, "Courts," 205; Swedenburg, *Memories of Revolt*, 92, 118–20.

61. Minutes, Cabinet committee on Palestine, April 20, 1939, TNA CAB 24/285/11. In this meeting the Cabinet essentially agreed to the Arab states' remaining demands; see Cohen, *Retreat from the Mandate*, 82–83.

62. Home Secretary Samuel Hoare and Chancellor John Simon, leading proponents of appeasement, were especially animated by the Guiana idea. Minutes, April 20, 1939, TNA CAB 24/285/11; and April 26, May 3 and 10, 1939, CAB 23/99/3–6. On Guiana see also Penkower, *Palestine in Turmoil*, 618–20, 656.

63. Hay, *Man of Genius*, 47–48. Two days earlier Weizmann had met Chamberlain in an unpleasant, if not as heated, encounter; notes in WA 8–2149B. See also Rose, *Gentile Zionists*, 202–4; Dugdale, *Baffy*, 137.

64. Like many other Zionist sympathizers in government, the elder MacDonald's sentiments were mixed with anti-Semitism. After an early visit to Palestine he wrote that Zionism offered a healthy alternative to the "rich plutocratic Jew." J. Ramsay MacDonald, *A Socialist in Palestine* (London: Poale-Zion, 1922), 6. Sanger, *Malcolm MacDonald*, 171–72. Bethell, *Palestine Triangle*, 67.

65. Minutes, May 17, 1939, TNA CAB 23/99/7.

66. "Cmd. 6019: Statement of Policy by His Majesty's Government" (His Majesty's Stationery Office, 1939). For earlier drafts: Minutes, April 13 and 26, 1939, TNA CAB 24/285/1, 24/285/19. Technically the text allowed for ten thousand immigrants annually for five years, plus twenty-five thousand more as a contribution to the refugee crisis.

67. After the London conference the British continued talks with the Arab states in Cairo, where they relinquished the Jewish veto idea. On changes between St. James's and the White Paper, see Cohen, *Retreat from the Mandate*, 85–86, and *Britain's Moment*, 301; Caplan, *Futile Diplomacy*, 109–13; Penkower, *Palestine in Turmoil*, 642, 648; *FRUS, 1939*, vol. 4, document 811.

68. Dugdale, *Baffy*, 137. "Jewish Agency Statement; A 'Breath of Faith,'" *The Times*, May 18, 1939. Weizmann, *Letters*, series A, vol. 19, 95ff. MacMichael to MacDonald,

May 18, 1939, TNA CO 733/406/12. Ben-Gurion, *Zichronot*, 284ff. See also Teveth, *Burning Ground*, 720; this chapter's name is taken from the evocative title of that book.

69. Roosevelt to Hull, May 17, 1939, FDR, PSF 16. "Palestine," *New York Times*, May 18, 1939.

70. Izzat Tannous, *The Palestinians: Eyewitness History of Palestine* (New York: I.G.T. Co., 1988), 309–10. Some accounts say other AHC members (Jamal Husseini, Hussein Khalidi) also opposed the White Paper. Khalidi, *Exiled from Jerusalem*, 321; Porath, *Palestinian Arab*, 292.

71. See for example Hanna to Levy, various letters, March and May 1939, ISA P-695/6. Nashashibi, *Jerusalem's Other Voice*, 107. The mufti's own explanation was: "The conference failed because of the obstinacy of the English on one hand and the American intervention for the benefit of the Jews on the other." Husseini, *Mudhakkirat*, 44–45; see also Elpeleg, *Through the Eyes of the Mufti*, 39.

72. Sanger, *Malcolm MacDonald*, 159, 164–75. Before the debate Dugdale tried to "do all we can to shake MacDonald's nerve. He is weak and pitiable. It might be done." Dugdale, *Baffy*, 137–39.

73. Despite his denunciations, Churchill abstained from the vote. Cohen notes that he had not even planned to join the debate, and did so "only after being roused to anger on the first day." MacDonald later wrote that Churchill told him he would have supported the measure if not for the Arab veto. Michael J. Cohen, *Churchill and the Jews*, 2nd ed. (London: Routledge, 2003), 179–84, 302; Cohen, "Churchill-Gilbert Symbiosis," 215–16, 226n34.

74. HC Deb, May 22, 1939, vol. 347, col. 1937–2016; HC Deb, May 23, 1939, vol. 347, col. 2130–2197. See also Beckerman, *Unexpected State*, 129–31.

75. In June the League of Nations Permanent Mandates Commission unanimously rejected the White Paper as a breach of the Mandate as hitherto interpreted. It referred the case to the League Council, but the world war intervened. MacDonald called the commission "somewhat pro-Zionist." Cabinet minutes, May 23, 1939, TNA CAB 23/99/8.

76. In Chamberlain's oft-quoted phrase to the Cabinet, "If we must offend one side, let us offend the Jews." Minutes, April 20, 1939, CAB 24/285/11. In his unpublished memoir, MacDonald called his efforts on Palestine among his "crashing failures in statecraft." Quoted in Sanger, *Malcolm MacDonald*, 170, 175.

77. Hanna to Levy, May 18 and July 22, 1939, ISA P-695/6.

78. Nashashibi to MacMichael and MacMichael to MacDonald, May 30, 1939, CO 733/406/12. Nashashibi, *Jerusalem's Other Voice*, 106–9; Porath, *Palestinian Arab*, 291–94; Boyle, *Betrayal of Palestine*, 269–72. On Alami and Antonius see also Joel Beinin, "Arab Liberal Intellectuals and the Partition of Palestine," in Dubnov and Robson, *Partitions*, 204–9, passim.

79. "To every Arab of a living conscience," contained in MacMichael to MacDonald, July 1, 1939, TNA CO 733/406/12. Yasin, *Thawrah*, 226.

80. AHC statement, May 30, 1939, ISA 1054/15. In a sympathetic biography of the mufti, Philip Mattar wrote that in refusing the White Paper he was "putting personal considerations and his idealism above practical politics." Alami's biographer similarly

deplored Amin's "usual all-or-nothing mentality." Rashid Khalidi—a historian and Dr. Khalidi's nephew—called it the costliest decision the mufti had made until that point. Mattar, *Mufti of Jerusalem*, 84; Furlonge, *Palestine*, 126; Rashid Khalidi, *The Iron Cage: The Story of the Palestinian Struggle for Statehood* (Boston: Beacon Press, 2007), 114.

81. Jabotinsky learned of the Biyar Ades attack in *The Times*. He protested to Irgun leaders that he was not opposed in principle to "mass actions," but women and children remained out of bounds. MacMichael to MacDonald, July 21, 1939, TNA CO 935/22; Battershill to MacDonald, June 13, 1939, CO 733/398. "Eighteen Injured by Bombs in Jerusalem Cinema House" and "The New Terror," *Palestine Post*, May 30, 1939. Niv, *Maarchot*, 238–52; Hoffman, *Anonymous Soldiers*, 94–97. Ohevet-Ami (born Habshush) was sentenced to life in prison and amnestied seven years later.

82. MacMichael to MacDonald, July 5, 1939, TNA CO 733/398/1. In spring and summer the Irgun also executed three Jews suspected of working with police intelligence. Its attacks on Arabs continued through July. On August 26 it laid a mine that killed Ralph Cairns and Ronald Barker, heads of the Jewish and Arab detective sections, respectively; see Morton, *Just the Job*, 60–62.

83. The "special" branch began around late February, as MacDonald revealed his proposals at St. James's, but began major actions (including anti-British sabotage) after the White Paper. It disbanded once the world war began. The site of Balad al-Sheikh—including Qassam's tomb—is now within the Israeli city of Nesher; Kibbutz Lavi stands on lands formerly belonging to Lubya. Slutsky, *Sefer Toldot*, 2:830–33, 848–50; 3:70–72, 1615–16. Niv, *Maarchot*, 245–47. MacMichael to MacDonald, July 21, 1939, TNA CO 935/22.

84. MacMichael's imperiousness extended to the Arabs as well: "I am afraid that the emblem of the race should be the double-cross. To be content with having a good day's work they must have played off A against B, demonstrated their cleverness by deceiving both, and eaten a series of cakes while still having them all in hand." MacMichael to MacDonald, July 5, 1939, TNA CO 733/398/1.

85. "Prophecy," Wingate note, April 5 and 28, and Haining report, July 10, 1939. Wingate memo, "Palestine in Imperial Strategy," May 6, and Ironside reply, June 8, 1939. All in BL M2313. Ironside would be named Chief of the Imperial General Staff on September 3.

86. Hamilton, *Monty*, 307. "Bredin," IWMSA 4550/3–4. "Woods," IWMSA 23846/1. Keith-Roach, *Pasha of Jerusalem*, 193–95. Anglim, *Orde Wingate*, 77, 85–88.

87. Hanna to Levy, December (no date) 1939, ISA P-695/6.

88. Ben-Gurion, *Zichronot*, 6:67, 233, 403ff. Slutsky, *Sefer Toldot*, 3:19–37. Ben-Gurion to Weizmann, April 26, 1939, WA 15–2146B. On "combative Zionism" and turning to America, see Teveth, *Burning Ground*, 640, 668, chap. 38–39.

89. Reinharz and Shavit, *Road to September 1939*, chap. 6; Dugdale, *Baffy*, 147; Weizmann, *Trial and Error*, 508–9; Rose, *Chaim Weizmann*, 354; Ben-Gurion, *Zichronot*, 6:526.

Epilogue

1. "Jewish losses during the Holocaust by country," United States Holocaust Memorial Museum, https://encyclopedia.ushmm.org/content/en/article/jewish-losses-during-the-holocaust-by-country. "Estimated Number of Jews Killed in the Final Solution," Jewish Virtual Library, https://www.jewishvirtuallibrary.org/estimated-number-of-jews-killed-in-the-final-solution.

2. Rami Hazan to author, August 16 and October 3, 2017. Yad Vashem's database has a Soviet file showing the death of Rukhlya Tabachnik of 54 Krasniya Armiya Street in Lutsk; Ben-Yosef's letter is addressed to 54 Pilsudski Street—its name before passing from Polish to Soviet control. Yad Vashem, https://yvng.yadvashem.org.

3. "My Sheindele, they killed her . . . you don't understand a thing," Ben-Gurion thundered later when accused of callousness for negotiating German reparations. Segev, *State at Any Cost*, 338, 372n, 617; Meir, *My Life*, 157–58; Teveth, *Burning Ground*, 617.

4. Arthur Koestler, *Thieves in the Night: Chronicle of an Experiment* (New York: Macmillan, 1946). Koestler, *Promise and Fulfillment: Palestine 1917–1949* (New York: Macmillan, 1949), 53–54. See also Koestler, *The Invisible Writing: An Autobiography* (Boston: Beacon Press, 1954), 377–81; Richard J. Watts, "Koestler's Novel of Zionism," *New York Times*, November 3, 1946.

5. MacMichael to Lord Lloyd, October 14, 1940, TNA CO 733/443–444.

6. Churchill removed MacDonald as colonial secretary within a year, and in 1941 appointed him envoy to Canada, ending his political career. Bethell writes, "Great was the Zionists' rejoicing at MacDonald's departure across the Atlantic." Bethell, *Palestine Triangle*, 72–73, 101; Sanger, *Malcolm MacDonald*, 170.

7. Pressed by the Iraqis, Husseini reluctantly accepted the White Paper on condition that independence come immediately and not after a ten-year transition. Churchill, opposed to the White Paper and loath to inflame Jewish opinion in America, balked. Joseph Nevo, "Al-Hajj Amin and the British in World War II," *Middle Eastern Studies* 20, no. 1 (January 1984): 6–14. Mattar, *Mufti of Jerusalem*, 86–94.

8. Husseini, *Mudhakkirat*, 123–24, 127–28, 194. Gilbert Achcar, *The Arabs and the Holocaust: The Arab-Israeli War of Narratives* (New York: Metropolitan Books, 2009), 150–58.

9. Quoted in A. J. Kellar (MI5) to J. T. Henderson (Foreign Office), November 10, 1945, TNA CO 968/121/1.

10. Husseini, *Mudhakkirat*, 164. Achcar, *Arabs and the Holocaust*, 155–58.

11. Postwar, Hourani was also Alami's deputy in the Arab League's public-diplomacy office in London. Boyle, *Betrayal of Palestine*, 284–86, 290–91. Elath, "Conversations," 55. Ajami, *Dream Palace of the Arabs*, 19–24. Various correspondence on Antonius's debts, ill health, and death, 1941–1943, ICWA. Dubnov and Robson, *Partitions*, 209, 214.

12. On the feuding between Alami and the mufti in this period, see Daniel Rickenbacher, "The Arab League's Propaganda Campaign in the US Against the Establishment of a Jewish State (1944–1947)," *Israel Studies* 25, no. 1 (spring 2020): passim. On the mufti's enduring popularity in the early postwar years, see Achcar, *Arabs and the Holocaust*, 158ff.

13. Nashashibi, *Jerusalem's Other Voice*, 68.

14. Furlonge, *Palestine*, chap. 10, 158. Daniel Rickenbacher, "Arab States, Arab Interest Groups and Anti-Zionist Movements in Western Europe and the US" (PhD thesis,

University of Zurich, 2017), 134. Rashid Khalidi laments the tendency in Palestinian-nationalist circles to dismiss "the manifestly successful nation-building efforts of Zionism." See Khalidi, *The Hundred Years' War on Palestine: A History of Settler Colonialism and Resistance, 1917–2017* (New York: Metropolitan Books, 2020), 216.

15. Achcar calls the mufti an "architect of the Nakba"; Achcar, *Arabs and the Holocaust*, 158–62. See also Walid Khalidi, "On Albert Hourani, the Arab Office, and the Anglo-American Committee of 1946," *Journal of Palestine Studies* 35, no. 1 (October 1, 2005): 64–70.

16. "Musa Bey Alami's Statement," August 30, 1947, ISA P-3220/19. The mufti's voice is audible in Alami's strident railing against the Zionists' "utterly worthless" case as a "body of invaders" with no rights whatsoever.

17. Roza El-Eini writes, "The Peel Plan proved to be the master partition plan, on which all those that followed were either based, or to which they were compared." El-Eini, *Mandated Landscape*, 331, 369. The UN offered the Jews much of the Negev, but not the heavily Arab central Galilee. It also abandoned population transfer and the linking of Arab Palestine with Transjordan. On similarities and differences between the 1937 and 1947 plans, see Sinanoglou, *Partitioning Palestine*, 168–72.

18. For a concise account of the two phases of the 1947–1949 war, see Morris, *Righteous Victims*, 191ff.

19. Ibid., 159–60, 191–92. For a map of the Wall and Tower settlements founded during the revolt, see Naor, *Yamei Homa u-Migdal*, 209.

20. Ben-Gurion recalled, "The Hagana's [*sic*] best officers were trained in the Special Night Squads, and Wingate's doctrines were taken over by the Israel Defense Forces." Ben-Gurion, "Britain's Contribution to Arming the Hagana" and "Our Friend: What Wingate Did for Us"; in Khalidi, *From Haven to Conquest*, 371–74, 382–87.

21. Haim, *Abandonment of Illusions*, passim. Shapira, *Land and Power*, 270.

22. Rashid Khalidi, "The Palestinians and 1948: The Underlying Causes of the Failure," in *The War for Palestine: Rewriting the History of 1948*, ed. Eugene L. Rogan and Avi Shlaim, 2nd ed. (Cambridge: Cambridge University Press, 2007), 30, passim. Khalidi, *Iron Cage*, 123 and chap. 4, passim.

23. Musa Alami, "The Lesson of Palestine," *Middle East Journal* 3, no. 4 (October 1949): 373–405. Elath, "Conversations," 34–35. Walid Khalidi called the book "a devastating exercise in Arab self-criticism"; see Khalidi, "On Albert Hourani," 78.

24. Yoav Gelber, *Palestine 1948: War, Escape and the Emergence of the Palestinian Refugee Problem* (Brighton: Sussex Academic Press, 2006), Appendix II, 314–15, passim. For a detailed, cogent reappraisal see Eliezer Tauber, *The Massacre That Never Was: The Myth of Deir Yassin and the Creation of the Palestinian Refugee Problem* (London: Toby Press, 2021), 152–66, 229, passim.

25. Alami, "The Lesson of Palestine," 373–405. On Alami and the war see also Furlonge, *Palestine*, chap. 11.

26. Walid Khalidi described Tal as "Musa's aide-de-camp, carrying his briefcase and opening the car door for him"; Khalidi, "On Albert Hourani," 77. Alami's ex-wife was by Tal's side when he was assassinated by Palestinian gunmen in 1971.

27. In 1955 Alami's farm suffered a massive attack by refugees who had been incited to believe he was a "traitor" seeking to resettle them permanently in the West Bank. Had he

been present, his biographer writes, "he would certainly have been murdered." Furlonge, *Palestine*, chap. 12, 189–206, 214–16.

28. From Yariv Mozer's film *Ben-Gurion, Epilogue* (Go2Films, 2016).

29. Ben-Gurion diary, June 12 and 19, 1967, BGA. Segev, *State at Any Cost*, 658.

30. Ben-Gurion diary, November 29, 1967, BGA.

31. Ambassador Remez to Hillel (Foreign Ministry), June 11, 1969, BGA. Avi Shilon, *Ben-Gurion: His Later Years in the Political Wilderness* (Lanham, MD: Rowman & Littlefield, 2016), xv, 52–53, 199n85–86.

32. Alami gave differing accounts of Ben-Gurion's remarks and his own reaction. Per Elath ("Conversations," 71), the former was "encouraged" by the latter's stance and disappointed Israeli leaders had not heeded it. According to Nasser Nashashibi (*Jerusalem's Other Voice*, 183–85), the former found the latter's flexibility diminished with each meeting, and considered his attitude "impertinent."

33. In Shilon's view, the talks' "very existence is enough to reveal a previously untold side of Ben-Gurion: his recognition de facto of the existence of [a] Palestinian people." Shilon, *Ben-Gurion*, xv, 52–53.

34. From Ben-Gurion's 1970 *Moked* interview, via Israel Broadcasting Authority archive, https://www.youtube.com. On his repetition of the anecdote, see Segev, *State at Any Cost*, 256–57, 405, 507: "Ben-Gurion told that story over and over in the years that followed, until his final days. . . . Apparently, over the years, Ben-Gurion amplified Alami's response into a seminal experience of his life."

35. Elpeleg, *Grand Mufti*, 165. Achcar, *Arabs and the Holocaust*, 162–63.

36. Shahid, *Jerusalem Memories*, 223–26.

37. E. C. Hodgkin, "The Last Palestinian," *The Spectator*, June 30, 1984. Hodgkin, a British journalist, was chair of the Arab Development Society.

38. Lazar, *Six Singular Figures*, chap. 1. Elath notes that in conversation Alami "constantly stressed the Mufti's basic trait—extremism"; see "Conversations," 53. Alami worried aloud that if he criticized him, "the Mufti might seek revenge—and, who knows, he might have me killed"; Nashashibi, *Jerusalem's Other Voice*, 194.

39. Elath, "Conversations," 31, 73–74. On Alami's role raising funds and arms, see Goglia, "Il Mufti e Mussolini," 1220ff.

40. Civilians accounted for about two-thirds of the up to two hundred Israeli fatalities through 1993. Morris, "Mandate Palestine in Perspective," 138, and *Righteous Victims*, 565–603. Stein, "Intifada and the 1936–39 Uprising," 70–81. See also "Fatalities in the first Intifada," B'Tselem, https://www.btselem.org/statistics/first_intifada_tables.

41. Israeli measures were based on the 1945 Emergency Regulations, themselves based on the 1937 Emergency Regulations enacted during the revolt. Laleh Khalili writes that today, "the rules under which Palestinians held in 'administrative detention' without trial are only marginally modified versions the punitive detention laws the British used in the 1930s." Khalili, "The Location of Palestine in Global Counterinsurgencies," *International Journal of Middle East Studies* 42, no. 3 (August 2010): 424.

42. The *New York Times* reported at the time: "Many Palestinians fear that such violence will be the revolt's undoing, as happened with the Arab revolt of the 1930's." See Swedenburg, *Memories of Revolt*, 173, 198; Stein, "Intifada and the 1936–1939 Uprising," 64–66, passim; Kimmerling and Migdal, *Palestinian People*, 303–6.

43. Shai Lachman wrote in 1982: "To this day, military units named for . . . Qassam may be found in almost all Palestinian organizations," including Fatah and the Marxist Popular Front for the Liberation of Palestine (PFLP). In Kedourie and Haim, *Zionism and Arabism*, 87, 99n214. Weldon Matthews adds, "It is a cliché . . . to observe that al-Qassam's killing gave Palestinian Arabs an example of heroic self-sacrifice that no one in the leadership had approached. The observation, however, is no less true for being so frequently made." Matthews, *Confronting an Empire, Constructing a Nation: Arab Nationalists and Popular Politics in Mandate Palestine* (London: I.B. Tauris, 2006), 245. Hamas was the first Palestinian group to wage suicide bombings, though Lebanese Hezbollah had preceded it; Qassam rockets were first fired in 2001.

44. Khalidi, *Hundred Years' War*, 213–16.

45. Nimr, "Nation in a Hero," 141. In her version the sniper killed "ten soldiers," though in fact three were civilians.

46. See for example Kevin Connolly, "Charles Tegart and the forts that tower over Israel," *BBC News*, September 10, 2012, https://www.bbc.com/news/magazine-19019949.

47. Rashid Khalidi asks "whether these bombings were meant to achieve anything more than blind revenge," noting "the terrible violence of the Second Intifada erased the positive image of Palestinians that had evolved since 1982 and through the First Intifada and the peace negotiations. . . . Israelis ceased to be seen as oppressors, reverting to the more familiar role of victims of irrational, fanatical tormentors." Khalidi, *Hundred Years' War*, 213–16.

48. Kimmerling and Migdal, *Palestinian People*, 393, 415. On parallels between the revolt and the two intifadas, see also Jonathan Schanzer, "Palestinian Uprisings Compared," *Middle East Quarterly* 9, no. 3 (Summer 2002): 27–37.

49. Smotrich, Bezalel (@bezalelsm), Twitter, April 23, 2021, 1:13 a.m., https://twitter.com/bezalelsm/status/1385356221859966976.

50. Kopty, Abir (@KoptyAbir), Twitter, May 17, 2021, 11:34 p.m., https://twitter.com/AbirKopty/status/1394390926974459905. See also Rami Younis on Democracy Now! (@democracynow), Twitter, May 18, 2021, 4:06 p.m., https://twitter.com/democracynow/status/1394640483876487168.

51. Kabha and Serhan, *Sijil al-Qadah*, 21, 29. Kabha, *The Palestinian People: Seeking Sovereignty and State* (Boulder, CO: Lynne Rienner, 2014), 21.

52. Nimr, "Nation in a Hero," 143, 155. Kadoorie was founded in the 1930s by Baghdad-born Jewish tycoon Ellis Kadoorie. A sister school for the Jews sits beside Mount Tabor in Israel; its alumni include Yigal Allon and Yitzhak Rabin.

53. For a recent summary see Mohammad Qutob, "Resilience through the Decades: The Arab Development Society," *This Week in Palestine*, June 2021, https://thisweekinpalestine.com/resilience-through-the-decades.

54. Mozer, *Ben-Gurion*.

Selected Bibliography

Archives

Ben-Gurion Archive, Sde Boker, Israel (BGA), including Shabtai Teveth Archive (STA)
British Library, London (BL)
Central Zionist Archives, Jerusalem (CZA)
Franklin D. Roosevelt Library, Hyde Park, New York (FDR)
Government Press Office, Jerusalem (GPO)
Haganah Archives, Tel Aviv (HA)
Imperial War Museum Sound Archive, London (IWMSA)
Institute of Current World Affairs Archive, Washington (ICWA)
Israel State Archives, Jerusalem (ISA)
Jabotinsky Institute, Tel Aviv (JI)
Labor Party Archive, Beit Berl, Israel (LPA)
Library of Congress, Washington (LOC)
Middle East Center Archive, St Antony's College, Oxford (MECA)
National Archives and Records Administration II, College Park, Maryland (NARA II)
The National Archives, London (TNA)
National Library of Israel, Jerusalem (NLI)
National Portrait Gallery, London (NPG)
Weizmann Archives, Rehovot, Israel (WA)
Weston Library, University of Oxford (WL)

Newspapers

English

Evening Standard
Jewish Telegraphic Agency (JTA)
The Guardian (Manchester)
New York Times
Palestine Gazette
Palestine Post
The Times (London)

Hebrew
Davar
Do'ar Hayom
Haaretz

Arabic
Al-Difa
Al-Jamia al-Islamiya
Al-Liwa
Filastin

Books and Articles

Abboushi, W. F. "The Road to Rebellion: Arab Palestine in the 1930's." *Journal of Palestine Studies* 6, no. 3 (Spring 1977): 23–46.

Achcar, Gilbert. *The Arabs and the Holocaust: The Arab-Israeli War of Narratives*. New York: Metropolitan Books, 2009.

Alami, Musa. "The Lesson of Palestine." *Middle East Journal* 3, no. 4 (October 1949).

Alfassi, I., ed. *Irgun Zvai Leumi (National Military Organization): Collection of Archival Sources and Documents April 1937-April 1941*. Vol. 1. Tel Aviv: Jabotinsky Institute, 1990.

Anderson, Charles W. "State Formation from Below and the Great Revolt in Palestine." *Journal of Palestine Studies* 47, no. 1 (November 1, 2017): 39–55.

Anglim, Simon. *Orde Wingate: Unconventional Warrior: From the 1920s to the Twenty-First Century*. Barnsley, South Yorkshire: Pen & Sword Military, 2014.

Antonius, George. *The Arab Awakening*. New York: Lippincott, 1939.

Arielli, Nir. *Fascist Italy and the Middle East, 1933–40*. Houndmills, Hampshire; New York: Palgrave Macmillan, 2010.

———. "Italian Involvement in the Arab Revolt in Palestine, 1936–1939." *British Journal of Middle Eastern Studies* 35, no. 2 (August 2008): 187–204.

Arnon-Ohanah, Yuval. *Mered Arvi be-Eretz Israel 1936–1939* [The Arab Revolt in the Land of Israel, 1936–1939]. Jerusalem: Ariel, 2013.

Bell, Gawain. *Shadows on the Sand: The Memoirs of Sir Gawain Bell*. London: C. Hurst, 1983.

Ben-Gurion, David. *My Talks with Arab Leaders*. Edited by Misha Louvish. Translated by Aryeh Rubinstein. New York: Third Press, 1973.

———. *Zichronot* [Memoirs]. Vol. 1–6. Tel Aviv: Am Oved, 1971.

Bethell, Nicholas. *The Palestine Triangle: The Struggle for the Holy Land, 1935–48*. New York: G. P. Putnam's Sons, 1979.

Bierman, John, and Colin Smith. *Fire in the Night: Wingate of Burma, Ethiopia, and Zion*. 1st ed. New York: Random House, 1999.

Black, Ian. *Enemies and Neighbors: Arabs and Jews in Palestine and Israel, 1917–2017*. New York: Atlantic Monthly Press, 2017.

———. *Zionism and the Arabs, 1936–1939*. London; New York: Routledge, 1978.

Bowden, Tom. "The Politics of the Arab Rebellion in Palestine 1936–39." *Middle Eastern Studies* 11, no. 2 (1975): 147–74.

Boyle, Susan Silsby. *Betrayal of Palestine: The Story of George Antonius*. Boulder, CO: Westview Press, 2001.

Cahill, Richard. "Sir Charles Tegart: The 'Counterterrorism Expert' in Palestine." *Jerusalem Quarterly* 74 (Summer 2018): 57–66.

Caplan, Neil. *Futile Diplomacy*. Vol. 2. London; New York: Routledge, 2015.

Chamberlain, Neville. *The Neville Chamberlain Diary Letters*. Edited by Robert C. Self. Vol. 4. Aldershot, Hampshire; Burlington, VT: Ashgate, 2005.

Chazan. "The Dispute in Mapai over 'Self-Restraint' and 'Purity of Arms' During the Arab Revolt." *Jewish Social Studies* 15, no. 3 (2009): 89–113.

Chetrit, Shlomi. *Rishonim Leha'ez: Plugot ha-Layla ha-Meyuhadot shel Orde Wingate* [First to Dare: Orde Wingate's Special Night Squads]. Mikveh Israel: Yehuda Dekel Library, 2017.

"Cmd. 5479: Report of the Palestine Royal Commission." His Majesty's Stationery Office, 1937.

"Cmd. 5854: Palestine Partition Commission Report." His Majesty's Stationery Office, 1938.

"Cmd. 6019: Statement of Policy by His Majesty's Government." His Majesty's Stationery Office, 1939.

Cohen, Hillel. *Army of Shadows: Palestinian Collaboration with Zionism, 1917–1948*. Translated by Haim Watzman. Berkeley: University of California Press, 2008.

Cohen, Michael J. *Britain's Hegemony in Palestine and the Middle East, 1917–56: Changing Strategic Imperatives*. London; Portland, OR: Vallentine Mitchell, 2017.

———. *Britain's Moment in Palestine: Retrospect and Perspectives, 1917–48*. London; New York: Routledge, 2014.

———. *Palestine, Retreat from the Mandate: The Making of British Policy, 1936–45*. New York: Holmes & Meier, 1978.

"Col. 134: Palestine Royal Commission: Minutes of Evidence Heard at Public Sessions." His Majesty's Stationery Office, 1937.

Courtney, Roger. *Palestine Policeman*. London: Wyman & Sons, 1939.

Danin, Ezra, ed. *Teudot u-Demuyot mi-Ginze ha-Kenufyot ha-Arviyot bi-Me'ore'ot 1936–1939* [Documents and Portraits from the Arab Gangs' Archives in the Arab Revolt in Palestine 1936–1939]. Jerusalem: Magnes Press, 1981.

Dayan, Moshe. *Story of My Life*. New York: Morrow, 1976.

Dubnov, Arie, and Laura Robson, eds. *Partitions: A Transnational History of Twentieth-Century Territorial Separatism*. Stanford: Stanford University Press, 2019.

Dugdale, Blanche E. C. *Baffy: The Diaries of Blanche Dugdale, 1936–1947*. Edited by Norman Rose. London; Chicago: Vallentine Mitchell, 1973.

Eisenberg, Laura Zittrain. *My Enemy's Enemy: Lebanon in the Early Zionist Imagination, 1900–1948*. Detroit: Wayne State University Press, 1994.

Elath, Eliahu. "Conversations with Musa al-'Alami." *Jerusalem Quarterly* 41 (Winter 1987): 31–75.

El-Eini, Roza. *Mandated Landscape: British Imperial Rule in Palestine, 1929–1948*. London; New York: Routledge, 2015.

Elpeleg, Zvi. *The Grand Mufti: Haj Amin al-Hussaini, Founder of the Palestinian National Movement*. Portland, OR: F. Cass, 1993.

———, ed. *Through the Eyes of the Mufti: The Essays of Haj Amin*. Translated by Rachel Kessel. London; Portland, OR: Vallentine Mitchell, 2009.

Eltaher, Mohamed Ali. *'An Thawrat Filastin Sanat 1936: Wasf wa-Akhbar wa-Waqa'i wa-Watha'iq* [On the 1936 Palestine Uprising: Description, News, Facts, and Documents]. Cairo: al-Lajnah al-Filastiniya al-Arabiya, 1936. https://www.loc.gov/item/2017481891/.

Eshkol, Yosef. *A Common Soldier: The Story of Zwi Brenner*. Translated by Shmuel Himelstein. Tel Aviv: MOD Books, 1993.

Eyal, Yigal. *Ha-Intifada ha-Rishona: Dikui ha-Mered ha-Arvi al-Yede ha-Tsava ha-Briti be-Eretz-Yisrael, 1936–1939* [The "First Intifada": The Oppression (*sic*) of the Arab Revolt by the British Army, 1936–1939]. Tel Aviv: Maarachot, 1998.

Fergusson, Bernard. *The Trumpet in the Hall: 1930–58*. London: Collins, 1971.

Foreign Relations of the United States (FRUS), 1937–1939. Vol. 2. Washington: Department of State, 1954.

Furlonge, Geoffrey. *Palestine Is My Country: The Story of Musa Alami*. London: Praeger, 1969.

Galnoor, Itzhak. *The Partition of Palestine: Decision Crossroads in the Zionist Movement*. SUNY Series in Israeli Studies. Albany: SUNY Press, 1995.

Gelber, Yoav. *Jewish-Transjordanian Relations, 1921–48*. London; Portland, OR: F. Cass, 1997.

Gilbert, Martin. *Churchill and the Jews*. London: Pocket, 2008.

Goglia, Luigi. "Il Mufti e Mussolini: Alcuni documenti italiani sui rapporti tra nazionalismo palestinese e fascismo negli anni trenta [The Mufti and Mussolini: Some Italian documents on the relationship between Palestinian nationalism and fascism in the 1930s]." *Storia Contemporanea* 17, no. 6 (1986): 1201–53.

Goren, Tamir. "The Destruction of Old Jaffa in 1936 and the Question of the Arab Refugees." *Middle Eastern Studies* 55, no. 6 (November 2, 2019): 1005–19.

———. "The Judaization of Haifa at the Time of the Arab Revolt." *Middle Eastern Studies* 40, no. 4 (July 2004): 135–52.

Habas, Bracha, ed. *Me'ora'ot Tartzav* [The 1936 Events]. Tel Aviv: Davar, 1937.

Hacohen, David. *Time to Tell: An Israeli Life, 1898–1984*. New York: Cornwall Books, 1985.

Haim, Yehoyada. *Abandonment of Illusions: Zionist Political Attitudes Toward Palestinian Arab Nationalism, 1936–1939*. London; New York: Routledge, 1983.

Hamilton, Nigel. *Monty: The Making of a General, 1887–1942*. New York: McGraw-Hill, 1981.

Heller, Daniel Kupfert. *Jabotinsky's Children: Polish Jews and the Rise of Right-Wing Zionism*. Princeton, NJ: Princeton University Press, 2017.

Hoffman, Bruce. *Anonymous Soldiers: The Struggle for Israel, 1917–1947*. New York: Knopf, 2015.

Horne, Edward. *A Job Well Done: (Being a History of the Palestine Police Force 1920–1948)*. Lewes, East Sussex: Book Guild, 2003.

Hughes, Matthew. *Britain's Pacification of Palestine: The British Army, the Colonial State, and the Arab Revolt, 1936–1939*. Cambridge: Cambridge University Press, 2019.

———. "Terror in Galilee: British-Jewish Collaboration and the Special Night Squads in Palestine during the Arab Revolt, 1938–39." *Journal of Imperial and Commonwealth History* 43, no. 4 (August 8, 2015): 590–610.

———. "The Banality of Brutality: British Armed Forces and the Repression of the Arab Revolt in Palestine, 1936–39." *English Historical Review* CXXIV, no. 507 (April 1, 2009): 313–54.

Husseini, Amin al-. *Mudhakkirat al-Hajj Muhammad Amin al-Husayni* [The Memoirs of Hajj Amin al-Husseini]. Edited by Abd al-Karim al-Umar. Damascus: Al-Ahali, 1999.

Jankowski, James P. "The Palestinian Arab Revolt of 1936–1939." *Muslim World* 63, no. 3 (July 1973): 220–33.

Jawhariyyeh, Wasif. *The Storyteller of Jerusalem: The Life and Times of Wasif Jawhariyyeh, 1904–1948*. Edited by Salim Tamari and Issam Nassar. Translated by Nada Elzeer. Northampton, MA: Olive Branch Press, 2014.

Kabha, Mustafa. "The Courts of the Palestinian Arab Revolt, 1936–39." In *Untold Histories of the Middle East: Recovering Voices from the 19th and 20th Centuries*, edited by Amy Singer, Christoph K. Neumann, and Selçuk Akşin Somel. London; New York: Routledge, 2011.

———. *The Palestinian People: Seeking Sovereignty and State*. Boulder, CO: Lynne Rienner, 2014.

———. *The Palestinian Press as Shaper of Public Opinion 1929–1939: Writing Up a Storm*. London; Portland, OR: Vallentine Mitchell, 2007.

Kabha, Mustafa, and Nimer Serhan. *Sijil al-Qadah wal-Thuwar wal-Mutatawi'in li-Thawrat 1936–1939* [Lexicon of Commanders, Rebels, and Volunteers of the 1936–1939 Revolt]. Kafr Qara, Israel: Dar Elhuda, 2009.

Kahn Bar-Adon, Dorothy. *Writing Palestine 1933–1950*. Edited by Esther Carmel-Hakim and Nancy Rosenfeld. Brookline, MA: Academic Studies Press, 2017.

Kanafani, Ghassan. *The 1936–39 Revolt in Palestine*. London: Tricontinental Society, 1972.

Kedourie, Elie. "Great Britain and Palestine: The Turning Point." In *Islam in the Modern World and Other Studies*. New York: Holt, Rinehart and Winston, 1981.

Kedourie, Elie, and Sylvia G. Haim, eds. *Zionism and Arabism in Palestine and Israel*. London; New York: Routledge, 2015.

Keith-Roach, Edward. *Pasha of Jerusalem: Memoirs of a District Commissioner under the British Mandate*. Edited by Paul Eedle. London; New York: Radcliffe Press, 1994.

Kelly, Matthew Kraig. *The Crime of Nationalism: Britain, Palestine, and Nation-Building on the Fringe of Empire*. Oakland: University of California Press, 2017.

Kessler, Oren. "'A dangerous people to quarrel with': Lloyd George's Secret Testimony to the Peel Commission Revealed." *Fathom*, July 2020. https://fathomjournal.org/mandate100-a-dangerous-people-to-quarrel-with-lloyd-georges-secret-testimony-to-the-peel-commission-revealed/.

Khalidi, Hussein Fakhri. *Exiled from Jerusalem: The Diaries of Hussein Fakhri al-Khalidi.* Edited by Rafiq Husseini. London: I.B. Tauris, 2020.

Khalidi, Rashid. *The Hundred Years' War on Palestine: A History of Settler Colonialism and Resistance, 1917–2017.* New York: Metropolitan Books, 2020.

———. *The Iron Cage: The Story of the Palestinian Struggle for Statehood.* Boston: Beacon Press, 2007.

———. "The Palestinians and 1948: The Underlying Causes of the Failure." In *The War for Palestine: Rewriting the History of 1948*, edited by Eugene L. Rogan and Avi Shlaim, 2nd ed. Cambridge: Cambridge University Press, 2007.

Khalidi, Walid, ed. *From Haven to Conquest: Readings in Zionism and the Palestine Problem until 1948.* Washington: Institute for Palestine Studies, 1987.

Kimmerling, Baruch, and Joel S. Migdal. *The Palestinian People: A History.* Cambridge, MA: Harvard University Press, 2003.

Klieman, Aaron S. *A Return to Palliatives.* The Rise of Israel Series, Vol. 26. New York: Garland, 1987.

———. "The Divisiveness of Palestine: Foreign Office versus Colonial Office on the Issue of Partition, 1937." *Historical Journal* 22, no. 2 (1979): 423–31.

Koestler, Arthur. *Promise and Fulfillment: Palestine 1917–1949.* New York: Macmillan, 1949.

———. *Thieves in the Night: Chronicle of an Experiment.* New York: Macmillan, 1946.

Krämer, Gudrun. *A History of Palestine: From the Ottoman Conquest to the Founding of the State of Israel.* Princeton: Princeton University Press, 2011.

Kramer, Martin. "Ambition, Arabism, and George Antonius." In *Arab Awakening & Islamic Revival: The Politics of Ideas in the Middle East.* Piscataway, NJ: Transaction Publishers, 2009.

Kroizer, Gad. "From Dowbiggin to Tegart: Revolutionary Change in the Colonial Police in Palestine during the 1930s." *Journal of Imperial and Commonwealth History* 32, no. 2 (May 2004): 115–33.

Lazar, Hadara. *Six Singular Figures: Jews and Arabs under the British Mandate.* Translated by Sondra Silverston. Oakville, ON: Mosaic, 2016.

Lesch, Ann Mosely. *Arab Politics in Palestine, 1917–1939: The Frustration of a Nationalist Movement.* Ithaca, NY: Cornell University Press, 1979.

Mattar, Philip. *The Mufti of Jerusalem: Al-Hajj Amin al-Husayni and the Palestinian National Movement.* Rev. ed. New York: Columbia University Press, 1992.

Matthews, Weldon C. *Confronting an Empire, Constructing a Nation: Arab Nationalists and Popular Politics in Mandate Palestine.* London: I.B. Tauris, 2006.

Morris, Benny. "Mandate Palestine in Perspective." *Bustan: The Middle East Book Review* 5, no. 2 (January 1, 2014): 136–45.

———. *Righteous Victims: A History of the Zionist-Arab Conflict, 1881–1999.* 1st ed. New York: Knopf, 1999.

Morton, Geoffrey J. *Just the Job: Some Experiences of a Colonial Policeman.* London: Hodder & Stoughton, 1957.

Nafi, Basheer M. "Shaykh 'Izz al-Din al-Qassam: A Reformist and a Rebel Leader." *Journal of Islamic Studies* 8, no. 2 (February 1, 1997): 185–215.

Naor, Mordechai, ed. *Yamei Homa u-Migdal 1936–1939* [Days of Wall and Tower 1936–1939]. Jerusalem: Ben-Zvi Institute, 1987.

Nashashibi, Nasser Eddin. *Jerusalem's Other Voice: Ragheb Nashashibi and Moderation in Palestinian Politics, 1920–1948*. Exeter: Ithaca Press, 1990.

Nicosia, Francis R. *The Third Reich and the Palestine Question*. 2nd ed. New Brunswick, NJ: Transaction Publishers, 1999.

Nimr, Sonia. "A Nation in a Hero: Abdul Rahim Hajj Mohammad and the Arab Revolt." In *Struggle and Survival in Palestine/Israel*, edited by Mark LeVine and Gershon Shafir. Berkeley: University of California Press, 2012.

Niv, David. *Maarchot ha-Irgun ha-Tzvai ha-Leumi* [Battle for Freedom: The Irgun Zvai Leumi]. Vol. 2. Tel Aviv: Klausner Institute, 1975.

Norris, Jacob. "Repression and Rebellion: Britain's Response to the Arab Revolt in Palestine of 1936–39." *Journal of Imperial and Commonwealth History* 36, no. 1 (March 2008): 25–45.

Parsons, Laila. *The Commander: Fawzi al-Qawuqji and the Fight for Arab Independence, 1914–1948*. 1st ed. New York: Hill and Wang, 2016.

———. "The Secret Testimony of the Peel Commission (Part I): Underbelly of Empire." *Journal of Palestine Studies* 49, no. 1 (Autumn 2019): 7–24, 142–45.

———. "The Secret Testimony of the Peel Commission (Part II): Partition." *Journal of Palestine Studies* 49, no. 2 (Winter 2020): 8–25.

Penkower, Monty Noam. *Palestine in Turmoil: The Struggle for Sovereignty, 1933–1939*. Vol. 2. New York: Touro College Press, 2014.

———. "Shlomo Ben-Yosef: From a British Gallows to Israel's Pantheon to Obscurity." In *Twentieth Century Jews: Forging Identity in the Land of Promise and in the Promised Land*, 311–56. Boston: Academic Studies Press, 2010.

Porath, Yehoshua. *The Palestinian Arab National Movement, 1929–1939*. London; New York: Routledge, 2015.

Rose, Norman. *The Gentile Zionists: A Study in Anglo-Zionist Diplomacy, 1929–1939*. London: F. Cass, 1973.

Royle, Trevor. *Orde Wingate: A Man of Genius, 1903–1944*. Barnsley, South Yorkshire: Pen & Sword Military, 2010.

Sakakini, Hala. *Jerusalem and I: A Personal Memoir*. Amman: Economic Press, 1990.

Sakakini, Khalil. *Kadha Ana ya Dunya* [Such Am I, O World]. Beirut: Al-Ittihad, 1982.

Sanagan, Mark. "Teacher, Preacher, Soldier, Martyr: Rethinking 'Izz al-Din al-Qassam." *Welt Des Islams* 53, no. 3–4 (2013): 315–52.

Sanger, Clyde. *Malcolm MacDonald: Bringing an End to Empire*. Montreal: McGill-Queen's University Press, 1995.

Schechtman, Joseph B. *Fighter and Prophet: The Last Years: The Life and Times of Vladimir Jabotinsky*. Silver Spring, MD: Eshel Books, 1986.

Schleifer, Abdullah. "The Life and Thought of 'Izz-Id-Din Al-Qassam." *Islamic Quarterly* 23, no. 2 (1979): 60–81.

Segev, Tom. *A State at Any Cost: The Life of David Ben-Gurion*. Translated by Haim Watzman. New York: Farrar, Straus and Giroux, 2019.

———. *One Palestine, Complete: Jews and Arabs under the British Mandate*. New York: Henry Holt, 2001.

Seikaly, May. *Haifa: Transformation of a Palestinian Arab Society 1918–1939*. London; New York: I.B. Tauris, 1995.

Shahid, Serene Husseini. *Jerusalem Memories*. Edited by Jean Said Makdisi. Beirut: Naufal, 2000.

Shapira, Anita. *Land and Power: The Zionist Resort to Force, 1881–1948*. Oxford; New York: Oxford University Press, 1992.

Sharett, Moshe. *Yoman Medini* [Political Diary]. Vol. 1–4. Tel Aviv: Am Oved, 1968. http://www.sharett.org.il/.

Shepherd, Naomi. *Ploughing Sand: British Rule in Palestine, 1917–1948*. New Brunswick, NJ: Rutgers University Press, 2000.

Shilon, Avi. *Ben-Gurion: His Later Years in the Political Wilderness*. Lanham, MD: Rowman & Littlefield, 2016.

Shindler, Colin. *The Rise of the Israeli Right: From Odessa to Hebron*. Cambridge: Cambridge University Press, 2015.

———. *The Triumph of Military Zionism*. London; New York: I.B. Tauris, 2006.

Shlaim, Avi. *Collusion Across the Jordan: King Abdullah, the Zionist Movement, and the Partition of Palestine*. New York: Columbia University Press, 1988.

Sinanoglou, Penny. *Partitioning Palestine: British Policymaking at the End of Empire*. Chicago: University of Chicago Press, 2019.

Slutsky, Yehuda. *Sefer Toldot ha-Haganah* [The Haganah History Book]. Vol. 2–3. Tel Aviv: Maarachot, 1963. http://www.hahagana.org.il/database/books/.

Stein, Kenneth W. "The Intifada and the 1936–39 Uprising: A Comparison." *Journal of Palestine Studies* 19, no. 4 (July 1, 1990): 64–85.

———. *The Land Question in Palestine, 1917–1939*. Chapel Hill: University of North Carolina Press, 1984.

Swedenburg, Ted. "Al-Qassam Remembered." *Alif: Journal of Comparative Poetics*, no. 7 (Spring 1987): 9–24.

———. *Memories of Revolt: The 1936–1939 Rebellion and the Palestinian National Past*. Minneapolis; Fayetteville, AR: University of Minnesota Press; University of Arkansas Press, 1995.

Sykes, Christopher. *Crossroads to Israel*. A Midland Book, MB-165. Bloomington: Indiana University Press, 1973.

———. *Orde Wingate, a Biography*. London: Collins, 1959.

Teveth, Shabtai. *Ben-Gurion and the Palestinian Arabs: From Peace to War*. Oxford; New York: Oxford University Press, 1985.

———. *Ben-Gurion: The Burning Ground, 1886–1948*. Boston: Houghton Mifflin, 1987.

Thawrat Filastin Ama 1936 [The Palestine Revolt 1936]. Jaffa: Matba'at al-Jamia al-Islamiya, 1936. https://lccn.loc.gov/2015421420.

Totah, Khalil. *Turbulent Times in Palestine: The Diaries of Khalil Totah, 1886–1955*. Edited by Thomas M. Ricks. Jerusalem; Ramallah: Institute for Palestine Studies; PASSIA, 2009.

Wagner, Steven B. *Statecraft by Stealth: Secret Intelligence and British Rule in Palestine*. Ithaca, NY: Cornell University Press, 2019.

Weizmann, Chaim. *The Letters and Papers of Chaim Weizmann, Series A*. Edited by Barnet Litvinoff. Vol. 17–19. Jerusalem: Israel Universities Press, 1979.

———. *The Letters and Papers of Chaim Weizmann, Series B*. Edited by Barnet Litvinoff. Vol. 2. New Brunswick, NJ; Jerusalem: Transaction Books; Israel Universities Press, 1983.

———. *Trial and Error: The Autobiography of Chaim Weizmann*. New York: Schocken, 1966.

Yasin, Subhi. *Thawrah al-Arabiyah al-Kubra* [The Great Arab Revolt]. Cairo, 1959. http://dlib.nyu.edu/aco/book/nyu_aco001361/10.

Yazbak, Mahmoud. "From Poverty to Revolt: Economic Factors in the Outbreak of the 1936 Rebellion in Palestine." *Middle Eastern Studies* 36, no. 3 (2000): 93–113.

Zuaytir, Akram. *Yawmiyat Akram Zuaytir* [Diaries of Akram Zuaytir]. Beirut: Institute for Palestine Studies, 1980.

Research Dissertations

Chetrit, Shlomi. "Ha-Milhama ha-Ktana be-Yoter: Ha-Ma'avak ha-Tzvai ha-Briti Neged ha-Mered ha-Arvi be-Eretz Yisrael, 1936–1939 [The Biggest Small War: The British Military Struggle against the Arab Revolt in Palestine, 1936–1939]." Bar-Ilan University, 2020.

Nimr, Sonia. "The Arab Revolt of 1936–1939 in Palestine: A Study Based on Oral Sources." University of Exeter, 1990.

Taggar, Yehuda. "The Mufti of Jerusalem and Palestine: Arab Politics, 1930–1937." University of London, 1973.

Index

About the Author

Oren Kessler is a journalist and political analyst based in Tel Aviv. Previously he was deputy director for research at the Foundation for Defense of Democracies in Washington, DC, a Middle East research fellow at the Henry Jackson Society in London, an Arab affairs correspondent for the *Jerusalem Post*, and an editor and translator at *Haaretz* English edition.

Kessler's work has appeared in outlets including *Foreign Affairs*, *Foreign Policy*, the *Wall Street Journal*, the *Washington Post*, and *Politico*. Raised in Rochester, New York, and Tel Aviv, he holds a BA in History from the University of Toronto and an MA in Diplomacy and Conflict Studies from Reichman University (IDC Herzliya). *Palestine 1936* is his first book.